Jews and Magic in Medici Florence

The Secret World of Benedetto Blanis

Jews and Magic in Medici Florence

The Secret World of Benedetto Blanis

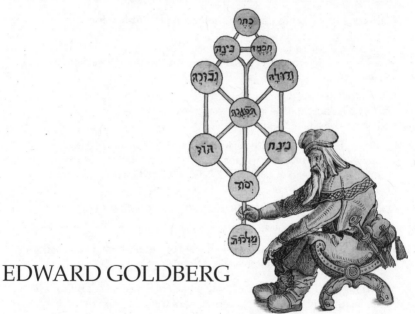

EDWARD GOLDBERG

UNIVERSITY OF TORONTO PRESS
Toronto Buffalo London

© University of Toronto Press Incorporated 2011
Toronto Buffalo London
www.utppublishing.com
Printed in Canada

ISBN 978-1-4426-4225-6

Printed on acid-free, 100% post-consumer recycled paper with
vegetable-based inks.

Toronto Italian Studies

Library and Archives Canada Cataloguing in Publication

Goldberg, Edward L., 1948–
Jews and magic in Medici Florence : the secret world of Benedetto Blanis /
Edward Goldberg.

(Toronto Italian studies series)
Includes bibliographical references and index.
ISBN 978-1-4426-4225-6 (bound)

1. Blanis, Benedetto.   2. Medici, Giovanni de', 1567–1621.   3. Jews – Italy –
Florence – Social life and customs – 17th century.   4. Florence (Italy) – Social
life and customs – 17th century.   5. Jews – Italy – Florence – Biography.
I. Title.   II. Series: Toronto Italian studies

DG738.23.G64 2010   945'.5100492409032   C2010-906136-5

This book has been published with the aid of a grant from the Lila Acheson
Wallace–Reader's Digest Publications Subsidy at Villa I Tatti.

University of Toronto Press acknowledges the financial support for its
publishing activities of the Government of Canada through the Book
Publishing Industry Development Program (BPIDP).

University of Toronto Press acknowledges the financial assistance to its
publishing program of the Canada Council for the Arts and the Ontario
Arts Council.

 Canada Council   Conseil des Arts
for the Arts   du Canada

 ONTARIO ARTS COUNCIL
CONSEIL DES ARTS DE L'ONTARIO

University of Toronto Press acknowledges the financial assistance to its publishing program of the Canada Book Fund.

To my mother,
Lillian Kemelhor Goldberg,
with love

Contents

Acknowledgments

I have been working in Florence for the past thirty-five years, mostly in the Archivio di Stato. Along the way, I have carried out an expanding range of research projects, addressing increasingly complex archival problems – pulling together more and more kinds of information from diverse documentary sources. The present book and its companion volume, *The Letters of Benedetto Blanis* Hebreo *to Don Giovanni dei Medici: 1615–21*, represent the most complex challenge that I have faced to date.

In the course of my long work, I have had the opportunity to run up an enormous debt of gratitude to individuals and organizations – above all to the Archivio di Stato di Firenze. This extraordinary institution is both a treasure house of historical documentation and a scholarly community. Looking back over the years, I see that it has been the one essential constant in my research and writing.

How do I thank everyone on the staff of the Archivio who deserves to be thanked? This requires an archeological excavation of a very personal and gratifying kind. First, there is the succession of distinguished directors who have made my work possible: Giuseppe Pansini, Maria Augusta Timpanaro Morelli, Paola Benigni, Rosalia Manno Tolu, and now Carla Zarrilli. Then there are the various curators who have managed the Archivio's unique resources, particularly: Vanna Arrighi, Anna Bellinazzi, Giuseppe Biscione, Angelo De Scisciolo, Irene Cotta, Roberto Fuda, Concetta Giamblanco, Orsola Gori, Francesca Klein, Marina Laguzzi, Loredana Maccabruni, Piero Marchi, Francesco Martelli, Simone Sartini, and Rossella Zazzeri. Also, there are those on the essential front line of the Archivio's daily operation: Linda Bussotti, Sonia Cafaggini, Rita Capelli, Tommaso Cecchi, Ettore Clinco, Marianna Conti, Filomena Fazio, Egidio Giannini, Giovanni Iaccino, Milvia

Masciarelli, Leonardo Meoni, Giuseppina Meccia, Paola Peruzzi, Adolfo Pinzani, Alessandra Pissilli, Cecilia Pistolesi, Sandro Righi, Riccardo Rossi, Sonia Santoni, Antonio Scognamiglio, Cristina Sorbi, Daniela Tatini, and Carla Tilli.

What about the broader archival community, the hundreds – perhaps thousands – of scholars who come and go for longer or shorter periods of time? 'Arno River Fever' is a renowned and mostly welcome contagion. Those infected never leave Florence – at least not more than they have to, due to the practical exigencies of life. Meanwhile, there is also 'Archive Fever' – with 'Archivio di Stato Fever' constituting a particularly virulent strain.

I can only begin to list my many friends and colleagues in and around the Archivio di Stato di Firenze – all of whom played a role in my ongoing work: Cristina Acidini, Lorenzo Allori, Maurizio Arfaioli, Alessio Assonitis, Nicoletta Baldini, Sheila Barker, Paola Barocchi, Karen-edis Barzman, Molly Bourne, William Bowen, Elena Brizio, Suzanne Butters, Malcolm Campbell, Niccolò Capponi, Robert Carlucci, Alessandro Cecchi, Marco Chiarini, Elena Ciletti, Luciano Cinelli, Janie Cole, José Luis Colomer, Rita Comanducci, Bernard Cooperman, Gino Corti, Elizabeth Cropper, Suzanne Cusick, Stefano Dall'Aglio, Charles Dempsey, Brendan Dooley, Bruce Edelstein, Konrad Eisenbichler, Caroline Elam, Anna Evangelista, Daniela Ferrari, Marco Ferri, Anna Forlani Tempesti, Francesca Funis, Lisa Goldenberg Stoppato, Richard Goldthwaite, Mina Gregori, Margaret Haines, Enriqueta Harris Frankfort, Rab Hatfield, Kelley Helmstutler di Dio, Pamela Jones, Dale Kent, Warren Kirkendale, Deborah Krohn, Susanne Kubersky, Stephanie Nadalo, Wanda Lattes Nirenstein, Joseph Levi, Amanda Lillie, Dora Liscia Bemporad, Burr Litchfield, Peter Lukehart, Federico Luti, Michele Luzzati, Peter Martin, Anthony Molho, Lucia Monaci, John Monfasani, Roberta Morselli, Marilena Mosca, Fabrizio Nevola, Alana O'Brien, Giuseppe Parigino, Linda Pellecchia, Elizabeth Pilliod, Brenda Preyer, Antonio Ricci, Michael Rocke, José Luis Rodríguez de Diego, Salvador Salort Pons, Brian Sandberg, Stefanie Siegmund, Marcello Simonetta, Louise Stein, Christina Strunck, Corey Tazzara, Anatole Tchikine, Nicholas Terpstra, Patrizia Urbani, Leonella Viterbo, Nicholas Wilding, Thomas Willette, and Ugo Zuccarello.

While researching this book, I made selective forays into other archives: the Archivio Arcivescovile di Firenze (with particular thanks to Rossella Tarchi), the Archivio della Congregazione per la Dottrina della Fede in Rome (Alejandro Cifres, Daniel Ponziani, and Fabrizio De Sibi – as well as Francesco Bustaffa, a fellow researcher), the Archivio dell'Opera del Duomo di Firenze (Lorenzo Fabbri), and the Sala di Manoscritti della Biblioteca Nazionale Centrale di Firenze (Rosaria D'Alfonso, Carla Pinzauti, Paola Pirolo, Anna Russo, Piero Scapecchi, and Isabella Truci). I also consulted various libraries, including: the Biblioteca Berenson at Villa I Tatti, the Biblioteca Marucelliana, the Biblioteca Nazionale Centrale di Firenze (especially the Sale di Consultazione), the Biblioteca Riccardiana-Moreniana, the Library of the Kunsthistorisches Institut in Florenz, and the New York Public Library (especially the Dorot Jewish Division).

A number of scholars read and commented on my work at various stages in its evolution: Robert Bonfil, Lucia Frattarelli Fischer, Shulamit Furstenberg Levi, Rosemarie Mulcahy, and two anonymous evaluators for the University of Toronto Press. Jill Foulston – a truly gifted editor – repeatedly saved the narrative from wandering off track. At the University of Toronto Press, Ron Schoeffel, Anne Laughlin, and Suzanne Rancourt kept a benevolent eye on the development of this book and the accompanying critical edition of the Blanis letters. Kate Baltais and Harold Otto brought essential rigour and clarity to the final manuscript. Joseph Connors and Louis Waldman at Villa I Tatti were continually on hand – encouraging me to share my discoveries with a wider public.

I could not have undertaken a project of this magnitude without the generous assistance of several funding institutions: the American Council of Learned Societies (Research Fellowship, 2005–06), the National Endowment for the Humanities (Research Fellowship, 2009) and the Lila Acheson Wallace Publications Fund (under the auspices of Villa I Tatti). They made it possible for me to venture beyond my usual work on art patronage and art collecting – into the sometimes daunting field of Italian Jewish history.

I have been fortunate – to say the very least – in the unstinting support of friends and family whose dedication and commitment have withstood the test of time, especially: Dennis Crowley, Lilly Morgese, Joanne Riley, and Dorothy Schwartz, my brother and sister Lyle and Rhonda Goldberg and my mother Lillian Goldberg – to whom this book is dedicated.

Illustration Credits

1 Detail from Stefano Buonsignori's *Map of Florence* (first edition 1584, reissued 1594 and again ca. 1660). The present negative of the third edition is in the Fototeca of the Kunsthistorisches Institut in Florenz.

2 *Piazza della Fonte nel Ghetto di Firenze prima della sua distruzione*, photograph ca. 1890. Archivi Alinari, Florence (Brogi Collection).

3 *La piazza del Mercato Vecchio*, photograph ca. 1880. Archivi Alinari, Florence.

4 Giovanni Grevembroch, *Abiti dei Veneziani* ..., vol. 3, no. 62: *Ebreo*. Museo Civico Correr, Venice.

5 Giovanni Grevembroch, *Abiti dei Veneziani* ..., vol. 3, no. 63: *Ebreo da Levante*. Museo Civico Correr, Venice.

6 Agnolo Bronzino, *Cosimo I in Armor*. Galleria degli Uffizi (Polo Museale), Florence.

7 Ludovico Cardi 'il Cigoli' (attributed), *Don Giovanni dei Medici*. Luigi Koelliker Collection, Milan.

8 Scipione Pulzone, *Christine de Lorraine*, Galleria degli Uffizi (Polo Museale). Florence.

9 Justus Suttermans, *Maria Magdalena von Habsburg, Cosimo II dei Medici and Ferdinando II dei Medici*. Galleria degli Uffizi (Polo Museale). Florence.

10 Letter from Benedetto Blanis (Florence) to Don Giovanni dei Medici (Venice), 1 January 1616 (Florentine style). Archivio di Stato di Firenze, Mediceo del Principato 5150, f. 205 recto.

11 Letter from Salamone Blanis (Florence) to Don Giovanni dei Medici (Venice), 3 October 1620. Archivio di Stato di Firenze, Mediceo del Principato 5150, f. 32 verso.

Notes on Sources

CONCERNING THE BLANIS LETTERS

In the Archivio di Stato di Firenze: Mediceo del Principato 5150 (ASF MdP), there is a crucial series of over 200 letters – now available in a critical edition, The Letters of Benedetto Blanis Hebreo to Don Giovanni dei Medici: 1615–21 (University of Toronto Press, 2011). Many are cited here and they are cross-referenced by their document numbers in the critical edition. For example: ASF MdP 5150, f. 123r (9 April 1616) [Letters, no. 40].

CONCERNING FLORENTINE DATING

In Florence at the time of Benedetto Blanis, the year changed on 25 March (not 1 January). For nearly three months (January, February, and most of March), the Medici Grand Dukedom operated with the date of the former year, as reckoned in Rome and most other places. This system remained in place until 1750 (after the end of Medici rule).

In the text of this book, all dates are expressed in modern (not Florentine) style. In the notes, both forms are offered: the Florentine dates inscribed in the documents and the normalized dates. For example: ASF Otto 258, f.144r (12 January 1617/18) describes a Florentine document dated 12 January 1617 (otherwise 12 January 1618).

THE BLANIS FAMILY

Dr Moyse Blanis de Lerda
(in Orvieto by 1512; died by 1536)

Samuel
(in Monte San Savino
by 1564)

Dr Laudadio
(doctorate in Perugia 1530;
in Florence by 1566;
m. Stella)

Jacob

Dr David
(in Florence
by 1560)

Dr Agnolo
(doctorate in Perugia 1547;
in Florence by 1571;
m. Bellotia Montolmo 1558)

Dolce

Salvatore
(in Massa by 1581)

Agnolo

Giuseppe — Salustro — Ginevra

Laudadio
(m. Laura or Reche Blanis;
died 1632)

Two daughters
(Laura and Reche)

Benedetto
(born c. 1580: died 1647
Wife 1 (died 1617)
Wife 2 (m. 1618)

David
(m. Mirra Galli
Franzesis 1611)

Salamone

Lelio/Agnolo
(m. Porzia Finzi
1595; m. Ricca
Finzi 1611)

Daughter
(m. Moisé
Lattone)

Daughter
(m. Salamone
Finzi)

Daughter

Daughter
(died 1616)

Daughter
(m. Dr Morino)

Daughter

Jews and Magic in Medici Florence
The Secret World of Benedetto Blanis

chapter one

The Piazza

You are standing in the middle of downtown Florence in the vast and vacant Piazza della Repubblica, an echoing no man's land bordered by oversized cafés, tourist shops, and five-star hotels. There is hustle and bustle of a kind, but not the hustle and bustle of locals doing real things in the course of a real day. Tour groups shuffle from museum to church to museum, with the aimless aggressiveness of their sort. Taxis come and go, horns blaring, as they plow through this supposedly pedestrianized zone.

Over the rooftops, just offstage, loom the towers and cupolas of the city of Florence – right there where they are supposed to be, all the familiar postcards from the land of the Renaissance. A few hundred steps in one direction would take you to the red-domed cathedral, a few hundred steps in another to the castellated town hall. But here in Piazza della Repubblica there is another story to tell – as inscribed on the ponderous triumphal arch at the back of the square:

L'ANTICO CENTRO DELLA CITTÀ
DA SECOLARE SQUALLORE
A VITA NUOVA RESTITUITO
1895

THE ANCIENT CENTRE OF THE CITY
RESTORED TO NEW LIFE
FROM AGE-OLD SQUALOR
1895

So, urban renewal struck with a vengeance and the ensuing century scarcely softened the shock of impact. But what ancient centre? What former squalor? What alleged new life?

For many generations, in fact, another inscription surmounted another portal near this same site:

COSMUS MED. MAG. ETRURIAE DUX
ET SERENISS. PRINCEPS F. SUMMAE IN OMNES
PIETATIS ERGO HOC IN LOCO HEBRAEOS
A CHRISTIANORUM
COETU SEGREGATOS NON AUTEM EIECTOS VOLVERUNT
UT LEVISSIMO CHRISTI JUGO CERVICES DURISSIMAS
BONORUM EXEMPLO DOMANDAS FACIEE
ET IPSI POSSINT
ANNO D.M. DLXXI

COSIMO DEI MEDICI, GRAND DUKE OF TUSCANY
AND HIS SON THE MOST SERENE PRINCE FRANCESCO
MOTIVATED IN ALL THINGS BY GREAT PIETY
WILLED THAT THE JEWS BE ENCLOSED IN THIS PLACE
SEGREGATED FROM THE CHRISTIANS BUT NOT EXPELLED
SO THAT THROUGH GOOD EXAMPLE THEY MIGHT COME
TO BOW THEIR STUBBORN NECKS TO CHRIST'S LIGHT YOKE.
YEAR OF THE LORD 1571

Cities are defined as much by what is missing as by what is present. Two thousand years ago in this very place there was the forum of the Roman colony of Florentia. Then, from the Middle Ages until nearly the present day, the Mercato Vecchio, Florence's central market. And on the edge of this market, the Jewish Ghetto, as decreed by the Medici grand dukes of Tuscany.

Scant traces of the Roman forum remain below ground. The central market has since moved twice – first to nearby San Lorenzo and then to distant Novoli. The Jewish Ghetto ceased to exist as a physical place more than a hundred years ago, when its buildings were razed in the late nineteenth century. It survives, however, as an historical fact and perhaps even as a state of mind.

Rather than brick and stone, the primary evidence for the Florentine Ghetto now consists of words on paper, preserved for centuries in local archives – usually Christian archives, not those of the Jews themselves. For years, the leaders of the Jewish community periodically obliterated their own history, clearing out the old documents on their shelves to make space for new ones. If we want to discover the Ghetto as it was and trace the lives of its inhabitants, the place to begin is the vast Medici Granducal Archive with its police files, judicial records, legal contracts, government deliberations, and literally millions of letters.

Sometimes there is an extraordinary trove waiting to be found – words on paper that seem to cancel the intervening centuries and bring us face to face with the past. Between 1615 and 1620 Benedetto Blanis (c.1580–c.1647), a Jewish scholar and businessman in the Florentine Ghetto, sent 196 letters to Don Giovanni dei Medici (1567–1621), an influential member of the ruling family. In the Medici Granducal Archive, we can read these letters more or less as Benedetto wrote them – in pen and ink, with all of the peculiarities of their time.[1] Now we can also read them in print, in a full critical edition – with transcriptions, footnotes, and indices.[2]

Here, in *Jews and Magic in Medici Florence*, we follow this same man on another archival journey – one that is longer, less direct, and less clearly mapped. It takes us to the farthest reaches of the Medici Granducal Archive and then beyond, moving from document to document of every imaginable kind. Benedetto served Don Giovanni as librarian – managing his palace library, organizing and cataloguing its contents, acquiring books from various sources, and sharing his patron's most recondite interests. Together they ventured into dangerous and often forbidden territory: astrology, alchemy, and the Kabbalah.

Along the way, we see Benedetto Blanis living life on the edge, in a strange no man's land between the Ghetto and the Medici Court. He was a scholar by choice but a businessman by necessity and his commercial ventures, especially loan sharking and debt collection, made him many enemies. Benedetto's worst foes were other Jews and the very worst his own in-laws and cousins – recent converts to Catholicism.

Benedetto played a daring game of brinksmanship in the realm of the occult, trusting in his patron's power and influence to set things right. He traded in esoteric writings, especially works on the Inquisition's *Index of Prohibited Books*, and he was incarcerated twice, first for two weeks and then for several years. After one particularly stormy encounter with Monsignor Cornelio Priatoni, the Father Inquisitor in Florence, Benedetto Blanis reported to Don Giovanni dei Medici: 'I was a bad Jew, he said, because I went from one condition to another and did not stay Jewish. That, he said, was his definition of a bad Jew.'

Benedetto may have been a good Jew or he may have been a bad one, but he was undeniably a brilliant and provocative individual. Thanks to his personal letters and a host of other documents in the Medici Granducal Archive, we can follow him closely, day by day, as he struggled to make a life for himself against daunting odds.

chapter two

The Palace

The Medici Family

Florence and the Medici... The Medici and Florence... For five centuries their destinies were inextricably linked. Even today, they are still an inevitable presence in their former capital – in its streets and squares, its churches and palaces, and most of all, its incomparable museums.

Originally farmers and small landowners, the Medici left the backwoods territory of the Mugello in the late thirteenth century to make their fortune in their adopted city. With Giovanni (1360–1429), his son Cosimo the Elder (1389–1464), and his grandson Piero the Gouty (1416–1469), they rose from shopkeepers and money changers to great international bankers. Along the way, they involved themselves in government affairs – first as civic officials, then as leaders of local factions, then as political bosses. By the time of Giovanni's great-grandson Lorenzo the Magnificent (1449–1492), the Medici had become de facto heads of state and legendary patrons of the arts.

During these years Florence was evolving as well. When the Medici first appeared, they found a turbulent city-state wracked by dissension between social classes and political cliques. Florence was also in conflict with most of her neighbours, including Prato, Pistoia, Pisa, Lucca, Arezzo, and Siena. As generations passed, and the Medici overtook other rival families, their home town emerged as the dominant power in the region.

With historical hindsight, it seems inevitable that the Medici should become rulers of a united Tuscany with Florence as its capital. But meanwhile, the struggle on the ground was intense and often deadly... In 1478 Lorenzo the Magnificent was wounded and his brother Giuliano killed in a conspiracy led by the Pazzi family. After Lorenzo's natural death in 1492, his son Piero (1472–1503) held on to power for only two years before he was expelled from the city. Then – in rapid succession – the old Florentine Republic was re-established in 1494, quickly becoming a religious dictatorship under Frate Girolamo Savonarola in 1496, who was deposed and executed in 1498. A secular republic under Leader for Life Piero Soderini was established in 1502, but terminated in 1512 when the Medici re-entered Florence. Alessandro dei Medici (1511–1537), the illegitimate great-grandson of Lorenzo the Magnificent, was elected duke in 1532, only to be assassinated by his cousin Lorenzino in 1537. Almost immediately, another cousin Cosimo dei Medici (1519–1574) was named duke of Florence in his place.

Contrary to every available precedent, Cosimo I ruled for thirty-seven years, until his death in 1574, and then he was succeeded by six direct descendents over five generations. Florence, for centuries a tempestuous republic, had become an absolute monarchy and a substantial territorial state. In 1555 Cosimo conquered Siena after a long siege, making himself master of the entire region. In 1557 he was proclaimed duke of Florence and Siena, then in 1569 grand duke of Tuscany.

The Medici were now hereditary princes presiding over a regal court, and so they remained until the extinction of the dynasty in 1743. In Florence their trajectory is marked by a sequence of increasingly grand palaces. In 1444 Cosimo the Elder built the first great Palazzo Medici, demonstrating his family's ascendancy in the quarter of San Lorenzo. In 1540 his great-great-grandnephew Cosimo I expropriated the former town hall (Palazzo della Signoria) as his ducal residence. In 1549 Cosimo's wife Eleonora de Toledo (1522–1562) acquired the Pitti Palace on the other side of town. Then, a few years later, the Medici made their next decisive move.

Palazzo Pitti

When Benedetto Blanis was a boy growing up in the Florentine Ghetto, the Pitti Palace was already a very big building – nearly a third the size of today's immense structure. Located across the river in the Oltrarno district, the chief Medici residence and its vast gardens occupied some twenty times the space of the tiny Jewish enclave in the centre of the city.

In 1591 Francesco Bocchi described the Pitti Palace in his guidebook, *Le Bellezze della Città di Firenze* (*The Beauties of the City of Florence*), offering an appreciation that was echoed by innumerable visitors over the centuries: 'This edifice is unequalled in magnificence and indeed superior to all others, demonstrating the ultimate power of the art of architecture and the beauty it can achieve. In this way, the palace corresponds to the grandeur of spirit of those who live there.'[1]

The Pitti Palace was continually growing, with its rooms and their contents in constant flux, but it was always lauded as the supreme expression of Medici splendour. In 1558 the architect Bartolommeo Ammannati extended the façade and added a monumental central courtyard: 'Entering [the chief portal],' Bocchi noted, 'you find three great loggias that enclose an ample *cortile*, 80 braccia [48 yards] long, forming a capacious theatre. Jousts and other noble spectacles are held there, produced in truly royal style.'[2]

While beautiful and splendid, the palace was also a functioning environment for affairs of state – ranging from routine meetings to great festive and ceremonial events. On 11 May 1589 an overwhelming spectacle was produced in Ammannati's great courtyard for the wedding of Grand Duke Ferdinando I and Christine de Lorraine. The architect and engineer Bernardo Buontalenti staged a series of extravagant mock combats followed by a lavish pyrotechnical display. Then, after a sumptuous dinner, he flooded the *cortile* for a dramatic naval battle between Christians and Turks, against a backdrop representing the City of Constantinople.

Nothing that visitors saw in the Pitti Palace and the other Medici residences happened by accident. Cosimo I (ruled 1537–1574) and his son Francesco I (ruled 1574–1587) created a system of workshops to produce the lavish necessities of princely life – everything from clothing and jewelry to tapestries and table decorations to paintings and sculptures by the most celebrated masters of the day. In 1588 Ferdinando I (ruled 1587–1609) transferred most of these workshops to the recently completed Uffizi Palace and coordinated their operation. The distinctive style of the Medici Court was essential to the family's identity and it survived as long as they did, until the death of Anna Maria Luisa in 1743.

The Pitti Palace was the principal showcase of Medici splendour, but it remained a construction site for most of its history, with the scaffolding barely concealed. On 16 February 1619, while living in Venice, Don Giovanni dei Medici received an update on the latest building campaign: 'His Highness [Cosimo II] will be staying in his nearby villas and in the old palace in the piazza [Palazzo Vecchio, formerly Palazzo della Signoria]. Meanwhile, they are adding a major extension at Pitti.'[3]

This was the court of an absolute monarch – the grand duke of Tuscany. While he did not make all the decisions nor formulate all the laws, everything that mattered was carrried out in his name and subject to his approval. In the Medici Granducal Archive, a standard formula appears at the bottom of many thousands of documents: 'His Most Serene Highness says in his rescript, *Let this be done.*'

Behind the scenes – and behind the legendary magnificence – the Florentine court was a notably compact and efficient operation. The principal members of the Medici family normally lived in the Pitti Palace, working closely with a small group of secretaries and advisers.[4] People came and went in this inner circle, but *We, the Grand Duke of Tuscany* remained an unchanging presence – especially for those outside the closed doors of the audience and council chambers.

Benedetto Blanis' life spanned the reigns of four Medici grand dukes. He was born around 1580, in the time of Francesco I (1574–1587) son of Cosimo I and co-founder of the Florentine Ghetto. He then lived through the reigns of Francesco's brother Ferdinando I (1587–1609) and Ferdinando's son Cosimo II (1609–1621), dying around 1647, halfway through the long reign of Cosimo II's son Ferdinando II (1621–1670).

Benedetto Blanis' letters to Don Giovanni dei Medici document his adventures in and around the Florentine court during a time of crisis. Cosimo II ascended the throne in 1609, at the age of nineteen and died in 1621, at the early age of thirty. Although intelligent and cultivated, he was ailing and weak-willed – so his authority devolved upon two strong and decisive women, his mother Christine de Lorraine (1565–1636) and his wife Maria Magdalena von Habsburg (1589–1631). Cavaliere Camillo Guidi (1555–1623), secretary to Dowager Grand Duchess Christine,[5] was an influential figure in the government, along with various chaplains and confessors, especially the French Augustinian Leonard Coquel.[6] Together they formed an ad hoc council of government that became all-powerful during the last years of Cosimo II's life. At first Christine and Maria Magdalena assisted the grand duke during his audiences, then they deputized for him during his protracted final illness. Meanwhile, petitions arrived by way of Secretary Guidi and the religious advisers. By the time of Cosimo II's death, *We, the Grand Duke of Tuscany* had been reduced to a mere signature.

Florence, meanwhile, was a small city where the people who mattered saw each other every day. The government was ostensibly autocratic, but the Medici themselves were readily accessible to those with the right connections. Even Benedetto Blanis, a Jew from the Ghetto, could find his way in and around the Pitti Palace – with the help of his friend and patron Don Giovanni dei Medici.

Don Giovanni dei Medici

Don Giovanni dei Medici (1567–1621) was the second to last of Cosimo I's fifteen children. Born out of wedlock to the Grand Duke's mistress Eleonora degli Albizzi, Giovanni soon won his father's affection and favour. Although not quite seven years old at the time of his sire's death, in 1574, the boy had already been legitimized and handsomely endowed with money and a Florentine palace of his own.

At the age of twelve, he represented the Medici in the first of many diplomatic missions – travelling to Venice when his half-brother Francesco I married his long-time Venetian mistress Bianca Cappello (1548–1587), complicating relations between the two states. On 11 July 1579 the young Don Giovanni offered Francesco a very mature account of his reception:

> Yesterday morning, I appeared before the assembly and I was greatly honoured by those gentlemen and by the Doge himself, since I am the brother and servant of Your Most Serene Highness. I carried out your instructions as diligently and respectfully as I could and I owe you the greatest devotion and obligation for this opportunity. While executing your mission, I encountered all the grandeur and greatness that I could have wished, and I was overwhelmed by the honours that these gentlemen accorded me. I hope that my obedience will always bring you satisfaction, since your satisfaction is the chief incentive in my life.[7]

In 1587 Don Giovanni joined the Spanish army in Flanders, launching a military career that lasted more than thirty years. He moved from one theatre of war to another, serving the governments of Spain, France, and the Holy Roman Empire, particularly in their struggles with the Turks in Central Europe and the Mediterranean.

In 1610 Don Giovanni was commissioned as general by the Venetian Senate but he settled permanently in Venice only in June of 1615. Until his death, on 19 July 1621 he served as governor and captain general of their armies, spending much of his time in combat in the border territory of the Friuli. He had a residence in Venice on the Grand Canal and a villa at Palvello near Padua. Meanwhile, he maintained his Florentine palace in Via del Parione and a villa just outside the city at Montughi[8] – but he visited neither during the last six years of his life.

While commanding the Venetian forces, Don Giovanni made good use of his inside knowledge and contacts, assisting the Tuscan government with local affairs. He was a paid employee of the Venetian state, and there was already an accredited Tuscan ambassador in Venice, but Don Giovanni was the most visible representative of the granducal family – with ample scope for conflict of interest. 'I warned Your Highness' ambassador that he should not be seen visiting me,' Don Giovanni advised his nephew Cosimo II in the spring of 1616. 'I live right in the middle, between the Spanish Ambassador and the agent of the Holy Roman Emperor, whose house is in fact across from mine ... So, it might well seem that he [the Tuscan Ambassador] is conferring with me before he meets with them.'[9]

Don Giovanni was widely acclaimed as a military engineer, designing and building fortifications in Florence and Livorno, in the south of France, and in the Eastern Veneto. On 17 March 1592 he wrote Grand Duke Ferdinando I, describing his hands-on work at the new fortress in Livorno: 'We are now completing the model and Maestro Raffaello Pagni arrived at just the right moment to help me, as soon as he finished taking the measurements. We don't yet have bricks or stones, and it is impossible to bring them here due to the bad weather. Meanwhile, we are levelling the site and doing what we can, and I will not leave here until the model has been completed.'[10]

He was also a skilled civil architect, involved in various Florentine projects – including the new façade for the cathedral, the chapel at the Forte di Belvedere, and the Cappella dei Principi (Chapel of the Princes), his family's grandiose tomb at San Lorenzo.[11] In December of 1615 he sent Cosimo II a copy of Vincenzo Scamozzi's newly published, *Idea dell'architettura universale* (*The Concept of Universal Architecture*) – by personal request of the celebrated Venetian architect.[12]

Don Giovanni collected works of art and cultivated a passion for music and, above all, the theatre.[13] He was a voracious reader, assembling extensive libraries at his various residences and leaving over seven hundred volumes at his villa in Palvello at the time of his death.[14] A cursory inventory of his Florentine palace cites leather wall coverings, weapons of various kinds, paintings, books, and drawings. In his laboratory (*fonderia*), he left a plentiful supply of glass vessels for distillation and other experimental processes.[15]

Throughout his life, Don Giovanni was dedicated to the arcane, maintaining a full alchemical workshop in his Florentine residence. When he moved to Venice, he entrusted its operation to his nephew Cardinal Carlo dei Medici (1586–1666), younger brother of Cosimo II. However, he was soon disappointed to learn that the young prelate was only a recreational alchemist, not a true adept of the occult. On 22 June 1620 the manager of his household in Florence commented, 'In my opinion, His Lordship [Cardinal Carlo] does not intend to embark seriously on such pursuits but means only to entertain himself – passing the time pleasantly by making fragrant and health-giving distillations, compounding sugar preserves and other such princely trifles.'[16]

There was at least one Medici relative who shared Don Giovanni's commitment to esoteric studies, his nephew and alter ego Don Antonio (1576–1621). Only nine years younger than his uncle, Don Antonio was born out of wedlock to Grand Duke Francesco dei Medici and his mistress (later Grand Duchess) Bianca Cappello. Don Antonio's own laboratory and alchemical library at the Casino di San Marco in Florence[17] attracted many seekers of cosmic secrets, including Jews like Benedetto Blanis and Doctor Samuel Caggesi from Fez.[18]

Not only in his pursuit of hidden knowledge did Don Giovanni push the limits of the permissible, indulging a fundamental recklessness throughout his life. At the age of twenty, on 6 June 1587, he begged his half-brother Francesco I to excuse an unspecified excess of youthful spirits: 'Pardon my error, for the love of God, since it oppresses my very soul to have so displeased you. Have compassion for my youth and for the straits in which I now find myself – particularly since the police did not recognize me for who I am, as you can easily ascertain.'[19]

Less than a year later, on 5 March 1588, he explained away his predilection for gambling, in a letter from Antwerp to Grand Ducal Secretary Belisario Vinta: 'If it is reported in Florence that my disorders here are due to gambling, I hope that as a gentleman you will treat these rumours as false and malicious and affirm this to His Highness. We never gamble in my house unless it has been ordered by the doctors to amuse me during my convalescence … and I usually come out ahead rather than losing.'[20]

Don Giovanni's transgressions did not cease with his youth. At the age of forty-four, on 6 July 1611, he asked his nephew Cosimo II to excuse his latest violent outburst – the killing of a man in Florence on a hot summer's night:

After dinner, Don Garzia di Montalvo and I withdrew to my rooms, where there was a certain young woman with whom I have a certain friendship. Don Garzia said that he had no idea how we could manage to sleep, unless we took a turn around town in order to tire ourselves ... So, I ordered a small carriage for an after-dinner drive with Don Garzia and the young woman ... We headed towards the Baptistry and when we were near the cross there, three men came over to our carriage. One of them stuck his head in the window and said, 'Carry on! Have a good trip!' meanwhile looking closely at all of us. So, I commented to Don Garzia, 'What sort of manners are these anyway?' and Don Garzia replied, 'It's just some drunk.' While we were making the loop for the sixth time, I told the coachman to go back to the house ... At that very moment, however, those three men spotted us and that same one put his hand on the carriage and announced, 'Off you go now! It's time to head home, that's the best thing. So do as I tell you!' I drew my sword and flourished it in the face of that character, who backed off. Then I threw open the door and jumped out of the carriage which was still moving.[21]

His greatest lapse was not the folly of a moment. Around 1609 Don Giovanni entered into a relationship with Livia Vernazza (1590–1655), the daughter of a Genoese mattress-maker who was already burdened with a husband and a history of public prostitution in Lucca and Florence. Indeed, Vernazza was presumably the 'certain young woman' in the carriage with him on the evening of 6 July 1611. Eccentric unions were not unknown in the Medici family,[22] but this was an indulgence that someone in Don Giovanni's position could ill afford. Although a respected and even beloved figure, he was still a legitimized bastard – a scion of a princely house but not quite a prince in his own right.[23] He did not figure in the granducal line of succession, did not have an apartment in the Pitti Palace, and was unlikely to marry a legitimate member of another ruling dynasty. However, he could certainly have married any number of socially presentable women with family, money, and connections.

Benedetto Blanis offered a typically sordid account of the first meeting of the two lovers – claiming the best possible inside source, Livia Vernazza herself:

I am qualified to talk about this ... since I frequented the home of His Most Excellent Lordship Don Giovanni – eventually in order to read the Hebrew language to His Excellency. This allowed me to develop a friendly acquaintance with the aforementioned Livia, who recounted her arrival in the City of Florence to me in the following terms: Having fled her husband's home [in Genoa], she took refuge in that of her brothers. Through violent means, they tried to force her to return to her husband, so she sought shelter in a Genoese convent. There she arranged for a male friend to remove the key from the porter's lodge at night ... and with that particular friend, she left the convent and travelled to Lucca. From there, she continued on to Florence where she began a relationship with a man from the Gabburri family. Then, she began a relationship with Signor Giulio Ricasoli who introduced her to Signor Don Giovanni. I heard it said that she lived in a generally immoral manner before her friendship with His Excellency, offering her services to various men.[24]

Grand Duke Cosimo II expressed the prevailing assessment of Livia Vernazza in a letter to his sister Caterina dei Medici-Gonzaga, Duchess of Mantua, on 7 February 1619: 'I consider that woman to be nothing less than a whore… [and] I find it difficult to believe that a man of such prudence and wisdom could be capable of so great an error.'[25]

Livia might well have been no better than a whore. She was, at very least, 'an available woman (*donna di partito*),'[26] in the language of the time – passed from hand to hand by leisured gentlemen of the Florentine patriciate. There was, however, no arguing the violence of Don Giovanni's passion nor the extremity of his error: 'I am your most Illustrious Ladyship's truest, most affectionate, and most obligated servant, and I humbly adore you, being your very slave, Don Giovanni dei Medici.'[27]

Don Giovanni married Donna Livia on 25 August 1619, after the granducal family tried and failed to block the annulment of her previous marriage.[28] By then the couple's absence from Florence had become a practical necessity. Don Giovanni dei Medici still enjoyed prestige and influence in his native city—but he did not, and probably could not, return.

Benedetto Blanis at Court

On Saturday, 20 June 1615, after sunset and the conclusion of the Jewish Sabbath, Benedetto Blanis wrote his first letter to Don Giovanni dei Medici:

At Your Excellency's departure, as you know, I was so overcome by anguish as to be rendered speechless. Seeing myself deprived of your noble and divine presence, I felt my heart burst from my breast and my soul depart from my body, leaving me drained of my very life blood. Aided however by imagination and memory, I summoned up the glad hope that you would make me worthy of your service and that I would fully experience your favour. This encouraged me to take up my pen and write these few badly composed lines, which do not deserve to be read by Your Excellency unless Your Excellency, in your graciousness and goodness, renders them worthy by reading them. In this way, I hope for a return to life by way of your kind reply, informing me of your happy arrival at your destination.[29]

For both the sender and the recipient this was more than a quaint exercise in ingeniously servile hyperbole. In the time of Benedetto and Don Giovanni, the proudest claim that a person could make was, 'I am in the service of …,' flourishing an appropriately potent name. At various phases of his life Don Giovanni could have cited the doge of Venice, the king of France, the king of Spain, and the Holy Roman Emperor, not to mention his own relatives, the grand dukes of Tuscany. Benedetto Blanis, in his more limited sphere, had Don Giovanni dei Medici.

A princely court or a noble household was conceived as an extended family in which every member had his or her place, through loyalty and mutual dependence if not through blood. The relationship of patron to client and client to patron was assessed in intensely personal terms, and it presupposed an unquestioning exchange of favour and support that conditioned all aspects of a person's life. Members of old and established Christian families – those in the mainstream of Florentine affairs – normally took such relationships for granted, thanks to generations of reciprocal interests and concerns. Those outside the mainstream – like the Jew Benedetto Blanis – needed ability, inventiveness, and sheer determination to get a foot in the door.

Benedetto's relationship with Don Giovanni began in the realm of commerce, the perpetual hurly-burly of Jewish buying and selling:

In Florence, Don Giovanni bought a house in [Via del] Parione right across from his own palace and he installed the aforementioned Livia, providing all of the necessary household goods. I sold her a set of Venetian brocade hangings and other things, as I did for His Excellency on a daily basis. I also supplied everything for the personal use of that lady, as His Excellency ordered – textiles and trimmings and other such items … His Excellency maintained her in a style worthy of any lady or indeed any princess. With her carriages, footmen, and pages, she enjoyed the same state as His Excellency – or perhaps even more. When I needed to deal with His Excellency or do business with him, I usually found him in Lady Livia's house, so I know of what I speak.[30]

By the summer of 1615 Benedetto was ready to complete an ambitious trajectory – from ghetto trader to public scholar and court Jew. Don Giovanni had set a strategy in place before his departure, and Benedetto moved quickly to put it into effect:

> In the course of my business affairs and in order to carry out some commercial dealings that were entrusted to me, I spoke with that man again that Saturday evening … placing myself at his disposal, since Your Excellency had recommended me to him that very morning. I will be seeing him again and I will keep you informed, obeying whatever instructions you give me. If it had not been Sabbath (*Sabato*)[31] my passionate spirit, my sincere affection, and my desire to serve you would certainly have induced me to set aside every other consideration.[32]

The concrete meaning of Benedetto's letter turns on the identity of 'that man.' The Jew already had commercial dealings with him, and he hoped to take their relationship to another level through his connection with Don Giovanni dei Medici. In fact, 'that man' was no less than Cavaliere Camillo Guidi, secretary to Dowager Grand Duchess Christine de Lorraine. A month later, on 21 July 1615, Benedetto briefed Don Giovanni on his emerging relationship with one of the most influential figures at the Medici Court:

> Every day or two, I stop by to see him and I have sold him 12 braccia [23 feet] of damask, light silk, taffeta, and other such things. I often beg him to favour me by rectifying the false opinion that the Padroni [the 'bosses,' referring to the granducal family] have of me … Last week he said these exact words, 'An opportunity arose with the Padrone [Grand Duke Cosimo II], who spoke a world of evil of you and your doings.' At that time, he assured the Padrone that he had no better subject than me, leaving aside my Judaism. All of this emerged when I went to offer a set of bed hangings that I had seen in Genoa and for which I was prepared to pay 800 scudi.[33]

Benedetto was perpetually anxious regarding his image at the Florentine court which (like most courts) was an insidious rumour mill: 'I have not been easy in my mind lately, since I don't like having the kind of equivocal reputation that I seem to have.'[34] Although Florence was the Tuscan capital, it operated like a small town and most matters – especially Jewish matters – landed up in the hands of the Medici sooner or later. Not only did the grand duke allow Jews to reside in his Ghetto, he owned the very houses in which they lived.

There were many ways that a Jew could develop an unsavoury reputation. Since most Jews were in business, they often ran up bad debts, received stolen goods, and loaned money illegally.[35] In addition, some gambled, got into fights, and abused their families. Christians, of course, did all of these things too – but unlike Jews, they were not constantly suspected of religious and moral subversion. Back in 1571 the presumption of Jewish iniquity figured prominently in the edict establishing the Florentine Ghetto: 'The Most Serene Grand Duke of Tuscany and the Most Serene Prince Regent ... both know how easy it is for these Jews ... to lure the souls of simple Christians into their own vain superstition and execrable perfidy.'[36]

Although simple Christians might well have been susceptible, some of the most sophisticated members of the Medici Court were also strongly attracted to Jewish superstition. On 21 July 1615 Benedetto Blanis described the latest approach by Secretary Camillo Guidi:

> In recent days, that man [Camillo Guidi] asked me if I had noted any particular properties of the psalms ... On another occasion, he asked me if I understood some letters or characters which I am enclosing in this letter so that Your Most Illustrious Excellency [Don Giovanni] can see them. I ask, however, that you return them immediately, so that I can give them back when he asks for them. To make a long story short, I replied that I would be able to understand them if they were letters but I knew nothing about characters, and we continued to skirmish in this way. I said that we were dealing with a sin and an offence to God. He answered that David had done as much with his psalms and that with a certain psalm, and lighting certain small candles, it was possible to bring death to an enemy. I replied that this was just a joke and that it would be a sin to try to force God to do one's will.[37]

Benedetto hedged his bets and played dumb when the granducal secretary pumped him for inside information regarding an extreme form of Practical Kabbalah verging on black magic. The characters in question, as any educated Jew would have known, came from *archangelic alphabets* of the kind used in Kabbalistic amulets.[38]

Benedetto's most valued attributes were his knowledge of Hebrew and his presumed mastery of Jewish mysticism. For orthodox Catholics, Hebrew was a sacred language essential for advanced study of the Old Testament.[39] For others – less orthodox – it was also an essential tool for exploring the occult. Many Kabbalistic texts were in Hebrew, and the language itself was the prime material for mystical intervention. Since Hebrew letters have numerical equivalents, elaborate numerological tables were devised to reveal the hidden meanings of words and names, fixing them in a broader cosmic scheme.

Don Giovanni had at least a rudimentary knowledge of Hebrew – enough to copy passages of 'Sacred Scripture' in his own hand.[40] He was now grooming Benedetto Blanis as a teacher at the Medici Court, and his chief pupil was to be Don Carlo, a younger brother of the grand duke destined for an ecclesiastical career. On 1 August 1615 Benedetto recounted Camillo Guidi's latest lobbying efforts, demonstrating a remarkable eye for setting and ear for dialogue:

> On Tuesday evening at the 24th hour [around sunset at 7 p.m.], I encountered the Cavaliere at the foot of Ponte Vecchio and he said, 'Come see me tomorrow.'
>
> 'I will come,' I said, 'whenever Your Lordship commands.' So, I went the next day after lunch, and the Cavaliere told me that he had been negotiating with Prince Don Carlo for me to give him lessons in the holy language. He found the Prince very well disposed and then took up this matter with his mother Madama Serenissima [Christine de Lorraine].
>
> After some discussion, the Cavaliere said to her, 'Your Highness should confer with your confessor, so that you can be fully informed.' Madama didn't trust me and asked the Cavaliere who I was. The Cavaliere replied, 'This is that Benedetto ... etc.'
>
> Madama then replied, 'I need no further information since I already know him. He is a man of great merit and an upright person.' The Cavaliere took much pleasure in communicating this good news to me, saying, 'I am pleased that you are held in such high regard.'[41]

Benedetto was gratified yet bewildered by this precipitous turnaround: 'To me this sudden alteration seems worthy of note, since I was formerly viewed in a particular way but now I am reputed a man of merit ... Meanwhile, I am waiting for you to return those characters that I sent you with my letter. Every day I fear that the Cavaliere will ask for them back and I do not wish to annoy him.'[42]

Like many court officials, Camillo Guidi lived in the Oltrarno district only a few minutes' walk from the Pitti Palace. Benedetto did not hesitate to call on him at home, then he promptly re-enacted their encounter in a letter to Don Giovanni dei Medici:

Last Monday [21 September 1617], I wanted to write to Genoa [regarding the bed hangings] so I went looking for the Cavaliere at his current house in Via Maggio but I didn't find him there and I went over to the Pitti Palace. No sooner did I enter the Palace than I ran into him under the loggia [in the courtyard] but saw that he was heading in the direction of his house. So, I accompanied him back home to collect some documents and then I returned with him to the Pitti Palace, leaving him at the stairs that go up to Madama Serenissima's apartment ... While walking down the street with the Cavaliere, I asked him if he had seen the Confessor in order to discuss the matter that concerns me, and he replied that he hadn't seen him in the Palace. I then observed that I would dearly love to know more about the waters in which I was fishing and that it was not my personal inclination to be a shopkeeper or a merchant. He assured me that I was in Madama's good graces, as he had previously told me, and that I was very well thought of.[43]

Florence was a place where a Jew from the Ghetto could dog the footsteps of one of the most powerful officials at the Medici Court. According to Benedetto, it was also a place where the local rulers peered out the windows of their palace to see what was happening in the streets below:

I went back to see the Cavaliere on Thursday [25 September 1615] and after discussing various matters, he said with evident amazement, 'There is something that I need to tell you but now I can't remember what it is!' 'Is there news?' I asked. 'Yes,' he replied. 'Please, by all means, tell me!' I responded.

Then he recounted the following, 'The day before yesterday [23 September], I was with the Grand Duke in the presence of the Grand Duchess[44] [Maria Magdalena von Habsburg] and Bardino [Attorney General Mario Bardini[45]]. The Grand Duke said to me, 'What were you doing with that man? Maybe you were running through your catechism?'

The Cavaliere replied, 'Where did you see us? This ground floor window is the biggest spy-hole you have! The Jew of whom we speak is one of the greatest virtuosi and one of the most worthy men that you have in your state and, I might even say, in all of Italy. He is the one who is eager to teach the holy language to Prince Don Carlo, to understand it in three lessons, not just read it but understand it, and usually it is no small thing to understand it in even three or four months.'

'I recommended him,' the Cavaliere said to Madama, 'and Your Highness can find out more about him from your Confessor.' She said, 'He has already told me and I know that we are talking about a man of great merit and an upstanding person.'[46]

Benedetto – it would seem – had been replaying Guidi's reported conversation over and over in his mind. Then he worked it up as a vivid, almost theatrical scene with full dialogue (the crossfire of 'he said' and 'she said' is quite remarkable in an early seventeenth-century letter).[47] Unfortunately, Benedetto's efforts soon bogged down in everyday reality – notwithstanding Guidi's high-level public relations work. On 8 November 1615 he assessed the situation for Don Giovanni dei Medici:

> As usual, I am busy with my studies for the sermon that I have to preach every week. Meanwhile, out of necessity and contrary to my personal inclination, I attend to business in order to maintain myself and my family. Every day I give a lesson to Madama Serenissima's Confessor[48] although I earn nothing from this. Meanwhile, there have been no new developments regarding that other matter of mine by way of either the Confessor or the Cavaliere.'[49]

Benedetto managed to sign up Christine de Lorraine's confessor for unpaid Hebrew lessons, although the grand duke's brother eluded him entirely. On 6 December 1615 he accompanied the Jewish delegation when they called on Don Carlo at the Pitti Palace, congratulating him on his election as cardinal and his impending journey to Rome.[50] The 'other matter' to which Benedetto refered was a failed attempt to expand his living space in the Ghetto by annexing the backyard of a nearby tavern.

As Benedetto frequently lamented, his personal inclination was not to be a shopkeeper or a merchant. However, it was difficult for Jews to earn a living in any other way, apart from a few actors, musicians, and medical doctors. Benedetto could claim an impressive range of qualifications including a mastery of Hebrew, a working knowledge of Latin, and a proprietary interest in the Jewish occult. What he needed was a patron like Don Giovanni dei Medici who could put these pieces together and shape them into a career.

chapter three

The Ghetto

Benedetto at Home

'My Most Illustrious and Excellent Lord and Patron,' Benedetto Blanis
wrote Don Giovanni dei Medici on 16 August 1615,

> As Your Excellency knows, having visited my room for that evening party,
> it receives light from two windows that overlook a small courtyard be-.
> longing to the landlord of the Tavern of the Piovano. As you also know,
> this room is where I do my preaching every Saturday. The courtyard in
> question is very small, measuring roughly 4 braccia [7.65 feet], and they
> set out tables there, so there is much insolence from drunken and imperti-
> nent people and much scandalous behaviour. In fact, there were two friars
> who behaved so outrageously two weeks ago that I had to stop my sermon
> until the noise died down. Also, we hear filthy and shameless expressions
> all day, including words not uttered even in Via del Giardino[1] [Florence's
> most notorious centre of prostitution]. Since I have three female children,
> one of whom is ten years old, there is an obligation to set this situation
> right – and we can accomplish this readily with the help of Your Most Il-
> lustrious Excellency. The solution is for the Grand Duke's property admin-
> istration to buy this little courtyard with the room above it, and then rent it
> to me for 100 scudi in the usual way... Then I would be able to spread out
> a bit, since my only habitation is this one room.[2]

For Benedetto, his wife and children these were the realities of daily
life in the Florentine Ghetto. In their single room, they hosted parties,
presented learned discourses, and received at least one of the Medici in
a social setting. Despite their cramped quarters and the indignities that

surrounded them, the Blanis were distinguished representatives of the local Jewish aristocracy.

This Ghetto was a concrete place – a distinct enclave within the Tuscan capital. There was an inner courtyard and a narrow street and two gates that were locked at night. Four hundred and ninety-five men, women, and children inhabited this meagre space, according to the official census of 1622. This was less than 1 per cent of Florence's total urban population of 60,059.[3]

The Florentine Ghetto began operation in 1571, and Benedetto Blanis was born there just a few years later, around 1580. But life in the local ghetto was only one chapter in the long history of the Blanis family. Who were they before 1571?

The Blanis Family

The name 'Blanis' is Hispanic in origin and still common in Catalonia and Valencia.[4] Benedetto's ancestors were presumably swept up in the great expulsions of 1492 (Spain) and 1497 (Portugal) that liquidated the ancient Jewish communities of the Iberian Peninsula. The earliest known family document, dated 2 July 1512, regards a doctor of medicine named Moyse Blanis de Lerda (evidently from Lerida) who had recently established himself in the Umbrian city of Orvieto in the Papal State. Moyse was Benedetto's great-great-grandfather.[5]

What about Moyse and his family in the years between 1492/1497 and 1512? Like many Iberian Jews, the Blanis might have suffered forced baptism and lived secretly as *marranos* for a time while weighing their options for escape. Or else, they might have fled immediately – which would mean that Benedetto's ancestors had never compromised their identity as open and practising Jews. One possibility is that Moyse landed first in the south of Italy, then made his way north to Orvieto after the banishment of the Jews from the Kingdom of Naples in 1510–11 – but this is only playing the odds of historical probability.

What we do know – as documented fact – is that Moyse Blanis de Lerda arrived in Orvieto in grand style, with a prestigious education, powerful connections, and financial resources. On 2 July 1512 the papal administration in Rome ratified an agreement between the government of the city of Orvieto and this Jewish doctor, allowing him to lend money at interest and exempting him from all authority except that of the papal chamberlain.[6] Our last glimpse of Moyse occurs two decades later, in a legal petition dated 6 January 1536. His son Laudadio was suing to reclaim some valuable rings, after Moyse Blanis de Lerda had been robbed and murdered near Vetralla, also in the Papal State.[7]

Laudadio – Benedetto's great-grandfather – led the Blanis family to the pinnacle of its fortune in Italy. On 22 April 1530 the authorities in Rome granted the young Jew a special dispensation, allowing him to take a university examination in medicine and the liberal arts.[8] Doctor Laudadio went on to establish a prestigious practice in Perugia, the chief city of Umbria – becoming personal physician to the governor, Cardinal Tiberio Crispi.[9]

Like his father Moyse, Laudadio Blanis managed an impressive range of business ventures. He lent money at interest,[10] sold textiles,[11] manufactured mattresses, blankets, and pillows in partnership with other Jews,[12] acquired agricultural land, and produced and sold wine.[13] Along the way Laudadio consolidated an eminent position in the local Jewish community and was regularly assigned the task of collecting the taxes imposed by the Christian authorities.[14] In 1545 he was given permission to host a synagogue in his own home in Perugia.[15]

Laudadio carved out as secure a niche for himself and his descendants as any Jew could have imagined at that time. In addition to money and connections, he had four sons – Jacob, David, Salvatore, and Agnolo – and one daughter, Dolce, on whom he could base his hopes for the future. In 1547 Agnolo Blanis[16] (Benedetto's grandfather) followed in Laudadio's footsteps, earning a degree in medicine from the University of Perugia, through the patronage of Cardinal Crispi.[17] A year later, in 1548, Laudadio took a decisive step to protect the family fortune – compelling his four sons to renounce gambling for high stakes on pain of forfeiting their inheritance.[18]

More than enough risks and reversals were already looming on the horizon for Laudadio and his heirs. In 1555 the fiercely anti-Jewish Gianpietro Caraffa was elected as Pope Paul IV, and he moved quickly to construct a ghetto in Rome – beginning an inexorable process that culminated in 1569 with a general expulsion from the papal territories, including Umbria.[19] Laudadio Blanis saw the handwriting on the wall well before the final cataclysm, and he began shifting the family's base of operations to the nearby Medici State. By 1564 he and his brother Samuele were running a bank in the Tuscan town of Monte San Savino[20] while Laudadio resided in the city of Florence. In 1567 a census of Florentine Jews registered this snapshot of the Blanis household:

In Gualfonda:
The doctor Maestro Laudadio, 60 years of age.

Stella, his wife.

His granddaughter Laura, 15 years of age.

His [nephews/grandsons] Joseph and Salamone, aged 15 and 11.

Moyse and his servant are in Bologna but often come to stay.

Here they have a synagogue.[21]

Laudadio's home in Gualfonda, a remote and sparsely settled area in the north of the city, functioned as the nucleus of a large extended family. At the time of the census, none of his four sons was living in Florence, and he had assumed personal responsibility for three younger relatives.[22] Laura was the daughter of Laudadio's son Salvatore – and either Benedetto's future mother or his maternal aunt.[23]

Laudadio hosted a synagogue, as he had in Perugia, attracting others of Iberian origin.[24] According to the 1567 census, there were ninety-seven Jews distributed around the city with at least two centres of worship, 'where these Jews of Florence gather.'[25] In 1570, on the eve of ghettoization, another census noted 710 Jews dispersed throughout the cities and towns of the Florentine territory, ranging from one in Arezzo to ninety-four in Pisa. [26] Eighty-six Jews were recorded in Florence itself, with 'Doctor Blanis Physician' heading the list with a substantial household of nine.[27]

Around 1571 Laudadio son of Moyse Blanis and his dependents moved from the gardens and orchards of Gualfonda to the close confines of the new Ghetto near the central market (Mercato Vecchio). Although the distance was less than a mile, Laudadio and his household suffered a precipitous decline in their standard of living as measured in terms of light, space, and freedom of movement.[28] Also, for the first time in their lives, they had to coexist on a daily basis with other Jews – if not quite as equals, at least as neighbours. Doctor Laudadio Blanis had seldom, if ever, prayed in a public synagogue until the opportunity was forced on him by Cosimo I and Crown Prince Francesco.

Some four hundred Jews came to live in the Florentine Ghetto, mostly refugees from disbanded settlements in the Medici State.[29] Meanwhile, at least three hundred others voted with their feet and went elsewhere, particularly those who might have been Doctor Laudadio's social and economic peers. Most conspicuous in its desertion was the old banking elite, with charters from the Medici allowing them to lend money at interest outside Florence (where usury was forbidden). When their charters lapsed, they lost their incentive to remain in Tuscany – so they took their liquid capital and moved on.

Before the creation of the Florentine Ghetto, there had been no organized Jewish presence in Tuscany, apart from the households of its more affluent and influential residents. With the departure of most of these, Laudadio Blanis found himself leader by default of a newly mandated community. In 1572, 1574, and 1575 he served as one of the governors of the Ghetto, helping put social and administrative structures in place where none had previously existed. A more immediate challenge was the economic survival of his own family, since the Blanis had been pushed out of the banking business by the Tuscan government. Although Doctor Laudadio could still practise medicine, he was already well into his sixties. In Florence the textile trade was the obvious answer, and Laudadio joined the Silk Guild (Arte della Seta) in 1572.[30]

The next generation of the Blanis family – Jacob, David, Salvatore, and Agnolo – did not settle easily into the new scheme of things.[31] Laudadio's eldest son Jacob (Benedetto's great-uncle) was living in Monte San Savino in 1570, then for a few years he was relatively active in the Ghetto – serving as a governor in 1573 and 1578. In 1575 Jacob Blanis matriculated in the Linen Guild (Arte dei Linaioli) as a *rigattiere* or seller of second-hand goods – but he evidently left Florence around 1580, after a series of rancorous disputes with other members of the emerging Jewish community.[32]

Doctor David Blanis matriculated in the Florentine Apothecaries Guild in 1560, but died or left town before 1571.[33] Salvatore (Benedetto's maternal grandfather and great-uncle) transferred to the tiny border state of Massa Carrara, engendering a collateral branch of the Blanis family closely aligned with their Florentine kin.[34] Doctor Agnolo[35] (Benedetto's paternal grandfather and great-uncle) made the move to the Ghetto but apparently died soon after, leaving at least four children who had been born on the outside: Laudadio, Giuseppe, Salustro, and Ginevra.

Agnolo's eldest son – Laudadio – married a cousin – Laura or Reche, one of the daughters of his uncle Salvatore. Then around 1580[36] Benedetto was born – into the first native generation of the Florentine Ghetto.

The Creation of the Ghetto

In 1571 the Medici did not merely legislate the creation of the Florentine Ghetto, they developed it as a private real estate venture. Agostino Lapini, a local diarist, witnessed the sudden transformation of the squalid underbelly of his home town:

Our Lord Crown Prince Francesco dei Medici began to construct the site where the Jews now live after buying up houses, shops, warehouses, brothels, and other residences long occupied by prostitutes of the most common sort ... There he created all of the habitations and shops that now form the Place of the Jews (Piazza dei Giudei). In that area, there had formerly been vile places of commerce and the squalid rooms of the lowest of whores, so Our Lord Prince removed them and rebuilt these premises, spending many thousands of scudi. It is shut up every evening, earlier or later according to the time of year.[37]

The Ghetto, according to Lapini, was a classic exercise in urban renewal and a bold venture in social engineering. The Medici cleared an unsightly slum in the heart of their capital – only a few minutes' walk from the cathedral, the baptistry, and the archbishop's palace. This underperforming property became the Place of the Jews, and the rulers of Tuscany marketed it directly to their new captive constituency. On the evenings of 22 and 26 April 1575 Medici agents staged a dramatic auction in the recently constructed synagogue, allocating fifteen newly available rental properties:

It is the wish and intention of their Lordships that the stated houses and shops in the Ghetto of the City of Florence be rented for two years beginning on the first of May 1575. They will be auctioned by candle, according to the norms and customs of such auctions, with each property adjudicated to the highest bidder [when the candle burns out]. The terms of this auction will be published by proclamation in the Ghetto and in the Synagogue ... and it will be carried out by their Lordships' agents ... Matteo, the Public Herald of the City of Florence, will announce each offering by blowing a trumpet ... This auction will take place in the presence of the Corporation of the Jews (*Università delli Hebrej*) in their Synagogue.[38]

The scene had undeniably picturesque elements and would have made a compelling subject for a local painter with a taste for the curious and exotic. In real terms, however, the Medici government was cynically forcing their tenants to bid against each other, maximizing income from a limited stock of Ghetto accommodation.[39] The Jews had been presented with a stark choice: they could quit the Medici State or make the best of their drastically reduced circumstances. By the time of Benedetto Blanis, there were approximately a hundred rental properties in the Ghetto, comprising apartments, simple shops, and shops with living quarters.[40] His father Laudadio Blanis rented two apartments and a shop in his own name – including the room occupied by Bene-detto, his wife and daughters.[41]

When Cosimo I and Crown Prince Francesco announced their crea-tion of the Florentine Ghetto, on 31 July 1571, they conspicuously failed to mention urban renewal and property speculation. Since the Medici were the hereditary rulers of a Catholic state, they preferred to voice grander principles – at least in public:

> The Most Serene Grand Duke of Tuscany and the Most Serene Prince Re-gent ... both know well the difference between the abominable laws and customs of the Jews and those that are desired and required from true Christians. They also know how easy it is for these Jews, through con-tinuous intercourse (*conversazione*) and assiduous familiarity, to lure the souls of simple Christians into their own vain superstition and execrable perfidy. This results in great dishonour to God and the loss of souls and also to the total disparagement of the Christian Faith, which as religiously devout princes they are compelled to guard with all possible care and at-tention. As true observers of the holy canons and true supporters of sacred and civil law, they wish to remove insofar as possible the opportunity for such intercourse (*conversazioni*), especially secretly and by night.[42]

This was a notably restrained variation on a familiar theme, at least by contemporary standards, which the Medici rulers of Tuscany could eas-ily have pumped to the level of sexual hysteria but did not. True, they played with the ambiguous term *conversazione* – which could mean al-most anything from 'discussion' through 'interaction' to 'lascivious in-tercourse.' In fact, far more incendiary language had been on the table less than a year earlier in an official report commissioned by the grand duke and the crown prince:

> The Jews have persisted in their dealings and intercourse (*conversazioni*) with Christians, and they have kept Christian serving men and serv-ing women, as well as Christian wet-nurses. They have gambled, eaten, and amused themselves together, all of which is forbidden by the sacred canons under pain of excommunication ... This is without even mention-ing love affairs and sins of the flesh, which must weigh heavily on the conscience of anyone who allows or abets such intercourse (*conversazi-one*).[43]

When it came down to it, the Tuscan government was motivated less by religious zeal than by reasons of state (*ragione di stato* in the austerely Machiavellian language of the time; our present-day term would be 'political expediency'). The Medici had few strong feelings on the Jewish question but they needed to placate powerful allies, including the vociferously anti-Hebraic Pope Pius V Ghislieri and King Philip II of Spain. So, they formulated a tactical compromise – opting to 'segregate but not expel,' as inscribed over the main gate to the Ghetto. In the final analysis, the Medici had nothing to gain by inflaming mob reaction, since their goal was to make money while creating a minimum of social and economic disruption. So, they moderated the rhetoric in their official decree – casting themselves, not as ideologues, but as the prudent rulers of a well-regulated state:

> The intolerable licentiousness of the Jews has in recent times introduced a great and abominable confusion (*confusione*). Due to their similar and even identical dress, it has become virtually impossible for human judgment to discern between Jews and Christians. This often gives rise to detestable improprieties and nefarious excesses, which any prudent prince must seek to remedy and obviate. So that Christians and Jews will no longer have any excuse, and so that Jews of both sexes will be recognized everywhere and by everyone, we decree the following within ten days of the publication of the present edict: All Jewish men who have come or will come to live in the city of Florence are required to wear a cap or hat in any yellow fabric except fine silk at all times and in all places. All Jewish women are required to wear a right sleeve of this same colour ... And in order to allow no confusion (*confusione*) in such matters and to remove all doubt in the future, Their Highnesses order all Jewish males who have reached fifteen years of age to pay an annual tax of 2 gold scudi in cash.

With this new Jewish tax, moral realignment and revenue enhancement found common ground in the Florentine Ghetto. The yellow hats and yellow sleeves were not surprising developments – since the Medici had mandated a similar code four years earlier in 1567 – but then they immediately granted a host of special exemptions.[44] Benedetto Blanis faced dire tribulation throughout his life, but it is unlikely that he wore a yellow hat, a yellow badge, or even a yellow ribbon for a single minute. At least in Florence, this was a fate reserved for another class of Jew entirely.

Segregation, Conversation, and Confusion

Conversazione and *confusione* were the two favourite shibboleths of anti-Jewish rhetoricians. There were a lot of both, it would seem, in Benedetto Blanis' Florence – especially if we take *conversazione* in the general sense of social intercourse, as people 'gambling, eating, and amusing themselves together.' Jews certainly ate and drank in Christian taverns, and this habit worried the Jewish authorities enough for them to temporarily ban it around the year 1620.[45] Jews also gambled with Christians in taverns – as recorded by the Florentine police, since gambling was an illegal and vigorously prosecuted activity. On 18 June 1624, for example, Giovacchino son of Salamone and Benedetto son of Abram – both Jews – were convicted of playing *morra* (a variety of blackjack or twenty-one) in a tavern with Maestro Ercole di Monte, a Christian tailor from Bologna. All three were sentenced to two hoists of the rope in public.[46] In Florence, this was a common crime and a common punishment and Jewish-Christian *conversazione* was not cited as an aggravating factor.[47]

Although Medici guests of honour appeared only rarely at Ghetto entertainments,[48] the general influx of visitors became a practical problem for the Jews if not a moral problem for the Christians. In 1608 the Jewish governors ruled that no one from outside the Ghetto could attend wedding celebrations and evening parties unless explicitly invited by the host.[49] Such festivities were probably viewed as an exotic diversion by many in Florence, as well as a convenient source of free food and wine.

Some Jews, like Benedetto Blanis, seem to have gone wherever they wished, while others were trapped in a hostile city, particularly after dark. Abram, son of Samuel, was tried by the Florentine criminal court on 24 October 1616 – apprehended at two hours after nightfall, without a badge on his hat, on the corner of Via Nuova: 'He fled when the constable spotted him, immediately removing his hat and putting it under his arm, and he was then seen going into a house in Via di Gualfonda.'[50]

Abram denied these charges but was found guilty on the testimony of three constables and two female witnesses. He was then fined 50 scudi[51] – a quarter of which was paid to the constables who made the arrest.[52] The Florentine police were authorized bounty hunters, which had an inevitable effect on the quality of law enforcement.

With the prevailing fear of illicit *conversazione*, it was profoundly risky for Jews to be in the wrong place at the wrong time, particularly if they were wearing the wrong clothing. On 1 February 1617 Moisé Ulliesco was arrested in the most compromising situation imaginable. At three in the morning, he was found dressed as a Christian in the house of a certain Laura, *donna di partito* (available woman or woman on the game). The magistrates gave Moisé a break, since it was carnival season and 'he had not gone to that house for sexual relations (*comercio carnale*) but in order to retrieve the masquerade costume that he had rented to the aforesaid Laura.'[53]

Apart from the sporadic rhetoric of their edicts, the Medici took an eminently practical view of the yellow hat, the yellow badge, and its variants. Over the years many Jewish requests for preferential treatment made their way through the granducal bureaucracy. On 27 August 1618 the administrators approved a typical appeal:

> Prospero Marino, a Jewish banker from Rome, wishes to come and do business in the state of His Most Serene Highness. Since wearing a badge could be detrimental to this activity, he requested an exemption extending to his family and his designated agent. The petition came back from His Highness [Cosimo II] with the following rescript, 'Grant this to him and his son'... Prospero Marino and his son Davitte are therefore granted an exemption from the badge normally worn by Jews.[54]

The yellow badge was certainly a sign of Jewishness – but even more, it was a sign of poverty and powerlessness. Since Prospero and Davitte Marino were coming from Rome, they could have been subject to harassment while travelling, especially by superstitious peasants and domineering officers of the law. Then, once they arrived, no one was going to do serious business with a Jew so blatantly lacking in money and connections as to be reduced to wearing the *segno* (the 'sign' or 'mark,' as it was called).

When problems arose, the Medici usually favoured moderate solutions that confirmed the status quo while emphasizing their ultimate power and authority. A typical case occurred in the autumn of 1621, during a crackdown on Jews in general and the Blanis family in particular. Benedetto's relatives had long been exempt from the segno, in tacit recognition of their social distinction. Jewish commercial families often extended these exemptions to their chief employees – but the Blanis erred in taking such prerogatives for granted: 'For many years, without express permission, Laudadio [Benedetto's father] has worn a black hat without a *segno*. Then more recently, in the last six or seven years, he has had Agnolo [son of Donato Tedesco] wear a black hat as well, claiming that Agnolo was his agent and representative.'[55]

The granducal administration accused everyone of fraud and misrepresentation – but after the initial tough talk, they opted for business as usual, leaving Laudadio's privileges intact along with those of his immediate family. Then a few months later – by explicit order of Cosimo II – Agnolo was allowed to buy his own exemption from the segno in return for a 50 scudi contribution to the Monastero delle Malmaritate (a religious hospice for abused wives).[56] The grand duke demonstrated that he was the sole source of all Jewish privileges, and the money expended on good works could reinstate the moral and social imbalance caused by an undesignated Jew. Fifty scudi might have been the going rate since this was also the fine levied on Abram son of Samuel when he was cornered at night on the streets of Florence without a segno.

What about *conversazione* and *confusione* of the most serious kind? Jewish men were certainly having sex with Christian women – as in the case of Daniele, son of Giuseppe d'Israel and Donna Diamante. This came to trial on 20 March 1625, and the magistrates rose to the occasion with suitably portentous language:

> Last December ... tempted by diabolic spirits and unbridled lust, contravening both divine and human law, they had a carnal exchange (*comercio carnale*), each committing adultery with the other since the Christian woman has a husband and the Jew has a wife ... Seeing the charges brought against the Jew Daniele and taking his failure to appear as a true and legitimate confession of his guilt, the said Daniele is to be led through the city on a donkey with a sign reading 'For Carnal Exchange with a Christian Woman' and a red hat on his head instead of the usual mitre, so that everyone will know that he is Jewish. Then he is to be sent to the galleys for five years. This sentence will be suspended for fifteen days so that he can appear and present his arguments.

This had the makings of a nicely choreographed public spectacle, explicating the dangers of *conversazione* and *confusione*. It would probably also have been Daniele's first experience of discriminatory dress, since he came from a family of affluent and privileged Levantines – Jewish merchants of Iberian origin who resettled in the Ottoman Empire. The guilty party went underground while his family and friends did the necessary, directly petitioning the grand duke. On 23 January 1626 Daniele presented the magistrates with a full reprieve – issued by Ferdinando II dei Medici in return for a 200 scudi donation to the Mendicants' Hospital.[57]

The woman's case was heard on 29 April 1625, with interesting results. The magistrates began with the usual formulas, registering their social and moral outrage: 'Donna Diamante, an easy woman (*zimarrina*), wife of the rope-maker Domenico ... tempted by diabolic spirits, contravening both divine and human law, had a carnal exchange with the Jew Daniele, thereby committing adultery since she has a husband and the Jew has a wife.' Then came the surprise ending: 'The said Diamante confessed to a carnal exchange with a man represented to her as Portuguese. She denied knowing or suspecting that he was Jewish and maintained this under torture. Considering her denial and the lack of evidence to the contrary, the said Diamante was absolved.'[58]

In the course of their carnal exchange, it is always possible that Donna Diamante did not notice that her Portuguese admirer was circumcised. The authorities might also have made a mental reservation, since she was a married woman and perhaps only a casual prostitute. At the most basic level, however, she must have been telling a plausible story – meaning that *confusione* was still a clear and present danger fifty years after the institution of the Florentine Ghetto.

Ghetto Goverŋmeŋt

The Jews were forced into the Ghetto against their will in 1571 – but once they arrived, the Medici gave them considerable scope to manage their own affairs. The rulers of Tuscany preferred to hear as little as possible about these newly assembled subjects, as long as they paid their head tax, paid their rent, and stayed out of trouble – particularly trouble involving Catholics and the Catholic faith.

Jewish matters were best confined to the Ghetto, along with the Jews themselves – but the Ghetto needed to fit into the prevailing scheme of Tuscan government. The grand duke presided personally over the administration of his realm, assisted by an inner circle of confidential advisers. He appointed the executive committees (usually called *magistrati* or magistratures)[59] that processed the day-to-day business of state; then he and his proxies modified their decisions through written rescripts and other less formal means.

Two magistratures were assigned direct responsibility for the Jews of the new Ghetto: the *Nove Conservatori del Dominio e della Giurisdizione Fiorentina* (Nine Preservers of the Florentine Dominion and Jurisdiction) and the *Otto di Guardia e Balìa della Città di Firenze* (Eight Magistrates for the Protection and Supervision of the City of Florence).[60] The Nine Preservers supervised the general operation of the various towns and villages in the Florentine territory – among which the Ghetto was now included. The Eight Magistrates enforced day-to-day criminal justice and debt collection in the capital city – of which the Ghetto was also part.[61]

On their arrival in 1571 the Jewish settlers had to cope with the social, economic, and psychological effects of sudden dislocation. They also had to transform themselves quickly into a functioning unit within the Medici Grand Dukedom of Tuscany. On 30 July 1572 the Nove Conservatori ratified the first election of Ghetto officials while approving a general scheme of governance:

> Every year they will elect and delegate ten of their Jews for their own Magistrature (*magistrato*), and these will serve as Officers (*offitiali*) and Heads (*capi*) of their Corporation (*università*) for one year ... These Ten will take office by swearing in the appropriate form in front of the Chancellor (*cancelliere*) of their Corporation, promising to execute their office faithfully for the service of God and the benefit of that Corporation. Then these Ten will elect two of their number as Overseers (*soprastanti*), and they will serve for the same period of one year.[62]

Year after year the Jewish electors regularly submitted the names of their new officers for ratification – as they did in June of 1609:

> They [the Nine Preservers] approved the resolution of the 16th of this month by the Assembly of the Ghetto of the Jews of Florence (*congrega del ghetto delli ebrei di Firenze*) as registered (*rogato*) by their Chancellor (*cancelliere*) Isach Gallico, wherein they elected Salvadore Teseo, Servadio Sacerdote, and Crescenzio son of Salvadore as Governors of the Ghetto of Florence for one year, with the usual obligations and exemptions.[63]

By 1580 the Jews were registering only four officials rather than ten, then by 1600 the number was further reduced to three.[64] The leaders of the Ghetto might have been streamlining their operation, at least on paper, but the original concept remained in place – a limited body of decision-makers (usually called the *Congrega* or Assembly) chose a few executive officers (usually called *governatori* or governors).[65]

In the Florentine Ghetto relatively few men (and presumably no women) had the right to attend meetings, the right to speak, the right to vote, or the right to stand for elected office.[66] In 1611 twelve members of the voting or office-holding elite (*Congrega*) sent a petition to the

Nove, identifying themselves as the majority of sixteen.[67] In these years the Ghetto was variously described as a *Commune* (Commonwealth), a *Università* (Corporation), and a *Repubblica* (Republic) – but universal suffrage was the farthest thing from anyone's mind.

At least in theory, the officers of the Ghetto acted as spokesmen for a largely self-governing community – one that policed itself, arbitrated its own disputes, and resolved its own quarrels without troubling the grand duke or his surrogates. In Florence, however, Jewish autonomy remained an elusive goal – mostly due to the Jews themselves. A contemporary observer summed up their options: 'Almost everywhere in the world, the chief rabbis act as judges should differences arise and litigation ensue. Otherwise, the Jews effect voluntary compromises through the mediation of two or three mutual friends ... In criminal matters, however, they obey the ruling princes of the places where they live.'[68]

Voluntary compromises were notoriously difficult to achieve in the overheated atmosphere of the Florentine Ghetto, and for nearly forty years there was no designated rabbi. So Jews entrusted major financial agreements – contracts, dowries, and wills – to Christian notaries, sued each other for debt in Christian courts, and denounced each other to the Christian police.[69]

Decades later an elderly Jewish man recalled the essential tenuousness of Ghetto authority: 'The Jews [here in Florence] had jurisdiction and acted as judges when the Jews themselves agreed to submit their cases to them. Otherwise, they went to the Eight.'[70]

Benedetto's Neighbours

Jews represented less than 1 per cent of the total Florentine population, but at times they seem to dominate the records of the local police court. In the Bargello Palace – headquarters of the Eight Magistrates (Otto di Guardia e Balìa) – there was a constant stream of Jewish plaintiffs, Jewish defendants, Jewish witnesses, and Jewish informants.[71]

On 4 January 1622 the Eight Magistrates heard yet another ridiculously petty Jewish case – one that they were probably glad to get on and off the docket as quickly as possible:

At 6 hours after sunset [around 11 p.m.] on the night of 16 November 1621, Leone [son of Salamone from Prato] threw a stone at the windows of Ventura, a German Jew in the Ghetto. Leone would have thrown other stones if he had not been overtaken by Raffaello Levi, also a Jew and the son-in-law of the said Ventura. Raffaello and his wife had been dining in Ventura's house, and Raffaello knew that Leone wished to harm Ventura out of spite. Leone had an amorous inclination for this woman, that is to say, Raffaello's wife and Ventura's daughter, but she did not share his inclination ... The Magistrates considered the testimony of the witnesses who were examined in this case, and they considered Leone's denial that he threw the stone or committed any other punishable act. Since there was no evidence to the contrary, they absolved Leone for lack of proof.[72]

The matter did not end there, and pressure continued to build over the following months – as pressure will in any tightly contained urban space. Then on 22 May 1622 Raffaello and Leone were back in court, with a large supporting cast. There were seventeen defendants in this one case – at a time when there were only 495 inhabitants (including children) in the Florentine Ghetto. These seventeen were all Jews, but they had been funnelled into the Ghetto from a wide variety of places, in Italy and abroad:

Raffaello son of Samuelle Levi, Mantuan [from Lombardy]
Davitte son of Prospero son of Marino, Roman
Leone son of Asdrubale Levi, Roman
Donna Sarra, German, wife of Ventura and mother-in-law of the above
   Raffaello
Salamone son of Abram, German, and
Isache son of Abram, German
– These are all Jews on one side of the case.

Zaccheria son of Jacobbe from Alba [in Piedmont]
Leone son of Salamone from Prato [in Tuscany, near Florence]
Benedetto son of Simone Levi
Israelle Castellani, Roman
Benedetto Sezzi, Roman
Sforzo son of Lione from Pesaro [in the Marche, on the west coast of the
   Papal State], who is blind
Salamone son of Leone from Prato
Lione son of Moisé from Prato
Jacobbe son of Moisé from Prato
Samuelle son of Isache from Prato, and

Lessandro son of Salamone Alpellingo [Spanish by way of Empoli, near
   Florence]
– These are all Jews on the other side of the case.[73]

Most of these seventeen were more or less fixed residents of the Florentine Ghetto, although it is difficult to know for sure. Jews were habitually on the move, and the geographical labels attached to their names
often referred to family origin, not place of current or recent habitation.
The Blanis were not implicated on this particular occasion, nor were
any privileged Levantines – but the defendants were generally solid
citizens from families that produced Ghetto governors:

On the night of 13 April 1622, Zaccheria from Alba, Lione son of Salamone, Benedetto Levi, Israelle Castellani, Benedetto Sezzi, and Sforzo son of
Leone were playing *bazzica* [*bézique* or pinochle] in the house of the aforesaid Zaccheria. Although Raffaello, the first defendant, had sworn several
months ago to keep the peace with Leone son of Salamone from Prato,
he went to Zaccheria's house, accosted Leone, and started punching him.
Leone fled to a bedroom and locked himself in, then Raffaello tried to force
the door. Davitte son of Prospero, Leone son of Asdrubale, and Donna
Sarra wife of Ventura all hurried to lend their support to Raffaello. The
aforementioned Davitte also tried to force open the door.
   In the course of their efforts, Raffaello and Davitte cursed repeatedly
invoking the name of God, saying 'whore, body and blood of God.' Once
they got the door open, Davitte started punching Leone from Prato, while
Leone son of Asdrubale and Donna Sarra started beating him with a slip-
per. The same Davitte also started punching Zaccheria, the master of the
house, and also Donna Sarra, who was Zaccheria's mother.[74] In this confrontation, Davitte and Raffaello were on one side, and Benedetto Levi,
Israelle Castellani, and Benedetto Sezzi on the other. They were then separated, so nothing else occurred at that time, although Leone from Prato
was left with various bruises on his face and various bloodless wounds
to his head.[75]

It is difficult to imagine that Raffaello and Davitte did not swear, in
one way or another, while breaking down Zaccheria's door in pursuit
of Leone – although 'body and blood of God' is a distinctly Christian
mode of cursing. On the following morning (14 May), after an overnight
lull in the hostilities. Salamone from Prato, Leone son of Moisé, Jacobbe

from Prato, Samuelle from Prato, and Lessandro Alpellingo were all standing around together in the Ghetto. They saw Raffaello and Davitte at a window and started shouting that Raffaello was a 'fucking cuckold (*becco fottuto*).' Then they challenged the two of them to come out for a new altercation.[76]

In the days that followed witnesses and defendants confronted each other angrily in the courtyard of the Bargello Palace. But on 22 May the magistrates closed the case, opting for minimal involvement. Raffaello was fined 50 lire for punching Leone at night-time, and Moisé from Prato was fined 10 lire for injuring Raffaello verbally – but the fifteen others were absolved for lack of credible evidence.[77] Ghetto mayhem was viewed as a kind of domestic violence, and Florence was already a turbulent enough place without worrying about Jews beating up other Jews. Tensions often boiled over, and sometimes the police had to take notice – but for every Ghetto incident that came to trial, many others certainly did not.

What was this conflict really about? It began, so far as the court was concerned, with Leone's sexual jealousy and the affronted honour of Ventura and Raffaello. That was the point of the mass heckling in the Ghetto – calling Raffaello a 'fucking cuckold,' even though his wife had repulsed Leone's advances. But neighbourhood squabbles are seldom simple, especially when the neighbourhood consists of a small piazza and a single street. The men of the Ghetto were constantly in each others' faces – competing for the same scant business, vying for the same few synagogue honours, and lusting after the same few Jewish women.

Every year the Republic of Italian Jews (*Repubblica di Ebrei Italiani*) in the Florentine Ghetto elected three governors to lead their community. In the winter of 1614 the police were called in to impose order on the current incumbents:

On the evening of 11 February, the defendant Donato son of Isac Tedesco [i.e., the German], Moisé son of Aronne, and Laudadio Blanis gathered in the Synagogue of the Ghetto along with other Jews at two hours after nightfall. This meeting had been scheduled on the previous day in order to announce that no firecrackers or other fireworks would be shot off in the Ghetto this Lent (*Quadragesima*) nor would ball games be played. Donato began by saying that he wouldn't agree to giving up the firecrackers. Moisé then asked him why he had changed his mind and suggested that he had done so in order to make his son happy. Donato replied that it had nothing to do with his children, and Moisé observed that they must all be princes. Donato answered that they were better than him in every way, which Moisé denied. At that point, Donato slapped him and they attacked each other verbally.[78]

Ball games and presumably fireworks were normally forbidden in the Ghetto[79] but this incident took place on the Monday preceding *Martedì Grasso* (Fat Tuesday or Mardi Gras).[80] Since Carnival is a Christian festivity, its celebration in the Ghetto might easily arouse strong feelings among some Jews. However, a silly quarrel of this kind with the kids in the middle could have erupted in any village where the neighbours saw too much of each other. The magistrates evidently shared this view, dismissing the charges out of hand.[81]

On that occasion, Benedetto's father Laudadio Blanis remained above the fray but there had been a family battle at Donato's Ghetto shop only a few years earlier, duly noted by the Florentine police:

On 26 October 1611, insults were exchanged by Donato's sons [Moisé and Agnolo], subsequently joined by Donato himself, and Laudadio's sons [Lelio, Davitte, and Benedetto] with the involvement of Laudadio. Donato said to Antonio his workman, 'Kill one of these scoundrels for me.' Antonio then got up from a seated position with a pair of tailor's scissors and injured Lelio, with a bloody wound to his ear and a bloodless blow above his wrist. Benedetto was also injured with a bloody wound to one finger.[82]

The confrontation was dramatic but the damage was slight and the case did not come to trial for over four years, demonstrating a lack of urgency on everyone's part.[83] On 13 January 1616 Laudadio, Lelio, Benedetto, Davitte, Moisé, and Agnolo were each fined a mere 10 lire for their exchange of insults. Meanwhile, the burden of guilt was shifted onto Antonio Mazzuola, the only Christian in the case, who was fined 500 lire 'since Donato's order to him, subsequently denied by Donato, did not constitute a justification for his action.' No one could possibly expect a hired workman to find that kind of money, and Antonio had already disappeared from sight – probably fleeing to his native Bologna. Donato Tedesco, recently deceased,[84] was exonerated for lack of evidence.

It would be easy to imagine that the Blanis and the Donati (as the German family was often called) were inveterate enemies locked in a dire feud. Life, however, went on in the Florentine Ghetto, and Laudadio and Donato served together as governors while their case was pending.[85] The two families also shared business interests, with Donato's son Agnolo (another defendant) acting as Laudadio's agent.[86]

Judging from the police records, the Jews of Florence seldom if ever killed each other or did each other lasting bodily harm.[87] Still, in terms of day-to-day life, the Ghetto was both a community of faith and a human pressure cooker. Even the Christian magistrates could sometimes feel the tension building, then erupting at night after the gates of the Ghetto were shut:

> The Jew David son of Abram from Siena and the Jew Michele son of Aronne were incarcerated for injuring each other verbally on various occasions. The following also occurred on the 22nd of the present month [July 1616], beginning a half hour before sunset and continuing later that night: First they had a fistfight in the Ghetto, then Michele went off and got a short stick one braccio [23 inches] in length. Since David was waiting for him on the little terrace in front of the synagogue, Michele used it to give him a painful blow to the left shoulder. Then the stick was taken away from him, and they had another fistfight and continued to injure each other verbally. Michele was left with a bruise to his left eye and a bruise to his right arm.[88]

The magistrates recognized this for what it was – just another Ghetto scuffle – and they sentenced David to the minimum statutory fine of 25 lire. Also, they chose to disregard Michele's use of a prohibited weapon 'since he took up the stick in the heat of the brawl, which was in the place where the defendants live, and the defendants subsequently made peace.'

Even the Jewish elite, represented by Benedetto's younger brother David Blanis, showed no snobbish reserve when it came to mixing it up with the lower orders, represented by the same Michele son of Aronne:

> On 23 January 1618, according to the accusation, David [Blanis] went to the rooms where the Jew Michele son of Aronne lives, called him a spy along with other injurious expressions, then punched him, scratched him, bloodied his nose, and gave him a slight contusion on his left brow. Later, David engaged Michele in a fistfight in the piazza of the Ghetto ... The Magistrates considered David's verbal testimony and Michele's deposition along with his scratches and his contusion. David confessed that he engaged in a fistfight with Michele in the piazza, and this was substantiated by two independent witnesses. Since David denied the rest under

questioning, he was sentenced only to the statuary fine of 50 lire for the punches that drew blood.[89]

Thanks to his frequent brushes with the law, Michele son of Aronne is one of the best documented Jews in early seventeenth-century Florence. An infamous troublemaker, in the spring of 1614 the magistrates imprisoned him 'for correction' at the behest of the three governors of the Ghetto, including Benedetto's father Laudadio Blanis.[90] In the summer of 1618 a restraining order was filed against him by Benedetto's older brother Lelio:

> The Jew Michele son of Aronne from Viterbo is to be released from prison. He was detained on behalf of the Jew Lelio son of Laudadio [Blanis] until he could post a bond of 100 scudi. However, considering this Michele's poverty and the fact that he cannot post even the smallest bond, he must promise not to offend the aforesaid Lelio on pain of 100 scudi fine plus a year of forced residence in Livorno and its district.[91]

When he was not in jail, this Hebraic ne'er-do-well ran errands and did odd jobs around town. Marginal as his career might have been, even that came crashing down on 30 April 1619:

> It is alleged that Michele son of Aronne, a Jew in the Ghetto, was sent by others to the Florentine post where he obtained a letter addressed to Procurator Ottavio Landini ... When questioned, Michele confessed that he was indeed there on the evening when the postal official claims to have given him that letter but only in order to collect other letters ... Then, he maintained his denial under repeated torture with the rope, specifically to determine who sent him ... In conclusion, the Magistrates convicted Michele and sentenced him to be led through the city on a donkey, wearing a mitre and a sign reading 'For Intercepting the Letters of Others.' Then he is to be exiled for life from the dominion of His Most Serene Highness and if he does not comply, he is to be sent to the galleys.[92]

Michele went to the post office to collect mail for various people, and he used this pretext to obtain a letter fraudulently – a letter addressed to a public official, no less. Apart from Michele's lack of elementary street smarts, we have to wonder about his basic instinct for survival. On 9 May 1619 his sentence was suspended for a month, giving him the opportunity to appeal – an opportunity that he evidently ignored.

Finally, on 10 June, 'The penalty with the donkey was carried out, as reported by Corporal Pepe. Then Pepe escorted Michele out through the Pinti Gate.'[93]

This should be the last that we hear of this notorious Ghetto bottom-feeder, since the authorities could not have made it clearer that he had worn out his welcome in Florence. However, by 16 November 1620, Michele was back in town and back in jail:

> The Most Honourable Eight Lords of Protection and Supervision of the City of Florence assembled in a sufficient number in their accustomed meeting place [in the Bargello Palace] and considered the incarceration of Michele son of Aronne, a Jew in the Ghetto. He was apprehended by Lieutenant Sabatino [Ronconi] on the evening of 7 November and charged with failing to observe the sentence pronounced by these Magistrates. On 30 April 1619, they exiled him for life from the dominion of His Most Serene Highness with the galleys as penalty for non-compliance ... They considered the police report and the apprehension of the suspect, then they considered Michele's acknowledgment that he failed to observe the sentence of exile, alleging that he returned to see his mother. Due to his failure to comply with the sentence of exile, they decided to send him to the galleys.[94]

Michele's filial piety failed to move the judges, and he was now a galley slave for life. What on earth could have possessed him to return to Florence? Did he imagine that he might pass unnoticed in a town with only a few hundred Jews – after the public exposure of his final donkey ride? The sad fact is that Michele had no money, no skills, and no frame of reference for putting his life on another track. His family had presumably been cut loose from Viterbo near Rome during the 1569 expulsions from the Papal State. Then, fifty years later, he found himself adrift in the floating population of rootless Jews with no place to go.

Life in the Florentine Ghetto was far from ideal, but it was not the worst available option. Some Jews never even made it through the gates of the city, like two wandering Germans on 11 April 1617:

> The Magistrates considered the incarceration of the Jew Isac son of Libello from Vienna and the Jew Gioiello son of Moisé, also German, who were arrested as knaves and vagabonds at the San Niccolò gate ... They then considered the report by the constable on duty at that gate... and they ex-

amined the two Jews. In conclusion, they decided to exile Isac and Gioiello from the dominion of His Most Serene Highness for as long as His Highness wishes, with the galleys as penalty for non-compliance.[95]

Throughout Europe, there were countless undesirables uprooted by war, famine, religious strife, or sheer poverty. They shifted from place to place, living by their wits and often by crime until they were chased away to try their luck elsewhere. Only a small percentage of these undesirables were Jews – but they had fewer options than most since so many territories were closed to them. Sometimes we can hear gate after gate slamming shut, as in the Florentine police records on 28 January 1619:

The Magistrates considered the incarceration of the Jew Jacob son of Cipriano who was arrested in the city of Florence for failing to respect the terms of the permit granted him by His Most Serene Highness [Grand Duke Cosimo II]. Since this Jacob had been banned from the State of the Church, he was allowed to live only in the territory of Siena ... It emerges from the report and other documents that he was subsequently expelled from Siena as seditious, scandalous, and criminal in behaviour. It also emerges that he was banned from Rome and its territory for being the accomplice of thieves. By way of justification, Jacob claimed that he had come to Florence in order to petition His Highness for a new residence permit. However, the Magistrates decided to exile him from this dominion, with the galleys as penalty if he does not comply. Within three days of his release from prison, he must vacate this dominion and never return.[96]

The Jews themselves were no less eager to exclude Jewish undesirables, as recorded on 9 July 1619:

The Magistrates have considered the incarceration of the Roman Jew Durante Leno Sestiero and the Jew Benaiù Anticoli, also from Rome, as requested by the Masters and the Assembly of the Jews of the Ghetto. Since these two have neither wives nor families nor trades, the Jews want them evicted [from Florence] and then exiled from the dominion of His Most Serene Highness ... Furthermore, they are scandalous people with disreputable habits and criminal connections ... The Magistrates have heard this Durante and this Benaiù in person, noting that Beniaù is not allowed in Rome and that Durante was previously fined 10 lire for possession of

stolen property ... These two are to be released from prison, then immediately escorted outside the gates of the city with an official ban lest they
dare re-enter.[97]

There was no space in Florence's tiny Ghetto for those extraneous Jews
who were likely to cause trouble or place an undue burden on the community. Benedetto Blanis and some five hundred others lived in close
proximity in a mandated enclave in the heart of a busy city – but they
were a diverse group of individuals, far more varied in their personal
histories than the general population that surrounded them. They came
from distant countries, spoke many languages, practised various trades
and professions, and achieved different levels of economic well-being.
They were all Jews – needless to say – and that was a crucial bond. It
was also a daily source of stress and strain, of crisis and contention.

chapter four

The Synagogue

The Synagogue as It Was

When the Ghetto opened its gates in 1571, there was already an officially mandated synagogue. From the very beginning, this was the essential focus of Florence's tiny Jewish community – the institution that
gave it order and meaning.

The original *scuola* (as it was usually called) did not survive into the
age of photography, and there are no drawings, plans, or even descriptions of the place as it was in the days of Benedetto Blanis. The Corporation (*Università*), Assembly (*Congrega*), or Magistrature (*Magistrato*)
– as the internal governing body of the Florentine Ghetto was variously
known – regularly discarded the records in its chancery when they
were no longer of practical use.[1]

What we do have is a scattering of documents from the Christian
side, preserved in the Medici Granducal Archive – government deliberations, judicial transcripts, and even personal letters, including those
of Benedetto Blanis himself. These offer intriguing glimpses inside the
local synagogue – but not a complete picture of the place and what
went on there.

Then we have another source – the most authoritative yet elusive
source of all. This is the cumulative evidence of accepted Jewish practice. From Benedetto's day to our own, the basic tenets of Jewish observance have changed remarkably little, although we cannot always
document what we assume was true in a particular community at a
particular moment.

Religious, moral, and civil law in the Jewish tradition (*halakha*) is expressed in a vast and varied literature going back thousands of years.

This begins with the commandments of the Torah (traditionally defined as 613 in number), followed by the authoritative interpretations of the Talmud, then the discernments of later rabbis inscribed in compendia and many thousands of surviving *responsa*. These responsa (*She'elot u-Teshuvot* in Hebrew, 'questions and answers') often reflect the practical realities of Jewish life in specific places and times, including the ghettoes of sixteenth- and seventeenth-century Italy. However, they were written for other Jews – people who already knew what Jewish observance was all about – so there was little need to explain the fundamental 'whats,' 'hows,' and 'whys.'

Laudadio Blanis the Elder – Benedetto's great-grandfather – was the most distinguished resident of the new Florentine Ghetto and a commanding presence in its scuola. In the generations that followed, the story of the Blanis family was inseparable from the story of their synagogue – and by extension, the story of their entire community. This was a turbulent passage marked by crisis and contention, culminating in a near revolution.

Leone da Modena, the celebrated Venetian scholar and preacher, figured in the Florentine synagogue at a crucial moment in its history. In 1609–1610 he served as the first official rabbi, nearly forty years after the scuola began operation. Leone da Modena (1571–1648) and Benedetto Blanis (c.1580–c.1647) were almost exact contemporaries. They had ample opportunity to know – and probably loathe – each other, since Rabbi Leone was brought to Florence to spearhead the anti-Blanis reaction.

Leone da Modena is the author of an influential treatise, *On the History of Jewish Rites* (*Historia de Riti Hebraici*).[2] In 1614, a few years after Modena's return to his native Venice, the English ambassador invited him to explain Jewish religious customs to the Christian public, including his master King James I. In this extraordinarily clear and concise work, Modena begins at the very beginning, explicating issues that would have been self-evident to those of his own faith.[3]

Regarding places of worship, Modena starts with a wry acknowledgment of the prevailing restrictions of Ghetto life: 'The Jews construct their *sinagoghe* – or *scuole* as they are usually called – as best they can, large or small, on the ground floor or on upper floors, free-standing or in residential buildings, since they do not have the opportunity to create conspicuous and sumptuous structures.' Then he emphasizes the universality of Jewish observance: 'The arrangement of these *scuole* might vary in detail, reflecting differences in location, country, and ethnicity (*nazione*) but they are all in the form that I describe.'[4]

In the Florentine Ghetto, the scuola was located on the top floor of an unremarkable building in the main piazza, its entrance set off by a small terrace or landing. (This *terrazzino* figures in the local police files as the site of a violent brawl in 1618.[5]) Leone's description of a typical synagogue evokes its interior:

> The walls are white or else lined with panels or wainscotting, with verses or other sayings written across them exhorting attention to prayer. Benches are arranged along the walls, and there are small cabinets in some of these for storing books, mantles, and other items. Up above, there are many lamps or chandeliers illuminating the place with oil or wax. At the doors, there are boxes or small chests for those who wish to leave money as alms for the poor.[6]

When the Florentine scuola was inaugurated in 1571, there was already a cash box for charitable donations[7] and several more were soon added. The benches along the walls faced inward (as described in the 1608 Ghetto by-laws) and the 'mantles' in the cabinets below would have been prayer shawls (*talith*) for the men. Unlike the painted and sculpted decoration that characterized Catholic churches, there would have been white walls and wooden panelling and devotional inscriptions, reflecting the Jewish ban on sacrilegious representation: 'Neither figures nor images nor statues are kept in the home, much less in the synagogues and sacred places, according to Exodus Chapter 20, "Thou shalt not make to thyself a graven thing, nor the likeness of any thing."'[8]

The axis of the scuola, architecturally and ritually, would have been defined by the Ark (*Aròn*) on one side and the reading platform (*bimah* or *tevah*) on the other:

> There is an Ark or Closet at the eastern end which is called the *Aròn* in imitation of the Ark of the Covenant that was in the Temple. The Pentateuch is kept there, that is to say, the first five books of Moses, written by hand with great diligence in squared letters on parchment with specially prepared ink ... This is not in the form of the books that are normally used today but in the ancient style, with pieces of parchment attached lengthwise and sewn with the nerves of approved animals, not thread. It is rolled and unrolled on two wooden sticks, and for the sake of conservation, there are wrappings of linen or silk and also a silk covering. The women decorate this with the finest embroidery, sheathing the Book in beauty. Sometimes the protruding ends of the sticks, called *Hez Haim* [*Etz Chaim* or Tree of Life], are capped with silver objects, either in the form of pomegranates

called *Rimonim* or little bells or some other device. Sometimes it is even
encircled with a crown of silver … Raised up in the middle of the room or
else at the other end, there is a small altar in wood [connected to the Ark]
by a little passageway. This is where the Book is read and where one leans
while preaching.[9]

The women of the community embroidered the Torah coverings but
were otherwise isolated from the chief functions of the synagogue:
'There is a separate place with wooden blinds, up above or adjoining,
and this is for the women. They go there to pray and see what is going
on but without being seen by the men or mixing with them. In this way,
the women will not distract the men from their devotions with sinful
thoughts.'[10]

In Florence, the women's galleries were called *le scuole delle donne*, as
if they were distinct entities of their own apart from the main body of
the scuola.[11] This scheme of segregation and subordination was clearly
expressed in the 1608 Ghetto by-laws: 'The *scuola* where the women go
is shared by all the women. On the Sabbath and holidays, the [*male*]
Governors of the Ghetto are to select two women who will see to their
placement, so that disagreement and discord does not arise, and they
can be quiet and peaceable.'[12]

Meanwhile, the men in the sanctuary below had their own rules, their
own disagreements, and their own recurring breaches of the peace. Not
only was the scuola a place of prayer and reflection, it was the seat of
Ghetto government and the nexus of local power and prestige.

On the Bench

On 17 July 1608 the leaders of the Republic of Italian Jews of the City
of Florence issued their fifth set of by-laws in less than forty years.[13]
Like the earlier regulations of 1571, 1572, 1578, and 1595,[14] this was a
generally shapeless piece of legislation – urgent in tone but unclear in
direction. Once again, we hear the local power brokers thinking out
loud, pondering difficult solutions to complex problems. Article 26 is
a case in point:

Laudadio de Blanis is permitted to sit on the bench in the *squola* (*scuola*) in
the place reserved for the doctor (*dottore*), if no other doctors (*dottori*) are
present nor other men of authority and quality. The rest of the bench, from
there to the corner, is to be used for seating old men or others. No more

than two of Laudadio's sons [Lelio, Benedetto, David, and Salamone] can then sit around the corner on this same bench, and visitors from elsewhere are not allowed to sit near them, unless they [Laudadio's sons] choose to relinquish their places.[15]

This was a blatant move to hedge the prerogatives of the Blanis family in the Florentine synagogue and by extension in the Ghetto community – but why suddenly then in 1608? From the very beginning it had been taken for granted, by Jews and Christians alike, that the Blanis family came first. In 1570, on the eve of ghettoization, Doctor Blanis, Physician (*Dottor Blanis fisico*), headed the official census list of eighty-six Jews then living in Florence.[16] This was Laudadio the Elder, whose grandson and namesake was grudgingly allowed the seat reserved for 'the doctor' thirty-eight years later. Then on 30 July 1572 the granducal administration ratified the first ten-man council elected by the inhabitants of the new Ghetto. The first name on the list (somewhat garbled by Christian bureaucrats) was *Maestro Lalda iddio hebrais Medico* – Master Laudadio, the Jewish Medical Doctor.[17] A year later, on 31 July 1573, Laudadio's eldest son Jacob took his illustrious father's place at the top of the new roster (*Jacob di maestro Laudadio de brandes*).[18] Then, on 30 July 1574 and 30 July 1575, Laudadio himself was back in position (inscribed as *Maestro Laudadio de Brandes*[19] and *Maestro Laudadio Ebrais*[20]).

The scuola was at the heart of Ghetto life, the designated site for group worship and community affairs. The men gathered there for daily prayers – with the women as well, safely segregated, on the Sabbath and holidays. In the scuola, they elected their leaders, formulated their by-laws, bid on rental properties, bid on ritual honours, pledged pious donations, filed legal documents, and presented disputes for arbitration. Placement on its benches was the public scoreboard for status and authority – but who was really in charge in the Florentine synagogue and by extension in the Florentine Ghetto? In Article 26, we see a shifting mass of doctors, men of authority, men of quality, old men, and visitors – along with Laudadio Blanis the Younger and his sons.

Men of Authority

In 1608 there was no designated rabbi in the Florentine Ghetto – nor had there been from the very beginning, back in 1571. Rabbis occasionally passed through without stopping for long, moving on to other places or even converting to Catholicism.[21] Meanwhile, the community operated as best it could under the uncertain and increasingly resented leadership of the Blanis family.

In a functioning Jewish community, there is one ultimate source of authority: the Law that came from God by way of Moses. Men of authority, with the rabbis normally in first place, are those who have accessed this Law through long and diligent study. 'They [the Jews] consider the study and explication of the Holy Scripture to be the most pious endeavour that one can undertake,' Leone da Modena explains in his *Historia de Riti*: 'This is stated in the Sixth Chapter of the Book of Deuteronomy, "and thou shalt meditate upon them [the laws] sitting in thy house, and walking on thy journey."'[22]

There are three layers of Jewish law: the Written Law, the Oral Law, and the Law of Custom. Time and attention was devoted mostly to the Oral Law, 'the pronouncements made by Rabbis and Doctors (*Rabini e Dottori*) throughout the ages concerning the Written Law of Moses ... which are gathered in an ample volume [the *Talmud*].'[23]

> There are a few who study *Cabalà* (Kabbalah), which is revealed speculation and the secret theology of the Scripture. Others study philosophy and still others natural and moral science. Such studies, however, are all applied to the understanding of the Scripture, since they would otherwise be considered pernicious, apart from those who study in order to take doctoral degrees in medicine (*addottorarsi in medicina*). The most common and usual study is that of the *Ghemarà*, which is more properly called *Talmud*, in those lands where it is permitted to have the Talmud. In other lands, they study compendia and various things by the Sages.[24]

Authority, in the Jewish tradition, depends as much on individuals as books. Over the centuries, Rabbi Leone's predecessors had defined the Oral Law in a body of written teachings. There was the *Talmud* – now banned by papal decree – and more recent compilations including the *Mishneh Torah* of Maimonides, the *Arba'ah Turim* of Yaakov ben Asher, and the *Shulhan Arukh* of Yosef Karo. Paralleling these authoritative written sources, there was an unbroken line of descent from rabbi to disciple:

> Rabbis don't take degrees (*esser dottorati*) or undergo examinations. Indeed, they consider it an act of shameful pride when someone seeks to do so. Therefore, when people are seen to be suitably learned, that is to say, experienced and well versed in the Oral Law above all, they are con-

sidered to have achieved their goal. In the Levant, they are recognized by common usage with the title of *Cacham* (*Hacham*), which means Sage. In Italy and Germany, older Rabbis confer titles either in writing or by oral pronouncement. *Caver* (*Chaver*) of the *Rau* (*Rav*) means Companion of the Master. *Morenu* means Preceptor, and *Rau* (*Rav*) means *Maestro* (Master or Teacher).[25]

In the daily life of any Jewish community, the rabbis are the acknowledged authorities on matters of interpretation and observance:

The *Cacham*, the *Rau*, or the *Morenu* decides all questions regarding permitted and prohibited things. They issue written opinions and findings, also in civil cases. They celebrate marriages and divorces. They preach, if they have this talent, and they are the heads of the academies [i.e., Yeshivot]. They take the first place in synagogues and other gatherings. They punish the disobedient through excommunication. Therefore, it is a point of obligation for everyone to treat them with respect in every situation.[26]

The rabbi normally occupied the seat of honour in recognition of his personal status and authority but he was not necessarily the designated prayer leader nor a salaried officer of the synagogue.[27] There were usually two such paid employees: the cantor (*Chazan* or *Cantarino*) and the caretaker (*Shamas* or *Servente*).[28] Modena evokes the dynamics of group worship in a typical synagogue: 'They await the assembly of ten men aged at least thirteen years and a day, since otherwise the prayers cannot be sung with full ceremony. The *Cantarino* or *C[h]azan* then goes to that little altar [the *tevah* or *bimah*] or in front of that closet [the ark or *aròn*] and he begins to sing in a loud voice, with everyone following him more softly.'[29]

In describing a Jewish wedding, Modena defines the pattern of authority under the Law, including the relative roles of the rabbi and the cantor: 'The rabbi of that place, or else the cantor of that particular synagogue, or else the closest relative ... pronounces the benediction to God who created man and woman and ordained matrimony ... The groom then puts the ring on the bride's finger in the presence of two witnesses who are normally rabbis, saying, "You are my wife, according to the rite of Moses and of Israel."'[30]

Rabbis lent their authority to the rite of marriage, witnessing the correct observance of the sacred commandments and witnessing a formal contract between members of the community. Their presence, however, was not obligatory since they were not dispensing sacraments like a Catholic priest. For Jews the hallowing or consecrating force was inherent in the very act of observance – which meant that a community could function without a rabbi, as long as it had ten men over the age of thirteen. For nearly forty years, this was the story of the Republic of Italian Jews of the City of Florence. Not only was there no rabbi, the local Jews did not even hire a cantor, so the men of the governing class led the synagogue services themselves.[31] By 1578 there was at least a caretaker or *shamas* (*tavolaccino* in Florentine usage).[32]

When the synagogue opened its doors in 1571, Benedetto's great-grandfather Laudadio Blanis the Elder presumably occupied the seat of honour and presided over its operation. Not only was he the leading resident of the Ghetto, he was a medical doctor, and he had already hosted synagogues in his homes in Perugia and pre-Ghetto Florence. In 1608, according to the latest by-laws, this seat was still destined for the *dottore* – although this honourable title could have many meanings. In the Christian context, 'Doctor' was normally reserved for men with university degrees, which some Jews duly obtained from Christian universities (where only medical faculties would admit them[33]). Benedetto Blanis came from a long line of university-accredited doctors. His great-great-grandfather, Moyse Blanis de Lerda, was a physician, as was his great-grandfather Laudadio son of Moyse, his grandfather Agnolo son of Laudadaio, and his great-uncle David son of Laudadio. This proud tradition then came to an abrupt end – undermining the family's status inside and outside the Ghetto. Laudadio the Younger did not become a medical doctor, nor did any of his sons (Lelio, Benedetto, Davide, and Salamone).[34]

In the Jewish context, the title of 'Doctor' could also be attributed more generally to men of learning, that is, scholars of Hebrew texts and Judaic Law, whether *Rav*, *Hacham*, *Morenu*, or less. Under this rubric, Laudadio the Younger and his son Benedetto could perhaps pass as *dottori* – just barely, 'if no other doctors are present nor other men of authority and quality.' Leone da Modena denigrated rabbis who took university degrees in medicine, perhaps for the very good reason that he did not have one himself while many other rabbis did. In his day, the rabbi-physician was a well-known and widely esteemed figure who enjoyed exceptional prestige in both the Jewish and the Christian worlds.[35]

The Jews of the Florentine Ghetto did not need an ordained rabbi to carry out their basic religious obligations – prayers in the synagogue, weddings, and so forth – but they desperately needed one if they were to function on their own terms as an organic community. For forty years the sole figure with ongoing authority was the *cancelliere* or chancellor, and he was an extraneous Christian imposition – even if the Jews selected him from among themselves. New governors came and from every year, but there were only four successive chancellors from 1572 until 1613: Raffaello di Cipriano, Leone da Pesaro, David Bettarbò, and Isacche Gallico.[36]

According to the 1572[37] and 1608 Ghetto by-laws, 'All of the documents prepared by the *Cancelliere* of that Corporation (*Università*) will be accorded the authority of public documents.'[38] The chancellor was meant to function as the Ghetto's internal notary – drawing up contracts, swearing affidavits, and filing official copies in the chancery (*cancelleria*) attached to the synagogue.[39] He also reported the annual election of Ghetto officers, then swore them in after their approval by the Nove Conservatori.[40]

Every town, village, and corporate body in Tuscany had a chancellor, so he was an essential figure in the Ghetto, as far as the granducal administration was concerned. Jews, however, did not share the legalistic culture of their Christian neighbours with its proliferation of notaries, sworn documents, and registered oaths – however much they focused on the Law of Moses and its emanations: 'Among themselves, they [the Jews] do not recognize the authority of public notaries, although the scribe can act as a witness and two witnesses can validate any document.'[41]

The swearing of oaths was the crux of the problem. Christian notaries registered their acts 'in the name of God,' followed by elaborate formulas that might include Jesus Christ, the Holy Spirit, the Virgin Mary, and various saints. For observant Jews, 'in the name of God' was already courting blasphemy by virtue of the Third Commandment[42] while the rest had no moral or legal meaning.

An extensive body of Christian law and legal custom evolved over the centuries regarding the issue of sworn testimony 'in the Jewish manner (*more judaico*).' This took bizarre forms in Germany and Eastern Europe, where a Jew might be required to stand on a bloody sow's skin with his breast bared and his hand on the Five Books of Moses, calling down every imaginable Old Testament curse on himself.[43]

In Florence there were less extreme options. On three occasions Benedetto Blanis testified in an ecclesiastical court 'touching a pen, as is the custom of the Jews.'[44] When a Christian judge needed to depose witnesses in an acrimonious Ghetto dispute – another one that the Jews were unable to resolve themselves – their chancellor agreed to administer the oaths 'according to the Jewish rite, physically touching their *tefilim* (*tefilin* or phylacteries). And so each of them touched their *tefilim* and swore physically to tell the truth.'[45]

Leone da Modena described another custom that was practised between Jew and Jew: 'At the conclusion of every contract, each of the parties touches the hem of the robe or some other garment of the witnesses, almost as if they were taking an oath. This is called *Chiniam Suddar*, which means the acquisition of the garment.'[46] Even inside the Ghetto, it would have been difficult to enforce obligations of this kind – without a rabbi on hand to invoke the threat of excommunication.

Quarrels and Dissension

'It was necessary to stipulate many rules and provisions,' stated the electors of the Florentine Ghetto on 17 July 1608, 'in order to quiet the current quarrels and dissension between various individuals in this Republic and for the practical well-being and tranquility of the Assembly.'[47]

Reading through their new by-laws, thirty-eight in number, we see a community that was in imminent danger of ceasing to be a community at all, in spite of the essential bond of Jewish observance. Men were disrupting prayers in the synagogue to register complaints. ('When the Deputy goes to officiate at the usual services, that is to say, in the morning, then at nightfall and in the evening, it is forbidden for anyone of whatever rank or class to discuss any matter or create any disturbance while the service is being said.') Men were offending their own elected leaders. ('Respect and reverence must be accorded the Deputies and Governors of the Ghetto, and they must not be insulted nor ridiculed nor mocked.') Men were attacking each other during formal meetings of the governing council. ('No one is permitted to insult his comrade in the discussions and deliberations of the Assembly ... All discussions must take place calmly, with everyone seated, and everyone honouring everyone else.')[48]

There had been quarrels and dissension in the Republic of Italian Jews of the City of Florence from the very beginning, and few of these regulations were entirely new. Back in 1572 previous leaders had already ruled that 'it is not permitted for anyone to make bird calls or otherwise mock or outrage any of the Ten Officials or their Syndic.'[49]

Then in 1595 they ruled: 'No one, whether male or female, shall dare set upon or beat their comrades in the Ghetto… nor make vile allegations nor otherwise impugn the honour of their comrades.'[50] But in 1608 the legislators faced an unprecedented level of disorder and contention, expressed in the sheer number of regulations: eight in 1571, seventeen in 1572, six in 1578, twelve in 1595, and thirty-eight in 1608.[51]

The framers of the new by-laws had no difficulty identifying the root of their problem: 'Most of the quarrels, dissension, and discord comes from the creation of governors. In some cases, individuals want to be made governors and are not but still wish to have things their own way. Others, meanwhile, do everything they can to avoid being made governors. As a result, there is usually disorder and confusion, which leaves the government of this republic divided and conflicted while control remains in the hands of only one or two.'[52] These unnamed power brokers were dominating Ghetto affairs through backroom politicking, which the 1608 legislators moved to block with a terse and probably inadequate ruling: 'It is not permitted to resolve issues in advance before the Assembly meets nor form cliques in order to impose one's will.'[53] The governors were also instructed to settle internal disputes quickly and decisively: 'Should discord arise among the men of the Assembly, the governors are obliged to pacify them and adjudicate their differences within three days and then let the matter rest.'[54]

In 1608 the leaders of the Florentine Ghetto took a hard look at seating arrangements in their synagogue, especially the place reserved for 'the doctor' but tentatively occupied by Laudadio Blanis. The Blanis dynasty was the most visible expression of the current malaise – whether they were still a vital political force or merely a discredited relic of the past. The obvious solution was to bring in a new man of authority from outside, dislodging Laudadio from his inherited place of honour and giving the community a strong religious focus and a positive sense of direction.

Their first hire was not a success. In Venice the Florentine electors discovered a prodigiously gifted scholar and preacher currently thwarted in his rabbinical career and in desperate need of money. This was none other than Leone da Modena, the soon-to-be author of the *Historia de Riti Hebraici*. They brought him to Florence with an impressive annual salary of 200 ducatoni but a heavy burden of obligations that included teaching, leading prayers, and delivering sermons.

Leone da Modena was undeniably brilliant and sporadically charismatic – but not an easy man to get along with and certainly not the consensus-builder that the Florentine Ghetto needed. Modena, in fact, was rapidly approaching the advanced age of forty without finding a senior rabbi to ordain him and, as a mere *Chaver*, he lacked the authority to issue rabbinical decisions in his own name. Modena was not happy in Florence – which was admittedly a Jewish backwater compared with Venice – and judging from his autobiography, he did not suffer in silence:

> I arrived in Florence at the beginning of the month of Iyyar [early in May of 1609] ... [and] I was welcomed into the home of Abraham To-desco of blessed memory, and I recuperated there. I stayed in his house for a month, honoured and esteemed, until my wife and children arrived on the eve of the holiday of Shavuot [7 June 1609]. After the holiday I settled into my house, teaching and preaching. That summer I was sick for about a month with a boil at the base of my throat. I was also afflicted on my left hand. On the High Holidays [29 September to 8 October 1609] I quarrelled with the aforementioned Abraham and some other members of the community. Meanwhile, the air bothered my eyes and my wife's, and we constantly longed for Venice and yearned to return there. Finally, after Passover [ended 15 April 1610], almost exactly one year to the day since my arrival in Florence, I departed and came back to Venice.[55]

On the plus side, Leone da Modena did not register any outbreaks of his notorious gambling addiction during his scant year in the Florentine Ghetto.[56] After his departure the local electors resumed their improvisation while seeking a permament replacement as unlike Modena as possible. For a time they paid a monthly salary to an unnamed cantor and prayer leader,[57] then on 1 June 1612 they hired Hayyim Finzi from Pesaro. Finzi was anything but a problematic celebrity, and he seems to have published nothing in the course of his life (unlike the breathtakingly prolific Modena), issued no rabbinical decisions (*responsa*), and corresponded with none of his learned contemporaries.[58] However, he was doubly qualified to occupy the place of the doctor in the synagogue, being both a physician and a *Hacham* (a mid-level man of learning, one step above a *Chaver* but one step below a top rabbi or *Gaon*).[59]

Finzi was not walking into an easy situation, since his congregants were at each other's throats. On 3 August 1611 Moisé son of Aronne, an influential member of the sixteen-man Ghetto Assembly, had filed an injunction with the Nove blocking the installation of the latest set of Ghetto governors.[60] On 19 August the Nove ratified this contested

election, ruling against Moyse and in favour of twelve other assembly-
men, while setting aside a controversial new scheme of electoral procedures.[61] Violence then erupted on 11 October 1611, when Donato son
of Isach Tedesco (a relatively recent arrival from Germany) ordered an
attack on Laudadio Blanis and his sons.[62]

Rabbi Hayyim Finzi was clearly the right man for the job, when it
came to resolving differences and formulating solutions. He remained
in Florence until his death in 1621,[63] with his salary regularly paid by
the *Compagnia della Misericordia* (or *Gemilut Hassadim*), the chief philanthropic organization in the Ghetto.[64] Finzi soon took over the job of
chancellor, making himself chief administrative officer as well as spiritual leader. He was now a real man of authority in the rabbinical mode:
arbitrator, judge, and witness, as well as scholar, preacher, and teacher.
On 8 October 1613 Finzi reported the election of a new government of
Ghetto unity. The three governors – promptly ratified by the Nove –
were the lately deposed Laudadio Blanis, the rebellious Moisé son of
Aronne, and the fractious Donato son of Isach Tedesco.[65]

The Republic of Italian Jews of the City of Florence weathered a
storm in the years 1608 to 1613, but it was not always smooth sailing
afterwards. On 11 February 1614 Laudadio, Moisé, and Donato – the
agents of the new regime – came to blows over the issue of Carnival
fireworks, and their scuffle was reported to the Otto di Guardia e Balìa
by a Jewish informer.[66] Against the odds, the Blanis family emerged
from the Ghetto revolution with its prestige diminished but not quite
extinguished. The scuola, however, ceased to be their dynastic pre-
serve, and by 1615 Benedetto was preaching Sabbath sermons in his
own single room.[67]

Italians and Levantines

In 1608, along with other major and minor rulings, the leaders of the
Republic of Italian Jews of the City of Florence took a strong stand regarding liturgy in their synagogue: 'Services are not to deviate in any
way from the Italian mode nor are they to be sung other than in the Italian style, as is the custom and as is set down in the books called *Magaz-
zor Bolognesi*, recently reprinted and available also in previous editions.
Whoever contravenes this order or dissimulates [in obeying it] will be
banned from reciting the service for six months.'[68]

The core of Jewish belief and Jewish observance is universal, but there
are many variations in ritual expression. 'In every city, there is one, two,

six, ten, or even more synagogues or *scuole,*' Leone da Modena explains in his *Historia*, 'depending on the number of Jews who live in that place and can be accommodated there. The Levantine, German, and Italian nations (*nazioni*) differ more in their mode of praying than in anything else and everyone, it seems, wants a synagogue in his own style.'[69] 'The Germans tend to sing more than the others,' Modena specifies, 'while the Levantines and Spaniards have a cantorial style that inclines to the Turkish. The Italians, for their part, are simpler and more restrained in manner. The nature of the service and its words are generally determined by the sequence of ordinary days and holidays but there are differences even in this.'[70]

The Republic of Italian Jews of the City of Florence implicitly banned Sephardic (that is, Iberian and Levantine) and Ashkenazic (northern European) practices from their synagogue while authorizing a prayer book published in Bologna in 1540.[71] This exclusionary ruling might seem strange since many leading members of the republic had come upon their Italian identity only recently. The Blanis were immigrants from Spain and ultimately rooted in the Sephardic rite. The Tedesco, as their name implies, came from Germany in the Ashkenazic sphere. As for the Levantines, their intrusion in the Italian synagogue should not have been a problem, since they already had a place of their own by 1608.

According to the Jewish census of 1567 there were at least two 'synagogues' in Florence – one in the home of Lazzero Rabeno and another in the home of Doctor Laudadio Blanis.[72] Prayer and/or study took place in other households as well, on a more or less organized basis – acknowledging both Italian and Iberian customs.[73] The situation was evidently a fluid one, but it came to an end with the opening of the Ghetto in 1571. By official decree, a single place of worship was then mandated for the entire population – the scuola of the Italians and neo-Italians – which absorbed the Blanis family along with everyone else.

Twenty-five years later, on 14 November 1596, a small group of newly arrived Levantines petitioned Ferdinando I dei Medici for a separate prayer space:

The Levantine Jews living in Florence as humble servants of Your Most Serene Highness express with all due reverence the fact that their mode of prayer is different from that of the other Jews. For that reason, they customarily pray in a place of their own wherever they happen to live, and they beg Your Highness to grant them one of the empty apartments in the

Ghetto for which they will pay the usual rent. This will be a convenience for them and for those who arrive from the Levant and other places to do business in this city. It will also serve those who come to live in Pisa and Livorno and might then pass through Florence. So that the other Jews in the Ghetto will not disturb them and impede their worship, the Levantines ask that Your Highness enjoin these others from going to pray there.[74]

Secretary Lorenzo Usimbardi granted all their requests on behalf of the Grand Duke, with particular reference to the exclusion of disruptive non-Levantine elements.[75] This precaution soon proved inadequate, and in 1601, the Levantines swore out a legal injunction against the Italians. The Levantine scuola was only a place of prayer while the Italian scuola was also the seat of Ghetto government. So, the Republic of Italian Jews seized on issues of liturgical style in order to impose their hegemony on the newcomers:

> They [the Levantines] are disturbed every day by these other Ghetto Jews. Lest anyone dare pray in that place [the Levantine scuola] at any time, they [the Italians] continually issue orders and impose arbitrary penalties with no legal basis. These orders and penalties apply to those who prayed there in the past and those who might wish to pray there in the future, including women and children. Their goal is to ban this place of worship and abolish the freedom that is customarily accorded the various nations.[76]

On 7 March 1601 the granducal administration strongly asserted the rights of the new non-Italian minority: 'These orders [by the Italian Jews] are hereby annulled, and this present finding will be enforced through legal penalties administered by the Chief Constable (*Bargello*) and any other necessary means. Furthermore, those who are active merchants (*mercanti reali*) will be treated in every situation as distinct from the Jews of the Ghetto. Therefore, the officers (*massari*) of the Ghetto have no authority over them, and they will be punished if they contravene this order by harassing them.'[77] Lest there be any confusion, the secretary of the Eight Magistrates summoned the three (Italian) governors of the Ghetto a week later, on 14 March, and communicated this new ruling in person.[78]

The Tuscan government took an authoritative stand on what might seem an internal religious question within the Ghetto community. However, there was a good deal more at stake than liturgical custom, as indicated by the references to Pisa, Livorno, and 'active merchants.'

In these very years, the grand dukes were pursuing a Jewish agenda of their own – one that would soon shrink the Florentine Ghetto and its warring governors into near irrelevance.[79]

For centuries Pisa had figured as the biggest and busiest of the Tuscan seaports, and in the Jewish census of 1570 it registered the largest Hebraic presence in the Medici State, with ninety-four individuals, including many important bankers and merchants. At that time there were only eighty-six Jews in the city of Florence, and they were generally poorer than their Pisan counterparts, due to a ban on Jewish moneylending in the Tuscan capital. In 1570 there were evidently no Jews in Livorno, which was only a small garrison town in the swamps south of Pisa.[80]

Then, in the next few decades, the situation shifted dramatically. In 1571, with the creation of the Florentine Ghetto and the wholesale expulsion of Jews from the rest of the dominion, the Pisan community briefly ceased to exist. By 1573 a few privileged Jews began resettling there, by special permission. Then in 1591 and 1593[81] Grand Duke Ferdinando I formally reconstituted the community and circulated official letters of invitation (the so-called *Livornina*), summoning 'merchants of whatever nation, *Levantini* and *Ponentini*, Spanish, Portuguese, Greeks and Germans, Italians, Jews, Turks and Moors, Armenians, Persians, and others.'[82]

The grand duke's motives were unabashedly economic: 'We are moved ... above all by our desire to act for the public good by encouraging and facilitating foreigners who might participate in business and commerce in our beloved city of Pisa and our port and depot of Livorno.' Ferdinando I seemed to be targeting a mixed bag of nations and creeds, but these foreign merchants were mostly Jews from different places operating under a variety of names. He was especially keen to attract those of Iberian origin – *Levantini* (Jews from the east) who had settled in the Ottoman Empire after the expulsions of 1492–97 and *Ponentini* (Jews from the west) who had remained in Spain and Portugal as ostensible New Christians. Such Levantini and Ponentini were far more likely to bring money, skills, and commercial contacts than their Italian and German co-religionists.

The Ponentini also brought a vexing religious and legal problem to the Tuscan state. There had been no openly practising Jews in Spain since 1492 nor in Portugal since 1497, so anyone coming to Pisa or Livorno from the west was in fact a baptized Catholic. Since the Inquisition regularly punished backsliding with death, Ferdinando I took a bold stand in his 1591/93 letters of invitation, blocking Inquisitorial intervention at the very outset.[83] For all intents and purposes, anyone could arrive in Pisa or Livorno as a Jew with no questions asked. The Medici then quickly ceased to talk about Ponentini at all – developing the blanket label of Levantino to cover any privileged Jew in any circumstance.

In some ways, Grand Duke Ferdinando's Livornina was less radical than it might seem, since his father Cosimo I and his brother Francesco I had been issuing privileges to both Jews and crypto-Jews for many years – on an ad hoc basis, with a stunning array of legal and mental reservations.[84] In 1545 the young Cosimo dei Medici (then only Duke of Florence) offered safe haven (*luogo e sicurezza*) in Pisa to Diego Mendes and his family, immensely wealthy Portuguese 'New Christians' who had relocated to Antwerp. For Mendes and his ilk, the principal guaranty was that of confidentiality, 'that their customs and habits not be scrutinized too closely.'[85]

On 15 January 1549[86] Cosimo extended a more general privilege to 'Portuguese' who might wish to settle in Pisa, tacitly admitting that many were secret Jews or at least Jewish sympathizers. A generation later a Medici secretary summarized these political and legal strategies for Cosimo's son, Grand Duke Francesco I:

> Beginning in the year 1548, the Portuguese obtained many privileges from His Highness [Cosimo I], should they wish to come live in the State of Florence. They could not be detained or imprisoned for crimes of heresy committed outside this State. For crimes of that kind committed here, they could only be prosecuted as a result of direct accusation [i.e., not Inquisitorial investigation] ... This largely contradicts the precepts of Sacred Law and the findings of Church Councils, and one would not necessarily grant privileges of this kind now.[87]

The old Medici solution could be characterized as 'Don't ask. Don't tell. And above all, don't put anything in writing.'[88] On 7 May 1602, a full decade after the Livornina, the same secretary commented wryly on the pragmatic habits of the Tuscan rulers when it came to Jewish matters:

> The Prince [Ferdinando I] must do what he thinks most convenient and appropriate, so that he can have his cake and eat it too [literally, *salvare la capra et cavoli* – save both the she-goat and the cabbages]. This was also the custom of His Most Serene Predecessors [Cosimo I and Francesco I] but

they never put pen to paper, so we cannot find precedents or records in any of the magistratures or archives in Florence.[89]

Under the new mandate of 1591/93, openly Jewish merchants in Pisa and Livorno were not to be locked up in a Ghetto nor forced to wear yellow hats, yellow badges, or other discriminatory forms of dress – unlike their brethren in Florence.[90] This venture proved to be a miracle of enlightened self-interest both for the Levantines and the Medici State. Livorno quickly became the new hub of the Tuscan carrying trade and a vibrant centre of Jewish life and culture – where Jews of various origins lived more or less freely, surrounded by representatives of every nation in Europe and the Mediterranean. In 1606 Livorno was incorporated as a city, and by 1622 it had achieved a population of 14,500, including 711 Jews. Pisa, a city of similar size, had 394 Jews and Florence 495 Jews out of a total population of 60,056.

In his Livornina, Ferdinando I left the door open for a wholesale extension of these privileges: 'You can reside in our city of Pisa and in Livorno, also doing business freely in other parts of our dominion.' This fine print did not escape the notice of Jewish merchants eager to enjoy the same exemptions while living and trading elsewhere in the Medici State, especially Florence.[91] Three years later, in 1596, there were already enough Levantines passing through and even settling for them to request a separate place of prayer. Their presence then increased precipitously in the first years of the seventeenth century, leading up to the new Ghetto by-laws of 1608.

In the summer of 1607, for example, 'Davit Alben Azzor, Jewish Levantine Merchant,' petitioned the Grand Duke. He represented himself (in the third person) as a businessman from the east who could do well for himself and his family while doing well for the Tuscan economy:[92]

Davit, your most humble servant, was here [in Florence] last year in order to negotiate important affairs with Your Highness. He then returned to Constantinople to make the necessary arrangements ... and is now ready to put this business into effect. He therefore appeals to Your Highness with all humility, asking that he and a Levantine Jewish partner and their families be allowed to enjoy in Florence and throughout your realm those privileges granted to Levantine Jews and others who come to live in Pisa and Livorno ... Not only will they be able to conclude the initiatives that are already under way but one initiative will lead to another, and their enterprise will grow.[93]

The Medici administration quickly granted Alben Azzor's request and confirmed his appointment of 'Emanuel Lattone, Levantine Jew,' as his agent in Florence. This was only one of many such petitions in those years, resulting in a rapid pile-up of legal precedents:

> The petitioner [Davit Alben Azzor] and his partner Emanuel Lattone, along with their families ... will have all of the privileges, concessions, and favours currently enjoyed by Abram [son of] Josef Isdrael and Sala-mone da Cagli throughout the realm of His Most Serene Highness even though they are residing in Florence ... These Levantine Jews in Florence can live outside the Ghetto, as stipulated in a petition from Abram Isdrael in 1589... Similarly, they can bear such arms as are permitted in Florence both during the day and night, as was granted to Giuseppe Isdrael on 5 July 1599 ... They can keep a shop outside the Ghetto without paying guild matriculation fees ... as His Most Serene Highness granted Josef Isdrael on 4 November 1606.[94]

These escalating concessions soon created two classes of Jews in Florence – the privileged Levantines and the unprivileged Italians. In effect, the Levantines took the rights of Pisa and Livorno with them wherever they went. Also, the Levantines answered directly to the grand duke in most legal matters, without the intervention of the Ghetto adminis-tration. They were even exempt from local professional organizations, especially the powerful Silk Guild (Arte della Seta) – unlike the Blanis family and other Italian traders.

Since the yellow *segno* was not worn in Pisa and Livorno, its dispen-sation elsewhere was easily granted. And since there was no Ghetto in Pisa or Livorno, the Levantines in Florence could live wherever they wished, at least in theory. In practice, we do not hear of many Levan-tines with houses and shops dotted around the city of Florence. Even the privileged lived mostly in the Ghetto or its immediate periphery,[95] and in the early years of the seventeenth century there was continuing con-struction in both the Inner and Outer Ghettos to create suitable housing for the new non-Italian elite.[96] The right to live outside the Ghetto had as much to do with jurisdiction as place of residence, since the Levantines could live 'in the Ghetto' without being 'of the Ghetto' – not answerable to the Italian governors. In July of 1612, only a month after the arrival of Hayyim Finzi in the Italian synagogue, the others began a major re-building of the '*schola* of the Levantine Nation.'[97]

There were ethnic Levantines in Tuscany but also jurisdictional Levantines, who could come from the north as well as the east and west, without any attachment to the Sephardic rite. In the summer of 1607, while the Medici were considering the petition of David Alben Azzor from Constantinople, they had a similar request from a blatant Ashkenazi. This was Donato son of Isach, often called Donato Tedesco or Donato Donati:

> Donato Donati, a German Jew (*hebreo alemanno*) who currently lives in Modena, has started up an enterprise in this dominion and ... might wish to reside in Florence or some other place. With this in mind, he and his family would like to enjoy everywhere the same privileges that the Levantines and other nations enjoy in Pisa. His Most Serene Highness says in his rescript, 'Let this be granted to him ... along with his four sons and his son-in-law.'[98]

Newly arriving kin of old Ghetto families could qualify for Levantine privileges by establishing pro forma residence in one of the coastal ports. In 1613 Moisé, son of Samuel Blanis – a somewhat distant cousin of Benedetto's – registered 'in that book which is kept in the Maritime Chancery in Pisa, listing all the Jews that settle in Pisa or Livorno.' This was ratified by the Florentine customs administration on 22 October 1613: 'His Serene Highness [Cosimo II] ... thus grants him all of the favours and exemptions that are enjoyed by Levantine Jews, as if he actually lived there in Pisa.'[99]

For a time, at least, these Levantines floated above the system, evading many of the obstacles and restrictions of Ghetto life. Meanwhile, Benedetto's family created a place of its own within this amorphous scheme of Italians, ethnic Levantines, and jurisdictional Levantines. Although Iberian in origin, the Blanis had long been a mainstay of the Italian synagogue in Florence – and so they remained, even after the putsch of 1608. They continued to appear regularly in the list of Italian governors: Laudadio in 1610, 1613, 1615, and 1617; then Benedetto in 1619, and then Benedetto's younger brother Salamone in 1623.[100] The German Donato Donati and his sons served along with them, choosing the non-Levantine side when it came to prayer and politics. In 1621 the 'Levantine' Moisé Blanis became chancellor of the Ghetto and rabbi in the Italian synagogue – further straining this tenuous web of differences and distinctions.[101]

Benedetto's family worshipped and voted with the Italians, but they were more likely to find their social and economic peers among the emerging non-Italian elite. Moisé Lattone *Levantino*, son of David

Alben Azzor's partner Emanuel Lattone, married one of Laudadio's daughters[102] and became Benedetto's brother-in-law. Even the Florentine authorities sometimes assumed that the Blanis were all de facto Levantines, considering their prestige and relative wealth. When Benedetto's younger brother David was caught with an illegal knife in 1615, the magistrates exonerated him, 'in view of ... the privilege granted to Levantine Jews among whom this David is included.'[103]

chapter five

Memory and Survival

The Jewish Year

On Saturday, 2 April 1616, Benedetto Blanis explained a few essentials to his great Christian patron Don Giovanni dei Medici:

> Your Most Illustrious Excellency should not be surprised that this letter is in an unfamiliar handwriting. On Friday afternoon, I sat down to write and was overtaken by the Sabbath because the day was cloudy and I did not have a clock to rely on. Friday evening was also the beginning of Passover, and it was still Passover on Saturday evening [after the conclusion of the Sabbath]. I am thus unable to write with my own hand but I did not feel that I could put off acknowledging that gracious letter [which you sent me] ... and once Passover is done, I will finish sorting out this matter.[1]

There is no reason to doubt Benedetto's basic story. His letter was written by someone else and the Sabbath began at sunset on Friday, 1 April 1616, coinciding with the arrival of Passover. Still, it is hard to imagine a Ghetto-dweller taken unaware by a major holiday – especially one who was living with his wife and daughters in a single room in a communal apartment.

In those same years Leone da Modena described the frenzy leading up to even a normal Sabbath:

> New tasks are not begun on Friday, unless it is generally possible to finish them before nightfall. Then about an hour before sunset, all of the food cooked for the next day is put on the fire to heat up, and every regular task

is laid aside. Then a half hour before sunset, in many cities, a crier goes around to announce that the holiday is drawing near, so that people can hurry up and finish whatever they are doing. At the 23rd hour, about half an hour before sunset, the holiday is understood to have begun, with all of its prohibitions. In the home, the women are then required to light an oil lamp with at least four or six wicks, and this burns until late at night. They set the table with a white cloth and cover the bread with another long narrow cloth. This, they say, is in memory of the manna which came down and was covered by dew both above and below, since it never rained on the Sabbath [during the forty years in the desert].[2]

Over the centuries the rabbis evolved an intricate system of precepts and regulations, distinguishing the Jews from other peoples and emphasizing their collective history and identity. Thirty-nine activities were strictly forbidden during this weekly holiday while many others were banned by association or analogy. It was forbidden to work, write, touch money, kindle or extinguish fires, wash oneself, walk more than a mile – or do anything associated with ordinary non-Sabbath practice.

As recorded in a Florentine court case on 12 November 1621, Emilia Finzi (widow of the recently deceased Rabbi Hayyim Finzi) refused to handle money on a Saturday morning. A Christian serving woman had brought Donna Emilia 2 scudi and a pawn slip for an allegedly stolen fork and spoon, 'and she ordered her to put it under a cup in the sink, since it was Sabbath.'[3]

Benedetto Blanis obeyed the stricture against writing on the Sabbath, calling in a non-Jew to pen his letter to Don Giovanni dei Medici. He was generally ingenious when it came to looking after his own interests – adapting his ways to those of the Christians around him while sticking to the letter of Jewish law. Networking, for example, was a seven-day-a-week job, although Benedetto would stop short of closing a deal or putting it in writing – as he commented to Don Giovanni on 20 June 1615:

In the course of my business affairs, and in order to carry out some commercial dealings that were entrusted to me, I spoke with that man again on that Sabbath evening … I placed myself at his disposal, since Your Excellency had recommended me to him that very morning … If it had not been Sabbath, my passionate spirit, my sincere affection, and my desire to serve you would certainly have induced me to set aside every other consideration.[4]

Five years later, on 26 September 1620, Benedetto was languishing in solitary confinement in the Bargello prison with no evident hope of release. Through bribery and inside connections, he managed to smuggle a brief, desperate message to Don Giovanni dei Medici: 'I entrust my family to you, in hope that you will resolve the calamitous misfortune that afflicts it. May God bring you every happiness. *Pasqua*. Benedetto Blanis.'[5]

For Benedetto, *Pasqua* was the holiday of *Pesach* or Passover, which had ended five months earlier, on 26 April 1620. It was always current, however, as an emblem of deliverance from captivity and other evils – serving, perhaps, as an emergency code between him and his patron.[6]

'On the 15th day of the month of Nissan, which is more or less April, there is the first day of the holiday of *Pasqua* called *Pesach*, in memory of the departure from Egypt.'[7] In the annual cycle of holidays, Passover offers the most intensely mythic affirmation of Jewish identity – which Leone da Modena cautiously understated for his Christian readers:

> For the duration of these eight days, they are forbidden to eat leaven or leavened bread or keep it in their houses or even in their possession, eating only unleavened bread (*pane azimo*), as stated in the 12th Chapter of the Book of Exodus, 'Seven days shall you eat unleavened bread; in the first day there shall be no leaven in your houses,' etc. Before Passover, with meticulous care and diligence, they remove from their homes and their possession anything associated with leavened or fermented flour. They cleanse and bleach everything ... and they acquire cooking and eating utensils that are entirely new or else scrubbed or made of reforged metal ... Before the holiday, they provide enough unleavened bread, called *Mazzod*, to last them for eight days. From the moment the flour is ground, they make sure that it does not become wet or heated so as to induce leavening. Then they knead flour and water, making flatbreads in various forms which are then baked immediately.[8]

Why do Jews do these things? The Jews themselves, along with those few Catholics[9] who had read the Book of Exodus, knew that Passover was a recurring act of self-identification. On the evening before their hasty flight from slavery in Egypt, the Children of Israel had no time to let their bread dough rise. Modena, however, cut the passage short with his 'etc.'[10] – skipping over the crucial words, 'whosoever shall eat anything leavened, from the first day until the seventh day, that soul shall perish out of Israel.'[11]

> In the evening, they go to pray and then return home. They sit around the table which was laid in advance before sunset, with as much grandeur as possible. In the 12th Chapter of the Book of Exodus, the eating of the Paschal Lamb is specified, 'And they shall eat it, etc., and unleavened bread with wild lettuce.' In place of this ceremony, they prepare a basin or basket with some lamb or kid and unleavened bread and bitter herbs, like celery, endive, or lettuce, and also something in memory of the mortar or clay with which they constructed buildings in Egypt.[12] There are glasses of wine and they recite a certain narrative called *Hagadà* which includes the memory of the massacres that were suffered and the miracles through which God preserved them. So, they praise God for the benefits they received and they recite psalms … and they dine.[13]

Modena tells his Christian readers everything except what really matters. The Jewish nation, coming out of Egypt, was forged in blood – exemplified by that of the Paschal Lamb. God ordered the head of every household to find an unblemished lamb, slaughter it, daub its blood on the doorframe of his house, and then, with his family, eat its flesh with unleavened bread and wild herbs. During the night, God passed through the land of Egypt and slaughtered the firstborn, 'passing over' the blood-marked houses of the Jews. Then on the next morning, the Children of Israel began their forty-year return journey to the Promised Land.

All of this is set out in the *Hagadà* (*Haggadah*), which was far more than 'a certain narrative,' as Leone da Modena knew well. It was the script for the annual re-enactment of the origins of his people. Their myth, however, was an uncomfortable one in the lands of the diaspora – casting the Jews as a dangerous and disruptive presence, with the local rulers in the role of Pharaoh.

Even worse, the Paschal Lamb had been identified by Christians as a prefiguration of Christ – allegedly killed by Jews in another drama of death, blood, and redemption. In Italian, *Pasqua* signifies both Passover and Easter, deriving from the Hebrew *Pesach* (literally *pass over*, in reference to God and the firstborn of Israel). Passover and Easter were parallel holidays with shared historical roots, so they normally took place at more or less the same time.[14] Since the Middle Ages, the

Passover-Easter season had been rife with anti-Jewish mayhem, exemplified by the infamous 'blood libel' (the perennial accusation that Jews murdered Christian children and made *matzoh* with their blood). It is not surprising that Leone da Modena kept explanation to a minimum – and left out blood entirely – presenting Passover as an innocuous feast of thanksgiving.

In the Florentine Ghetto shops remained closed for the Sabbath, for the full eight days of Passover[15] and for the duration of most other Jewish holidays. In addition to the festivals themselves, time was often needed for planning and preparation. On 25 September 1616 Benedetto Blanis apologized for his delay in completing an inventory of Don Giovanni's library: 'I now have to draft that list and would already have done so if our Feast of Huts (*Festa delle Capanne*) had not intervened this week.'[16] This was *Sukkot*, another major affirmation of Jewish national identity:

On the 15th day of the month of Tisri (Tishri), there is the Feast of Bowers or Tabernacles or Huts, which they call *Succod*. This commemorates their departure from Egypt, since they lived in dwellings of this kind in the desert. In the 23rd book of Leviticus, it is written, 'And you shall dwell in bowers seven days, etc., [you] shall dwell in tabernacles.' At his home, everyone therefore makes one of these bowers, covering it with green branches from trees, surrounding it with a trellis, and embellishing it as best he can.[17]

Benedetto was writing on the day before the holiday, so he must have been busy constructing an open-air shelter for himself and his family in some corner of the Florentine Ghetto – perhaps on an upper-level terrace,[18] like the one outside the synagogue. Finding outdoor space for all of these 'bowers,' 'tabernacles,' or 'huts' could not have been easy for him and his neighbours in their crowded urban enclave.

On 29 September 1619 Benedetto offered Don Giovanni another apology, for his delay in forwarding the latest instalment of an arcane work in Hebrew, tentatively attributed to Ramón Llull, the thirteenth-century founder of Christian Kabbalah: 'Your Most Illustrious Excellency has not been sent those sheets due to the nine days of holidays.'[19] In 1619 Rosh Hashana fell on 9 September with Yom Kippur on 18 September, closely followed by Sukkot on 23 September.

The Jewish year is based on a lunar calendar and consists of twelve months of twenty-nine-and-a-third days, with each month beginning with the new moon. In order to reconcile lunar and solar reckoning, a thirteenth lunar month is added to the calendar every two or three years as needed. The New Year is celebrated on the first and second day of the seventh month of Tishri and is called Rosh Hashana (Head of the Year), followed by Yom Kippur (Day of Atonement) ten days later. Leone da Modena evokes the emotional intensity of this passage in the Jewish year:

> The first and second day of the month of Tisri (Tishri) is a festival called *Ros asanà* [Rosh Hashana] ... On this day, tradition has it, God judges the doings of men in the past year and determines what will befall them in the year to come, almost as if it were the birth of the world. They review the old year with minute attention and begin their penance in advance, during the preceding month of Elul ... On the eve of this holiday, many wash themselves and have themselves beaten with thirty-nine lashes, as written in Chapter 25 of Deuteronomy ... When arriving at the synagogue on the first evening of the New Year, they say to each other, 'May you be inscribed for a good year,' and everyone replies, 'And you as well.' The custom is to put honey and raised bread on the table and various things that refer to growth and a sweet year ... On the mornings of these two days, they go to the synagogue, and many wear white as a sign of cleanliness. Among the Germans, many wear the garment that they have set aside for their own use after death, and this is a sign of contrition.[20]

The momentum builds in the days that follow Rosh Hashana, leading to Yom Kippur, the Day of Atonement (or Day of Pardon, as it was often called in Italian). This period – popularly known as The Days of Repentance or even The Days of Awe – offers the last opportunity to mitigate the just sentence inscribed for each individual in the Book of Life. On 4 October 1615 Benedetto Blanis commented to Don Giovanni dei Medici: 'Your most recent gracious letter was brief, so it does not require a lengthy response. I should also mention that I spent this Saturday [yesterday] in continuous prayer, without eating or drinking, because it was a most significant day for us which we call the Day of Pardon (*Giorno del Perdono*).'[21] Leone da Modena offers a much fuller picture:

> After these two days [of the New Year] until the tenth day of Tisri (Tishri), they rise before dawn for prayer and penance. Then the tenth day of this month is the Day of Pardons (*Giorno delle Perdonanze*), called *Iom Achipur*

(Yom Kippur), as ordered in Chapter 23 of Leviticus ... All work and all business is forbidden, as it is on the Sabbath, and they fast, eating and drinking nothing at all ... Many cleanse themselves in the bath and discipline themselves with the thirty-nine lashes. Those with a troubled conscience give back whatever belongs to others, ask pardon of those whom they have offended, pardon those who have offended them, give alms, and do whatever is required for true penance ... Eating ceases at sunset, then many dress in white or in mortuary clothes and go to the synagogue barefoot or at least unshod. The synagogue is illuminated with a great many oil lamps and wax tapers. For at least three hours, they say numerous prayers of repentance and they utter many confessions, each ethnicity (*nazione*) according to its own usage. Then they leave in order to sleep, although some sleep very little, remaining in the synagogue to recite prayers and psalms. Then, at dawn, they all return to the synagogue, dressed as before, and they remain there until nightfall, saying prayers, psalms, and confessions, praying that God will pardon their sins.[22]

For Benedetto Blanis, there was the Sabbath, Passover, Sukkot, Rosh Hashana, and Yom Kippur, plus all of the other major and minor feasts and fasts that he observed but failed to mention to Don Giovanni dei Medici. Benedetto might have adapted his ways to those of the Christians around him but he was still living in a parallel universe – with his home in a separate Jewish quarter and the rhythm of his life that of a separate Jewish year.

Home and Family

On 16 August 1615 Benedetto Blanis commented to Don Giovanni dei Medici, 'I have three female children, one of whom is ten years old.'[23] Six months later, on 27 February 1616, he updated the tally, 'A fourth girl was born to me today, which is a goodly number by any reckoning.'[24] Then on 4 November 1616 he scratched one of the four from the list: 'I have had to stay in my house all week, mourning the death of a little daughter of mine.'[25]

Benedetto's family is a constant presence in his letters to Don Giovanni. Again and again, we hear about his father Laudadio, his elder brother Lelio, and his two younger brothers David and Salamone – their quirks of personality, their business affairs, and their frequent brushes with the law. Meanwhile, the women in his life – two successive wives and four daughters from his first marriage – remain discreetly off-stage.

He tells of their births and deaths but little else. In fact, we don't even know their names.

In practical terms, the Blanis clan was an ongoing joint venture. Their family business operated out of a single Ghetto shop with Benedetto, his father, and brothers sharing responsibilities and risks[26] – dividing up deals and trading investments back and forth. Meanwhile, their enterprise slotted into a broader network of cousins, nephews, and in-laws – throughout Italy and possibly abroad.[27]

By necessity, Laudadio, his sons, and their dependents lived a more or less communal life in the Florentine Ghetto. Benedetto's father rented a shop and two apartments in his own name,[28] and they used this limited space as best they could. Cooking and eating together would have made excellent sense, and cousins as well as siblings were probably sharing beds. This strategy lent the Blanis clan an essential resilience and stability, particularly since the men were often away from home – travelling or in jail.

Outside the Ghetto, many Christian families made similar arrangements, but the Jews were playing for higher stakes against longer odds. Economic and material survival was the immediate challenge, but so was spiritual survival – and ultimately, the survival of an entire people. In his description of the Jewish home in exile, Leone da Modena evokes the essential dislocation at the heart of religious observance, based on the hallowing of daily life in a land that is not one's own:

> As the rabbis remind us, if anyone builds a house, he must leave some part of it incomplete or unfinished in memory of Jerusalem and the Temple which remain desolate. It is said in the 136th Psalm, 'If I forget thee, O Jerusalem, let my right hand be forgotten.' So, as an expression of sadness, they leave unplastered a square measuring at least a quarter of a braccio [5.75 inches] in which this verse is written in capital letters, or at very least the words *Zecher Lachorban*, that is to say, *In Memory of the Desolation*.[29]

For Benedetto Blanis and those around him, marrying and begetting children was more than a personal choice – it was a sacred duty:

> Every Jewish man is obligated to take a wife, and the rabbis have determined that the appropriate time for doing so is at the age of eighteen, certainly not going beyond the age of twenty. He who passes this limit without a wife is said to be living in sin for various reasons. First, because he is required to generate offspring, as God said to Adam in the First Book

of Genesis, 'Increase and multiply, and fill the earth,' etc. By having at least one male and one female child, he is understood to have fulfilled this precept. Second, he must marry in any case in order to avoid the sin of fornication.[30]

God's commandment could extend to polygamy, particularly among Jews with links to the Muslim cultures of the east: 'Taking more than one wife is permitted and indeed, as many wives as one wishes, since this is authorized in many passages of the Scriptures. The Levantines do so, although the Germans neither allow nor practise it. In Italy it is very rare and only occurs when a man has had a first wife for years without producing children.'[31] Benedetto had at least one neighbour with multiple wives, although they were strategically deployed in different towns. Doctor Samuel Caggesi from Fez arrived in Florence in 1609 and was granted a privileged residence in the Outer Ghetto.[32] In April of 1616 the Moroccan travelled to Massa Carrara, 'where he has a second wife who will soon give birth.'[33]

Benedetto, unfortunately, had no sons and his multitude of female dependents constituted a daunting burden. In the patriarchal society of the time, women had few opportunities to generate money on their own, and they needed to be provided with dowries. Meanwhile, the mortality rate was high for both children and childbearing wives, and men often ran through several of the latter in the course of their marital careers. In a letter to Don Giovanni on 18 November 1617 Benedetto sorrowfully noted the death of both his wife and his mother-in-law.[34] Then a year later, he remarried.[35]

Like any such union, this began with a series of financial negotiations: 'Once an agreement has been reached, the groom and the relatives of the bride draw up a written contract. The groom then goes to touch the bride's hand, thereby recognizing her officially.' At that time, a date could be set for the actual wedding, after the bride's menstruation and subsequent purification in the ritual bath (*mikveh*):[36]

> At the appointed time, the couple comes together in a room or chamber under a canopy. There is music and in some cases there are young boys around them holding lit tapers and singing. The people surround them and the heads of the groom and bride are covered, using one of those square mantles with fringes called *Taled* [talith]. The rabbi of that place, or else the cantor of that particular synagogue, or else the closest relative, takes a carafe or cup of wine in his hand and pronounces the benediction

to God who created man and woman and ordained matrimony, etc. The groom and the bride drink, then the groom puts the ring on the bride's finger in the presence of two witnesses who are normally rabbis, saying, 'You are my wife, according to the rite of Moses and of Israel.'[37]

On 23 December 1618 Benedetto shared his good news with Don Giovanni dei Medici: 'According to the ancient Jewish law and rite, my home has been assigned to me as a sweet and voluntary prison during this time of my nuptials, and I cannot leave it for any reason for eight days.'[38] This was an exclusively male ritual, an ongoing post-bachelor party. 'In some places,' Leone da Modena explains, 'the custom is for the groom to remain in his house for seven days, beginning on the day of the wedding, in pleasure and recreation with his friends.'[39] Married life then ensued with its usual variables – all according to the prescribed rite.

Observance

On 10 March 1615 Benedetto's younger brother David Blanis was arraigned in the Florentine police court. Due to a peculiar concatenation of circumstances, he had been apprehended while carrying an illegal weapon in the city:

> On the morning of 5 March a knife measuring more than a quarter of a braccio [5.75 inches] with a spring closure was found on the person of the Jew Davitte son of Laudadio Blanis. At that time he was in the changing room of the Prison of the Bargello preparing to enter that prison in regard to another matter ... He confessed that he had been out of Florence for a few days and had been using that knife to kill pigeons and do other things that Jews normally do. Then that morning, while on his way to Cosimo Baroncelli's villa at Mezza Strada, he was summoned to appear before the Magistrature, which he did without stopping to leave his knife. He always carries it with him when he goes out of the city, since it is forbidden for him to use the knives of Christians.[40]

It must have been difficult enough for David Blanis to observe the dietary laws at home in the Ghetto, let alone keep kosher on the road.[41] Jews can only eat land animals that chew their cud and have a divided hoof like cattle and sheep, or else poultry. This excludes rabbits and particularly pigs, in a place and time where rabbits were cheap and pork was the principal meat. Jews can only eat sea animals that have fins and scales, which excludes eels and every sort of shellfish. Permitted land animals, including pigeons, can be eaten only if they are slaughtered in the approved way by slitting the jugular and draining away the blood: 'This needs to be done by an experienced person ... using a sharp knife with no nicks. And it needs to be done quickly, so that the blood flows in a steady stream, falling on dry earth or ashes, where it is then covered with the same earth or ashes.'[42] There was a slaughterhouse (*macellaio*) in the Florentine Ghetto and a designated slaughterer (*sciattatore*), as noted in the 1608 by-laws. Meanwhile, individuals like David Blanis cut their own meat and even killed their own animals.[43]

Then there was the issue of pots and pans, of cutlery and other utensils. Meat and milk (including all dairy products) could not be eaten together nor even cooked or served with the same implements.[44] In Jewish kitchens, two distinct sets were carefully separated – from each other and from external pollution:[45] 'For this reason, things cannot be eaten if they are cooked by other peoples. Neither can their cooking vessels be used, for fear that forbidden foods have been placed inside. Neither can knives belonging to other peoples be used.'[46]

It is relatively easy to observe the Jewish dietary laws when everyone else is doing so as well, but where Jews are a tiny minority surrounded by other peoples, keeping kosher becomes a dominant concern that defines daily life. Jews must avoid all obviously forbidden foods (pork, shellfish, mixed meat and dairy), as well as the meat of otherwise permitted animals that have been improperly slaughtered. Then, by extension, Jews must avoid anything that has come into contact with these – creating a vast grey area of possibly or probably forbidden items of unknown origin or suspect handling.

On 25 September 1607 a member of a distinguished Ghetto family was sued for a large unpaid grocery bill: 'Carlo son of Giuliano, a *pizzicagnolo* in the market, requests 45 lire 16 soldi and 8 piccioli from Abramo Liucci, a Jewish perfumer, for merchandise obtained from Carlo's shop.'[47] A *pizzicagnolo* was a delicatessen seller who dealt primarily in cured pork – ham, sausage, and so forth – and this one operated in the Mercato Vecchio, right outside the Ghetto. Abramo and his family did not necessarily eat such things, since Carlo could have supplied them with cheese or other merchandise off his shelves. Even then, there was the danger of contamination through contact, and cheese was an especially troublesome item:

They do not eat cheese unless they have seen it being made and seen the coagulant. This is for fear that milk from a forbidden animal might have been used, or that animal membrane has been beaten to produce rennet (*quaglio*) which is considered meat, or that it has been heated in a cauldron used to cook forbidden food. Those who have overseen the making of the cheese designate it with a mark, so that it can be identified clearly.[48]

Leone da Modena was writing in his home in the Venetian Ghetto, surrounded by several thousand Jews who evidently constituted a ready market for authenticated cheese. Florence, meanwhile, had barely five hundred keeping kosher, probably without their own producers and suppliers, or even their own food shops.[49] As a result, the Blanis family and its neighbours did not always have the luxury of the highest observance when it came to kosher and not kosher – following up all possible doubts and suspicions.

According to the 1608 by-laws of the Florentine Ghetto, 'On the Sabbath and other holidays, no one is permitted to eat and drink in taverns and *greco* shops [*greco* was a light white wine] on any pretext. Neither is it permissible to have wine brought into the Ghetto on the Sabbath.'[50] This would have involved commerce, the carrying of loads, and the handling of money on holy days – but otherwise, it was apparently normal to eat food and drink wine that was not strictly kosher, prepared by Christians in Christian establishments.

Wine presented special problems since it had long been associated with the idolatrous rites of foreign races:

Some maintain that there is an ancient rabbinical stricture forbidding Jews from drinking wine made or even touched by non-Jews, and this precept is observed by Levantines and Germans. In Italy, however, this is not the case and it is held that those rabbis were surrounded by idolaters and that they issued their ban in order to stop interaction with such people. Now, however, the Jews find themselves among people of a different kind, as these people have amply demonstrated.[51]

Leone was writing in Italian for a Christian public, so he was unlikely to propose the Holy Eucharist as an idolatrous rite. Wine, in any case, was an essential food in Italy,[52] and Benedetto's great-grandfather Laudadio Blanis had produced it in Perugia for several years.[53] By the time of Benedetto, however, the only choice was to drink Christian wine or no wine at all.

Viewed from outside, the Jewish dietary laws are primarily about prohibitions, a complicated list of things that Jews must not eat. Viewed from inside, every meal becomes a shared exercise in national memory and a quasi-sacramental rite. Not only are the animals that Jews consume living beings created by God, they are links to the sacrifices offered in former times in the Temple in Jerusalem. Leone da Modena describes the conclusion of an appropriate Jewish meal:

> When they have finished eating, they wash their hands, and then they remove the knives from the table, since it represents the altar and iron could not be left on it. Many customarily recite the psalm which the Levites recited that weekday in the Temple followed by Psalm 66, 'May God have mercy on us,' etc. If three or more have eaten together, one of them washes a glass and then fills it with wine. Rising from the table, he says in a loud voice, 'Gentlemen, let us bless Him whose food we have eaten.' Then the others reply, 'And let us also bless that which we have eaten of His, since it is by His bounty that we live.' Then they continue with the blessings, thanking God who gives everyone his sustenance and who gave the Promised Land to the fathers of old. They pray that God will rebuild Jerusalem and that he will bless the master of the house. Finally, they pray for peace. When that is done, the speaker gives everyone a bit of wine from the glass, then he himself drinks. Then everyone rises from the table.[54]

Jewish observance consists of many single rules that cohere into an integrated way of life. Its defining theme is the constant recognition of God's presence in every aspect of existence: 'The Rabbis have established the obligation of reciting benedictions and offering praise to God, not only in the course of prayer and for favours received but also in response to every special occurrence.' There are prescribed blessings on waking in the morning, on washing one's hands, on studying the Law, on eating bread or fruit, on smelling a fragrant odour, on seeing mountains or the sea, on wearing new clothing and so on. 'In this way, they offer a benediction to God for every thing and for every action, sometimes before, sometimes after, sometimes both before and after. Since God is the Lord of all, it would be a sin of ingratitude to use or enjoy any thing in the world without first acknowledging Him through an act of praise.'[55]

The hallowing of daily life through meticulous observance is the key to Jewish religious practice, as Benedetto Blanis and his neighbours knew well. But even educated Christians seldom suspected this seemingly obvious fact – fixating on the murky by-ways of the Jewish occult.

Justice and Commandments

By 1571 the leaders of the Florentine community had already instituted a *cassetta dei poveri* or poor box in their new synagogue.[56] By 1578 the use of such poor boxes was well established, with a strict rota for taking them around the Ghetto on a daily basis: 'The Jews who are called on each day to gather alms (*elemosine*) for the needy poor (*poveri bisognosi*) are required to do so when the caretaker (*tavolaccino*) entrusts the box to them. If they do not make the round, they must themselves give 2 lire in *piccioli* so that the poor will not suffer.'[57] This daily round with the collection box was part of the defining rhythm of Ghetto life, along with prayers in the synagogue at the prescribed times of day and the locking and unlocking of the gates.

In Hebrew there are no precise terms for such overwhelmingly Christian concepts as charity (*carità*) or good works (*opere buone*), not to mention alms (*elemosine*) and works of mercy (*opere di misericordia*).[58] For Jews operating in their own language, the crucial words are *tzdakah* (from *tzedek*, justice) and *mitzvot* (commandments), since these are acts of observance ordained by God, not optional gestures that bring added virtue to believers. Leone da Modena describes the context of this essential activity:

> No one can deny that this people [the Jews] are very pious and compassionate towards the poor, since there are so many of these among them. Indeed, the poor are their majority because this nation is subject to greater adversity than any other. Even those few [Jews] who might be considered rich have scant wealth, possessions, or income in real terms. Nonetheless, they all support everyone as best they can, doing whatever they can in every situation.[59]

In any ghetto, mutual support was doubly relevant. First, it was a defining aspect of Jewish identity, and without it other activities would have lost their meaning. Second, it was necessary for national survival since Jews were ineligible for Christian charity. Economic crises and medical emergencies could force many into conversion – if there were no alternatives at home:

In the big cities, on Fridays and on the evenings before major holidays, the poor go to collect at the houses of the rich and the middling alike, and everyone gives according to his ability. Also, the officials of the community, called *Parnassim* or *Memunim*, are responsible for sending support every week to the houses of those who do not make the rounds, particularly widows, the sick, and the unfortunate. Offerings are collected in every synagogue and given to the poor, along with the money that is deposited in the various cash boxes. Some of the proceeds from the sale of the right to officiate or participate in various ceremonies are used for this purpose.[60]

Fines were often destined for community support. According to the 1608 by-laws, any man who refused a governorship or other Ghetto office had to pay 25 scudi, 'half of which goes to the Granducal treasury and half to the five poor boxes that are used every day to collect alms.'[61] (Since they were writing in Italian, *elemosine* or *alms* was the best available word.) Fines for playing ball in the Ghetto also made their way to the poor boxes – and for talking during synagogue services, for failing to keep public spaces clean, for selling or working in public on Christian holidays, and for insulting Ghetto officials.[62]

Throughout Italy and elsewhere, the sale of synagogue honours – particularly access to the Torah – was an important source of benevolent funds: 'Out of devotion, everyone wishes to take part, particularly when it comes to removing and replacing that book [in the ark]. Those and other essential activities are therefore sold at auction during the time of prayer, to be carried out by those who pledge the most. The resulting monies are spent for the needs of the synagogue and for alms to the poor.'[63]

Special collections were often made in the synagogue, although pledges could not be realized on the spot: 'When a poor person, local or foreign, has an exceptional need or when it is necessary to marry off women, redeem slaves, or accomplish other things, the officers of the synagogue extract a promise from every individual, called *Nedavà*. The Cantor (*Cantarino*) makes the round and says to each, "May God bless so-and-so, who will give a particular sum as alms for this purpose." Since this occurs during the Sabbath, and it involves money, everyone promises verbally whatever seems appropriate and then pays promptly in the course of the week.'[64]

At least in Florence, prompt payment was an optimistic goal – since men were pledging righteous donations in the heat of the moment and then having second thoughts. The leaders of the Ghetto addressed this problem in the by-laws of 1572,[65] then again in 1608: 'Offerings made in the *scuola* of this Republic must be paid within one month, and those who do not pay will be subject to a penalty of one quarter of the sum. This penalty will be compounded for every month of non-payment, and those in authority are empowered to exact these payments.'[66]

Public welfare committees also collected and disbursed monies: 'In the big cities, there are various confraternities (*fraterne*), mostly for good works. Those that look after the sick and bury the dead are called *Ghemilud Hassadim*. Those that exist for simple almsgiving are called *Zedacà*. Those that redeem slaves are called *Pidion Seuuim*. Those that marry off girls are called *Hassi betulod*. And in each place there are others, in greater or lesser number, depending on the number of Jews.'[67]

By the early seventeenth century there was at least one confraternity operating in the Florentine Ghetto plus four benevolent funds – probably corresponding to the five 'poor boxes' cited in the 1608 by-laws. This confraternity was the equivalent of the *Ghemilud Hassadim* (*Gemilut Chasadim* or Work of Righteousness), although in the official Italian documents, it was called the *Compagnia della Misericordia* (Company of Mercy) – borrowing the name of the organizations that looked after the Christian sick and buried the Christian dead.[68] The other Florentine funds (which might or might not have had committees attached) were an all-purpose *Zedacà* (*Tzdakah*) account, a dowry account, an account for the education of boys, and an account 'for Jerusalem.'[69]

Donations for the Holy Land were an important link to the Jewish past and the hoped-for Jewish future: 'In every place where Jews are found, they send alms to Jerusalem every year for the maintenance of the poor people who live there and pray for the well-being of everyone. This money also goes to other places in Judea like Saffet (Safed), Tebbaria (Tiberias), and Hebron where there are the tombs of the Patriarchs Abraham, Isaac, and Jacob, with their wives.'[70] Jerusalem, Tiberias, Hebron, and Safed were the four holy cities of the Talmud. By the time of Benedetto Blanis, Safed was also the epicentre of Lurianic Kabbalah.[71]

Few Florentine Jews were rich, so few could afford to alienate family property – but community welfare figured prominently in the wills of several affluent women without children.[72] In a testament dated 5 May 1574 Benedetto's aunt Ginevra (daughter of Agnolo Blanis) provided for her own burial and allocated candles to be burned in the synagogue for her soul. She also gave the synagogue two durable gifts: a silver lamp and a curtain (bearing her name) for the ark. Then she made four focused philanthropic bequests: 10 scudi to the Misericordia of the Jews of the City of Florence, 10 scudi for the instruction of Jewish boys, 10 scudi for Jewish paupers, and 80 scudi for dowries for eight Jewish girls.[73] This was the first benefaction of its kind in the history of the Florentine Ghetto and one of the largest ever, totalling 160 scudi. In real terms, however, 160 scudi was a relatively modest sum, and 10 scudi the bare minimum for a humble dowry.

Resources were limited and need was extreme. So, the principle of social justice and the commandment to support the needy often came crashing into the hard reality of Ghetto life. Leone da Modena expressed the righteous ideal of Jewish solidarity:

> If some poor person has an urgent need that those of a single city are unable to supply, he addresses this matter to the principal rabbis. They draw up an affidavit stating that he is respectable and deserving (*da bene e meritevole*), and they call on everyone to help him. With this document, he visits every place where Jews live, and if it is only a village or a small settlement, he is given lodging, food, and drink for a day or two and then a bit of money at the time of his departure. When he is lodged in the big cities, he has his affidavit confirmed and signed by the local rabbis, then he visits the synagogues, addressing the Parnassim and the confraternities, or whoever else has authority in that place. In some way or other, he thus receives help and support.[74]

What about needy Jews without rabbinical affidavits – the ones who were neither respectable nor deserving? As the Florentine police files demonstrate, there was a steady stream of impoverished wanderers clamouring for admission at the gates of the Ghetto. The local Jewish leaders addressed this problem in August of 1571, in their very first set of by-laws:

> No scandalous or trouble-making Jew, without family in the Ghetto or business with the customs administration or one of the magistratures, can remain in Florence for more than three days. Should he wish to remain longer, he must notify the official designated by Your Highness [the Grand Duke] and then go with formal permission in hand to the two council-men (*consiglieri*) selected by the Jews. The Jews must send all of the others away, in order to avoid the scandals that frequently ensue. This is by their own request, since they want to enjoy the continuing good grace of Your Highness, for whose happiness and long life they all pray.[75]

The leaders of the Jewish community nervously repeated this basic formula in their by-laws of 1572 and 1608. Then we hear this same language, again and again, in the orders for expulsion processed by the local police court: 'Since these two have neither wives nor families nor trades, the Jews want them evicted [from Florence] and then exiled from the dominion of His Most Serene Highness.'[76] There were already enough poor Jews without bringing in more – especially rootless men without wives and children binding them to the ordained pattern of Jewish observance.[77] In the Florentine Ghetto, there was the Law of Moses and there was the law of survival, expressed in the daily struggle to earn a living against daunting odds.

chapter six

The Market

Shopping

You could buy almost anything you wanted in late Renaissance Florence – clothing and food, furniture and household goods, exotic luxuries from around the world, and the common necessities of everyday life.[1] You could buy it new or you could buy it used. You could buy it from the man or woman who made it or after it had been resold countless times. You could buy it in a grand shop or on a market stall or from an itinerant vendor. You could even buy it stolen, with or without questions asked.

If there had been a shoppers' guide to Florence in the days of Benedetto Blanis, the Jewish Ghetto would have been firmly fixed on the down-market edge of the map. You would probably have begun your tour of the city's commercial attractions at the Ponte Vecchio, the oldest of the bridges spanning the Arno River. This had emerged only recently as a prestigious shopping destination, when in 1593 Grand Duke Ferdinando I evicted the resident butchers and blacksmiths, bringing in goldsmiths and jewellers. An upgrade of this kind was essential for the image of the Tuscan court since the bridge was immediately adjacent to the newly constructed Uffizi Palace (1560–80) – housing the Medici art gallery, the granducal workshops, and the chief offices of the Florentine government.

At the foot of the bridge on the downtown side, you entered Por San Maria, the street of the Silk Guild, which brought you to Calimala, the street of the Merchants Guild. On your left, you passed the stately arcade of the Mercato Nuovo (New Market), built by Cosimo I in 1547–51 for the sale of costly textiles and other luxury goods. But then, after

Calimala, came a precipitous lowering of the commercial tone as you joined the milling crowd in the Mercato Vecchio (Old Market) – the gritty hub of the city.

For centuries the Mercato Vecchio had been simply the Mercato, until the construction of the fashionable new showcase of the Mercato Nuovo. The Old Market was then destined to remain the chief point of distribution for the often messy and smelly requirements of daily life. In its central pavilion and surrounding shops and stands, there was Florence's densest concentration of butchers, bakers, and greengrocers, as well as specialists in poultry, tripe, ham, sausage, and cheese, not to mention a shifting range of seasonal products. The fishmongers had a special facility of their own in a handsome arcade built by Cosimo I and Crown Prince Francesco in 1567. Meanwhile, other shops and stands offered a mixed array of clothing, textiles, and household goods – both new and recycled.

In 1570–71, when the Ghetto rose on the north side of the central market pavilion, it was bordered by the Street of the Second-hand Dealers (Via dei Rigattieri) – alternately known as the Street of the Rag Merchants (Via dei Stracciaiuoli). Just around the corner, there was the Street of the Scrap Iron Dealers (Via dei Ferravecchi). The Ghetto was conceived as an urban renewal project but the Jews did not transform the commercial scheme of things in that corner of town. Even after reconstruction, this remained the realm of recyclers and second-handers – rag merchants, iron scrappers, and so on.

Market and Ghetto

On Sunday 8 November 1615 Bendetto Blanis shared a recent drama in the Florentine Ghetto with Don Giovanni dei Medici:

> Yesterday we had a major commotion here, when a frightful conflagration broke out in the Mercato Vecchio in the shop of a chestnut roaster. He had left thousands of wrappers on top of his oven, and these ignited at the 14th hour [around 6 a.m.]. If this had happened at night-time, almost all of the Ghetto would have been at risk but thanks to God, we had no particular damage, neither to persons nor property. Two shops burned, that of the delicatessen seller[2] and the one next to it and also two stands, but we had time to save everything, thank God.[3]

In practical terms, the Ghetto and the Mercato Vecchio were extensions of each other. Not merely adjacent, they shared some of the same buildings. If one burned down, so did the other. The Inner Ghetto (Ghetto Interno) looked onto the Jews' small square and single street while the contiguous buildings of the Outer Ghetto (Ghetto Esterno) faced Florence's busy central market. There were Jews with stands and even shops on the outside. Meanwhile, Jewish pedlars circulated throughout the market, and Jewish touts worked to pull in trade for the shopkeepers inside.

Competition was intense, so the Ghetto legislators issued regulation after regulation to keep Jewish vendors out of each other's way: 'No one is permitted to station himself within 10 braccia [six yards] of the gates of the Ghetto with things to sell nor block buyers and sellers from entering the Ghetto[4] ... No one can put tables in front of his shop in the Ghetto square nor impinge in any way on the space of others[5] ... Unauthorized people are not allowed buy household goods in order to resell them in the Ghetto square[6] ... When someone is engaged in buying or selling, others must not intrude on any pretext, even outside the Ghetto in the houses of Christians.'[7]

The tensions of daily life within the Ghetto were aggravated by other tensions just outside the gates. On 4 February 1622 the Eight Magistrates for Protection and Supervision ruled on the case of 'Giulio son of Francesco from Arezzo, formerly delivery boy for Domenico Vanni, poulterer in the Mercato Vecchio' and 'Agostino son of Piero Lisi, formerly Domenico's shop assistant':

> An hour and a half after nightfall on 24 March 1621, the little brother of the Jew Jacob son of Moisé from Prato was heading from the gate of the Ghetto towards the Mercato Vecchio and the above-mentioned Giulio was allegedly bothering him. When Jacob called out, 'Why are you picking on him?' Giulio replied, 'Because I feel like it.' Jacob then started running but before he could catch up to them, Giulio picked up a stone and threw it but didn't hit him. The above-mentioned Agostino then came running to back up Giulio with a knife, key, or other such instrument in his hand. He struck Jacob with this under his right eye, resulting in a bump and a bloodless bruise.[8]

Agostino denied the charges and was absolved for lack of evidence while Giulio failed to appear and was fined 50 lire in absentia. This was an impossible sum for a poultry seller's delivery boy – so the police would not be collecting their usual cut and were unlikely to waste time looking for him. Meanwhile, there was no lack of criminality in that part of town, as the magistrates heard on 6 July 1619:

> Paolo son of Simone, a baptized Turk about twelve years of age, was arrested by one of the officers of the Florentine constabulary since an earthenware pitcher had been stolen from the well in the Ghetto. The officer received information that the said Paolo was responsible, and Paolo was then questioned and he confessed of his own accord. When tortured with the *ciuffoli* for one eighth of an hour, he further confessed to stealing a cloak worth 5 lire ... The Magistrates considered the evidence of these thefts and sentenced Paolo to fifty lashes – to be carried out by the appropriate public official at the column in the Mercato Vecchio. He is also to make restitution for his thefts ... On 22 August 1619, the whipping was carried out, as recorded by Constable Dreino ... On 4 September 1619, Paolo was released from prison since the earthenware pitcher had been given back to its owner.[9]

Petty theft was often ridiculously petty in early seventeenth-century Florence, and life was a constant struggle between those who had a little and those who had nothing at all. Paolo was either a baptized Turkish slave or the son of one – in either case, he had been cut loose after conversion and left to survive as best he could on the streets of Florence. In view of Paolo's tender age, he was treated gently by the Eight Magistrates for Protection and Supervision. He was subjected only to a second-grade torment (he had his fingers crushed between *ciuffoli* or splints of wood) and a second-grade penalty (whipping). If he had been a few years older, the prescribed mode of both judicial torture and corporal punishment would have involved the *fune* or rope. That is, he would have had his arms secured behind his back and thereby been hoisted into mid-air – dislocating all the joints of his upper body.

Trials were carried out behind closed doors at the headquarters of the Florentine constabulary in the Bargello Palace but non-capital punishments were usually inflicted publicly in the Mercato Vecchio. In Florence's central market, the most imposing feature was a tall granite column surmounted by a statue of Abundance (still visible in the present-day Piazza della Repubblica[10]), alluding to the plentiful supply of goods for those who could pay. Whippings were carried out at the base of this column, and malefactors were exposed to public scorn at the *gogna* or pillory.[11] Meanwhile, the *fune* was featured at the other side of the market square, where a permanent pulley structure had been erected near the southeastern corner of the Ghetto.

Most punishments were exemplary, as in the case of Cristofano, son (presumably illegitimate) of a laundress named Maria – tried by the Eight Magistrates on 1 December 1614:

> While serving as shop-assistant, this Cristofano pilfered from Francesco his master a half-ounce of gold trim, a bundle with five pieces of napped velvet, taffeta, cloth pouches, and other items worth 8 or 10 lire ... They therefore sentenced him to two hoists of the rope to be carried out in public with a placard at his feet reading 'For Theft.' Then he is to be confined for 18 months at the construction site in Livorno.[12]

In resolving other crimes against property, ridicule rather than pain was the main point:

> On 4 May 1607, the Magistrates considered the incarceration of Mariotto son of Federigo from Capalle in the jurisdiction of Campi who was arrested for damaging artichokes on the property of the Most Excellent Lord Verginio Orsini, having gathered twenty-five or thirty of them during the night ... He is sentenced to stay in the pillory at the column in the Mercato for one hour, with artichokes displayed on his person and a placard reading "For Damaging Produce."[13]

> On 22 February 1619, the Magistrates considered the incarceration of Lionardo son of Giovanni Folchi who was arrested for stealing a pull-over jacket belonging to Raffaello Nucci while the latter was unloading a pack animal ... Since this Lionardo is incapable of torment of any kind – being hunchbacked and twisted and sickly all his life – they sentenced him to give back what he stole and spend an hour in the pillory in the Mercato Vecchio with a placard reading 'For Theft.'[14]

In the Mercato Vecchio the daily dramas of Florentine life were played out on a public stage for all to see. There were crowds and noise. There was buying and selling. There were rich and poor. There was crime and retribution. And on the edge of it all, there was the Piazza dei Giudei – the designated *Place of the Jews*.

Half-in and half-out of the Mercato Vecchio, the Ghetto was an integral part of the city's shopping district – or so it seemed to the Christian bargain hunters who dropped in during business hours to buy things on the cheap. The Jews, inevitably, had their own more focused and pragmatic point of view. Having been excluded from most of the usual trades and professions, they were struggling to survive in an economic ghetto far more constraining than any architectural one.

Blanis and Sons

On 3 October 1619 the Eight Magistrates dealt with a typical incident of theft and thuggery originating in the Florentine Ghetto:

> They reviewed the lawsuit brought by the Jew David son of Laudadio Blanis against two men of no fixed occupation,[15] Niccolò son of Simone son of Piero del Garbo and Alessandro son of Zanobi, both Florentines. On 18 June, the two accused went to the shop belonging to the plaintiff and his father. Niccolò asked the plaintiff's mother to show him some buttons, then he took two or three strings of them and went off without wanting to pay. The plaintiff then followed the aforesaid Niccolò as far as Piazza delle Pallottole, telling him that this was no way to behave and that he should give back the buttons. Alessandro then took hold of the plaintiff while Niccolò worked him over with his fists or a knife or a key, leaving him with a scratched face and a bloody nose. Then Alessandro threw a stone at him, bruising his right knee ... The Magistrates absolved Alessandro for lack of evidence while Niccolò's failure to appear was taken as a legitimate confession of his guilt. He is therefore sentenced to give back the buttons and pay a fine of 150 lire for scratching the plaintiff's face and bloodying the plaintiff's nose, plus a fine of 50 lire for the bruise caused by the stone, arriving at a total fine of 200 lire.[16]

Niccolò and Alessandro might have been surprised by the Jew's persistence – thinking they were home free once they exited the Ghetto. David Blanis (Benedetto's younger brother) dogged them for several hundred feet – from the family shop, down the Ghetto's single street, out the main gate, then along the length of the cathedral into a small adjoining square. Persistence, however, was one of the keys to economic survival in the Florentine Ghetto, along with nerve, resilience, and ingenuity.

The Blanis were a distinguished and respected Ghetto family but there was nothing aristocratic about their day-to-day business. Benedetto's mother staffed the shop, offering buttons to low-class clients, while his brother David acted as enforcer when need arose. Buttons were an essential item of Jewish trade, produced right there in the Ghetto. Hand-carved or else turned on small wheels or lathes – mostly in common materials like horn, bone, and wood – they could be made almost anywhere by men, women, or children. Between 1605 and 1609 alone, seven Jews registered as button-makers, probably representing entire households.[17] Back in 1582, in the earliest years of the Ghetto, the governors banned the placement of workbenches 'with or without buttons' outside Ghetto shops.[18] Although there was good natural light in the street, the button-makers were blocking the passage of pack animals transporting charcoal and firewood.

The Blanis family's stock in trade was not limited to buttons. On 28 June 1620 Benedetto asked Don Giovanni's mistress Livia Vernazza to clarify her order for an unspecified quantity of *ermesino*, a lightweight silk fabric: 'I didn't send Your Most Illustrious Ladyship the *ermesino* immediately because you didn't tell me how much you required nor how you planned to fashion it. In Florence – I swear to you – we have such a variety of sleeves, that there could be a full braccio [23 inches] difference depending on the style.'[19]

On 5 February 1621 Benedetto's youngest brother Salamone explained to Don Giovanni's secretary in Venice: 'At this time, I am sending you some samples of taffeta of which I can get 6 or 8 or even 10 braccia [3.8 or 5.1 or 6.4 yards] for 3 lire 6 soldi 8 piccioli per braccio in cash – although it would cost at least 4 lire around the shops. I am also sending you a sample of gold thread ... of which I can get 5 ounces at 5 lire 5 soldi per ounce, more or less.'[20]

The Blanis family pieced together small consignments of generally luxurious materials for Don Giovanni and Donna Livia, also including gold and silver lace,[21] silk cording,[22] and silver thread. Venice was the best supplied commercial depot in Europe, but the Jews back home could get stuff cheaply, then send it off for free with the Medici post. When it arrived, Don Giovanni could ignore local customs duty – either as a foreign dignitary or as an agent of the Venetian government.[23]

The Ghetto was known as a good place to buy things at bargain prices, although not usually things of top quality. On 29 May 1621 Don Giovanni dei Medici heard from Cosimo Baroncelli, the manager of his household in Florence:

We have not yet been able to get the taffeta from the Jewish Ghetto. This is for two reasons: First, the Consuls of the Silk Guild have issued an injunction against them selling retail (*vendere a taglio*), so they can no longer operate in this way. Second, it is now the period of their Passover, and according to their law, they have to keep their shops closed and can't do business of any kind. Therefore, I got the taffeta from Codilungo's shop, and it is more expensive than in the Ghetto, although perhaps much better.[24]

The Codilungo family were big silk producers and pillars of their guild (the Arte della Seta) with a grand shop near Por San Maria. Laudadio and Lelio Blanis (Benedetto's father and older brother) were both members of this same guild, as had been Benedetto's great-grandfather Laudadio and his aunt Ginevra.[25] But even with their family tradition and their paid-up memberships, they were excluded from direct competition with Christians like these on the up-market side of town.

On 17 September 1580 – barely ten years after the creation of the Ghetto – the Silk Guild issued an exhaustive set of new by-laws running to over a hundred pages. They established six categories of 'Major Members,' beginning with Setaioli Grossi (Big Silk Producers) then running through Orefici e Banchieri (Goldsmiths and Bankers who keep goldwork, silverwork, and jewels), Ritagliatori (Retailers and warehouse keepers who sell cloth by measure that they have not made themselves), Battilori e Tiralori (Gold Leaf and Gold Thread Makers), Velettai (Veil Makers), and Linaioli (Linen drapers who also wish to stock merchandise in this guild's retail category).[26]

The Silk Guild – in actual fact – was a conglomeration of diverse trades including tailors, stocking-makers, mattress-makers, and button-makers. Its main focus, however, was on large-scale silk production, which was a mainstay of the Florentine economy. Policy was usually set by the Setaioli Grossi, exemplified by the Codilungo firm, which coordinated the activity of smaller operators, often in home workshops. According to the 1580 by-laws, these 'Big Silk Producers' were required to live and keep their shops in the area of Por San Maria, within 200 braccia (120 yards) of the guild headquarters[27] – effectively excluding the Blanis family and everyone else in the Ghetto. Near the end of a long discussion on procedures for guild registration, there was a special provision for Jews – the only reference to them in this laboriously crafted document:

> It might occur that there are some Jews who wish to carry out the trade of buying and selling, in houses, convents, and elsewhere … These Jews are required to keep an open shop – maintaining residence in the place that His Most Serene Highness designated for the Jews – and they must matriculate as members for retail selling (*membro del ritaglio*).[28]

The Blanis were operating as *ritagliatori*, 'retailers and warehouse keepers who sell cloth by measure that they have not made themselves.' As required, they kept an open shop in the Ghetto, rented in the name of Laudadio Blanis[29] who was a full member of the Silk Guild. Retailing, however, was only the beginning of their activity – which extended into the murky realm of second-hand trading and beyond.[30]

In Florence Jews were disparaged as much for their commercial habits as for their religious practices. In Ghetto shops and from Jewish pedlars, you could buy almost anything from anywhere – usually with special deals and attractive discounts. The guilds, meanwhile, sought to protect the old-fashioned values of regulated business – values that inevitably favoured the big producers. In their world, you bought cloth made to strict guild specifications directly from the person responsible for making it. Then, you took it to a tailor who fashioned it into clothing, with a minimum of extraneous handling along the way. Such handling, however, was exactly what allowed most Jews to earn a living.

There were two other Florentine guilds with a Jewish presence. One was the Physicians and Apothecaries Guild (Arte dei Medici e Speziali) which had merged with the Merchants Guild (Arte dei Mercatanti). By the time of Benedetto Blanis, it primarily enrolled Jewish makers and sellers of veils and buttons.[31] Then there was the Linen Guild (Arte dei Linaioli), another conglomerate organization. Although less grand and less influential than the Silk Guild, their interests often overlapped. Its key members were Linen Producers (Linaioli), but there were also Rigattieri (Second-hand Dealers or Resellers), Osti e Vinattieri (Tavern Keepers and Wine Sellers), Cuochi (Cooks), and Pollaiuoli (Poulterers). Still, their chief focus was on linen production and, like their comrades in the Silk Guild, they were uneasy about people who sold but did not make. On 23 July 1578 the Arte dei Linaioli issued a set of new by-laws. Almost as long and complicated as those of the Arte della Seta, these were even more explicit when it came to defending the reputation and dignity of their trade:

> The officers of this Guild and framers of these by-laws considered the damage that is done both to individuals and the general public by male and female resellers (*rivenditori e rivenditrici*) who go around the city and countryside selling linen cloth and other new and used things – including linen, linen wadding, and whatever else. They deceive and defraud many people regarding the nature and quality of their goods, often passing things off as something else ... In order to protect the worthy and punish

the scoundrels, it is hereby decreed that no one of any condition or gender will go around the city or the countryside in houses, streets, and markets, reselling things whether new or used, in any way or under any pretext – even if they are members of this Guild, unless this Guild has issued them an explicit licence to operate in this way.[32]

Jews are not mentioned among these itinerant resellers but their presence is strongly implied. Jews, in fact, are explicitly cited only once in the 1578 by-laws of the Linen Guild – in regard to their nefarious influence on the secondary market:

It is necessary to remove the cause of many disagreements that arise between those who bring cloth to be made up and those who make it up – that is to say, male and female tailors and resellers (*sarti, sarte e rigattieri*) ... In most cases of this kind, the garments are damaged because the tailors and the resellers (*rigattieri*) do not use the full quantity of cloth that they are given – so that cuttings will be left over for their own purposes. This is of great detriment to those who have things made up and would perhaps not occur if these tailors and resellers (*rigattieri*) were not able to dispose of the resulting cuttings by selling them to Jewish resellers (*rigattieri giudei*) or others. Wishing to rectify this situation insofar as possible, the officers of this Guild – who are the authors of these by-laws – order that in the future no male or female tailor or reseller (*rigattiere*) nor their assistants, apprentices, workers, or others, can sell cuttings of any cloth or material. Neither can any Jewish reseller (*rigattiere giudeo*), nor anyone else under the authority of this Guild, buy such things without an express licence from the Consuls of this Guild.[33]

There was a lively demand for anything that could be put to some kind of use – even scraps of fabric – supplying a population of remakers and resellers who were characteristically but not exclusively Jewish. According to the by-laws of the Silk and Linen guilds, this amorphous sector included *rivenditori* (resellers), *ritagliatori* (retailers), *venditori al taglio* (sellers by measure or by the piece), and finally *rigattieri*. In modern Italian, *rigattiere* means junkman or old clothes dealer – but a few centuries ago, it could include almost anyone who recycled goods whether new, used, or reconditioned. In the by-laws of the Linen Guild, for example, there were rigattieri who produced clothing alongside tailors – presumably for the ready-to-wear market – and sold their leftover cuttings to Jewish rigattieri who somehow fashioned them into salable items.

For rigattieri, finding goods to recycle was as big a challenge as finding customers to buy them. Their stock often came from outside Florence and even outside the Medici State – so Jewish shopkeepers were
constantly harassed by customs officials on the hunt for contraband.
In the spring of 1615, for example, *doganieri* raided the Ghetto shop of
Daniello Calò and seized forty pairs of reconditioned silk stockings,
claiming that Daniello had brought them secretly to Florence without
paying duty. They were then forced to return them – when his son Isac
Calò demonstrated that 'he himself bought these stockings openly from
an Armenian in the Crown Tavern (Osteria della Corona) by way of
an authorized middleman (*sensale*) and having acquired them, remade
them here in Florence.'[34]

Jews were not always hapless victims of the Florentine customs
administration, and the Blanis family could take credit for one of
the boldest failed scams of all time. In May of 1611 the Maestri della
Dogana heard a case against 'Agnolo son of Salvadore Blanis,[35] a Jew
from Massa, and Lelio son of Laudadio Blanis, a Jew in the Ghetto of
Florence':

> On 4 March 1611, Agnolo brought to Florence by way of Lucca a large
> quantity of goods including clothing for men and women of small,
> medium, and large size, in textiles of various kinds and colours ... The
> Most Illustrious Signor Rodrigo Alidosi had been away on an ambassa-
> dorial mission, and the accused Agnolo and Lelio took advantage of the
> arrival of that gentleman's personal property on that very day. They trans-
> ported their own things into Florence as if they belonged to Signor Rod-
> rigo – without taking them to the Dogana and without paying duty as they
> should have done with trade goods ... At night, they brought these things
> to the Ghetto – to the house of Lelio and his father Laudadio – where they
> were subsequently found and removed along with the other inventoried
> items.[36]

The Blanis family operated in Florence and Massa di Carrara – a small
independent principality between Tuscany and Liguria, where Benedetto had relatives on both his father's and his mother's side. Don Rodrigo Alidosi was a distinguished Tuscan diplomat, sent as ambassador
in 1610 to the Court of Lorraine. Whether Agnolo and Lelio plotted
their sleight-of-hand or merely rose to the occasion, the authorities had
cause to admire their nerve and ingenuity. The case, however, was out-
rageous by any standard – generating an intense search of the Ghetto,

many court appearances, and much legal documentation.[37] Eventually, the Maestri della Dogana ordered the forfeiture and sale of the seized items, along with the pack animals that had carried them into the city.

The inventory of Blanis contraband fills two densely written pages, detailing dozens of items of good second-hand clothing. There were men's long cloaks (*zimarre*), men's sleeveless overcoats (*ferraioli*), and women's skirts (*sottane*) – in wool and silk, in taffeta, damask, and velvet, with embroidered, brocaded, and applied decoration. In addition, there were bedcovers and bed hangings and innumerable pairs of stockings. The Florentine Surrogates Court (Maestri dei Pupilli) auctioned the entire lot, realizing nearly 2,500 lire in silver (355 scudi in gold). This would have been a grievous loss for any merchant – let alone a family of Jews living by their wits on the edge of the Florentine economy.

In the months that followed the Alidosi caper, Laudadio and his four sons Lelio, Benedetto, David, and Salamone all spent time in jail while the Maestri della Dogana sifted the evidence for other infractions. On 18 August 1611 Laudadio and Lelio were further charged with smuggling a used cloak in black velveteen and a set of bed hangings in white and golden figured silk – passing them off as personal property rather than trade goods:

> Laudadio carried a valise on horseback from Massa, containing various items including a cloak that had been given to him [in Massa] by his son Benedetto for delivery to his other son Salamone. Laudadio then conveyed this cloak into the city of Florence without paying duty ... The bed hangings, Laudadio confessed, had also been brought to Florence as tax exempt, allegedly forming part of the trousseau of his daughter-in-law Mirra [bride of David Blanis].[38]

Salamone quickly sent the cloak to auction, realizing 10 scudi. The bed hangings were passed on to another second-hand dealer (evidently a Christian), who found a ready buyer at 70 scudi. In the end, the authorities cut the Blanis family a major break, fining them a mere 22 scudi – the value of the cloak and Laudadio's horse. These Jewish rigattieri, it would seem, had already taken enough hits from the Florentine Dogana.

Rigattieri were not at the absolute bottom of the secondary market, and some rigattieri – like the Blanis – were remaking and reselling in quite a big way. The *ferravecchi* were the ultimate commercial underclass – scrap iron dealers by name but really itinerant traders in almost

anything. In their 1578 by-laws the Linen Guild treated these ferravecchi as semi-untouchables:

> The officers of this Guild – who are the authors of these by-laws – con-
> sidered that there are many *ferravecchi* who go around the city and the
> countryside buying and reselling things that pertain to this Guild, like
> feathers, linen, woolen fabric, and other such items, without paying any
> matriculation fee. Although their trade does not seem important enough
> to warrant matriculation, it is not suitable for these *ferravecchi* to go around
> buying and selling these things without paying a fee of some kind ... It was
> therefore decided that they should pay this Guild a mandatory fee of 30
> soldi every year in the month of January.[39]

Like the rigattieri, the ferravecchi were characteristically but not exclusively Jewish. On 22 December 1621 Moisé son of Emanuel Lattone
identified Sabato son of Vivante Ancherani in a legal deposition: 'The
aforesaid Sabato has two rooms in the Ghetto where he lives with his
wife, and he goes iron-scrapping (*va ferravecchiando*) around the outlying villages as do other Jews.' Moisé, for his part, was an affluent
Levantine (worth 1,000 scudi, according to his own statement)[40] and
also Benedetto Blanis' brother-in-law.

Most of these itinerant buyers and resellers led miserable lives, eking
out an existence from one small deal to the next. Meanwhile, they were
subject to abuse from the Christians on whom they depended for even
this marginal activity. On 10 July 1617 the Eight Magistrates for Protection and Supervision considered a case of gratuitous harassment:

> The Magistrates reviewed the investigation of Cosimo son of [father's
> name omitted] a mercer who resides in Borgo Ognissanti ... and of
> Camillo son of Giovanni Maria, a gold-thread maker who also resides in
> Borgo Ognissanti. On 30 March 1617, the two defendants met up in the
> tavern in Via Benedetta for the purpose of drinking. Out in the street, they
> heard Rubino son of Moisé and Elia son of Servadio – both Jews – crying
> out, 'Who has old gold?' Intentionally and by mutual agreement of the
> two defendants, Cosimo got up from the table and ran after the aforesaid
> Jews. He grabbed Elia by the arm and brought him into the tavern force-
> ably with punches. Cosimo then compelled Elia to sit down at the table
> between him and Camillo, closed in so that he couldn't leave. Then he also
> made Rubino sit down and told the Jews that he wanted them to pay for
> a flask of wine. After they had drunk, Cosimo and Camillo told the Jews

that it was time to pay up. Since the Jews said that they didn't have any money, they made them leave a pair of sleeves that was in the possession of the aforesaid Elia. The Jews then left but returned shortly thereafter in order to retrieve the sleeves. Words were exchanged, with Cosimo injuring Elia verbally. Cosimo then took hold of the shaft of a scythe, beat Elia with it until it broke, and chased the two Jews out of the tavern with kicks. [41]

Cosimo and Camillo were both found guilty in absentia and sentenced to fines that they presumably never paid. Meanwhile, Elia and Rubino continued to wander the city, turning over any items that came their way – doing what all Jews did to earn a living, even those with guild memberships and Ghetto shops.

By necessity, the Jews of Florence cultivated their narrow sector of the economy as intensely as they could – developing products outside the Christian mainstream of making and selling. This was an arduous way to earn a living, but not entirely impossible thanks to the insatiable demand for second-hand goods. Dress was an essential indicator of so-cial status in late-Renaissance Florence, but textiles and clothing were wildly expensive in real terms. As a result, most people went through their lives without ever owning a good suit of entirely new clothes. Even at the Medici Court, many were piecing together outfits with ef-fort and ingenuity in order to save face and make a good show.

Besides reconditioning and reselling clothing, Jews were also renting it. On 15 April 1614 Don Giovanni dei Medici wrote Granducal Sec-retary Andrea Cioli in order to help Laudadio Blanis with a business problem:

> Before going to Vada, Pierfrancesco Gabbrielli borrowed a velvet suit with gold trim from the Jew Laudadio, I don't know for what occasion. Not only has Gabbrielli not abided by the terms of their agreement, he hasn't even returned the suit. The Jew has kept quiet out of respect, but since this problem has been referred to me, I ask you to bring your authority to bear. I imagine that Gabbrielli would be pleased to have the matter end here, avoiding awkwardness and damage to his reputation.[42]

Providing costumes for festive and theatrical events was a natural ex-tension of Jewish second-hand dealing. After the Carnival of 1619 Bene-detto's older brother Lelio Blanis sued to recoup his fee for some exotic dress-up items, including 'two satin outfits in the Turkish style, a fine white turban, a mask, and a headband.'[43] Although the Medici Court was best known for its operatic spectacles with fabulous scenic effects, there was also a constant round of more modest entertainments. In the spring of 1618 the granducal property administration (Guardaroba) authorized two payments to Laudadio Blanis for the rental of 'various men's and women's costumes' used in improvised comedies at the Pitti Palace.[44]

The Jews themselves made buttons and women's veils, products only loosely controlled by the guilds.[45] Otherwise, they were firmly relegated to the secondary market – remaking, reselling, and renting. Then around 1620 the Silk Guild narrowed their sector even more drastically, excluding them from retail trade. Ghetto merchants, even guild members with open shops, could no longer sell new silk cloth by measure or by the cut piece. This was a grave financial loss to the Blanis and other Jewish families – and a blow to their already marginal status in the Christian world of Florentine business.

Stolen Goods

When thieves needed to recycle their loot, the Ghetto was often the first place that came to mind. The Jewish connection was an old one. On 10 April 1569, in the last months before the declaration of the Florentine Ghetto, the authorities cracked down hard on the circulation of stolen goods. In their edict, the words 'Jew' and 'fence' were treated as virtually synonymous:

> The Most Honoured and Worthy Eight Lords of Protection and Supervision of the City of Florence, on behalf of their Most Illustrious Excellencies the Duke and the Prince of Florence and Siena [Cosimo I and Francesco dei Medici], have considered the damage that is done through the voracious greed of those who make unjust profits from stolen goods. This applies to the Jews who live in the City of Florence and its Dominion and also to second-hand dealers (*rigattieri*), shopkeepers, and resellers of all kinds. They buy things from every sort of unknown person for irrational prices (*prezzi non ragionevoli*) – sometimes not even paying half what they are worth on the market.[46]

Another edict, fifty years later on 19 February 1619, was only slightly more subtle. This came after a rash of startling thefts of gold and silver by servants in the Pitti Palace:

> Thieves would not dare commit such crimes if people were not ready to

receive their takings, and those most implicated in the past have been goldsmiths, Jews, second-hand dealers (*rigattieri*), gold-leaf makers, gold-thread makers, and metal founders. Impelled by their insatiable craving for profit, they buy gold and silver from thieves for vile prices (*vilissimi prezzi*) with no compunction that such things are stolen.[47]

Both in 1569 and 1619 the magistrates offered an impeccable rule of thumb for spotting questionable merchandise: if the price is *non ragionevole* (irrational) or *vilissimo* (vile or inappropriately low), something is wrong. On 18 August 1623 the magistrates decided a typical case of this kind, involving Benedetto Blanis' younger brother David and a major theft from a posh silk shop in the Mercato Nuovo:

> On 13 May, Domiziano son of Baccio Cappelli authorized a locksmith to open up the shop of Marco Bartoli, a *setaiolo* (silk producer and dealer) in the Mercato Nuovo. This took place at noon, when the *setaioli* were off for lunch, and the accused told the locksmith that he had left his own keys inside the shop ... Domiziano then stole a piece of red worked damask measuring 62 braccia [40 yards] and worth approximately 80 scudi. He sold it to the Jew David Blanis who paid only 18 scudi knowing that it had been stolen ... although the Jew David subsequently maintained his denial under torture. The Magistrates therefore sentenced the said Domiziano to two years of forced residence in Livorno, one hoist of the rope in public, and restitution ... They exonerated the Jew David since he had cleansed the evidence of guilt by way of torture.[48]

David Blanis acquired a valuable piece of silk for less than a quarter of its true value, and the magistrates saw that justice was served – in spite of his de facto exoneration. The rightful owner regained his property, and the thief was duly punished. The Jewish receiver of stolen goods had a bad time as well. By standing up to torture, David Blanis repudiated any involvement – resulting in a dead loss of the 18 scudi he had presumably paid Baccio Cappelli.

Judging from the records of innumerable court cases, the Blanis family was not necessarily more crooked than anyone else in the Ghetto, nor indeed the rest of Florence.[49] Like other resellers, they had to assess every proposition that came their way, calculating the relative risks and gains. On 22 April 1622 the magistrates heard the case of Lorenzo Gori, a recently fired manservant who had expropriated two richly trimmed women's headdresses: 'He attempted to resell them in the Ghetto but was unable to put his plan into effect, since the Jews did not know him. Lorenzo was then arrested by the officers of the constabulary.'[50]

Second-hand dealers in general and Jews in particular laboured under a heavy presumption of guilt. If questions arose regarding their stock in trade, it was up to them to demonstrate due diligence and good faith. Many offerings were not merely suspicious, they were downright preposterous. In 1615 a knife sharpener and delivery man tried to sell five ounces of gold thread in the Ghetto – claiming that he had casually 'found' this precious material. The Jews noted that the gold thread had been removed from its marked spools and promptly called the police.[51]

Even with the best intentions and the keenest fear of criminal prosecution, it was not always easy for second-hand dealers to spot wrong merchandise. On 12 October 1618 the magistrates exonerated both a Christian and a Jewish reseller who had been duped by a thief called *il Romanino* (the little Roman):

> Last July, the said Romanino stole the following items: a doublet, a pair of trousers in black mocaiardo wool and another pair in tawny Perpignan wool, a waistcoat, and a deerskin collar. He dressed himself in the doublet and the mocaiardo trousers, then went and sold them to the Jew Rubino for 12 lire. Then he sold the other trousers, the waistcoat, and the collar to Cesare ... Rubino and Cesare both admitted to buying the said items in the said manner without suspecting that they were stolen, stipulating that they had bought them openly and then displayed them openly ... The Magistrates therefore absolved Cesare of all legal liability ... They also absolved the Jew Rubino since he bought the clothing off the back of the seller and could not be expected to conclude that it was stolen and not his own.[52]

Others, however, were far less scrupulous, and there was a lively Florentine underworld of Christian thieves and Jewish fences. On 12 January 1618 the magistrates heard a case involving five scoundrels of very mixed origin, operating out of the Fig Tree Tavern (Hosteria del Fico). The Christian thief was Bastiano Bartoli, a young shoemaker's helper from the Mugello region of Tuscany, and his accomplice was Valentino Maioranza, a Christian shoemaker from Trieste. The fences included one Florentine Jew Emanuello son of Agnolo da Pesaro, one Roman Jew Durante son of Leone del Sostiero, and one Mantuan Jew Rubino son of Moisé[53] (not to be confused with the Rubino in the preceding case who was the son of Agnolo):

Approximately two months before his incarceration, the first defendant Bastiano went at night-time to the shop of Jacopino Diociaiuti, a shoe-maker at the Canto del Giglio. He knew these premises well since he had served there as a shop-boy, so he reached through a gap where the upper and lower shutter closed badly. With a stick, he hit the latch several times from behind, managing in this way to open the shutter. Once inside, he found the key to a closet where there was a wooden bowl from which he stole six gold coins (*zecchini*), seven or eight silver coins (*testoni*), and a gold ring with a red stone. Then he went off and left the shop as he found it, closing the shutter in the same way that he had opened it. In the days that followed, Bastiano returned to Diociaiuti's shop on two occasions, stealing seventeen or eighteen fine chamois skins and five large chamois skins from the same closet. He allegedly sold three of the large skins at night-time for 10 lire to the third defendant, that is to say, the Mantuan Jew Rubino ... Then at the Hosteria del Fico, he allegedly sold the remaining large chamois skins and the seventeen or eighteen small chamois skins to the Jews Emanuel and Durante, the second and fourth defendants, for a total price of 2 scudi. Valentino, the fifth defendant, allegedly hid the skins for Bastiano and then brought them to the Hosteria del Fico concealed under his cape.[54]

Bastiano was not a criminal mastermind, repeatedly hitting the same establishment where he was the obvious suspect. He then went on to rob a cutler's shop where he stole mother-of-pearl spoons, simulated jewels, and women's hair clasps, giving them away to various friends. The magistrates had an open-and-shut case against Bastiano but they chose to moderate their sentence. Since he was young and too small for the galleys, they sent him instead to the government construction site in Livorno. Although a public whipping was also called for, they let him off because he had a marriageable sister and they did not want to harm her prospects by shaming the family.

The magistrates also had an open-and-shut case against the Floren-tine Jew Emanuello da Pesaro, since everything about the deal was wrong: 'In accordance with the law promulgated in 1569, he should have considered the quality of the person selling the goods and their low price, realizing that they might have been stolen. The Magistrates therefore sentenced him to a fine of 10 scudi and restitution of either the goods or their fair value.' Rubino, the Mantuan Jew, missed his court appearance and received the same sentence in absentia while Durante, the Roman Jew, was exonerated – somehow convincing the magistrates that he had innocently wandered onto the scene of the crime. They were not ready to extend the same benefit of the doubt to Valentino, the Christian shoemaker from Trieste, although he maintained his innocence under torture: 'The Magistrates found that he had received the chamois skins in his own shop and carried them under his own mantle to the tavern in question. Therefore, they sentenced him to a fine of 10 scudi and restitution, together with the aforementioned Emanuello.'[55]

Bastiano's thieving was amateurish in the extreme, but he could at least rely on the Jewish connection to liquidate his takings. The two foreign Jews were Ghetto riff-raff and presumably up for anything. Durante, the Roman, was a drifter 'with neither wife nor family nor trade,' and the governors finally had him expelled in the summer of 1619.[56] Rubino, the Mantuan, was also in and out of jail with no visible means of support. He was, in fact, the same Rubino son of Moisé who had been wandering the streets of Florence with Elia son of Servadio, shouting 'Who has old gold?'[57] Emanuello da Pesaro, on the other hand, was a substantial figure in the Ghetto, and he might have served as governor, only a few years after his arrest and conviction.[58]

When it came to stealing, no Jew was above suspicion – not even the son of Benedetto's cousin Moisé Blanis,[59] who succeeded Hayyim Finzi in 1621 as chancellor of the Ghetto and rabbi in the Italian *scuola*. On 19 July 1623 the magistrates shrugged off a particularly ludicrous case:

> They reviewed the investigation of the Jew Giuseppe son of Moisé Blanis and the Jew Simone son of Isac from Prato, in response to the lawsuit brought by Francesco, a *mutandaio* (purveyor of bathing drawers). It is alleged that the two of them went to bathe in the Arno River on the evening of 3 July 1623, at the place where the plaintiff lends bathing drawers. When they left, they allegedly pilfered a *lenzuolo* (sheet or towel) belonging to the plaintiff's establishment, as recorded on page 85 of the 488th Book of Lawsuits. The Magistrates considered this case and examined various witnesses, none of whom had testimony to offer against the accused. Considering their denial and the lack of evidence to the contrary, the Magistrates ordered them to be freed and fully absolved of the charges.[60]

By that time, Giuseppe and Simone had already spent two weeks in jail awaiting trial.[61] Francesco, the *mutandaio*, presumably knew enough about Jewish business to imagine these two recycling sheets, towels, and anything else that came their way. Some Jews, however, were not quite living from rag to rag. And in any case, there were smarter ways to improve the profit margin in second-hand deals.

Scrocchi Barocchi

One of the most enduring Jewish stereotypes is that of the voracious moneylender exacting his pound of flesh from Christian victims. In the time of Benedetto Blanis, there were various 'shylocks' in the Florentine Ghetto. Perhaps the most notorious of these was Benedetto himself.

The legal and moral context of this activity was complicated, to say the least.[62] Usury – taking money for the use of money – had been sternly banned by the Catholic Church for most of its history, although Jewish outsiders were generally exempt from this prohibition. Christian bankers, in the meantime, proved endlessly inventive in their exploitation of loopholes in the dogma. The most sensational example was that of the Medici themselves, who made a huge fortune in international finance in an earlier phase of their rise to power.[63]

With the emergence of the Medici State, in the early sixteenth century, its rulers withdrew from commerce of this kind. Moneylending was largely relegated to Jewish pawnbrokers, who were granted special charters throughout the territory. Meanwhile, in the City of Florence itself, credit was provided by the Monte di Pietà, a quasi-charitable pawnbroking operation. This situation changed dramatically after 27 September 1570, when Grand Duke Cosimo I and his son Francesco seized on Jewish usury as a convenient pretext for mass expulsion and ghettoization:

> In the past, these Jews obtained the right to lend money for profit (*prestare ad usura*) and to operate banks in various towns in the Florentine Dominion ... subject to specific contractual agreements which these Jews subsequently violated, thereby causing grave harm to Their Highnesses' subjects ... They broke their contracts by lending money at interest on holidays; sometimes ... they took higher fees (*maggiore usura*) than were allowed; sometimes ... they expropriated items pledged by humble peasants; sometimes ... they defrauded widows and poor people.[64]

Jews were to cease lending money immediately and leave their places of residence. There was, however, a meagre escape clause:

If some Jews wish to remain in this State in order to live with their families and trade or exercise some other profession, they will be permitted to settle in the City of Florence in the neighbourhoods or localities that Their Highnesses set aside for them – subject to whatever terms and conditions Their Highnesses dictate.[65]

As expected, most Jewish bankers quickly left the Medici dominion in order to do business elsewhere, apart from a few notable exceptions, like Laudadio son of Moyse Blanis and his clan. They put down roots in the new Ghetto and set out to exercise some other profession, dealing second-hand, in various forms and guises.

This is not to say that the Blanis and their ilk stopped lending money at interest, since even in Florence there was still a pressing demand for credit. The Monte di Pietà was sanctioned by both church and state but grossly undercapitalized – unable to provide large or even medium-sized loans (except to the Medici, who floated the construction of the Ghetto on Monte di Pietà funds[66]). Making money from money continued to be the ultimate second-hand trade for Florentine Jews, and it was generally tolerated by the authorities – as long as they managed their lending discreetly and none of their Christian borrowers objected.

In 1582, more than a decade after the government banned Jewish usury, Vitale Medici preached two sermons in the Florentine Church of Santa Croce.[67] Vitale, formerly Rabbi Jachiel da Pesaro, had been an esteemed figure in the local Ghetto during its earliest years.[68] Now, as a very recent convert to Catholicism, he directed these sermons to his unredeemed brethren – developing a compelling double theme: Not only were Jewish business practices morally flawed, they embittered the lives of the Jews and placed them at odds with the dominant society:

You must perpetually struggle to earn a living, finding some means or other to turn a profit – by word or deed, licitly or illicitly, *per fas o nefas*. So there you are, constantly offending your neighbour, distraining his property contrary to the dictates of conscience. That is not the way to find salvation, even if your own vain [Jewish] law were good and true. Do not allow yourselves to believe that it is virtuous and legitimate to obtain property by fraud and to deceive Christians. That is not the way! That is not the way![69]

Per fas o nefas, 'as is permissible or forbidden by Divine Law,' is the weightiest phrase, heavy with implication for those on both sides of the religious divide. But in Florence, usury continued to flourish – very nearly in plain sight.

In the time of Benedetto Blanis, almost all of the financial suits heard by the Eight Magistrates involved Jews, and the majority of these were brought by Jews themselves. Cases usually focused on *cedole* or 'notes of credit.'[70] Christians – often from distinguished families – were signing notes of credit in considerable numbers, obligating themselves to deferred payments for a wide variety of goods.[71] Many then defaulted on their obligations, impelling the Jews to dun them in court.

On 17 August 1617 'the Magistrates reviewed the claim of the Jew Benedetto Blanis against Bonacorso son of Senator Giovanni Uguccioni and Giovanfrancesco son of Giovanfrancesco Falconi for the sum of 100 scudi each, deriving from a note of credit (*cedola*) ... dated 22 March 1617.' Uguccioni and Falconi had promised to pay 'the above-mentioned Jew or whoever else presents this note of credit' in two instalments in June and August of 1617. When they failed to do so, Benedetto swore out a warrant and the magistrates found in his favour. He could then proceed to the next stage of litigation and have the two gentlemen imprisoned for debt.[72]

In this particular case, Uguccioni and Falconi had contracted for a large quantity of linen, and this linen might even have existed in actual fact.[73] Often, however, the items in the *cedole* were merely notional – serving to disguise illegal cash loans. Substantial premiums were then built into the terms of deferred payment, resulting in significant profits for the lenders. Jewish usury – in other words – was alive and well and flourishing in the City of Florence. Since the notes of credit were transferable, there was also a lively market for discounted and recycled debts.

Loan sharking, whether thickly or thinly disguised, was still highly illegal under both civil and canon law. It was, however, one of the few ways that Jews could make their money work for them, and Christian borrowers seldom objected – thanks to a compelling lack of other options.[74]

On 15 November 1615 Benedetto Blanis asked Don Giovanni dei Medici to help him collect a heavily manipulated loan to a young patrician, Giovanfrancesco son of the late Cavaliere Pandolfo degli Albizi.[75] Along the way, this illicit transaction had been disguised as the sale of a fictive gold chain and pearl necklace:

In the copy of the documentation that I am sending you, you see that this gentleman acknowledges a debt to me. I promised to wait six months for part of it and eighteen months for the rest, and now the time has come for him to settle the balance of 170 scudi. Instead of paying me, however, this gentleman's man of business – a certain Matteo son of Michele Berti – is threatening me with legal action, saying he heard that I had bought up this debt for no more than 50 scudi. I replied that I knew Signor Albizi to be a gentleman who keeps his word, apart from the fact that I have his signature on the paper … To tell the truth, I bought this debt from a tailor for 115 scudi in cash – although this was just between him and me. Meanwhile, I put a gold chain and a string of pearls in the contract – which is what I will maintain if necessary. In any case, I believe that one can buy up a debt at any price.[76]

The file that Benedetto sent to Don Giovanni in Venice traces this deal back to 5 January 1607 – when Stefano Terzoni, a Christian tailor from Lucca, assumed an unspecified debt that Giovanfrancesco degli Albizi owed to the Capponi Bank in Florence. Albizi then obligated himself to pay Terzoni 340 scudi within two years, (presumably including a hefty premium on the original transaction). By July 1612 Terzoni had received 90 scudi from Albizi plus 19 scudi worth of textiles. A year later, 'I, Stefano son of Cherubino Terzoni tailor, relinquish and transfer the present credit to the Jew Benedetto Blanis for the value received in a gold chain of ten ounces and a pearl necklace of four strands totaling six ounces. I attest to the veracity of the present deed of conveyance in Florence on this day 29 November 1613.' Giovanfrancesco degli Albizi then signed a new note made out to Benedetto Blanis for 231 scudi – the unpaid balance of the recycled debt going back to 1607.[77]

Benedetto stood to make a hefty profit of 116 scudi if he could force Albizi to pay up – and this is where Don Giovanni dei Medici entered the picture: 'Your Excellency's graciousness and courtesy embolden me to impose a small task on you … In order to avoid argument, I beg Your Excellency to write a few lines in your usual way, telling Albizi that his man threatened me – or whatever you think best.'[78]

Don Giovanni was only a second-tier member of the Medici family, but in Florence he had considerable weight to throw around. He did not hesitate to do so – with overwhelming success, as far as Benedetto was concerned:

Your letter for Albizi was so effective that he came to Florence the instant it was delivered to him … visiting me in the Ghetto on Saturday morning

... That person [Matteo Berti] claimed that he only intended to take Signor Albizi's side, and he felt that he deserved praise for this. Albizi flew into a rage and went for that man's face with his hands, telling him that he had always valued his relations with me and did not wish to see me treated disrespectfully. He then discharged Matteo from his service, stating that he had been authorized to ask me for more time and nothing else.[79]

Benedetto was Jewish and the Albizi deal was illegal – but otherwise, Don Giovanni only did what any patron of the time would have done for a faithful client. Meanwhile, other properties were maturing in Benedetto's portfolio, as he reminded Don Giovanni on 22 November 1615:

> Let me describe the various affairs that I now have in hand: There are three credits here in Florence that I need to realize. In my last letter, I wrote you about one of these [involving Antonio Albertani], and I have already had a favourable decision from the Eight Magistrates, allowing me to act on his property and his person. There is no recourse without legal action, but we have no doubt regarding the ultimate verdict. The second collection is against Giovanbattista son of Francesco Michelozzi and I hope to resolve it this week, since it has been a serious drain on me. The third collection is against Daniello Bontalenti, and it is the most important of all. It has already exceeded all reasonable limits and is likely to drag on for at least another two months.[80]

Debt collection was an intensely adversarial process in early seventeenth-century Florence, and the usual method was to force a settlement by having the defaulter arrested and jailed. This required shrewd legal manoeuvring and influential friends – especially when dealing with eminent families like the Albertani, the Michelozzi, and the Bontalenti. By 6 December 1615 Benedetto had updated the essential paperwork in the nick of time, allowing him to imprison Antonio Albertani:

> I was soon set upon by a whole troop of knights and ladies, so it was a good thing that I was prepared. The Cavaliere Rimbotti[81] ... opposed me at the Magistrature of the Eight, swearing that Albertani had been arrested under one particular name while the notice of default from the Magistrature of the Nine was made out in yet another. Albertani – in other words – is documented as my debtor under two different names, and the one cited in the notice of default is not the one that is cited in the fugitive warrant

... However, I reminded Marsili [Giovanni Battista Marsili, Secretary of the Eight Magistrates] that no notice of default was needed, because I had renewed the fugitive warrant within one year ... Now – to make a long story short – Albertani will have to settle with me if he wants to get out of prison, and we have already begun discussions.[82]

Here we have the extraordinary spectacle of a Jew from the Ghetto wreaking havoc among the Florentine elite and thoroughly enjoying it. Not only did he outmanoeuvre the Albertani clique with his knowledge of the law, he overpowered them with his contacts. Through his connection with Don Giovanni, Benedetto was able to enlist the most influential official at the Medici Court, the secretary to Dowager Grand Duchess Christine de Lorraine: 'Signor Cavaliere [Camillo] Guidi helped me and favoured me with much affection. If I need anything, I only have to ask him for it.'[83]

For Benedetto Blanis, this heady rush of empowerment was relatively short-lived since the Michelozzi and the Bontalenti debts proved more difficult to collect. Moneylending was a risky business, since it took time and depended on the tacit collusion of the authorities. The magistrates, like everyone else, knew the real deal regarding the Jewish notes of credit that they were called on to enforce. Many or most of these would not stand up to scrutiny if anyone objected – but until that happened, it was not their duty to intervene. Benedetto, meanwhile, was counting on the unquestioning favour and support of Don Giovanni dei Medici – assuming that his great patron would always be there to turn the trick.

Benedetto's last major investment in aristocratic debt involved the distinguished Sernigi family. In 1614 Jacopo son of Andrea Sernigi signed a note of credit to Benedetto for 370 scudi and then left 130 scudi unpaid.[84] In the years that followed, Jacopo returned on various occasions to negotiate new deals. By 1620 the Jew held paper from him totalling 1,200 scudi – a huge sum, guaranteed by his mother Maddalena Martelli Sernigi.

In the past such ventures had been lucrative and relatively safe, since Benedetto could rely on Don Giovanni to manipulate the system and pull debtors into line. By 1620, however, the ground had shifted under Benedetto's feet. His patron in Venice was seriously ill and increasingly out of touch with Florentine affairs. Meanwhile, Benedetto had fallen under intense scrutiny in matters of faith and morals – becoming persona non grata in the ultra-pious circle of Christine de Lorraine.

As Captain Piero Capponi explained to Don Giovanni dei Medici, on 6 September 1620, there was not much that any of them could do for Benedetto and his family – at least in regard to the Sernigi case:

> I understand how fervently Your Excellency wishes to further the interests of the Blanis family and that they are counting on me when it comes to Signor Jacopo Sernigi's debt. However, I cannot even begin to put things in order. Signor Jacopo's mother appealed directly to Madama Serenissima [Christine de Lorraine], and usury was discovered in the contracts. Her Highness then referred the matter to the Attorney General (Auditore Fiscale) … Now that the nature of the debt has been revealed, it was strongly suggested that these particular Jews accept the same compromise as the others – dropping their suits against the mother and reducing the obligation by 40%. The Blanis, however, would not accept this proposal, and they turned to Your Excellency for help. I regret that I am unable to assist them on Your Excellency's behalf, but you see how matters stand.[85]

Benedetto's family made an extreme tactical error when they dug in their heels regarding the Sernigi debt. A widowed Christian gentlewoman was certain to receive a more sympathetic hearing than a gang of Jewish usurers, now that Christine de Lorraine was de facto ruler of Tuscany. Still, Maddalena Martelli Sernigi might well have welcomed a negotiated settlement. There was a real debt under the various layers of usury, and the Sernigi were just as guilty as the Blanis in fabricating these illicit agreements. Benedetto, for his part, was bargaining from a position of almost laughable weakness. In late July of 1620 he had been jailed for anti-Catholic activities and was being held incommunicado in the Bargello prison. Then, on 19 July 1621, Don Giovanni dei Medici died in Venice – eliminating Benedetto's last tenuous claim to special treatment.

With Benedetto out of circulation, his youngest brother Salamone took over his affairs. Although the influence of the Blanis family was at its lowest ebb, they refused to loosen their grasp on a stack of heavily manipulated notes of credit. The Blanis-Sernigi case dragged on for several more years – an ongoing triumph for the Sernigi family, since they were under no immediate pressure to settle their debts. When the magistrates finally ruled, on 30 August 1623, their summary of the evidence read like a textbook model of crypto-usury.

Benedetto had begun with an unspecified claim against Jacopo Sernigi for approximately 400 scudi. Then on 24 May 1617 he had

Jacopo cover this with two notes of credit totalling 450 scudi – one for an alleged set of satin wall hangings and another for an alleged string of pearls. Two years later, on 7 June 1619, Jacopo's mother substituted these with a 550 scudi note of credit, including a 100 scudi premium for a further twenty-month delay in payment. Meanwhile, Jacopo signed off on two further obligations to Benedetto Blanis totalling 450 scudi. On 11 December 1618 there was a note of credit for 217 scudi – for an alleged set of brocade wall hangings, to be paid by the end of May 1619. Then, on 10 February 1619, there was a note of credit for 233 scudi – for some alleged tapestries and chairs, to be paid by the end of March 1619. On 7 June 1619 Jacopo's mother took over these obligations as well, kicking up the total from 450 to 650 scudi in return for a further delay in payment. By that time Maddalena Martelli Sernigi owed the Jew Benedetto Blanis 1,200 scudi, including at least 350 scudi in interest – 'all of this by way of extortionate, twisted, and usurious practices (*scrocchi, barocchi et usure*).'[86]

Scrocchi, barocchi et usure is a colourful phrase, especially in a legal judgment. A *scrocchio* was an abusive deal in slangy Florentine, variously translatable as a 'squeak,' a 'scrape,' or a 'squeeze.' *Barocco* was basically a synonym for *scrocchio*, but with a primary meaning of 'twisted' or 'deformed.' *Usura* signified 'act of usury,' with a strong implication of 'wearing' or 'grinding down.'

Benedetto's youngest brother was running some *scrocchi* of his own, as the magistrates found at the same hearing on 30 August 1623. On 19 June 1617 Salamone Blanis registered a 150 scudi note of credit from Jacopo Sernigi, 'using the false pretext (*sotto finto nome*) of a basin and mug in gilded silver … and the false pretext of a small diamond set in a ring, to be paid within four months.' This generated a whole series of subsequent scrocchi, with further accommodations and further notes of credit for illusory textiles and a pearl necklace – all duly guaranteed by Maddalena Martelli Sernigi. In only two years, the initial debt had doubled from 150 to 300 scudi – 'by way of extortionate, twisted and usurious practices and illicit terms (*scrocchi, barocchi, usure, et patti illeciti*).'[87]

The essential problem for the magistrates was that the Blanis and the Sernigi were equally guilty before the law, since both families connived in illegal deals and registered fraudulent documents. Their solution, however, was elegant in its simplicity. After considering extensive testimony, ample documentation, and various legal precedents, the magistrates found in everyone's favour. First, they dismissed the suit

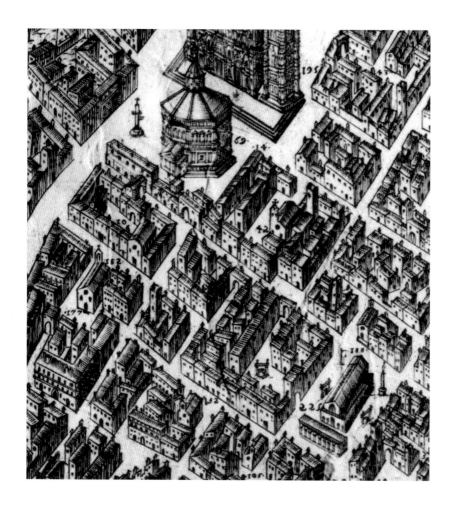

1 Florence at the time of Benedetto Blanis, showing the area from the cathedral and baptistry (*upper left*) to the Mercato Vecchio (*lower right*). The Ghetto is immediately to the left of the Market Pavilion (*number 225*), with two gates, a piazza, a well, and one street.

2 The piazza of the former Ghetto in the late nineteenth century (before demolition).

3 The Mercato Vecchio (before demolition), looking towards the former Ghetto.

4 A Jewish pedlar with his distinctive red hat.

5 A Levantine Jew in Turkish dress.

6 Cosmo I dei Medici, father of Don Giovanni.

7 Don Giovanni dei Medici.

8 Grand Duchess Christine de Lorraine dei Medici.

9 Grand Duchess Maria Magdalena von Habsburg and Grand Duke Cosimo II
dei Medici, with their son Grand Duke Ferdinando II dei Medici.

10 A typical letter to Don Giovanni dei Medici, signed 'Benedetto Blanis heb[re]o' – Benedetto Blanis the Jew – with the name of God in Hebrew characters.

11 A letter from Salamone Blanis (Benedetto's brother) to Don Giovanni, with casual drawings by Don Giovanni or his secretary, including a bearded Jew.

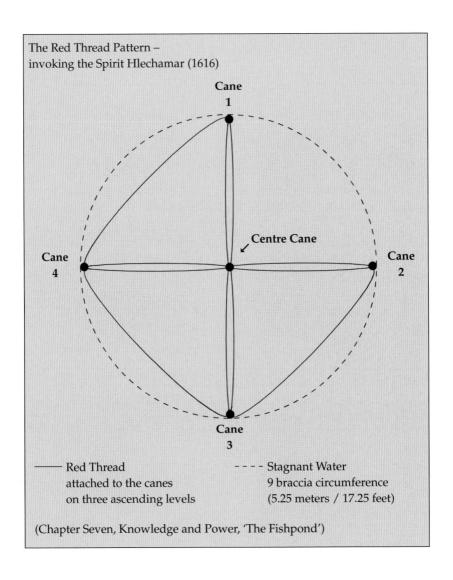

The Red Thread Pattern –
invoking the Spirit Hlechamar (1616)

Cane
1

Centre Cane

Cane
4

Cane
2

Cane
3

——— Red Thread
attached to the canes
on three ascending levels

- - - - Stagnant Water
9 braccia circumference
(5.25 meters / 17.25 feet)

(Chapter Seven, Knowledge and Power, 'The Fishpond')

12 To invoke the spirit Hlechamar, Benedetto Blanis created a network of red thread, attached to five canes, in a body of stagnant water (see in Chapter 7, 'Knowledge and Power,' the section: 'The Fishpond').

13 A Jewish Kabbalist with a *Tree of the Sephirot* (the ten emanations of God) from a sixteenth-century treatise.

14 Benedetto's last surviving message to Don Giovanni (measuring 2.85 by 3.55 inches), smuggled out of the Bargello prison, and enclosed in a letter from his brother Salamone Blanis (dated 26 September 1620).

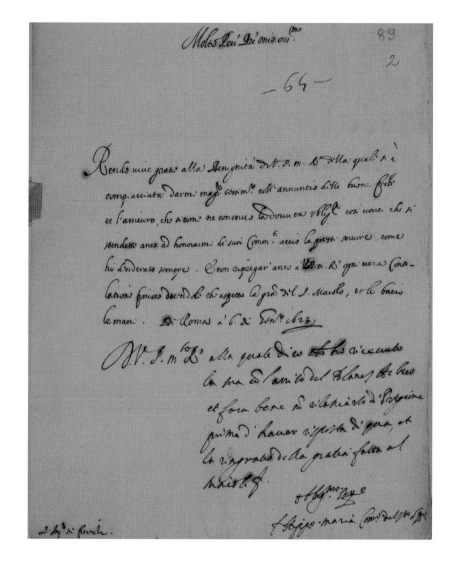

15 A holiday greeting from Filippo Maria Acquanegra (Commissioner of the Holy Office in Rome) to Cornelio Priatoni (Father Inquisitor in Florence): 'You would do well not to release the Jew Blanes from prison until you hear from us' (6 January 1623).

16 An old photograph of an isolation cell in the Bargello prison, where Benedetto Blanis spent several years.

for malfeasance which the Sernigi brought against Benedetto and Salamone Blanis. Then, they dismissed the suit for debt which the Blanis
brought against Maddalena Martelli Sernigi as guarantor for her son
Jacopo.[88]

As even-handed as this might seem, it was an unqualified victory
for the Christians, since all of the notes of credit authorized by Jacopo's
mother had been rendered null and void. If the Jews wished to start
from scratch with Sernigi's initial obligation, they were welcome to try.
But – as they finally learned – it was no longer the heyday of Benedetto
Blanis and Don Giovanni dei Medici.

Rich Jews

The Jewish second-hand dealer, the Jewish fence, the Jewish loan shark
– these were three of the faces of Ghetto business. Then there was the
most potent Jewish archetype of all, the super-rich international merchant. According to popular belief, these vastly wealthy cosmopolitan
Jews moved from country to country and place to place, their economic
power raising them above the vicissitudes of history and the prevailing misery of their people. Such individuals certainly existed but there
were not very many of them – not nearly as many as lived in the public
imagination.

The Blanis family and its peers were only moderately well-to-do by
prevailing Florentine standards.[89] Meanwhile, most of their Ghetto
neighbours were poor and some desperately poor. Jewish poverty,
however, had an illusory quality for both the Christian population and
the Tuscan government. No matter how poor Jews might seem, it was
generally assumed that they had access – somewhere, somehow – to
financial resources beyond the ken of simple non-Jews.

From time to time, the Jewish super-rich materialized in Florence
– passing through the Medici Court, without necessarily touching
ground in the local Ghetto. On 25 February 1608 the magistrates heard
a certain Diego Tessiera defend his interest in a 40,000 scudi deal involving Grand Duke Ferdinando I dei Medici. This was a fabulous sum
of money, equal to many millions of present-day dollars. Diego was
suing his former partners – four 'foreign Jews' identified as Davit Nunies, Isach Sus, Barugh Muslinest, and Barugh Piloso:

> Beginning last January, the said Tessiera negotiated a deal with these Jews
> on behalf of His Most Serene Highness [Ferdinando I] regarding various

merchandise totalling approximately 40,000 scudi. These Jews promised Tessiera a fee of 3% as stipulated in a written contract – but at the instigation of the said Davit Nunies, they managed to get their hands on this contract and tore it up. Although three of these Jews subsequently passed through Florence, they did not want to give Tessiera his fee, which amounted to some 1,000 scudi. Since these Jews are foreigners, Tessiera asked to have them imprisoned – particularly the aforementioned Nunies – so that they could not leave town without settling their debt to him.[90]

On 16 February 1608, a week before the magistrates issued their finding, Attorney General Paolo Vinta sent an advance warning to his brother, First Secretary Belisario Vinta – helping him manage an awkward situation: 'The court has acted on the Diego Tessiera deal and ruled against him. In regard to the various merchandise captured by His Serene Highness' galleon, there was no premium to be paid because that agreement never took effect.'[91]

This was state-sponsored fencing of the most exalted kind, recycling cargoes plundered on the high seas by the Knights of Saint Stephen (Tuscan pirates or Tuscan crusaders, depending on your point of view). There were deals within deals, involving the Christian della Fonte family among others – but the attorney general had no difficulty recognizing quintessentially Jewish business: 'Della Fonte acquired this merchandise in his own right, not acting on behalf of the Levantines. However, when you consider the risk of financial failure and when the range of prices is so unclear … it is certainly plausible that della Fonte intended to sell off this merchandise by way of the Levantines or somehow contract it out to them, since these are their sorts of things.'[92]

'I wanted to share our reasoning with you,' Paolo explained to his brother Belisario, 'so that you will be able to reply fully to Signor Diego, who seems a shrewd and sagacious man.'[93] Diego Tessiera – usually known as Diogo Teixeira Sampayo – was born in Portugal, and he made a brilliant career in commerce and at the Spanish Court (Portugal was then part of the Spanish Empire). Although not quite thirty in 1608, he was well placed to do a deal of this kind, especially since he was a secret or not-so-secret Jew. Davit Nunies, Isach Sus, Barugh Muslinest, and Barugh Piloso – his estranged associates – probably knew him by his Jewish name of Abram. Years later, in 1643, Teixeira was granted a patent of nobility by King Felipe IV. He then took his colossal wealth and reestablished himself in Hamburg – where he lived in princely style, openly practising his ancestral faith.[94]

When the grand duke wanted to do a 40,000 scudi deal, he went to four foreign Jews and a Portuguese crypto-Jew – not the designated *sensale* or broker in the Florentine Ghetto. The Blanis family and its neighbours were not operating on this level, and the prevailing attitude towards Jewish business was schizophrenic at best. Local Jews were habitually scorned as disreputable parasites, subverting the native economy with their second-handing and iron-scrapping, their *scrocchi, barocchi et usure*. Meanwhile, it was fervently hoped that other Jews would come in from outside and rescue local commerce with new skills, new capital, and – above all – access to new markets. Teixeira was only one of the international entrepreneurs, more or less Jewish, who appeared in the Tuscan capital in these years. There was also Maggino di Gabbriello,[95] David Alben Azzor,[96] and Isaac Lus[97] (presumably the 'Isach Sus' in the Teixeira case), plus many lesser figures.

The dream of a Jewish economic miracle was as old as the Medici State. For centuries the wool industry had been the chief source of Florentine wealth, but – by the time of Cosimo I – an alarming downturn occurred with no correction in sight.[98] The city counted on its emerging production of silk fabrics and accessories to fill the gap, but this was falling far short of the mark. Meanwhile, elsewhere in the Mediterranean, a critical mass of capital and commercial expertise had been turned loose with the expulsion of the Jews from Spain and Portugal in 1492 and 1497. Many went underground in their native lands, while others – including the Blanis family – made their way to Italy, northern Europe, and especially the Ottoman Empire.

Only eight years after becoming Duke of Florence, in 1537, the twenty-six-year-old Cosimo I was already looking to enlist such promising new business partners.[99] On 26 October 1545 his agent in Antwerp reported on opportunities among Portuguese 'New Christians' – many or most of whom were secret Jews:

One person … told me that if we made an effort in Portugal and spread the word there, we could attract many rich and substantial men – New Christians, that is to say – if they were given guarantees and shown that they could engage in commerce … He asked me how far Pisa was from Florence, since he had heard that Pisa was conveniently situated for Spain, Portugal, Naples, Rome, and other localities by sea and that it was a fine and abundant place to live … I also conferred with another man of substance who had recently returned from Portugal and is very well informed regarding things there … Attracting New Christians who have lots of money might really bear fruit, he said, as long as we could demonstrate that their persons and their property would be secure, that they would be treated well, and that their behaviour would not be scrutinized too closely.[100]

The Florentines knew that saving the textile industry was the key to saving their economy, and they eyed the vast, underexploited Turkish market. The Turks dominated an immense territory covering most of the southern and eastern Mediterranean, as well as the Balkans and the interior of Asia Minor. There was a major obstacle, however, to the expansion of Florentine trade. Throughout the sixteenth and seventeenth centuries, the Grand Duke of Tuscany was fighting a Holy War against the Sultan in Istanbul, along with various other Catholic rulers.

Since the Jews were neither Christian nor Muslim, they could rise above politics and sectarian strife to the commercial advantage of all. In 1551 Cosimo I appointed Servadio Greco, a Jew of Greek origin from Damascus, to coordinate Florentine commerce in the Turkish sphere.[101] After the death of Servadio in 1572, the position of *sensale* or broker was entrusted to Abram Baroch, whose family was well established in both Italy and Turkey.[102] Then in 1583 Abram Baroch was succeeded by Salvador Tesei,[103] whose descendants served the other Jews of Florence as *sensali* for the next forty years.

The ultimate goal of the Medici grand dukes was to create a permanent nucleus of Jewish exporters funnelling goods out of their country. To this end, Ferdinando I redrew the commercial map of Tuscany in 1591 – targeting Levantines and other Jews 'who might participate in business and commerce in our beloved City of Pisa and our port and depot of Livorno.'[104] Surpassing even the most 'enlightened' Italian rulers of his day, he encouraged would-be Jewish manufacturers (as well as merchants) with concessions, exclusive agreements, and start-up loans – further widening the gap between inland Florence and the entrepreneurial cities on the coast.[105]

Ferdinando's principal focus was on Pisa and Livorno, but he soon extended the privileges of these places to Levantines throughout his realm, especially those in his capital. This gave rise to an exempt class of foreign Jews who prayed in their own synagogue and answered directly to the grand duke, not to the Italian governors of the Ghetto. Disappointingly enough for government strategists, the Levantines in Florence tended to be only middling traders, not super-rich international merchants. Although families like the Isdraele, the Pernicca, the Lattoni, and the Tesei[106] were sending quantities of local textiles to northern Europe and the Ottoman Empire, their activity fell short of a commercial revolution.

The Florentine Silk Guild, meanwhile, was entering a phase of near panic – desperate to produce more fabric and dispatch it to foreign parts. On 13 August 1614 Cosimo II issued an edict revising the production standards for satin, 'so that these goods will satisfy those in the Levant and in other countries and kingdoms ... since they have not been enjoying the same success there as in the past.'[107] Then on 3 September 1621 the regents for the young Ferdinando II announced a 40,000 scudi line of credit, putting two hundred new silk looms into operation.[108] Finally, on 8 January 1622, the government published an exhaustive set of new guidelines for all categories of silk production 'in order to bring this craft back to its former stature ... and to please those in the Levant and in other countries and kingdoms who customarily request such things.'[109]

While the directors of the Silk Guild threw their weight behind this export drive, they also asserted their control of the domestic market – limiting Jewish non-exporters to second-hand goods in the narrowest sense of the term.[110] In the autumn of 1620 they launched a series of dramatic court cases, including one with thirteen defendants and another with twenty-seven – declaring open war on the laissez-faire habits of Ghetto commerce. They accused the Jews of fraudulent book-keeping and the sale of questionable goods. Most of all, they accused them of competing with Christians – targeting those 'who keep fixed shops in the Ghetto that stock only textiles, in the manner of the Big Silk Makers (*Setaioli Grossi*) in their shops.'[111]

Big Florentine Silk Makers had their share of problems, but local Jewish traders were thrown into full crisis. Then, in the autumn of 1621, the unthinkable happened. Guglielmo and Giuseppe Tesei – the designated brokers in the Ghetto – fled to Turkey by way of Venice[112] without paying the Christian producers who supplied them. In Florence, at least, the Jewish rescue fantasy was in ruins.[113] On 17 October the three governors of the Ghetto addressed the three consuls of the Silk Guild – making a strenuous effort to contain the damage:

> We realize that the absence of Guglielmo and Giuseppe Tesei has brought great displeasure to Their Most Serene Highnesses,[114] great damage to the creditors, and great harm to the Silk and Wool guilds. This situation afflicts us more than we can express and we want you to see that the actions

of our community match our sentiments ... According to our Jewish custom (*more hebreorum*), we now fear for the state of our souls and we also
wish for these guilds to recognize fully our good intentions.

Specifically, the governors of the Ghetto offered to send two representatives to Turkey, hoping to convince the Tesei to return to Florence
and settle their obligations. As envoys, they proposed Messer Davitte
Rimini and 'that excellent gentleman Doctor Moisé Blanis.'[115] Moisé
Blanis was Benedetto's distant cousin, chancellor of the Ghetto, and
father of the accused towel-stealer Giuseppe Blanis.

The Jews of Florence might have been eager to save their souls and
their commercial reputation – but by now, they were largely irrele-
vant to business that mattered. The real action had shifted to Pisa and
Livorno, depriving the Florentine community of much of its income as
well as its political cover. Throughout history, Jews have been tolerated
so long as they are useful. Unfortunately, Benedetto and his neighbours
were now feeding off the Florentine economy more than they were
feeding it – with their buttons, their masquerade costumes, and their
barely disguised usury.

chapter seven

Knowledge and Power

Books

By the summer of 1616 Don Giovanni dei Medici had been in Venice for a year, and he did not plan to return to Florence any time soon. He was therefore looking to rent his palace in Via del Parione, and he found a suitable tenant in Monsignor Pietro Valier, the new papal nuncio (ambassador) in the Tuscan capital. Benedetto Blanis had the tedious job of shifting Don Giovanni's library to a less accessible part of the building – to free up space for the renter while removing unsuitable items from the sight of a high Church official. In mid-July Benedetto offered his patron a running update:

> I won't move the books until I receive your instructions but will leave them in those same two rooms. Meanwhile, I will dust them and put them into some kind of order. Since I don't understand the current alphabetical system, and this has been applied only to some of the books in any case, I will continue to organize them by subject matter, making a descriptive label for each book, as was done at [your villa at] Montughi. I should also tell you that I happened to come across a volume of works elsewhere by Paracelsus including his most curious writings, that is to say, books IX, X, and XI discussing his Occult Philosophy. Since I know that Your Most Illustrious Excellency has the other works of Paracelsus with you, I thought that I should relay this information ... I could tell from the title that we were dealing with a curious work, and I know how jealous Your Excellency is when it comes to things of this kind. Indeed, you are quite right to be jealous since they are sometimes not to be had at any price.[1]

Benedetto failed to mention that he was writing his letter while holed up in Don Giovanni's own palace – along with other Jewish fugitives from the law during a sensational gambling scandal.[2] Meanwhile, he was taking advantage of this opportunity to study the premises at close hand, since he needed to choose between two relatively out-of-the-way spaces for the library: a small room behind the *fonderia* (foundry, distillery, and alchemical laboratory) and an upstairs writing room towards the Arno River.[3] Benedetto eventually settled on the second option, and he completed the laborious move three months later:

> I am sending Your Most Illustrious Excellency the list of your books, which took me a long time to compile, and even now, there is not the order and method that I should have liked. Since we had to move the library, we are making do with the available accommodation, and since there was no wish to build new bookshelves, I appropriated some old shelving that I found around the house. For now, I am leaving many of the titles half in Latin and half in the vulgar tongue [Italian] ... In any case, your books are in very good shape and you can immediately find the one you want. There is a small table in the middle of the room and the books are all around it, so the urge to study comes even to those who never had it before.[4]

Don Giovanni had thousands of books, and he kept them in at least four different places: at his palace in Via del Parione in Florence, at his Villa at Montughi north of the city, at his palace in Venice, and at his Villa at Palvello near Padua. Presumably he also took some of his favourites with him when he was in the field on military operations. Since he was constantly on the move, his librarian had to make sure that he had whatever reading and reference material he wanted wherever he might be. Benedetto therefore faced a constant succession of practical tasks: identifying titles and authors, searching the stacks in the palace library, tracking down items in other collections or on the market, and packing and shipping the latest consignments to Venice or elsewhere. 'Since there was no appropriate box for holding the books,' he wrote during Don Giovanni's first winter away from Florence, 'I had one made, and then I had it wrapped in waxed cloth and heavy canvas so that it won't be damaged by rain. Then I turned it over to [your servant Lorenzo] Ferroni, so that he can take care of transport and customs.'[5]

Books of every description passed through Benedetto's hands on their way to Don Giovanni. In his letters, he refers to a two-volume Greek-Latin dictionary,[6] Hippocrates' classic medical text the *Opus*

Novum,[7] a French grammar,[8] and the collected works of Rabelais.[9] Most of all, he discusses 'curious' and 'forbidden' writings, particularly arcana on the Inquisition's *Index of Prohibited Authors and Books* (*Index auctorum et librorum prohibitorum*) including Theophrastus Paracelsus' *Occult Philosophy*,[10] Ramón Llull's *Secrets of the Philosopher's Stone*,[11] and Heinrich Cornelius Agrippa's *Occult Philosophy*.[12] There were also various items of Jewish Kabbalah.

By prevailing scholarly standards, Benedetto's qualifications for the job of palace librarian were fragmentary, not to say eccentric. He had good Hebrew, functional Latin, possibly some Arabic but no Greek. His culture, in fact, was far more Jewish than classical or philological, as he commented to Don Giovanni in the autumn of 1616: 'I now have to draft the list of your books and would already have done so if our Feast of Huts (*Sukkot*) had not intervened this week. I still have to show someone four or five items in Greek since these didn't have dedications in Latin from which I could deduce the names of the authors, as I had done in many other cases.'[13]

What Benedetto Blanis could offer Don Giovanni dei Medici was absolute loyalty, a shared enthusiasm for arcane studies, and an aura of privileged access to the world of Jewish mysticism. Loyalty probably figured at the top of the list, since Don Giovanni was running a calculated risk in sharing the contents of his library with another person. Benedetto therefore promised total discretion when it came to making new labels for the books: 'I have been using a friend of mine, and I had him work in my home rather than going to your library. I dictated what he needed to inscribe, using a copy [of the book list] that I did not let out of my own hands.'[14]

Books were knowledge and knowledge was power. In Don Giovanni's libraries, there were books for reading and books for studying but also books for conjuring – for unmasking the secrets of nature, for telling the future, and even controlling it.[15] In the spring of 1616 Benedetto Blanis responded joyfully to the predicted birth of a male child to Don Giovanni dei Medici and his mistress Livia Vernazza:

My Most Illustrious and Excellent Lord and Most Honoured Patron, it is impossible to imagine the boundless satisfaction that I felt when I learned of your extraordinary result with that book, first and foremost because it proved so advantageous to the health of your lady and then to the well-being of the entire world. In my opinion, we can hope for the greatest man the world has ever seen, since the issue from such a unique couple can only be powerful and marvellous, that is to say, he who Isaiah called 'powerful and marvellous,' along with other titles, *'Parvulus enim natus est nobis et factus est principatus super humerum eius et vocabitur nomen eius Admirabilis Consiliarius, Deus Fortis, Pater future secoli Princeps Pacis* (For a child is born to us, and a son is given to us, and the government is upon his shoulder: and his name shall be called, Wonderful, Counsellor, God the Mighty, the Father of the world to come, the Prince of Peace).' This, I hope, will be the fruit of such a tree, and I doubt that there was a tree of such perfection even in the earthly paradise. May the Lord grant you the tree of life alongside this tree of knowledge, giving you health and long – rather, eternal – life by way of your progeny.[16]

Benedetto cites Isaiah in Latin,[17] expropriating a Messianic passage traditionally used to prefigure the birth of Christ. Then, for good measure, he adds the Tree of Life and the Tree of Knowledge from the Garden of Eden, compounding an arcane reference to eternal wisdom and eternal being. For six intense years Benedetto Blanis and Don Giovanni dei Medici shared this peculiar language – mystical and oracular, ingeniously erudite, but not quite Christian and not quite Jewish.

Tree of Kabbalah

The plan was for Benedetto Blanis to join Don Giovanni dei Medici in Venice as soon as possible so that they could resume their investigation of the occult. His patron, however, now had other more pressing priorities as supreme commander of the Venetian army. Again and again, their reunion was delayed, and seven months later Benedetto was still biding his time:

Your Excellency gives me good reason to hope that I will once again enjoy your noble and divine presence in the divinity of those studies, particularly since I am expecting that Tree from that Jew in Lippiano. The Tree comes by way of an uncle of mine who is a doctor,[18] so it will be easy to have it drawn and copied, if Your Excellency wishes. He and I have asked to borrow it for two weeks or a month.[19]

Benedetto soon repeated his enticement:

I am delighted to have so important a Tree of Kabbalah here in Florence, brought from Lippiano at my request. I am having it copied on vellum with great diligence, so it will not be inferior to the original in any way but even better. I hope that this Tree will please Your Most Illustrious Excellency and that we will be able to enjoy it together – but if not, I will see that it is finished as quickly as possible, and I will then send it to you.[20]

By way of his family network, Benedetto's connections extended to Lippiano – a tiny town on the border between Tuscany and Umbria in the independent Marchesate of Monte Santa Maria.[21] In the mid-sixteenth century, in the wake of wholesale Jewish emigration from Tuscany and the State of the Church, new communities formed in this and other minuscule border states, including Pitigliano (between Tuscany and Latium) and Massa Carrara (between Tuscany and the Republic of Genoa). In such frontier settlements, Jews tended to make their own rules, offering refuge to co-religionists who got into trouble elsewhere.

The Kabbalistic literature is full of charts and diagrams of many kinds[22] but in this case, Benedetto was proposing a *Tree of the Sefirot* – setting out the relationship between the ten emanations of God. Such *Trees* were the essential maps of the spiritual realm, revealing the path to the most exalted levels of Kabbalah. As artefacts, however, they were far from rare, even if he was offering an exceptionally handsome collector's piece.

By the time of Benedetto Blanis and Don Giovanni dei Medici,[23] the traditions of Jewish mysticism had been evolving for nearly two thousand years and had taken many forms, generally subsumed under the name of 'Kabbalah' or 'Received Knowledge.' This was a seemingly limitless field of inquiry, as broad and varied as human experience itself. Among its Jewish adepts, there was a fundamental but often unclear distinction between 'Speculative Kabbalah' and 'Practical Kabbalah.' While Speculative Kabbalah sought a mystical union with God, Practical Kabbalah sought to manipulate the natural order to achieve concrete results. In real terms, Practical Kabbalah could span all of the gradations from white to black magic. A telling example from the dark side was Secretary Camillo Guidi's fascination with 'bringing death to an enemy' by way of 'a certain psalm and lighting certain small candles.'[24]

In Kabbalah, God is the *Ein-sof*, the 'boundless' or 'unquantifiable one,' immutably perfect in its own being. Having no tangible qualities, God cannot be perceived by the human intelligence. Having no active characteristics, like thought, desire, intention, or will, God cannot be understood as a creative force. People, however, need to explain the perceptible world of created things that somehow partake of God's being. They need to reconcile this transcendent deity with the God of the Old Testament who made the universe and intervened directly in human affairs.

Over the centuries the Kabbalists defined an intermediate level of being between the infinite and the finite, between the unknowable and the knowable. This was the realm of the *Sefirot*, the emanations of God, which were eventually fixed as ten in number. 'The *Sefirot* emanate from the *Ein-Sof* in succession, as if one candle were lit from another without the emanator being diminished in any way.'[25] 'They are compared to a candle flickering in the midst of ten mirrors set one within the other, each a different colour. The light is reflected differently in each, although it is the same light.'[26]

These Sefirot were the key to advanced spiritual exploration. They also played a crucial role in the numerological, astrological, and alchemical practices that used Kabbalah as their point of reference. In Italy at the time of Benedetto Blanis, an exciting new current was that of Lurianic Kabbalah.[27] Isaac of Luria (1533–1572) settled in the town of Safed in Palestine in the mid-sixteenth century, along with other Jewish refugees from Spain and Portugal, including Moses Cordovero (1522–1570) and Hayim Vital (1543–1620). Traumatized by their collective experience of the expulsion and its aftermath, the sages of Safed sought to impose order on a disordered world through a complex system of hermetic practices that extended to amulets, incantations, and intricate permutations of names and numbers. Lurianic Kabbalah had much to offer votaries of the occult, particularly when divorced from its broader philosophical and spiritual context.

Meanwhile, there was also the growing authority of Christian Kabbalah. In the thirteenth century, the Catholic scholar and mystic Ramón Llull (1235–1315) recognized Jewish Kabbalah as a divine science with an essential role in forming the Christian consciousness. With Pico della Mirandola (1463–1494) in the fifteenth century, Kabbalah entered the mainstream of Christian speculation, giving rise to a new tradition that paralleled the Jewish one and found its most exalted expression in Florence in the neo-platonic circle of Lorenzo dei Medici (1449–1492).[28] In the course of the sixteenth century Christian Kabbalah came to focus more and more exclusively on practical applications, and by the time of Benedetto Blanis, Kabbalah had become synonymous with numerology and witchcraft in the minds of most Christians and even some Jews. The canonical text was Cornelius Agrippa von Nettesheim's *De*

Occulta Philosophia (1531), which offered an authoritative compendium of all the arcane sciences of the day.[29]

In his home in the Florentine Ghetto, Benedetto Blanis enlisted members of his own family and even Christians to copy esoteric works for Don Giovanni dei Medici.[30] In addition to the 'Tree of Kabbalah from Lippiano,' Benedetto replicated 'a small book in Hebrew in rabbinical script titled *Book of Ramón Llull Regarding the Secrets of the Philosopher's Stone.*'[31] 'I will have my brother Salamone do the writing,' he assured Don Giovanni, 'since I don't trust anyone else.'[32] Meanwhile, he had 'a priest who is a friend and confidant of mine' copy an intriguing text in Latin.[33] This was *The Fourth Part of Cornelius,*[34] a notorious sorcerer's manual that expanded on Cornelius Agrippa von Nettesheim's three-part *De Occulta Philosophia.*

A popular archetype of the time was the Jewish adept who inducted Christians into the cosmic mysteries – or more modestly, supplied them with amulets, curses, prophecies, and philters.[35] Don Giovanni was a passionate devotee of the occult, and Benedetto was quick to make the most of any opportunity that came his way. But how much magic did he actually know – white or black, speculative or practical, Jewish or otherwise?

If Benedetto Blanis was an accomplished master of some branch of the arcane, it does not emerge from his letters to Don Giovanni. Nor does he reveal more than a basic grounding in the principles of Kabbalah, such as any Jew might have absorbed along with a traditional rabbinical education. If he produced major – or even minor – books and writings, they do not survive. And if he influenced his learned contemporaries – Jewish or Christian – they did not cite him in their publications and scholarly correspondence.

'I frequented the home of His Most Excellent Lordship Don Giovanni,' Benedetto Blanis observed, 'eventually in order to read the Hebrew language to His Excellency.'[36] Benedetto, in fact, made his entry through the back door – as a Jewish tradesman offering the usual goods and services. He began by buying and selling clothing and textiles, then he expanded his range to include the Hebrew language and more. With time, he emerged as an adjunct member of Don Giovanni's household, available for freelance assignments of every kind.[37]

Jews were innately predisposed to supernatural practices – or so it was believed by Florentine courtiers, Church authorities, superstitious peasants, and many Jews themselves. As an aspiring scholar and an aspiring practitioner of the arcane, Benedetto Blanis was trading on the dangerous glamour of this forbidden other. When it got down to it, however, most of what passed through his hands – Ramón Llull, Cornelius Agrippa et al. – was only Jewish at many removes.

Medicean Planets

On the evening of 15 December 1618 Benedetto paid a hurried visit to Don Giovanni's palace in Florence: 'While I was writing, I received a letter from Your Most Illustrious Excellency. Although it was two hours after nightfall [around 7 p.m.], I immediately went to Parione where I found the astrological birth chart (*natività*) that Your Excellency requested along with the accompanying letter from Father Don Orazio. As you ordered, I immediately gave this to [your major-domo] Signor Cosimo Baroncelli so that he could send it with the latest dispatch that very evening. I read him the relevant portion of your letter, so that he would know to pack it well and make sure that it does not get wet.'[38]

Father Don Orazio was the eminent churchman Orazio Morandi (c.1575–1630). In 1590, after completing his university studies in Rome, Morandi entered the mother house of the Vallombrosan order at Vallombrosa, twenty-two miles southeast of Florence – a small but prestigious branch of the Benedictines founded by Saint Giovanni Gualberto in the eleventh century. When Morandi eventually assumed leadership as father general in 1617, he was responsible for approximately 250 Vallombrosan brothers in nineteen monasteries, largely concentrated in Tuscany and firmly under the control of the Medici family.[39]

Although the Abbey of Vallombrosa was and is famed for its sylvan tranquility, Morandi had from the beginning set his sights on an important career in the wider world. Since Medici patronage was the key to success, he spent much of his time at the Abbey of Ripoli on the outskirts of Florence, barely an hour's ride from the Pitti Palace. Above all, he sought to make a name for himself as a scholar and a man of culture, developing a formidable reputation in the areas of astrology and alchemy. Inevitably, he attracted the attention of Don Giovanni and his nephew Don Antonio, the two members of the Medici family who were most passionately devoted to arcane studies.

By the autumn of 1618 Father Orazio and Don Giovanni were already hard at work on the *natività* that Benedetto forwarded to Venice a few months later. Their initial task was to cast a horoscope, fixing the location of the sun, moon, and planets at the time of the subject's birth in relation to the stars associated with the signs of the zodiac. This could then serve as the basis for a full projection of the course of the subject's life, expressed in an analytical study (*discorso*). By 8 September 1618 Orazio Morandi had already prepared a preliminary version of the horoscope:

> For now, I am sending Your Excellency the birth chart that you were pleased to order from me, incorporating your own readings. It corresponds precisely to the complexion, temperament, nature, and emotions of the subject, as well as the circumstances of the birth. When I have some free time, I will say a bit more, and the subject of this birth chart has already asked me for my opinion. However, it is not suitable for me to say what I think, particularly in regard to matters of health. I will tell Your Excellency frankly that the conjunctions are very bad, with all of the signifiers badly placed ... In my opinion, we need greatly fear for the life of the subject in the thirty-fifth year, unless there are strong beneficent influences. In fact, this outcome is not difficult to predict since the subject's body is so weak that any unfortunate conjunction or passage could cause great harm during the fourth decade ... Meanwhile, I am eagerly awaiting ... some copies of those sheets of alchemy and Kabbalah that Your Excellency is having printed.[40]

The subject of this horoscope was Grand Duke Cosimo II (1590–1621). Although it was obvious to everyone that the ailing prince was not long for this world, Morandi was loath to inform a ruling head of state of his imminent demise, no matter how compelling the medical and astral evidence. As it happened, Morandi erred on the side of optimism since Cosimo II died at the age of thirty, not thirty-five, on 28 February 1621.

Orazio Morandi was only one of many who cast Cosimo II dei Medici's horoscope in those years. Celestial optimism was the theme for most astrologers, particularly those who got in early with hopes of a career at court. Cosimo became Grand Duke in 1609, at the age of nineteen. Then the very next year, Galileo Galilei (1564–1642) published the *Sidereus Nuncius* (*Starry Messenger*), announcing his sensational discovery of four previously unknown moons of Jupiter. Not only did Galileo obligingly name these the *Medicean Planets*, he used them as cosmographic evidence to enhance the young grand duke's prospects for a long and happy reign:

> It was Jupiter, I say, who at Your Highness's birth, having already passed through the murky vapours of the horizon, and occupying the mid-heav-

en and illuminating the eastern angle from his royal house, looked down upon Your most fortunate birth from that sublime throne and poured out all his splendour and grandeur into the most pure air ... Therefore, Most Merciful Prince, acknowledge this particular glory reserved for you by the stars and enjoy for a very long time these divine blessings carried down to You – not so much from the stars as the Maker and Ruler of the Stars, God.[41]

Galileo tactfully Christianized his starry message since the Church's attitude to astrology was ambivalent at best. In any case, his prognostication was gratefully received, and Cosimo II promptly recalled him from the University of Padua to the University of Pisa and named him First Mathematician and Philosopher to the Grand Duke. Galileo Galilei's emergence as an astronomical or astrological celebrity (at that time, there was no clear distinction between the two studies) was received with intense hostility by other practitioners in Florence, most notably Raffael Gualterotti.

Gualterotti (1543–1638) flourished at the Medici Court for nearly a century, through the reigns of five successive Grand Dukes.[42] Prodigiously talented as well as long-lived, he was an artist,[43] poet, and astrologer but above all, an entrepreneur and a Medici publicist. In 1579, at the time of the wedding of Francesco I and Bianca Cappello, Gualterotti pioneered a lucrative new literary genre, the festival book, issuing a lavishly illustrated volume less than a month after the event.[44] He wrote an eyewitness account of the ceremonies, composed celebratory verse, and prepared sixteen drawings to be rendered in etching – an innovative medium, far quicker than engraving or woodcut.[45] Gualterotti went on to produce similar works for Christine de Lorraine and Ferdinando I in 1589 and for Maria Magdalena von Habsburg and Cosimo II in 1608[46] – enjoying a virtual monopoly on the coverage of three successive granducal weddings.

In 1605 Raffael Gualterotti published two books, consolidating his reputation as the pre-eminent astrologer at the Florentine Court: *Concerning the Appearance of the New Star and the Three Eclipses of the Sun and the Moon that Occurred in 1605*,[47] and *Concerning the Play of Animal Spirits, with Reference to the Eclipse of 1605*.[48] He cited an impressive range of ancient and modern authorities in these works, documenting the influence of the heavens on human affairs. More immediately, he described the latest cosmic phenomena with subtle precision and lyrical power, offering some of the most evocative nature writing in the Italian language at that time.[49]

Galileo was able to discover the Medicean Planets thanks to his construction of a state-of-the-art telescope, incorporating the recent advances of the Neapolitan Giovanbattista della Porta and the Netherlander Hans Lipperhey. Gualterotti, meanwhile, knew exactly where credit was due – to himself first and foremost. On 24 April 1610 he fired off a letter to Galileo in Padua:

> I heard that Your Lordship saw the telescope (*cannochiale*) of that Milanese [sic], Messer Giovanbattista and accorded it some praise. However, I made such an instrument myself twelve years ago ... Then I heard a rumour that some Fleming took my lenses and my tubes and reassembled them and rethought their use and saw many things in heaven and on earth much better than with Messer Giovanbattista's device ... In any case, I am not saying all this to detract from Your Lordship's glory. However, Your Lordship owes me the praise that you saw fit to give that Belgian instead of someone from your own country.[50]

Gualterotti had already addressed this issue with Grand Duke Cosimo II a few weeks earlier, offering grudging admiration for Galileo's recent achievement and promising a heroic poem on the inspiring new theme of the Medicean Planets: 'I ask Your Highness to give me a larger subsidy than you do now, if you want me to live and continue with my work. I also beg Your Highness to leave the place where you are now [Pisa] as soon as possible because the atmosphere there is no longer good for you, and I see a certain level of danger when May comes.'[51]

'Here in Florence an enormous and terrifying comet was sighted an hour before daybreak,' Don Giovanni's major-domo Cosimo Baroncelli reported on 1 December 1618. 'Signor Raffael Gualterotti said that it was the biggest he had ever seen and that it foretells the overthrow of nations and grave illnesses. It was monstrous in appearance, with a tail like a great dishevelled bunch of linen fibres.'[52]

This was the last and most dramatic of three comets that appeared during the autumn of 1618 – seizing the attention of stargazers across Italy, including the Jesuits in Rome and Galileo Galilei at the University of Pisa.[53] In Venice, Don Giovanni was intrigued as well, as he informed Baroncelli on 8 December: 'Here too we could see that extraordinarily tailed comet, and there can be no doubt that it represents deaths and the shifting of nations. So, we need look at the constellation to which it belongs, its sphere of power, and the country it controls. Rather than getting up early to see the comet cross the horizon, I had it observed for me, and now I will do the calculations, give them some thought, and then write something. There is a significance here that I want to share with you, and I may not be Signor Gualterotti but I too have some talent in these matters.'[54]

At the Medici Court, such prognostications of illness and political upheaval could have only one meaning. Three days later, on 11 December 1618, Don Giovanni ordered the immediate dispatch of the dire horoscope that Father Morandi had recently cast for Grand Duke Cosimo II.[55] Benedetto forwarded this to Venice on 15 December, the moment his patron's request arrived.[56]

Knowledge was power, particularly in the political sphere, and astrology was prized as an essential means for taking control of world events. As Cosimo II drifted from one seemingly terminal illness to the next, the Medici Court lived on signs and portents, mostly supplied by the astrologers of the moment. Although Benedetto Blanis was himself no astrologer, he had an ambitious protégé Ferdinando Magnani – an aspiring priest, mathematician, and philologist sent by Don Giovanni to learn Hebrew. In January of 1619 Magnani made his move, offering Grand Duke Cosimo II yet another 'astrological discourse regarding His Highness' birth.'[57]

Silver, Gold, and Grappa

On 9 April 1616 Benedetto Blanis sent Don Giovanni dei Medici a sample of a metallic substance freshly compounded in the Florentine Ghetto. 'This consists of one third silver or perhaps even less, and it only costs three *giuli* an ounce, including materials and making the alloy. If it seems worthwhile, you can have some whenever you want. They say that it stands up to every test including that of the crucible.'[58] In the months that followed, Benedetto and his partners worked to improve the mixture. Although their product looked like silver and assayed as silver, Benedetto stopped short of claiming that they were actually making silver through secret alchemical processes. 'An even better alloy might yet emerge.' Benedetto explained. 'My idea is to use this material at home in order to make a good show while spending little, and Your Excellency will perhaps agree that it has some utility for prestige and display.'[59]

In Florence Benedetto Blanis was only proposing flashy ersatz silverware. In Venice, meanwhile, his old acquaintance Leone da Modena was considerably more daring in his claims. At that very time, the rabbi was recording his success in transforming nine ounces of lead and one ounce of silver into ten ounces of pure silver: 'Twice I myself have seen this happen, and I myself and no other sold the silver after having assayed it in the crucible.'[60] In the spring of 1615 Leone da Modena and his son Mordechai set up a laboratory in the Venetian Ghetto and began their experiments, using methods learned from a Catholic priest.[61] Notwithstanding Modena's reference to lead, the most frequent alchemical simulation of silver was copper arsenide – copper treated with arsenic to give it a white colour.[62] Word must have travelled quickly to the Florentine Ghetto, although Mordechai da Modena was already dying from arsenic poisoning.[63] Benedetto and his friends presumably imitated their product, then sought to re-export it to Venice – to Don Giovanni dei Medici.[64]

When it came to the fabrication of precious metals, Don Giovanni and his friends were busy as well. On 31 October 1615 Father Orazio Morandi wrote Don Giovanni from Rome, thanking him for a prized alchemical formula: 'I will thus be able to admire the great wisdom that allows you to add lustre to lead and make it look like gold.'[65] Apart from the obvious cash incentive for turning base metals into precious ones, there was also a crucial spiritual dimension, as the German alchemist Theophrastus Paracelsus had explained a century earlier: 'Alchemy is nothing else but the set purpose, intention, and subtle endeavour to transmute the various kinds of metals from one to another. With his own mental grasp, each person can thus select for himself a better way and art and thereby find truth.'[66]

Alchemy, at its most exalted, was a means of finding truth – a path to spiritual enlightenment and a transformational experience for the alchemist as much as the substances he transmuted. Like Kabbalah and astrology, however, alchemy was also rife with temptation and danger. In another letter of thanks to Don Giovanni dei Medici, Father Orazio Morandi revelled in the essential union of alchemy and power, using a Faustian language far removed from orthodox Christian pieties:

> The method and procedure of that operation is the most precious gift that ever a great prince could bestow, and with your immense liberality, you have exceeded Alexander the Great who merely gave away cities. Your Excellency, however, has given me the entire world, which will be mine if I succeed in carrying out this process. In regard to eventual difficulties, I seem to remember that Your Excellency told me in person that copper is the chief ingredient, and it has to be treated with iron. The mercury has to

be treated with antimony. Then the catalyst is *cemento regale*, that is to say, gold passed through antimony.[67]

Gold was the usual catalyst in operations seeking to make gold, so much of this precious material was inevitably wasted in the course of trial and error. In his absence, Don Giovanni had entrusted his Florentine *fonderia* (laboratory) to his young nephew Cardinal Carlo dei Medici, so he was understandably worried about the depletion of laboratory equipment and supplies. Don Giovanni's major-domo Cosimo Baroncelli reassured him on 13 June 1620:

> I told [the caretaker] what you ordered regarding the maintenance and conservation of everything in your *fonderia* ... Your Excellency should not worry, he said, because he will make sure that things remain as you left them, including the storage containers that were made for you and the instruments for working and carrying out operations. I know that some of the Cardinal's most devoted servants have already warned him about consuming gold in hope of finding it again. I really don't think that the Cardinal has embarked on activities of this kind although some of his favourites seem to have their heads amidst the *soffioni* (fire bellows or blow pipes). So, I suspect that they got him to spend a few scudi on this sort of experiment.[68]

'Il capo ne' soffioni (their heads amidst the fire bellows or blow pipes)' is an apt and amusing turn of phrase. 'Soffiare (to blow or pump air)' was a favourite slang expression for alchemical activity, most of which required the focused application of intense heat. As Paracelsus stated, 'Destruction perfects that which is good; for the good cannot appear on account of that which conceals it ... By the element of fire all that is imperfect is destroyed and taken away.'[69] Sometimes, it would seem, there was purifying fire but sometimes merely the blowing of air. Although alchemy was a personal passion for Don Giovanni dei Medici, it was also an aristocratic diversion about which he and his fellow adepts could freely joke.

On 7 March 1620 Cosimo Baroncelli ran a high-level errand at the Florentine Court. Don Giovanni wanted to negotiate a deal involving the Holy Roman Emperor Ferdinand II, beginning with his sister Maria Magdalena von Habsburg, Grand Duchess of Tuscany. Baroncelli wrote a lengthy report on their meeting, but frustratingly enough, he treated most of the specifics as given since they had come from Don Giovanni in the first place:

> I took the opportunity to read Her Highness the letter which Your Excellency wrote me so that she would be more fully informed … She received much of this with great merriment, and she told me several times, 'If anyone other than Don Giovanni had written a letter of this kind, I wouldn't have believed it. However, I must accept that the proposal is as he describes since Don Giovanni is so devoted to this family'… Then Her Highness asked me if I thought the proposal was related to alchemy, and I replied that I was sure it was not since Your Excellency does not use such arts to make gold but only to obtain health-giving remedies. In the course of this discussion, I saw that Her Highness wanted to strike at those who made or thought they could make gold.[70]

In fact, most of the recent products of Don Giovanni's *fonderia* were extracts and distillates of various sorts, prepared from herbs, flowers, fruits, and resins. He and his contemporaries, it would seem, recognized two distinct levels of practical alchemy. There was alchemical sorcery, from which Don Giovanni sometimes needed to distance himself, exemplified by the transmutation of base metals into gold. Then there was the permitted realm of what we would now call applied science or technology. Don Giovanni probably hoped to pitch some new scheme of industrial production to Emperor Ferdinand II, and in that case, the German connection would have been fundamental. Most of Europe's pioneering alchemists/chemists came from Germany, which was also the cradle of advanced metallurgy.

At least one historic technical advance, directly related to alchemy, was brought to Tuscany by German Jews. This was in the area of distillation. On 30 August 1619 Isach Calò, a long-time resident of the Florentine Ghetto, filed a petition along with two newcomers, Jacob and Mattia Donati: 'These Donati are of German nationality but they have been staying in Modena where they carried out the trade of making brandy from grape-pressings (*acqua vite tratta dalle vinaccie*), and they now wish to introduce this here.' Their product was in fact *grappa*, a clear and usually colourless distillate from the residue of wine-making, now popularly considered the most indigenous of Tuscan spirits. Calò and the Donati made two specific requests. Since they were introducing a new product, they asked for a proprietary monopoly. (This was granted for ten years.) Also, they needed special permission to remain outside the Florentine Ghetto for extended periods, so they could travel to Pisa, Prato, Pistoia, and elsewhere, in order to buy and process grape pressings. (This was also granted.)[71] The principal challenge was that they needed to begin production promptly since the grape harvest was close at hand. By 24 January 1620 they were able to register a notarized affidavit in Prato: 'We the undersigned swear that the Jews Isach son of Daniel Calò and Jacob son of Donato Donati have here in this locality at the Dolce Hospital constructed two furnaces with eight large copper boilers. For three months now, they have distilled and continue to distill grape pressings to make *acqua vite*.'[72]

The Fish Pond

On 6 February 1616 Benedetto Blanis wrote Don Giovanni dei Medici in Venice, sharing his latest adventures in the occult. In addition to the usual blend of astrology, alchemy, and Kabbalah, he could now add the fresh leaven of Arab demonology, thanks to one of his newer neighbours in the Florentine Ghetto. This was a Jew of Moroccan origin named Samuele Caggesi (alternately Chagez, Hagges, Hagis, Agies, and even Aes), usually referred to as 'Doctor Samuel from Fez':

> That friend could not delay any longer unless he had another outbreak of gout since he has not been out of bed these last ten days. Meanwhile, the phase of the waxing moon was coming to an end, so he ordered me to carry out the first stage of the operation, which I will now describe...[73]

Doctor Samuel was apparently a strategic hypochondriac, more than willing to leave the work and responsibility to Benedetto Blanis. Since Benedetto gave his patron none of the back story, they must have formulated their plans before Don Giovanni's departure from Florence, eight months earlier:[74]

> With my help, he had already selected a place with an accumulation of stagnant water and the other essential characteristics. There couldn't be running water or springs. There had to be trees in front of it. The body of water had to be at least one braccio [23 inches] deep and at least 1 1/3 braccia [30.6 inches] wide on each side. When he found the place he wanted, he praised it greatly and said that it could not be more suitable since it was 9 braccia [17.25 feet] around and more than 1 1/2 braccia [34.5 inches] deep.

And the bottom was just as he wished, with mud and earth, not slabs of stone or bricks.

Since his infirmity prevented him from going to that place in order to carry out the operation, he told me on Tuesday [2 February] that I should do so. He instructed me to mark the perimeter of that pit of water a half braccio [11.5 inches] beyond its outer margin. I did this by thrusting five canes into the ground, that is to say, four canes on the outside spaced at equal distances and one cane in the middle. The canes had to be long enough to include five nodes, with one node under ground and four above.

For each cane, I did a suffumigation by burning seven grains of coriander, putting the fire in the hole where the cane was to be thrust, and then doing a suffumigation of the cane above. Although our friend should now go and do the rest, he shows no sign of getting out of bed but has promised to give me further instructions tomorrow or the day after, so that I can continue on my own. In that case, I will be even more gratified by the succcess of this fish pond, if things work out as they should. That is to say, if there is the apparition of the fish and we can interrogate it and it responds.[75]

Suffumigation – the burning of aromatic substances like spices or incense – is a common feature of many religious and magical rites, serving to link the corporeal and the ethereal realms. With his references to fish and fish ponds, Benedetto was being very coy since their ultimate plan was to summon a familiar spirit who could answer questions from the world beyond. The chief Old Testament precedent was King Saul's visit to the Witch of Endor, who baulked at calling up the ghost of the Prophet Samuel – since Saul had personally expelled all magicians and soothsayers under a sentence of death.[76] The Book of Exodus was uncompromising in this regard: 'Wizards thou shalt not suffer to live.'[77]

In the present case, the fish pond was doing double duty for both a greater and a lesser rite of invocation:

Our friend [Doctor Samuel] attaches little importance to this current effort and is only doing it to demonstrate his abilities, since the big operation is much greater and requires ninety days, beginning on 7 February. It is true, however, that he has lost these last ten days and has now enlisted the greatest king who is currently in the ascendant and has great authority. If the small operation succeeds we can then be optimistic regarding the big one and Your Most Illustrious Excellency will be kept informed of everything that happens.[78]

Nervous optimism was the prevailing tone of Benedetto's letters, at least at this stage. He had something fresh and intriguing to offer his patron, but magic was a business where some ventures paid off while many did not. Benedetto wrote Don Giovanni again the very next day, striking a balance between superstitious credulity and cynical detachment – ready to jump in any direction, depending on the outcome of the initial operation:

> We are almost ready to experience a demonstration of what that Doctor Samuel has been chattering about, even though I never had any faith in him. He promises to show us great things soon, and all of this without extracting even a *crazia* [a small Florentine coin of copper-silver alloy] from us in advance. In fifteen or twenty days, all will be made clear if it was not already abundantly clear, and Your Most Illustrious Excellency will be informed of whatever happens.[79]

Week after week, with bated breath, Benedetto updated Don Giovanni – keeping a close eye on his patron's investment and protecting his own credibility as much as possible:

> [14 February 1616] I am getting to the bottom of things regarding that friend of ours. We now await the waxing of the moon and if he is unable to make anything happen, as I expect, this will soon be obvious. He must not receive even a *soldo* [a small Florentine copper coin] until he can show us some done deeds.[80]

> [21 February 1616] That friend from Fez is beginning to create problems, in order to drag things out, I imagine. In any case, we want to bring this to a rapid conclusion, perhaps within two weeks.[81]

> [27 February 1616] In my next letter, I hope to give Your Most Illustrious Excellency some news before the moon turns. I am pressing him as hard as I can, and meanwhile, I am holding firm to the principle that he does not see even a *soldo* until I see him deliver what he promises. In fact, it would suffice if he could deliver only one part in ten of all that.[82]

Benedetto then cushions Don Giovanni's expectations even further by lauding his patron's own achievements in the occult: 'Truthfully and without flattery, if we put all of the other practitioners together, I don't believe that we would arrive at even one part in a thousand of your own proficiency, that is to say, your doctrine, knowledge from books, practical ability, and mastery of the essentials. I would say that Your Most Illustrious Excellency has already achieved a thousand parts in a thousand.'[83]

To Benedetto's evident dismay, Doctor Samuel was pushing him deeper and deeper into the operation – playing on the mood of astrological urgency and his own alleged physical debility. By 13 March the magus was showing vague signs of improvement but was still far from ready to leave his bed, let alone visit the fish pond. He therefore promised his acolyte full working instructions,[84] and on 20 March 1616 Benedetto offered Don Giovanni a running update:

It seems that my presence was enough to trigger a recurrence of gout in our friend, and he has put off to Wednesday what he had been promising for Sunday. He says that the friend he is seeking to acquire, named Hlechamar [underlined in the original document], is solar, and since the celestial lights were put in place on the fourth day of creation, it would be well to wait until a Wednesday, since the first apparition needs to take place on that day. So, he instructed me to go to that place at that time and enclose those five canes with a red thread, beginning with one of the outer canes, then going to the one in the middle, then from the one in the centre to the second, then from the second to the third, then from the third to the centre, then from the centre back to the third, then from the third to the fourth, then from the fourth to the centre, then from the centre to the fourth, then from the fourth to the first, then from the first to the centre, and then from the centre to the second. The water would thus be divided up by the string into three parts. I carried this out, and when I reported back to him, he said that it could not have gone better. This was done near to the ground, and he promises that on Monday there will be a second similar operation at the middle of the canes and on Wednesday a third operation at the top of the canes. Then there is the incantation and he [Hlechamar] will instantly appear. I will advise you of the outcome immediately, and I will be ready to obey your every wish.[85]

The play on the days of creation from the Book of Genesis seems a direct borrowing from classic Kabbalah as does the manipulation of the red thread, traditionally used to exclude malignant spirits. As the weeks dragged on, Doctor Samuel continued to add an ever more eclectic range of supernatural elements, drawing freely on his Arabic background. The spiritual agent Hlechamar[86] was evidently Arabic himself, since the crucial incantation was in that language, not Hebrew. On 27 March Benedetto Blanis reported on his increasingly improbable journey into the secret world of the fish pond:

> I am yet to extricate myself from the prattle and procrastination of that man. Now, he has instructed me to carry out that same operation with the red thread but suffumigating each cane with seven spices including *curiandolo, pepe, bengiucii, mastice, almeghna, alfarach,* and *masias.* I don't know if the apothecaries have all these things, and I haven't had time to enquire. Since the red thread goes at the top of the canes in the third stage, people might be able to see it. So, I don't want to perform the second stage until he gives me the instructions for the third, which he promised for yesterday. This involves a long incantation in Arabic which he has begun to copy out for me, saying that I need to do it in this language and no other. Meanwhile, he says that he will personally oversee the ninety-day operation which has now reached its thirtieth day.

Doctor Samuel ordered the burning of seven aromatic substances which Benedetto lists in a hybrid mixture of Italian, near Latin, and near Arabic: *curiandolo, pepe, bengiucii, mastice, almeghna, alfarach,* and *masias.* Curiandolo and *pepe* are easily identified as coriander and pepper. *Masias* is probably *macis* or mace. *Mastice* is mastic, a resin from the tree *pistacia lentiscus,* and *bengiucii* is benzoin, a resin from the tree *styrax benzoin.* Almeghna is presumably *almèa,* the bark of the tree *styrax officinalis,* from the Arabic *almei'a. Alfarach* is yet another herb of Arab origin, perhaps alfalfa, from the Arabic *al-fasfasa.*[87]

Benedetto's official attitude was shifting rapidly to sarcastic exasperation: 'For my own part, I consider Your Excellency to be a most truthful prophet, and I do not have even the slightest faith in him.'[88] Don Giovanni had made the Moroccan's acquaintance at the Casino di San Marco, where his nephew and fellow alchemist Don Antonio dei Medici kept his celebrated laboratory and library. 'This is what Your Most Illustrious Excellency said from the very beginning, having recognized him immediately for what he was when you spoke with him at the Casino.'[89]

By this time Benedetto was anxious to liquidate his Caggesi connection, and Doctor Samuel considered it an opportune moment to get out of bed and also get out of town. However, the Jewish Passover (beginning 2 April 1616) and the Christian Easter (3 April) both intervened,[90] and an unnamed Christian patron[91] of the occult remained doggedly committed to the fish pond, even calling at the Blanis family's shop in the Ghetto to express his support: 'Out of courtesy to that gentleman, I had to ... pretend to believe in the big project since the little project with the canes and the pinwheels had come to nothing. Neither do I expect anything to come of the rest.'[92]

Doctor Samuel finally left Florence after several delays,[93] and by then Benedetto's frustration was boiling over. He noted, rather vindictively, on 17 April:

> Our friend is leaving on Thursday morning [21 April] for Massa di Car-rara where he has a second wife who will soon give birth, and he says that he will continue supervising the project. He wanted that gentleman [the unnamed Christian adept] to lend him his carriage as far as Massa, so that he could travel more commodiously with his gout. However, considering my firm resolution that he should not enjoy even a *crazia* of profit, I did not want the gentleman to spend 7 or 8 scudi on a hired carriage. He had done this previously so that our friend would not be seen inside his personal carriage with that robe of his and that beard like the Magus Falsirone. Therefore, I told him that the gentleman's carriage had already been lent to someone else. If he wants a scudo for a place in a public carriage, I might let him have it for the sake of hearing his response. But then again, I might not since I don't want to seem like a soft touch. Now I will wait to see what he does, and I will immediately inform Your Most Illustrious Excellency.[94]

With his preposterous robe and beard, Doctor Samuel looked like an outlandish necromancer, at least in Benedetto's eyes.[95] Although Falsirone was a subsidiary character in Ariosto's epic poem *Orlando Furioso*, there was the more immediate echo of the Italian word *falso* (meaning false or fake). The fish pond story trails off into nothing in Benedetto Blanis' letters to Don Giovanni dei Medici – and that was probably the writer's fondest hope:

> [(24 April 1616] Our friend with the project has had a daughter, and I believe that he will be returning here soon.[96]

> [8 May 1616] That man has not yet returned from Massa and if he never returns, it would scarcely matter.[97]

Not surprisingly, Benedetto was leaving out far more than he was including in his reports to Don Giovanni – at least regarding matters on the Jewish side. Not only was the border principality of Massa Carrara a flourishing centre for Jewish commerce,[98] it was an important base for both the Caggesi and the Blanis families. Samuel's second wife lived there as did many of Benedetto's relatives, presumably interacting on a daily basis.

Benedetto was eager to cast the Moroccan as an absurd charlatan – but we are only hearing one side of the story and that was heavily edited for Don Giovanni's consumption. In fact, Samuel Caggesi (or Chagez, Hagges, Hagiz, Agies, Aes) might well have been the most distinguished resident of the Florentine Ghetto in these years. His family had settled in Fez after 1492 along with other Jewish exiles from Spain, and in the generations that followed they had made their presence felt throughout the Mediterranean diaspora.

In 1597 a Rabbi Samuel Hagiz published two important works in Venice, a homilectic commentary on Deuteronomy and a series of sermons on the Pentateuch.[99] In the early years of the seventeenth century, a Samuel Hagiz lived in Pisa and served as rabbi of the Levantine community.[100] In 1609 a 'Dottore Samuele Hagges' settled in Florence along with other Levantine merchants, attracted to the Tuscan capital by special favours from the grand duke.[101] He was then allocated a prized apartment in the Outer Ghetto facing onto the Mercato Vecchio – enjoying free access to the city while the Blanis family was locked inside.[102]

In the final analysis, this startling tale might tell us more about Benedetto Blanis and his constantly thwarted occult ambitions than about the actual career of the alleged Moroccan sorcerer – who was also a leading businessman and perhaps a learned rabbi. We would certainly expect to have seen the last of Doctor Samuel, at least in Florence, after his ignominious flight to Massa in the spring of 1616. This intriguing figure did indeed vanish from Benedetto's letters to Don Giovanni dei Medici – but the man himself was soon back in town and back in the Ghetto, where he regularly paid his rent to the granducal administration for yet another twenty years.[103]

chapter eight

Games of Chance

Porta al Prato

The Ghetto had its own gates, two of them, which were locked at night after business hours – keeping Jews in and keeping other people out. It was, however, only a small enclosure within a much bigger one: the great City of Florence.

In the time of Benedetto Blanis, the Tuscan capital was surrounded by five miles of defensive walls with fifteen gates, delimiting a thousand acres of inhabited space. Some parts of the city were densely crowded – particularly the Ghetto where Benedetto lived – while others were green and open, almost rural in effect, with gardens, orchards, and scattered houses. The walls of Florence had been built three centuries earlier, just before the devastating plague of 1348, to protect a burgeoning metropolis of 100,000. This was nearly twice the population of the city that Benedetto Blanis knew.

Over the years, these walls were periodically renovated as military technology advanced. Florence, however, had not faced a direct attack since 1529–30, when Alessandro dei Medici borrowed an army from the Holy Roman Emperor, besieged the city, and installed himself as duke. Then for the next two centuries, these same walls helped Alessandro's successors maintain order within their capital. Soldiers were stationed at the gates, along with municipal policemen and customs officers. Together they stopped undesirables, Jews and Gentiles alike, from entering the city and apprehended delinquents fleeing their crimes. They collected taxes on rural produce bound for market and blocked most foreign manufactured goods. They even regulated the removal of works of art, 'so that the city will not be deprived of such ornament.'[1]

Each of Florence's fifteen gates had a distinct character. The Porta di San Gallo to the north was the first sight noted by Francesco Bocchi in his 1591 guidebook, *The Beauties of the City of Florence* (*Le Bellezze della Città di Firenze*), 'since this is where most visitors arrive when they come from Venice, France, and Germany.'[2] For those heading south, 'the voyage to Rome begins at the Porta di San Pier Gattolini, which is thus called the Porta Romana.'[3] The Porta di San Gallo and the Porta Romana were both prestigious entries to the city, frequently used by visiting dignitaries. By contrast, the southwestern Porta di San Frediano (which Bocchi fails to mention) was situated in a grim industrial wasteland that was going back to nature with the contraction of the wool and leather industries. Least attractive of all was the Porta alla Croce or 'Gate of the Cross' to the northeast. The outlying ground was the dreaded site of public executions and 'those arriving from La Verna or the Romagna'[4] skirted an infamous cluster of scaffolds, gallows, and gibbets, often featuring the dangling remains of the dead.

The Porta al Prato to the northwest, 'used by those who travel to or from Genoa, Lucca, Prato, and Pistoia,' had the most cheerful associations for the Florentines. Every June on the Feast of Saint John the Baptist, Patron of Florence, a dramatic race of Barbary horses took place on the *prato* or field just inside the gate. 'Many people gather merrily along the street and you can indeed say that most of Florence is there … This is the most honoured festival that the city has and the most magnificent spectacle.'[5] Outside the gate, there was a broad avenue leading to the nearby Cascine ('The Hamlets'), an extensive agricultural estate belonging to the Medici family. This was strictly private property, but the rulers of Tuscany admitted their subjects as a treat on special occasions.

One such occasion was 12 May, the birthday of Grand Duke Cosimo II, which fell on a Sunday in 1619. On the following Monday, four young Jewish men from eminent Ghetto families were apprehended by the police at the Porta al Prato:

> Gratiadio son of Lelio Blanis, Agnolo son of Teseo, Benedetto son of Lione, and Daniello son of Elia, all Jews, were arrested by constable Benedetto, nicknamed '*il Miglio*,' outside the Porta al Prato. They were returning from the Cascine, walking along the avenue playing a *tiorba* [*theorbo* or large lute] … allegedly violating the ban against setting foot in that place. The accused all confessed that they were indeed returning by way of the avenue since they had seen many other people walking there and were una-

ware of the prohibition. The Magistrates considered affidavits attesting that the accused were all under fifteen years of age. They also considered the testimony of a witness who swore that these Jews were incited to go to the Cascine in the first place by the constables themselves, who encountered them in the tavern at Ponte alle Mosse and told them that there was a big dance going on. The Magistrates therefore decided to absolve the Jews since they were just boys and they had no intention of breaking the law – and in fact, they were not engaged in anything illegal.[6]

These boys were as near to gilded youth as the Florentine Ghetto could offer, and their *tiorba* was a fashionable and expensive stringed instrument, invented at the Medici Court a few decades earlier.[7] Gratiadio Blanis was evidently Benedetto's nephew, son of his older brother Lelio, while Agnolo son of Teseo was a member of the Tesei family, the designated Jewish brokers in Florence.[8] The Tesei, in fact, had a villa on the edge of the Cascine at Ponte alle Mosse, near the tavern where the boys' adventure began.

The magistrates had no difficulty recognizing the incident for what it was – a blatant example of police entrapment. The records of their court are filled with such cases, which they normally dismissed with a minimum of comment. On 15 May 1625 they exonerated another young Jew:

> The Honourable Eight Lords of Protection and Supervision of the City of Florence ... reviewed the imprisonment of the Jew Davitte son of Abram Ricco, who is thirteen years of age. He was arrested by constable Felice, nicknamed '*Cice*,' who alleges that he found Davitte gambling with cards in the Piazza del Gran Duca on the 14th day of the present month. The Magistrates ordered that the prisoner be released without expense, considering his denial of the charges, his scant age, and the unlikelihood that he was gambling.[9]

In the Florentine criminal court, cases often dragged on for weeks if not months or years. Probably in response to Davitte's youth, the magistrates got him out of jail as quickly as possible, putting his case at the top of the docket on the day after his arrest. Little deliberation was needed, since there were no witnesses apart from the arresting constable. Also, Davitte was the only person charged, and it was difficult to imagine him gambling by himself in the bustling Piazza del Gran Duca (as the Piazza della Signoria was then known).

The Eight Magistrates for Protection and Supervision were all gentlemen, and they had few illusions regarding the constables (*famigli*) in their service. These were recruited from the dregs of Florentine society – the unemployed and unemployable – who came to enforce the law during intervals in their marginal and often criminal careers. On 14 January 1622 the magistrates heard a typical case regarding two of their own:

> The Magistrates reviewed the investigation of Giovanni son of Piero Fornaini nick-named '*il Beccaino*' (the Little Butcher) and Giovanni Battista son of Romolo Cianfani nick-named '*Cianfrona*.' During the four or five months that these two have been constables, they cursed habitually – invoking the holy name of God and the saints while gambling with cards … in the guardroom and other places in the palace of the constabulary [Palazzo del Bargello]. They said 'whore,' 'cunt,' 'body,' 'blood,' and 'great cuckold of God,' 'I fuck Saint Peter in the ass,' 'Saint Paul too,' and other such horrendous blasphemies … In accordance with the law against cursing, the accused are sentenced to fines of 200 lire each and the perforation of their tongues as well as exclusion from their office for six months.[10]

Despite their gambling and horrendous blasphemies, Beccaino and Cianfrona were only suspended from the constabulary for six months, not dismissed in shame for the rest of their lives. These two were neither better nor worse than expected, and few candidates were likely to represent an improvement.

In addition to being gentlemen, the magistrates were well paid for their services, earning 168 lire per quarter. The constables, meanwhile, received less than a third that amount, a mere 52 lire – but they could supplement their salary with a share of the fines generated by their arrests. Under the circumstances, it is not surprising that the constables were energetic in their apprehension of criminals, nor that charges were often dismissed on the spot with discreet pay-offs.

On the subject of low-level bribes, the magistrates considered a complicated gambling case on 14 December 1624 – separating the charges by the police from the charges against the police: 'On the 16th of last month, the constables of the Bargello arrested two of the accused, Bastiano and Simone, for gambling with cards. They had been bound and were being taken off to prison when Giovanni, the third accused … allegedly tried to corrupt the constables with money, offering them

6 giuli to let the prisoners go. Then, when the constables refused, the accused decided to make a break for it.'

The magistrates knew the game far too well, and they exonerated the would-be corrupter of the police on the grounds of basic improbability: 'In addition to the denial of the accused, it is difficult to believe that such people [the constables] would refuse money.'[11]

Direct pay-offs were a subversion of justice; they were also unfair to the higher-ups. On 9 February 1622 the magistrates issued a formal order on behalf of Captain Giovanni Milani, Chief Constable (Bargello) of Florence: 'The Captain wishes to avoid the frauds perpetrated by his Lieutenant, his Corporals, and his Constables in the course of their daily arrests ... resulting in a serious loss of money, since a share [of all fines] belongs to him.'[12] In the future, any policeman who failed to report an arrest was subject to two hoists of the rope in public – presumably to the immense satisfaction of the population that he harassed and victimized.

In the time of Benedetto Blanis, 'criminal justice' was a relative concept. Arrests were made on a speculative basis by agents who had a stake in the action, whether bounty hunters or outright crooks. Then, as soon as the arrest was made, a long process of mediation and favour-broking began. In most cases – or at least, most of the important cases – the real trial took place behind the scenes, in hallways, and antechambers throughout the city of Florence. The final court of appeal was at the Palazzo Pitti, not the Palazzo del Bargello, and the ultimate judges were the Medici themselves.

Risky Business

Gambling was seen as the root of many evils – social, moral, and economic. On 17 January 1586 the authorities issued a proclamation banning this pastime in no uncertain terms:

By express order of His Most Serene Highness [Grand Duke Francesco], the Eight Magistrates for Protection and Supervision of the City of Florence wish to prevent the numerous disturbances, improprieties, blasphemies, larcenies, and other iniquities that are caused every day by those who gamble with dice and cards. Defying previous orders and edicts, they are continually gambling, instead of working and attending to their business and their families ... In the future, no person of any quality, class, or condition ... will dare gamble with dice or cards along the Arno River, near the walls of the city, in any street or piazza, or in any shop. The penalty is one hoist of the rope for the first offence, then three hoists of the rope for the second offence, then forced service in the galleys for the third offence.[13]

Such laws were proclaimed with notable frequency and, judging by the magistrates' caseload, just as frequently ignored. The Florentines were evidently starved for stimulating diversions, and the risk of discovery must have been part of the attraction. In the Mercato Vecchio, a constant succession of apprehended gamblers (always male) were hoisted by the rope, occasionally dozens at a time.

In spite of the egalitarian language of the edict, gamblers of any quality, class, and condition were not the object of such exemplary public punishments. On 22 October 1616 the police broke up a card game in a tavern at Ponte a Greve. A miller and two other humble locals were sentenced to the rope, while 'Piero di Palla Strozzi, Citizen of Florence was absolved, notwithstanding his confession, because he was a gentleman.'[14]

In March of 1614 the lieutenant of the Bargello raided an aristocratic gaming establishment in Florence and imprisoned eighty-one players and onlookers, many from distinguished families. A mere greengrocer and two serving boys were each sentenced to two hoists of the rope in public while seventy-eight others were released because they were Florentine citizens – members of the voting and office-holding elite.[15]

Since people were not created equal, neither was the law. A generally accepted principle was that the lower orders were undisciplined and weak-minded while their betters could rise above most ordinary temptations. Nonetheless, the authorities were alarmed by the destructive behaviour of gentlemen who had cash to lose and good enough credit to go on losing. On 18 September 1606 Grand Duke Ferdinando I and the Magistrates issued yet another gambling edict – one that expressed unusual urgency and much good sense:

Although gambling might be tolerated in some cases as an honest recreation, it must not be allowed to destroy those who practice it ... Experience teaches that much harm, both past and present, derives from gambling on credit, including catastrophic loss and the ruin of whole families. It is therefore forbidden to furnish, lend, handle, or accommodate money on behalf of gamblers or those who facilitate their gambling, in any way or

under any pretext ... Let it be stated that all documents, all financial instru-
ments, and all obligations formulated for such purposes are rendered null
and void by law.[16]

On 26 March 1616 a local manuscript newsletter (*avviso*) offered a titil-
lating account of the latest scandal to erupt in the Florentine Ghetto and
a copy was duly forwarded to Don Giovanni dei Medici in Venice.[17] It
reads like a moral object lesson on the perils of gambling on credit:

> Jacob son of Juda Pernicca, a rich Jewish youth of nineteen or twenty
> years without even a hint of a beard, was left without a father a year ago.
> While at the villa of another Jew, Josef di Tiseo, near the Ponte alle Mosse
> in Florence, he began gambling on credit with the said Josef di Tiseo as
> well as Josef d'Israel and Moisé Lattone, all shrewd Jews. They won 1,500
> scudi from him on credit, and he then paid them off with cordovan leather
> stored as an investment in the customs warehouse and intended for com-
> mercial sale.

Josef Tesei, Josef Isdraele, and Moisé Lattone were all a generation older than the hapless boy. The Tesei were the designated brokers in the
Ghetto, and their villa outside the Porta al Prato on the border of the
Cascine was an extraordinary indication of their success. (This was five
years before the collapse of the family enterprise and Josef's flight to
Turkey.[18]) The Pernicca were Portuguese in origin (as were the Isdraele
and possibly the Lattone), and Jacob's father Juda had brought them
to Florence by way of the port city of Ancona,[19] where they still had
commercial interests. The Isdraele and Lattone were both established
households of Levantine merchants, and Moisé Lattone was Benedetto
Blanis' brother-in-law. Together, these families occupied the most privileged stratum of Florentine Jewish society.

The anonymous *avviso* writer told this sensational story with obvious
relish. Gambling was always a hot topic, and in this case there was a
rich young dupe, his false friends, a large sum of money, and an exotic
Jewish background. There was also a heroic protagonist, Jacob's widowed mother:

> The mother of the said Jacob was a woman of merit and had charge of
> her husband's property since he had left her mistress of her own affairs.
> She therefore brought legal proceedings against the Jews who had won
> at gambling, charging them with robbery since they had enticed and en-

trapped her son. For the sake of justice, she asked that they be made to give back the leather since she would otherwise be forced to go tell the story to Madama Serenissima [Christine de Lorraine] whom she hoped would come down hard on them.

Dowager Grand Duchess Christine de Lorraine was no lover of the Jews but as a widow and the grand duke's mother, she saw herself as the patron of women with families to protect. A few years later, Maddalena Martelli Sernigi would bring her appeal directly to Christine when her son Jacopo fell prey to Benedetto Blanis' usury.[20] In this instance, the Pernicca family had a very great deal at stake:

This young man, Jacob son of Juda Pernicca, inherited 20,000 scudi in cash from his father, and this was placed with the Riccardi bank and with the merchant Matteo Galli to be managed as an investment. Also, he was obligated to give a dowry of 2,000 scudi to each of his three sisters, who are of marriageable age. Since the mother was left lady and mistress (*donna e madonna*)[21] by her husband, her plan was to increase this money, not let it dwindle away as the young man started to do. In fact, it is said that he really lost 3,000 scudi at gambling, not merely 1,500. It is also said that the winners were all enemies of his father and jealous of his inheritance, which his father earned while doing business in this city over the course of twenty-five years.

If the *avviso* writer got his numbers straight and was not exaggerating for the sake of the story, Jacob Pernicca was breathtakingly rich for a Florentine Jew. Twenty thousand scudi was a huge inheritance and 2,000 scudi an impressive dowry even for a marriageable Christian girl. Whatever the actual figures, the Ghetto was a very small place, and the Pernicca case set the Jews who mattered at each other's throats.

When Benedetto Blanis made his pitch to Don Giovanni three months later, on 26 June 1616, he kept inconvenient facts to a minimum and put his own spin on things: 'Some months ago, my young brother-in-law [Moisé Lattone] was gambling with a certain Jew named Pernicca who played on credit after his cash ran out. Pernicca lost a few hundred scudi and they suspect that their adversary, another Portuguese named Giuseppe d'Israele, was acting as spy.'[22] If Don Giovanni had read and remembered the recent *avviso*, he might have raised an eyebrow. The sum of money had been knocked down from 3,000 scudi to a relatively inconsequential few hundred. Although Pernicca was barely twenty, it is the thirty-something Lattone[23] who is described as 'young.' Giuseppe Isdraele is cast as the leading villain and Jacob's mother does not figure at all, nor – most critically – does Don Giovanni's sister-in-law Christine de Lorraine.

Benedetto was now deeply involved in the case: 'My brother-in-law was supposed to go to jail and Sabatino [Sabatino Ronconi, lieutenant of the constabulary] was supposed to take him but decided to send him on his own. I personally accompanied my brother-in-law and encouraged him to flee, since he was lacking in spirit and hadn't thought of this on his own. So, he flung himself into that church in Via dello Studio, which was a ridiculous sight and left Sabatino looking like a fool.'[24]

The Jew Moisé Lattone took refuge in the ancient Church of San Benedetto, adjacent to the residence of the canons of the nearby cathedral. While Lieutenant Sabatino was coping with his embarassment, Benedetto had to decide what to do with the escapee. His first thought was to hide him in Don Giovanni's own palace in Via del Parione but he eventually sent him to Don Giovanni's ailing nephew, the alchemist Don Antonio, at the Casino di San Marco. Benedetto then dug himself in for a long and intense negotiated settlement, with everyone on all sides enlisting their most influential friends. 'It could only help us,' he observed, 'if Your Most Illustrious Excellency would write a few timely lines to Signor [Camillo] Guidi,' refering to Madama Serenissima's confidential secretary. Then in a postscript, he reminded Don Giovanni of their chief talking point: 'Those three involved in the gambling are all merchants and important dealers in textiles sent to the Levant and Germany. If the present matter is not resolved, business will be ruined.'[25]

Benedetto was soon on the lam as well, as the major-domo of Don Giovanni's Florentine palace explained on 2 July 1616: 'Messer Benedetto has secluded himself in Your Most Illustrious Excellency's palace since he fears that he will be examined by the Eight Magistrates in the gambling case brought against Pernicca and Moisé Lattone. Since this is not a grave criminal matter, I had Cencio give him a room as requested. It seemed appropriate to let him have this accommodation, since I know that he is your servant and there is the precedent of Moisé who withdrew to the Casino.'[26]

As the case escalated, few would have agreed that it was not a grave criminal matter. Benedetto was terrified at the prospect of being arrested and questioned under torture, which would not have been a new experience for him. On 10 July 1616 he renewed his appeal to Don Giovanni:

Your Most Illustrious Excellency will be doing me a favour if you assist me
in that gambling matter by writing to Marsili [Giovanni Battista Marsili,
secretary of the Eight Magistrates] on behalf of my brother-in-law Moisé
Lattone and against that Portuguese Jew Josef Israel whom the Bargello
says acted as spy. I also ask you to support me personally so that I will not
be put to the test as a witness, since the rope scarcely seems appropriate
under the circumstances. It is the custom here in Florence to use it against
witnesses, not against the principals in the case. This happened to me previously, and I would suffer any sort of martyrdom rather than jeopardize
someone else with my own tongue.[27]

While hiding out in Don Giovanni's Florentine residence, Benedetto
put his enforced leisure to good use, beginning a major reorganization
of the palace library. As major-domo Cosimo Baroncelli noted on 16
July, 'Messer Benedetto has been busy around the library but has had
no need of [the servants] Girolamo, Cencio, and Pagolino. Everything
is being done by him and two friends who have taken refuge in Your
Most Illustrious Excellency's palace. This work is helping them pass the
time and their idea, he tells me, is to … make a label for each book so
that it will be easier to find in its appropriate place.'[28]

Who were Benedetto's two friends? We can only wonder, since Moisé
Lattone had already been spirited out of the country a week earlier: 'On
Sunday [10 July] my brother-in-law left the state of Tuscany in a carriage belonging to Don Antonio [dei Medici], accompanied by one of
his men. He was heading towards Bologna and is now in a safe place.'[29]
In major Florentine legal cases, the usual practice was to get the central
figures out of the way so that negotiations could take place in a calm
atmosphere, with no one in jail and no one tortured. Giuseppe Isdraele
and Giuseppe Tesei had also disappeared from sight while the unfortunate young Jacob Pernicca remained in solitary confinement in the
Bargello prison.

In the weeks and months that followed, the wheels of justice ground
on and on. Fines and other penalties were levied in absentia to force
Lattone and Isdraele to appear and testify.[30] Don Giovanni brought
his influence to bear on Secretary Marsili, who made all of the right
noises. 'I already knew that you were much loved by Signor Don Giovanni,' Marsili assured Benedetto, 'and that he esteems you and values you greatly. Therefore, I could not trouble you in any way without
displeasing His Most Illustrious Excellency – which I would never do

under any circumstance. Therefore, you should not worry about anything at all.'[31]

Meanwhile, fate overtook Benedetto's arch-enemy Giuseppe Isdraele, testing the limits of Jewish solidarity under duress:

> I cannot fail to recount a miraculous occurence of Divine Justice, since God *supplantasti insurgentes in me subtus me* (hast subdued under me them that rose up against me).[32] Thus it happened with that Giuseppe d'Israel who was fined for his failure to appear in court, with the penalty of 200 scudi and two years of forced residence [in Livorno]. Since he did not take up his forced residence within fifteen days as decreed, he was in imminent danger of being sent to the galleys ... So he turned to me and begged me to let him stay for three or four days in that same room in Your Excellency's palace where I stayed with my brother-in-law. Although Giuseppe d'Israel does not even deserve a place in your stable, I could scarcely refuse to make this request to Signor Baroncelli, and he granted it.[33]

In the days that followed, while residing in Don Giovanni's palace, Isdraele worked the system and managed to quash all of the charges against him – probably proving Benedetto's assertion that he was a police informer.[34] When the Otto issued its finding on 22 August 1616, there were only three defendants left in the case: Jacob Pernicca, Moisé Lattone, and Giuseppe Tesei.

The magistrates clearly sympathized with the young man who had suffered a horrifying ordeal – beginning with a devastating betrayal by his elder peers in the local Jewish community: 'The said Moisé and Tesei took the said Jacob to various places, making merry with him and getting him more or less drunk. Then they used deceit to win 3,400 scudi from him in cash plus an additional 1,800 scudi on credit.' Jacob Pernicca was therefore sentenced only to a token fine of 100 scudi, 'considering his gullibility and simplicity and the fact that he is only around eighteen years old and also considering his imprisonment, torture, and great financial loss.'[35]

Even under torture, Jacob Pernicca steadfastly denied gambling with Tesei, Isdraele, and Lattone. Although his fortitude is to be admired, he effectively waived any legal right to recoup his losses. The magistrates, however, leapt to his defence, reinstating his option to sue at some future time 'since it is claimed that he was seduced and deceived by them.' Jacob was finally released from prison on 5 September 1616, having paid half of his fine while the other half was remitted by direct order of the grand duke – who tempered mercy with irony, earmarking this Jew's money for the construction of the new ceiling of Livorno Cathedral.[36]

Giovanni Battista Marsili, secretary of the Eight, assured Benedetto that he need not worry – but the court was not ready to condone Tesei and Lattone's despicable behaviour. Their failure to appear was taken as a full confession of their guilt, and they were each fined 2,000 scudi – somewhat more than their alleged winnings.[37] Benedetto immediately launched a round of emotional appeals to Don Giovanni on behalf of his family: 'If God does not help us obtain a pardon for the whole sum, or at least half of it with terms for delayed payment, this will result in utter ruin. My sister, who has four female children, is desperate.' And so on...[38]

Even under pressure, Benedetto never quite lost his peculiar sense of entitlement: 'Since they [Giuseppe Tesei and Moisé Lattone] were sentenced in absentia, this should make it easier for them to receive a pardon for the whole sum or at least part. They cannot be harmed in either their property or their persons since they are the sons of families that matter.'[39] In fact, Salvador Tesei (father of Giuseppe) and Emanuel Lattone (father of Moisé) quickly petitioned the grand duke, who personally reduced their fines by 75%. Each was assessed 500 scudi: 450 for the ceiling of Livorno Cathedral plus 50 for an unnamed police informant – perhaps their own neighbour Giuseppe Isdraele.[40]

Jew Made Christian

After his release from prison, Jacob Pernicca began distancing himself from other Jews – understandably enough. This passage in his life is documented only in two terse administrative notes. First, he requested and was denied permission to live outside the Ghetto, away from the people who had victimized him. 'His Highness wishes him to live in the Ghetto. He is to be granted all the privileges and prerogatives that his father enjoyed but only those ... 2 September 1617.'[41] Then, when that failed, he became Christian.[42] On 24 December 1618, the day before Christmas, he settled his final rent payment in the Florentine Ghetto: 'Three scudi received from Jacobbe son of Juda Pernicca, formerly Jew, now known as Gianlorenzo Laurenzi.'[43]

After his conversion, the former Jacob Pernicca married a Christian woman with whom he had at least one child who was duly baptized.[44]

He also pursued a fitful business career. On 27 March 1619, 'Gio. Lorenzo Laurentij ebreo fatto christiano (Giovanni Lorenzo Laurenzi Jew made Christian)' was exonerated along with several other defendants in a complicated but ultimately petty case of fraudulent trading.[45] Then in the autumn of 1622 he suffered a violent psychological breakdown:

> Giovanlorenzo Laurentij, Jew made Christian, is a perverse and malignant individual who respects neither God nor honour nor those around him. In his own home, he constantly threatened to kill his wife and the female servants and on various occasions, he indeed attempted to poison his wife. Arsenic and scamony were then found in his house. On various other occasions, he tried to sodomize his wife but she refused to consent. Having previously been an enemy of God, he continued behaving more like a Jew than a Christian, uttering infamous words against Christ our Saviour. Truly he showed himself to be an enemy of the Faith, saying 'Cunt of God,' 'Cunt of the Virgin,' 'Christ, I fuck you in the ass and your Apostles too,' 'Christ, you are a fucking cuckold,' and other such infamous and obscene expressions.[46]

Although the magistrates were keenly aware of Jacob/Gianlorenzo's Jewish background, converted Turks[47] and Christian beggars[48] were also subject to breakdowns of this kind – with uncontrolled swearing and sexual battery against their own spouses. It was, in fact, a characteristic behaviour of embittered men who had been wrenched from their natural place in society. Jacob/Gianlorenzo was sentenced to a fine of 200 scudi and the perforation of his tongue for blasphemy, then five years of forced residence at Portoferraio on the Island of Elba.[49] After the usual round of pleabargaining, the Grand Duke personally waived the horrible but normal corporal punishment.[50]

Meanwhile, the Pernicca firm went bankrupt. On 14 November 1622 the magistrates found in favour of the Christian banker Luigi Carnesecchi who was suing 'Salamone and Jacobbe Pernicca and partners, Jews of Ancona' for 632 scudi worth of unpaid merchandise sent to Ancona on their behalf. By then the Pernicca family had already left Florence, and Carnesecchi demonstrated this by posting a legal summons, three times, at the well in the Ghetto square.[51]

Even on paper that was probably Jacob Pernicca's last appearance in the Florentine Ghetto using his cast-off Jewish name. As Gianlorenzo Laurenzi, he remained in exile in Portoferraio for three-and-a-half years – until March 1626, when he was reprieved by the grand duke.[52] At that time, he was still only in his late twenties, so he might have gone back to Florence (if so, he stayed out of the hands of the police). He might have gone to Ancona to rejoin the family that he had previously repudiated. He might have gone almost any place in the world – as either a Christian or a Jew.

Jacob/Gianlorenzo's story is particularly distressing because he managed to wreck a promising life without the usual help of war, politics, natural disaster, or even religious persecution. Simply put, he inherited too much money at too young an age and fell in with the wrong crowd – which happened to be his own social set, the precarious elite of the Florentine Ghetto.

chapter nine

The Mirror of Truth

On the Road

Benedetto Blanis spent nine months in Venice with Don Giovanni dei
Medici, from February to October 1618. This was the most intense
phase of their long collaboration – when they could see each other every day,[1] exchanging confidences and venturing together into the farthest reaches of the arcane. Don Giovanni had moved to Venice in late
June of 1615, and only a month later, Benedetto was already planning a
clandestine visit to that city:

> After receiving your order, I considered how I might best serve Your
> Most Illustrious Excellency, and it came to mind that my brother David
> has some rental properties in the Venetian Ghetto that bring in about 100
> scudi a year.[2] When I was there in Venice with him four years ago, I took
> 400 scudi worth of merchandise in lieu of rent and this agreement has
> now reached its term. Since I arranged the matter with a certain Iacobbe
> d'Anselmo Levi, a Jew of Venice, I could tell people in Florence that it was
> necessary for me to make the trip now for this reason, showing whatever
> documents seem appropriate to you.[3]

Benedetto could tell people in Florence almost anything except the
truth: Don Giovanni was summoning him to Venice to resume their
exploration of the occult.[4] He was willing – nay, eager – to make the
journey since he knew that city and its Ghetto well, and he knew that
he had to fight for his patron's attention. Maguses, often more qualified
than he, were now at Don Giovanni's beck and call and arcana of every
sort could be had for the asking.[5]

Business was always a plausible excuse for a trip. Like other affluent Jewish families, the Blanis had learned the lessons of history, and they were keeping their options open and their assets strategically dispersed. The usual method was to place sons and daughters, brothers and sisters and cousins in distant cities, strengthening the family network come what may. During these years Benedetto and his brother David were in and out of Venice. Meanwhile, they had cousins in Massa Carrara, a sister in Ferrara, and business partners, related or not, in Pisa and Genoa. Benedetto was often on the road, as he noted with perhaps exaggerated casualness in 1615. 'Going to Venice, whenever Your Excellency pleases, is no more of a burden to me than another trip to Montughi,'[6] referring to his patron's villa on the outskirts of Florence.

Secrecy was a fragile commodity in the small world of the Florentine Ghetto, and Laudadio Blanis soon blew his son's cover while chatting with an aristocratic client in the family shop. Benedetto shared the resulting comedy of errors with Don Giovanni on 28 November 1615:

> I had started to mention to my father and other relatives that Your Most Illustrious Excellency wanted me in Venice for a few days. Then, as it happened, that gentleman stopped by my shop to buy a few odds and ends, and I had to run off to another shop on his behalf. While I was away, my father commented that Your Excellency had summoned me to Venice, not realizing that this was meant to be a secret ... So, the gentleman came back to see me the very next morning and he addressed me with great ceremony, 'Since you are my friend, I am grateful that God has chosen to favour you in this way, seeing how things are now going'... Then, it was almost as if God himself were speaking to me. When I started to say, 'I will have to go to Venice...,' that gentleman jumped right in without letting me finish. 'Yes, His Lordship summoned you! That's what your father told me yesterday.' So I carried on, as best I could under the circumstances, 'Actually, I need to manage some house rentals there but I really don't know when I can possibly find time...'[7]

As it happened, neither Don Giovanni nor Benedetto found time in the months and years that immediately followed. Don Giovanni was busy coordinating military strategy for the Venetian government, then he was on campaign with his army in the Friuli.[8] Benedetto, meanwhile, had a full docket of commercial lawsuits in Florence, family obligations throughout northern Italy, and various business trips. On 14 August 1617 he sent his patron a brief note from Pisa where he had gone to collect a major debt.[9] Their correspondence then ceased for three months, until 18 November 1617, when Benedetto emerged from an excruciating round of illnesses that devastated the Blanis family, claiming the lives of his wife, his mother-in-law, and very nearly his own:

> I offer infinite thanks for Your Most Illustrious Excellency's affectionate letter which brought me great consolation and touched on the essential point: Although God never sends us evil, we do not necessarily know what is for our own good. Therefore, we must always thank God in equal measure whether we are faced with seeming good or its seeming contrary. My wife's mother was anguished beyond all limits by the loss of her daughter and this resulted in her own death. We buried her yesterday, may God grant peace and repose to her soul.[10]

Benedetto's convalescence dragged on for another two months. On 21 January 1618 he offered a witty response to Don Giovanni's good wishes, quoting the Book of Proverbs in Latin. By this time, Don Giovanni was back in Venice, recovering from an illness of his own contracted in the field:

> Without flattery, I can surely say that Your Excellency's gracious and benevolent letter kept the fever from me. Friday was its predicted day of recurrence ... but it bothered me neither on Friday nor Saturday. So, I think that I have finally seen the last of it, thanks be to God. Soon I hope to receive health and life directly from your divine presence, recovering my full force and vigour: in *hilaritate vultus Regis vita et clementia eius quasi imber serotinus* (In the light of the king's countenance is life; and his favour is as a cloud of the latter rain). My only regret is that you are in bed yourself but I take consolation in the fact that your illness does not keep you from your studies. [11]

Benedetto was back on his feet and Don Giovanni, at long last, had a period of enforced leisure that he could devote to personal concerns. By 3 February 1618 Benedetto was busy packing: 'I received Your Most Illustrious Excellency's affectionate letter but I am making only a brief reply, since I will soon have the opportunity to talk with Your Excellency in person, particularly regarding that matter of ours.'[12]

Venice

Don Giovanni dei Medici first settled in Venice in the autumn of 1610, renting a palace from the noble Trevisan family at the Traghetto di San Geremia – directly across the Cannaregio canal from the principal entrance to the Ghetto. He remained in the Palazzo Trevisan for about a year, hiring grand furnishings (including tapestries, brocade wall hangings, and monumental beds) from a consortium of Jewish second-hand dealers.[13] Since Benedetto was in Venice at about this same time, their paths might well have crossed in the bustling Jewish quarter.[14]

The Ghetto was a favourite haunt of Venetian aristocrats who went there both for business and pleasure. Jews were prohibited by law from owning real estate, so they rented their homes and shops at inflated rates from Christian *padroni*. Thanks to chronic overcrowding, there was a lucrative market for Ghetto leases[15] among speculators of all faiths – including David and Benedetto Blanis. The Venetians also relied on Jews to make their money work for them in other ingenious ways, since they were adventurous traders with contacts throughout Europe and the Mediterranean. In Venice (unlike Florence), Jews could even lend money at interest, sometimes fronting investments for silent Christian partners.[16]

In addition to business opportunities, the Venetian Ghetto offered fashionable diversions for the rich and privileged. Christian men and women, including foreign dignitaries, flocked to the various synagogues to hear choral music[17] and sermons by celebrated rabbis. Leone da Modena noted a memorable occasion in the Spanish *scuola*: 'There was the brother of the King of France accompanied by some French noblemen and five of the most important Christian preachers ... God put such learned words into my mouth that all were very pleased, including many other Christians who were present.'[18]

Purim (the Feast of Esther) generally coincided with the Christian Carnival and was celebrated in the Ghetto by Jews and Gentiles alike. Then there was Simchat Torah (Rejoicing in the Torah), the conclusion and reinauguration of the annual cycle of Torah reading. Fra Giulio Morosini – Samuel Nahmias in the Venetian Ghetto before his conversion – evokes this festive event: 'In many places, especially in the city of Venice, that evening is almost like Carnival, in that many maids and matrons mask themselves to avoid being recognized, and go to see all the synagogues. At this time Christian ladies and gentlemen come to the synagogues out of curiosity almost more than on the other holidays, to see the outfitting and the wealth of the synagogues thus illuminated, and the foolish happiness of the Jews on that day.'[19]

The Jewish occult was an inevitable part of the Ghetto experience, and if a Christian required esoteric books, Kabbalistic amulets, mystic spells, or magical potions, he or she knew exactly where to go.[20] A discreet enquiry to a Jew in the street was enough to get things moving, and even the most distinguished members of the community treated cosmic secrets as part of their stock in trade. Rabbi Leone da Modena listed many occupations in his autobiography, including 'teaching arcane remedies and amulets' and 'selling books of arcane remedies.'[21] Rabbi Isaac Levi (Modena's nephew) offered a full range of occult goods and services – literary, alchemical, clairvoyant, and necromantic.[22]

Although Christians found much to intrigue them in the Venetian Ghetto, for Jewish visitors like Benedetto Blanis the experience must have been alternately overwhelming and exhilarating. This was the oldest Ghetto in Italy, founded in 1516, and the prototype for those that followed in Rome (1555), Florence (1571), and elsewhere. The Venetians even coined the word *Ghetto*, relocating their Jews to the area of the former municipal foundry – *geto* in the local dialect, from *gettare*, 'to cast metal.'[23] In Benedetto's day, it was the largest Jewish settlement in the peninsula, with as many as 3,000 inhabitants out of a total urban population of 150,000.[24] This made it six times the size of the Florentine Ghetto (495 inhabitants, according to the census of 1622), in a city two-and-a-half times the size of Florence (60,059 inhabitants).[25]

While the Florentine Ghetto was little more than an enclave, the Venetian Ghetto was an authentic city within the city. At home, Benedetto encountered Jews of various origins, including a violent German tailor,[26] a Moroccan sorcerer,[27] and a young Portuguese businessman with a gambling problem.[28] In the Jewish metropolis of Venice, the international presence consisted not merely of individuals and families but distinct functioning communities. There were three officially recognized 'nations,' each with its own governing body, synagogues, and schools: the German Nation (Ashkenazi Jews), the Eastern Nation (Levantini, Sephardic Jews from the Ottoman Empire, usually of Iberian descent), and the Western Nation (Ponentini, Sephardic Jews from Spain and Portugal, usually with a *marrano* past). There was also a population of Italian Jews, with their own synagogue but without distinct 'nation' status – chartered in tandem with the Germans. Within each of these groups, there were subtle distinctions of language and culture reflecting the infinite complexity of the Jewish Diaspora.

When Don Giovanni returned to Venice in June of 1615, he was entrusted with an arduous mission. As General, he had to plan and execute a land war against the Austrians, consolidating Venetian control of the Friuli, a strategic frontier zone to the northeast. In keeping with his official status, he rented an imposing palace on the Grand Canal from the Moro family[29] and was then busy for over a year organizing the political and logistical complexities of a major military campaign. In February of 1617 he joined his army in the field and remained there for eleven months – apart from an interlude in Udine with Livia Vernazza, his increasingly irrational and demanding mistress.

On 5 January 1618 he and Livia reappeared in Venice[30] with Don Giovanni much the worse for wear. Asdrubale Montauto, the Tuscan ambassador, commented to Grand Duke Cosimo II, 'He has aged considerably, I would say, and has lost a lot of weight. He is not in low spirits, however, but seems quite cheerful.'[31] Although seriously debilitated, with a massive swelling on his throat, Don Giovanni addressed the Venetian Senate on 8 January,[32] setting the stage for a long and acrimonious quarrel with his employers, whom he accused (like most military leaders) of underfunding his campaign and undermining his authority.

A physical collapse then ensued, followed by many months in bed. He quickly realized that the Venetian phase of his career was coming to an end but could not have guessed that he had already seen his last military engagement. In fact, Don Giovanni was facing an extended period of uncertain health and diminishing fortune, culminating in a premature death at the age of fifty-four on 19 July 1621. But – whatever the future might bring – he was now free to focus on unfinished business of a very unofficial kind.

The Mirror of Truth

Benedetto Blanis would have ample opportunity to look back on his nine months in Venice. On 26 September 1620, while in solitary confinement in the Bargello prison in Florence, he sent his patron an impassioned plea, compounding his current desperation with nostalgia for a lost golden age:

> If the tribunal calls on me to account for the time that I spent in Your Excellency's company reading, writing, and virtuously studying holy scriptures, you might do well to bring that most precious book, *The Mirror of*

Truth, which publicly demonstrates the veracity of all I say. In those print-ed pages of scholarly doctrine full of Hebraic, Greek, and Latin writings, they will see how you and I passed our time.[33]

Then on 19 January 1622 – still in prison – Benedetto registered a legal deposition:

In 1618, around the time of Fat Thursday [22 February], I travelled to Ven-ice having been summoned by His Excellency [Don Giovanni] … I stayed in his palace through the following September because he did not wish to let me go. Again and again, he had me look over a book – a work that he composed himself – because there were many authorities from Sacred Scripture written in His Excellency's own hand in the Hebrew language.[34]

For Benedetto, this abstruse work was the epitome of Don Giovanni's scholarly accomplishments:

From my own experience with Don Giovanni … and because I read to him in the Hebrew language, I always considered him to be a learned Prince in addition to his valour in arms. He had a solid grounding in all fields of knowledge (*tutte le scienze*) including philosophy, theology, and law … and he mastered various languages. I know that he was working on a compo-sition of his own called *The Mirror of Truth* (*Specchio della Verità*), since he showed it to me. This treated many and various fields of knowledge … and demonstrated clearly the attainments of that Prince. He showed it to me in the city of Venice during the three or four months that he was kept at home for medical treatment … It was in quarto, about six fingers thick.[35]

Benedetto was then a prisoner of the Inquisition, so he had good reason to emphasize 'Sacred Scripture' rather than the occult. Since their *Mir-ror of Truth* does not survive, we can only imagine its form and content. If it was six fingers thick in quarto, it was a substantial work, even in manuscript.

On 8 September 1618, shortly before Benedetto's return home, Fa-ther Orazio Morandi in Florence reminded Don Giovanni of a previous promise: 'I am eagerly awaiting … some copies of those sheets of alche-my and Kabbalah that Your Excellency is having printed.'[36] Morandi was Father General of the Vallombrosan Order, an accomplished as-trologer and alchemist, and one of Don Giovanni's most distinguished fellow travellers in the realm of the occult.

Nine months later, on 1 June 1619, Raffael Gualterotti considered the first samples of this work: 'I thank Your Most Illustrious Excellency for favouring me with the two prints which are drawn and engraved well and are full of noble mysteries. The Greek, however, is not done well and the Hebrew letters are faulty. For example, *amot* without the *aleph* signifies the contrary and has the force of *with* when placed above. In any case, many years have already passed since a book appeared in large folio format entitled *Teatrum divine sapiente*, with many engraved sheets containing many great mysteries with an abundance of Hebrew, Greek, and Latin verses. There one can find good and advanced knowledge. It was printed in Frankfurt.'[37]

Raffael Gualterotti was an admired writer, a celebrated astrologer, and an entrenched presence at the Medici Court. He was also a virulent enemy of Benedetto Blanis, so his slighting of the Hebrew was probably not coincidental. While damning their efforts with faint praise, Gualterotti lauded Heinrich Khunrath's *Amphitheatrum sapientiae aeternae christiano-cabbalisticum, divino-magicum, nec non physico-chemicum* (*Amphitheatre of Eternal Wisdom, Christian-Kabbalistic and Divine-Magical as well as Physical-Alchemical*). This compelling work of speculative alchemy (probably first printed in Hamburg, not Frankfurt, in 1595) offers a glimpse of what Don Giovanni and Benedetto could have had in mind for their own *Mirror of Truth*.

In treatises of this kind, the goal was to express a clear sequence of cosmic truths by combining diagrams and emblems with recondite inscriptions. This was a time-consuming and expensive process, since the ideators needed to work closely with each other and with their printmaker, monitoring each stage of design and execution. Even slight errors with characters and symbols (in Benedetto's Hebrew, for example) could have invalidated the entire mystical program.

Don Giovanni was closely involved with the leading printers and printmakers in Florence. At the time of the *Mirror*, he was helping Pietro Cecconcelli acquire type from Venice so that he could begin printing Greek and music.[38] Jacques Callot was producing a map of the *Siege of Gradisca* for Don Giovanni, publicizing the principal engagement of his war in the Friuli.[39] For reasons of practicality and discretion, *The Mirror of Truth* needed to be realized in Venice – but the project was evidently never completed, and then the work disappeared without a trace.[40]

After Don Giovanni's death, in 1621, the agents of the Tuscan Embassy in Venice struggled to bring order to his chaotic personal, political, and financial affairs. While dismantling his former residence, they

turned up cache after cache of startling items, including enough para-
phernalia to stock a sorcerers' warehouse. On 18 September 1621 Ambassador Niccolò Sacchetti shared the latest unsettling discovery with
Granducal Secretary Andrea Cioli:

> While organizing the sale of Don Giovanni's possessions, we came upon
> a strongbox and for the sake of His Excellency's memory and reputation,
> I regret having to send you the things that we found inside. We put eve-
> rything in a chest, especially a quantity of superstitious writings. I don't
> know if they have to do with Kabbalah or magic or perhaps both, but
> judging from the little that I saw while packing, these are troublesome
> items that could contaminate anyone who comes in contact.[41]

Sacchetti's strategy was to get Don Giovanni's amulets, charms, books,
charts, and manuscripts out of Venice as quickly as possible, avoiding
an itemized inventory at all cost. In Florence, the Medici regime – then
guided by the pietistic Christine de Lorraine and Maria Magdalena von
Habsburg – would know exactly how to manage troubles of this kind.
And that was presumably the last that anyone saw of the plates and
proofs of the *Mirror of Truth*.[42]

Ironically enough, this compelling title resurfaced in Venice only a
few years later on the cover of a very different sort of book. In 1626
Orazio Petrobelli, a local notary, published his own *Mirror of Truth*
(*Specchio di Verità*), and the author had a definite program that was neither Benedetto's nor Don Giovanni's: 'As Substantiated by Holy Scripture, by the Authority of the Rabbis, and by Cogent Reasoning, it is
Clearly Demonstrated that the Jews have Lost True Understanding of
the Holy Scripture. It is also Demonstrated that God is Triple in Person
but Unique in Essence, that the Messiah is both Man and God, and that
He Wished to Suffer and Die to Redeem Mankind...'[43]

At Home with Livia and Don Giovanni

In Venice, Benedetto resided in a noble palace on the Grand Canal –
outside any Ghetto.[44] He was part of the daily life of Don Giovanni's
household, which was also the household of Don Giovanni's notorious
consort Livia Vernazza:

> I saw how Signora Livia lived familiarly in His Excellency's palace [in
> Venice], eating at his table and served by all of his household servants and

courtiers, as if he and she were the same person. I remained there in His Excellency's palace [from February] through the month of September.[45]

Benedetto was at the same table, disregarding social convention and the Jewish dietary laws. 'I was constantly with His Lordship and Livia while I was in Venice ... eating and drinking with them.'[46] He had, in fact, become an all-purpose confidant in their unruly establishment, witnessing scenes that ranged from the inappropriate to the scandalous to the blatantly criminal.

Benedetto's host and presumably many of his host's friends were adepts of the occult. Don Giovanni was also a patron of the theatre and his house was full of actors, actresses, and their ilk:[47]

> In his household, Don Giovanni accorded Livia the status of wife and declared her to be his very own. On one occasion, she went out in a gondola with that actor (commediante) Flavio, who took her to another gondola belonging to various Milanese, where they drank together ... I don't know whether Flavio was with her or with these Milanese, but it was certainly Flavio who organized the encounter. Don Giovanni then asked me to take up the matter with Livia – as if I was doing this on my own, not letting on that His Lordship knew. I was meant to tell her that it was not appropriate for her to be taken around by some clown (buffone), considering her relationship with Don Giovanni and the declarations that he had made to her, as if she were his wife ... When I recounted all this to Livia, she burst out laughing and asked me who had informed His Lordship – which I didn't know.[48]

'Flavio' was the nome d'arte of Flaminio Scala, a celebrated Venetian actor-manager and the director of Don Giovanni's own Compagnia dei Confidenti. He was not himself the most obvious suspect for an amorous intrigue – already in his mid-sixties at the time of their aquatic excursion.[49]

'Actors, whores, and Jews' was a popular topos, and it certainly characterized Don Giovanni's eccentric ménage. Benedetto's hostess was a former whore or, at best, a formerly 'available woman.'[50] In any case, she still knew all the tricks of her trade – keeping her besotted lover in the perpetual throes of jealous passion: 'I was in the bedroom with Her Ladyship,' Benedetto recalled, 'when Don Giovanni came and knocked on the door of that room in the middle. His Lordship said to open up and Her Ladyship said not to. So I asked His Lordship what he wanted

me to do. "Obey her," he replied, "since she is mistress of the house."
Then he went away.'[51]

Scenes of this kind were anything but rare, with a Jew from the Ghetto in the midst of the action: 'It was not only in Venice that this happened but also in Florence. His Lordship would complain to her, "But
if Messer Benedetto can be there, why can't I?" She would reply to His
Lordship, "Messser Benedetto can see me however I am but I don't
want you to see me when I am not looking my best."'[52]

Even on the Jewish Sabbath, Benedetto might be found closeted with
Lady Livia:

> There was another occasion, a Saturday, when His Lordship was very
> busy writing up dispatches. Livia dug in her heels and insisted on going
> to Palvello [Don Giovanni's villa near Padua] but His Lordship resisted,
> citing his many obligations. When he finally saw that she was not going
> to let up, he threw together his dispatches as quickly as he could and gave
> orders to the various members of the household – who should stay [in
> Venice], who should go [with them to Palvello], and so on. He dressed [for
> the country] in a suit of beige goat-hair cloth (*baracane*) with silk bands,
> then he went to Her Ladyship and asked if she was ready to leave – and
> she replied that she no longer wanted to go. His Lordship begged her over
> and over again but she repeatedly refused. Then His Lordship, poor man,
> went down on his knees and protested that she was mocking him and that
> he had already given orders to the household.[53]

Don Giovanni was aging and ill and he was certainly enjoying – or at
least indulging – this erotically charged abuse more than was healthy.
'His Lordship was not well and his throat troubled him – swelling up
when he was angry. I had to go and bring him a glass of cold water,
which he drank in great quantity when he was angry.'[54]

What might seem privileged intimacy in some circumstances could
be seen as guilty knowledge in others – especially after Don Giovanni's
death, when the Florentine authorities were eager to cancel all traces
of the Vernazza régime. They began by annulling the annulment of her
first marriage to Battista Granara – invalidating her subsequent marriage to Don Giovanni and disinheriting their son. Benedetto Blanis
was an obvious 'person of interest,' despite his vague and unconvinc-
ing attempts to distance himself after the fact:

> I cannot say whether or not Don Giovanni was working to undo Signora

Livia's marriage [with Battista Granara] but, as I said previously, His Excellency wanted to overcome the sin of adultery [in his relationship with Livia]. On one occasion, Signora Livia showed me certain affidavits from Genoa, from three or four people – both men and women, if memory serves me. They attested that Signora Livia wept when she was married and stated that she did not wish to wed. I saw these affidavits, read them, and gave them back to Signora Livia. Then a few days later, she said to me – in more or less these words, 'Those affidavits are of no use because they were produced by the secular courts. They need to be done by the ecclesiastical courts.'[55]

Benedetto, it seems, was party to a good deal more than legal documents:

During the time that I stayed in Venice, one of Signora Livia's brothers was there. I don't know his name but I am sure that I could recognize him if I saw him. I found myself present while he was dealing with Antonio Ceccherelli. Among other topics, I heard Ceccherelli exhort him to find a way to free the aforementioned Livia – either by swearing a new affidavit or by killing her husband. However, I don't know how the brother replied or what agreement they might have reached. This was none of my business, and in any case, they soon withdrew so that I wouldn't hear.[56]

Antonio Ceccherelli was Livia's de facto secretary and he had been given a very full mandate to resolve the Battista Granara problem. Under stringent questioning, Benedetto eventually admitted that he had accompanied Ceccherelli to a tavern for a sub rosa strategy session with the Vernazza sibling – and he did not miss a word:

It seems to me that I went with Ceccherelli once or perhaps twice to an inn near the Rialto … I don't know the name of the innkeeper nor do I remember the sign … It was Ceccherelli who brought me to that inn and Livia's brother was there – but at the time, I didn't know that Ceccherelli intended to go to an inn nor why he wanted to go there … As I mentioned before, Ceccherelli discussed dissolving Livia's marriage … Yes sir, Ceccherelli reminded him about killing Livia's husband … 'I know what I need to do,' Livia's brother replied – but it was not clear if they had agreed on how to carry it out … No sir, I never heard Ceccherelli say that [he was acting on the order of Signor Don Giovanni].[57]

For all of Benedetto's omissions and reservations, this was dangerous business and he was right in the middle, whether he liked it or not. For him, Don Giovanni represented a boundless realm of wealth and power, intellectual liberation, and social access. But he was still a Jew from the Ghetto – playing a perilous game by other people's rules.

Fire at the Fair

'We arrived in Ferrara early this morning, which is Tuesday, but we didn't find the ambassador. So, we can expect him to appear this evening, on the road from Bologna.'[58] Benedetto Blanis wrote Don Giovanni dei Medici an emotional appeal on 21 August 1618 – the only surviving letter from his nine months in Venice.[59]

Benedetto had a sister to visit in Ferrara and a mysterious errand to transact. Luca Albizi, a ranking Tuscan diplomat, was making an overnight stop on his way to Venice,[60] and the Jew joined the welcoming party. Whatever Benedetto hoped to achieve,[61] his meeting was overwhelmed by a family catastrophe:

> I bitterly regret having come to Ferrara. Instead of rejoicing in the company of my sister, I find that I am here to weep with her in her misfortune. Her husband – my brother-in-law – was at the fair in Lugo di Romagna, which is a big and fine fair held every August on the Feast of the Madonna in a field that is like a vast marketplace. This year, alas, the entire fair went up in flames and was razed to its very foundations in only an hour ... All of the merchandise was destroyed and even the metals melted down, with an estimated loss of a million in gold.[62]

Ferrara had been one of the greatest Italian centres of Jewish life and culture until its annexation by the papacy in 1598. Many Jews then left, while others remained under increasingly difficult circumstances.[63] One of Benedetto's sisters[64] was married to a local merchant, Salamon Finzi, and the annual fair at Lugo was a major regional event that attracted both Jewish and gentile traders:[65]

> My sister's unfortunate husband had 2,000 scudi of his own merchandise with him. Even worse, he brought stock that was not yet paid for because he wanted to make a good show at the fair. So, he now owes three or four Jewish merchants an additional three or four hundred scudi. Considering

these circumstances, I beg Your Most Illustrious Excellency to write a letter of recommendation to the Papal Legate in Ferrara, Cardinal [Jacopo] Serra, asking him to grant my brother-in-law a respite for a number of years ... Even if he has nothing left, he is ready to scrimp and save day and night in order to satisfy those Jews who are his creditors. He only asks that they allow him a reasonable period of time and do not force him to flee.[66]

Having posted his letter, Benedetto quickly left town – following Luca Albizi back to Venice.

Florence

Benedetto's sojourn in Venice began with Don Giovanni's convalescence and ended with a dramatic worsening of his condition. On 15 September 1618 Ambassador Niccolò Sacchetti sent a grave message to Grand Duke Cosimo II:

We continually fear for the life of Signor Don Giovanni, and on Wednesday [12 September] the symptoms were so bad that I was ready to dispatch a courier to Your Highness. However, the members of his own household thought it premature to anticipate such bad news, so I held back. Last Sunday [9 September], His Excellency finally had that surgeon from Florence open the swelling at the middle of his throat, then the very next day he was attacked by a fierce fever and an inflammation of his entire chest. Now the fever seems to be abating but we are alarmed by occasional losses of blood from a burst or cut vein near the incision. Since the doctors dread a sudden hemorrhage, I decided to warn Your Highness by express messenger.[67]

This was not the moment for Don Giovanni to ponder arcane doctrine with a visiting Jew – on his presumed deathbed, with people fixated on his Christian soul.[68] He was surrounded by representatives of the Tuscan legation, observers from the Venetian government, a host of doctors, and selected priests. Captain Piero Capponi, one of Don Giovanni's oldest and closest friends, was sent from Florence[69] – to comfort him in his illness and (if worse came to worst) wrap up his affairs.

When Benedetto left Venice in mid-October, Don Giovanni was making a notable recovery – contrary to the best medical opinion – but his father Laudadio had suffered a major stroke:

I arrived in Florence on Wednesday [17 October] at lunch time, deluged by rain all the way from Bologna … I found my father in somewhat better shape, and he has recovered the use of his left side which he had lost entirely. He is still unable to speak and this is his chief handicap, although he expresses himself with gestures as best he can. He wants me continually at his side, and when I arrived, he held me in a tight embrace for a full hour, immediately asking with great emotion for news of Your Most Illustrious Excellency. He constantly complains about the doctors and he wants to drink good wine barely cut with water, so it is not easy to keep him happy. Still, I cannot help but admire his patience and endurance.[70]

Laudadio Blanis had always been a strong and decisive individual, so he did not adjust easily to his impaired state. Benedetto updated Don Giovanni several weeks later:

It brings tears to my eyes to see my father express his humble reverence for Your Most Illustrious Excellency in his mute way. He is watching even as I write this and has already kissed Your Excellency's signature twice, with tears and sighs that would make the stones weep. He gestures for me to request some remedy from you which would enable him to speak a few words. I ask Your Excellency to consider the plight of a man like my father, who always spoke so much and so well and is now struck dumb. Otherwise, he seems rather better and he came to listen to my sermon today for nearly an hour and a half.[71]

Benedetto was putting his life back on track after a tumultuous year. He was even ready to remarry, now that the anniversary of his first wife's death had passed. On 23 December 1618 he wrote Don Giovanni from the 'sweet and voluntary prison' of his home, where he and his male friends were celebrating his wedding 'according to the ancient Jewish law and rite.'[72]

Unfortunately, Benedetto's financial affairs were not flourishing and he was forced to borrow heavily from a Christian moneylender. Hoping to sell a consignment of gilded leather in Venice, he asked Don Giovanni's help. 'Business here is very slow and there is no other way to turn a profit … which will allow me to buy bread for myself and my children.'[73]

Don Giovanni instructed Benedetto to retrieve the books of astrology, alchemy, and Kabbalah that he had hidden before his recent trip – but there were difficulties, as the Jew explained on 6 January 1619:

Before I went to Venice to serve Your Most Illustrious Excellency, I had my father secure all of my prohibited writings and books. He concealed them in two different places but I only had to go to one of those when I first returned ... and I already knew where it was. Again and again, I asked my father about the second hiding place but we were unable to make ourselves understood. After receiving your latest letter, I tried once more and – thank God – my father finally understood me. His speech is still incomprehensible, so he took me there in person, and I am now sending you what you request, accompanied by my eagerness to serve you.[74]

For Benedetto Blanis, banned books and forbidden writings were an essential stock in trade. They were also his key to a fascinating and fast-moving world outside the Ghetto – one that he shared with some of the most powerful Christians in the land. There were thrilling discoveries, secret deals, comic misadventures, and breathtaking escapes – all for a man who lived life on the edge, by necessity or else by choice.

chapter 10

The Magic Circle

Fellow Travellers

The autumn of 1618 was a portentous time for devotees of the occult. In October, when Benedetto Blanis left Don Giovanni dei Medici in Venice, his patron had just survived a near brush with death and was more focused than ever on the secret world of the arcane. Back in Florence, local adepts were pondering the ultimate fate of the Medici dynasty as Grand Duke Cosimo II drifted from one medical emergency to the next. Meanwhile, three major comets were sighted in only two months, with the last and most dramatic on 31 November. Raffael Gualterotti, the doyen of Florentine astrologers, recorded 'an enormous and terrifying comet' that foretold 'the overthrow of nations and grave illnesses.'[1] Don Giovanni's major-domo Cosimo Baroncelli promptly relayed this news to Venice and Don Giovanni ordered Benedetto to forward the Grand Duke's latest horoscope, cast by Gualterotti's astrological rival Orazio Morandi.[2]

The Blanis family, in its lesser sphere, was also veering from crisis to crisis, dogged by ill health and economic adversity.[3] Benedetto, meanwhile, forged ahead with his esoteric pursuits, tracking down curious and forbidden writings for his patron in Venice. On 23 December 1618, in the midst of his own wedding celebrations, he dispatched a hasty note to Don Giovanni: 'Messer Ascanio Canacci tells me that he found the fourth part of Cornelio Agrippa written in pen.'[4] The Jew offered an update on 30 December, the moment he broke out of his 'sweet and voluntary prison':

In my last letter, I told Your Most Illustrious Excellency that I have a friend here [Ascanio Canacci] who has found a handwritten copy of the fourth part of Cornelio. Now I can add that he has also found a small book in Hebrew in rabbinical script titled *Book of Raimondo* [Ramón Llull], *Regarding the Secrets of the Lapis* [the Philosopher's Stone]. From what I can deduce, having seen it only briefly, this is the key to another book by Raimondo although I am not sure which one. It demonstrates that Raimondo was writing secretly in a coded language and offers a key for accessing that other book.[5]

On 6 January 1619 Benedetto pulled his own stash of forbidden books and writings out of secret storage with the help of his disabled father Laudadio.[6] A week later he promised to track down the *Fourth Part of Cornelius*,[7] noting that Canacci was staying at Cosimo Baroncelli's villa near Strada in Chianti.[8] He also offered to translate the Hebrew *Key to Raimondo* into Italian, if his patron wished. 'There is no need to wait for me to become a widower again, I assure you. I am always ready to respond to any request, since you are my absolute master and the master of everything I possess.'[9]

There are many shadowy figures moving in the background of Benedetto Blanis' letters – mostly Florentine devotees of astrology, alchemy, and Kabbalah. We see Jews and Christians, Medici courtiers and ranking churchmen, miscellaneous scholars, and failed magicians living by their wits. However little or much these people had in common, they were all fellow travellers in the realm of the occult.

The Late Cosimo Ridolfi

On 19 January 1619, three months after his return to Florence, Benedetto Blanis made a devastating announcement to Don Giovanni dei Medici:

> Your Most Illustrious Excellency has lost a faithful servant and I have lost a loving and affectionate friend in the person of Cavaliere Cosimo Ridolfi. He had been out at his villa for more than four months, so I did not have the chance to see him. I understand that he was struck down yesterday and then died during the night at the ninth hour [2 a.m.], suffocated by congestion. His wife and son are still at the villa.[10]

Cosimo Ridolfi was a commanding figure in his own little circle, although virtually unknown outside it. On that same day, Cosimo Baroncelli expressed his personal sorrow to Don Giovanni:

With pain in my heart and tears in my eyes, I must inform Your Excellency of the death of a dear and intimate servant, Signor Cosimo Ridolfi, while at his villa at Meleto. Abruptly and without warning, he was suffocated by an overflow of congestion in his chest. Our Blessed Lord, however, allowed him the grace of confession before he died, so we can infer that he was granted true pardon and repose. Father General Don Orazio [Morandi] spoke with me recently and told me that he had very strong premonitions regarding this year in Signor Cosimo's life and that he had warned him in person. Alas, we now see that Don Orazio was not wrong – although he would dearly love to have been wrong in this particular case.[11]

Cosimo Ridolfi was born in 1570 into the upper sphere of the Florentine aristocracy, son of Piero Ridolfi and Maddalena Salviati. In 1594 he became a Knight of Saint Stephen (thus the title of 'Cavaliere') and in his youth married Alessandra daughter of Alessandro Capponi, who died childless in 1595. Cosimo subsequently married Laudomine daughter of Giuliano Ricasoli, who gave him one child, Niccolò, who was six years old at the time of his death.[12] The Cavaliere had a residence in Florence and an important agricultural holding at Meleto (south of the city, near Castelfiorentino), where he and his family spent much of their time.

Ridolfi's sudden demise offered a chilling reminder of human mortality to those around him. After many years in the outer reaches of astrology, alchemy, and Kabbalah, they liked to think that their fellow traveller had kept his options open – leaving this world, albeit hastily, as a good Catholic. On 26 January 1619 Don Giovanni shared some more or less pious reflections with Cosimo Baroncelli, before taking ultimate refuge in astrological science:

I am older than Signor Cosimo, so I am now performing the offices for him that I thought he would eventually perform for me. I will never cease to pray God for his pardon and repose, as I would for a beloved brother, since I can desire no greater good for myself. Ah, Signor Cosimo, *ad hoc nati sumus* (it is for this that we were born)! ... Events like these must teach us to live worthily, hoping to rejoin our friend in glory when our own time comes. If Father General Don Orazio has the root of my horoscope, I would like him to tell me what he thinks about the cycle of the current year and the next year as well – and if he doesn't have the root, I will send it. When it comes to our own interests, none of us can easily discern the truth, so I will be very grateful to the Father General.[13]

Unlike many of his class, the Cavaliere did not pursue a public career of any note – diplomatic, ecclesiastic, or military. Instead, he lived the life of a rustic magus, as he described to Don Giovanni dei Medici on 25 June 1618 – using only the most lightly coded language:

> I did not reply to Your Excellency's letter sooner because I am taking my leisure at a villa far from the city ... I miss your conversation greatly, since I derived much benefit from it, back when I had the good fortune to serve you ... Your Excellency could remedy my loss – at least in part – by sharing some of your noble studies with me by letter ... I am thinking in particular of certain sorts of studies that you know well – studies to which I devote much of my time and take much pleasure. They allow me to see certain kinds of things – things denied to those in the everyday world who have only a lukewarm understanding and cannot navigate beyond the Pillars of Hercules, *sed deb.is havemus quia sapienti pauca* (which is due to us, the wise ones, for whom only a few words suffice). I appeal to you, great lord that you are, and ask you to favour me with news and information. Open the treasure chest of your sovereign intellect, for the sake of one who serves you with his heart and soul. This will be a great consolation to me, since I live the life of a hermit, sweet although this life may be.[14]

If the Villa of Meleto was Cosimo Ridolfi's magic island – in the uncharted seas beyond the Pillars of Hercules – who were the courtiers that gravitated around him? First, there were gentlemen adepts like Don Giovanni dei Medici, Cosimo Baroncelli,[15] and Orazio Morandi. Then there were eager freelancers – people hustling to earn a living – like Benedetto Blanis and Ascanio Canacci. Conspicuous by their absence from Ridolfi's entourage were two of the three pre-eminent astrologers then operating at the Medici Court: Raffael Gualterotti and Galileo Galilei.

Gualterotti, Morandi, and Galileo had been sniping at each other for years,[16] and Don Giovanni was quick to cast the latter as little more than a figure of fun. On 20 February 1616, at the height of the first Galileo trial in Rome,[17] Don Giovanni meditated on the advent of spring – and the rise and fall of his overrated compatriot:

> The weather is becoming milder as the moon advances. Galileo's propositions (*le preposizioni galileiche*) are based on nothing and will return to nothing, although they are propounded in a way that can easily deceive

people. Soon, it will become obvious that light things move and heavy things remain in place. Florence will thus stay in the Arno Valley in Tuscany and the Saint Gotthard Mountain will stay at the border between the Swiss and the Italians. What I want to say is that the snow is vanishing there [in Florence] as it is here [in Venice] and once again, couriers will be able to do their job without things going amiss.[18]

On 21 July 1618, just before the autumn comets, Morandi sent Don Giovanni an anti-Galilean diatribe, fully expecting a sympathetic response: 'I am sending Your Excellency two compositions, one by Galileo regarding the tides of the sea and one written in reply by my friend from Forlì. With your excellent judgment, you will be able to discern which of them is right and which is wrong.' Galileo Galilei's composition was the *Discorso sopra il flusso e il reflusso del mare* (*Discourse Regarding the Ebb and Flow of the Sea*) of 1615. A year later, Morandi's friend, the priest Francesco Ingoli (from Ravenna, not nearby Forlì), authored the anti-Copernican and anti-Galileian response, *De situ et quiete Terrae contra Copernici Systema Disputatio* (*On the Location and Stability of the Earth, Argument against the System of Copernicus*).

After the three comets of 1618, it was once again open season for stargazers throughout Italy. Galileo, however, did his best to remain above the fray. He was now keen to distance himself from practical astrology – the influence of the heavens on human affairs. For him, the chief issue was the location of the comets and their place in the world order, with the ultimate question of whether the sun orbited the earth or the earth orbited the sun. In Rome, the Jesuit Orazio Grassi immediately launched a series of lectures and publications promoting the old earth-centred view.[19] In Florence, Mario Guiducci – Galileo's pupil and designated spokesman – replied. In his *Discorso delle comete* (*Discourse on the Comets*) of 1619, largely ghostwritten by Galileo, Guiducci focused exclusively on technical matters – the observation of the stars, the use of the telescope, and the principles of physics. He pointedly referred to their constituency as *astronomi* not *astrologi*, an unusual distinction at that time.

The problem of separating astronomers from astrologers – or pure from applied science – would not have occurred to subsidiary members of the Ridolfi circle like Benedetto Blanis and Ascanio Canacci. They were merely second-stringers eager to get into the game, any way they could, and for them the game was practical astrology, practical alchemy, and Kabbalistic magic.

Ascanio Canacci was the quintessential freelancer, someone whom even a Jew in the Ghetto could view with tolerant amusement. Benedetto first mentioned him to Don Giovanni on 16 August 1615, treating him as an outright charity case:

> The priest Don Ascanio Canacci arrived in Florence with little money and no evident prospects. To me it seemed an act of charity to give him a bed in a room in your house as his first refuge, without rent since the room would otherwise remain empty ... Now it seems that Don Ascanio wants to keep company for a month or two with a brother of Saint Stephen, the one who makes those iron rings to prevent epilepsy. I therefore told him that he would need to take this up with [your major-domo] Signor Cosimo Baroncelli.[20]

Don Ascanio was the oldest member of the troupe (over seventy at the time of Cosimo Ridolfi's death[21]), an endearingly humble cleric and evidently the mascot of their magic circle. He eked out a marginal living as an agent or runner, brokering the sale of esoteric items. Also, he was a persistent house guest in the palaces and villas of the gentlemen adepts. By 1605 Canacci was already operating as a middleman for both Cosimo Ridolfi and Don Antonio dei Medici, Don Giovanni's nephew and a passionate alchemist. Don Antonio had offered to publish a curious work by Zefiriele Thomaso Bovio in Verona, entitled *The Theatre of the Infinite* (*Il teatro dell'infinito*), and Ascanio Canacci, then in Venice, negotiated the details with Cosimo Ridolfi in Florence.[22]

There was at least one other figure in the Ridolfi circle who was neither a gentleman adept nor an ingenious free-lancer – Cosimo's widow, the lady Laudomine Ricasoli Ridolfi. Marooned on the magic island against her will, she had entered into marriage as a patrician wife and mother in the normal Catholic style – not as the consort of a reclusive necromancer with strange habits and appalling friends. 'She took her husband's dedication to these studies very badly,'[23] Benedetto Blanis would have frequent cause to complain. 'Even after her husband's death, the lady still hates his comrades, out of sheer contrariness.'[24]

The Workshop

Barely a week after Cosimo Ridolfi's death, the freelancers were already hard at work, as Benedetto explained to Don Giovanni on 27 January 1619:

Don Ascanio has been ill at Signor Baroncelli's villa, aggravated by the loss of so great a friend as Signor Ridolfi. When it comes to matters of health, Don Ascanio can usually stand up to any task if he is not suffering from lack of food, and his chief complaint is a bit of gout. Unless the owner greatly values the *Chiave Raimondina* (*Key to Ramón Llull*), I think that we can have the original for 8 or 10 scudi. If you want a copy in the vulgar tongue [Italian], it will be necessary for me to read and have someone else write. My brother Salamone can do the writing, so there won't be any expense and I won't have to trust anyone else.[25]

The elderly priest soon left the Villa Baroncelli at Mezza Strada and re-established himself in Florence, staying with a tailor who gave him food and a place to sleep for 4 scudi a month.[26] Meanwhile, Benedetto's single room in the Florentine Ghetto did triple duty. He lived there with his new wife and the daughters of his previous marriage; he preached his weekly sermons; and he launched an occult scriptorium, enlisting members of his own family and various Christians – usually Catholic priests. At the outset, there were two works in production, both discovered by Ascanio Canacci: the *Chiave Raimondina* (*Key to Ramón Llull*) and the *Quarta Parte di Cornelio* (*Fourth Part of Cornelius*).[27]

Ramón Llull (1235–1315), known as *Doctor Illuminatus*, was a Spanish Franciscan philosopher, poet, and theologian. Deeply engaged with Arab culture, he devoted the last forty years of his life to the conversion of the Moors and was eventually stoned to death in Tunis at the age of seventy. Llull also had close Jewish contacts, and he is generally recognized as the initiator of Christian Kabbalah – the first to channel elements of the Hebrew mystical tradition into the mainstream of Catholic speculation. Llull was an astonishingly prolific writer, producing some three hundred works in Latin and Catalan. Numerous other compositions, mostly of an occult nature, emerged over the centuries and were associated with his name. Strangely enough, with the rise of Christian Kabbalah and its increasing identification with alchemy, astrology, and magic, Ramón Llull the Magus became the alter ego of Ramón Llull the Catholic Theologian. Even Llull's authentic writings could have a weird afterlife, honoured as magical scripts in their own right – as in the the the case of Benedetto and Ascanio's *Book of Raimondo Regarding the Secrets of the Lapis*.

The *Lapis Philosophorum* or 'Philosopher's Stone' was the ultimate goal of all seekers of arcane knowledge and power. On the material level, the *Lapis* was the alchemical substance that could turn base metals into gold and engender untold wealth. More sublimely, it could bring spiritual enlightenment, which was the true object of all higher magicians. Some Jew or Gentile,[28] it would seem, had imposed a Kabbalistic meta-language on a real or alleged work by Ramón Llull, hoping to extract the final secret of alchemy through a sequence of numerological permutations. For only 8 or 10 scudi, this 'small book in Hebrew in rabbinical script' was a very great bargain – if it delivered even a fraction of what it promised.

The other work in production in the Blanis scriptorium was the *Fourth Part of Cornelius* – referring to Heinrich Cornelius von Nettesheim from Cologne (1486–1535), usually known as Cornelius Agrippa.[29] In the course of his brief but eventful life, Cornelius passed through various courts and universities – without stopping for long or publishing much. His fame was almost entirely posthumous, propelled by one of his works, *The Occult Philosophy in Three Books* (*De occulta philosophia libri tres*). In 1509, at the age of twenty-three, Cornelius sent the manuscript to his teacher and mentor Johannes Trithemius, Abbot of Sponheim, the most authoritative occult scholar of the day. Trithemius read it with great enthusiasm, 'I wondered ... that you being so young should penetrate into such secrets as have been hid from most learned men.'[30]

In the First Book, *On Natural Magic*, Cornelius Agrippa described the material world – running through the hierarchy of created things from lower phenomena (like stones, metals, plants, and animals) to superior phenomena (like the elements and the stars). In the Second Book, *On Celestial Magic*, he defined the principles that structure nature, with particular attention to mathematics, numerology, musical harmony, and astrology. Then in the Third Book, *On Ceremonial Magic*, he explained how to control nature through ritual practices, including many derivations from Jewish Kabbalah. The *Occult Philosophy* remained unpublished for twenty-two years, until Cornelius issued a Latin edition in Antwerp in 1531. This immediately brought down the wrath of both the ecclesiastical and the temporal authorities, and in 1533, the beleaguered author escaped to France, fleeing a death sentence for heresy pronounced by Emperor Charles V. Cornelius Agrippa lived the last two years of his life more or less on the run, then in 1559 his writings were universally condemned by the Inquisition in its first *Index of Prohibited Authors and Books*.

As is often the case with banned books, Heinrich Cornelius von Nettesheim's *Occult Philosophy* became a perennial best-seller, spawning numerous translations and imitations. By the time of Blanis, Canacci, and Don Giovanni, it had figured for nearly a century as the most authoritative compendium of occult knowledge in Europe. Along the way, it was 'largely responsible for the mistaken association of the Kabbalah in the Christian world with numerology and witchcraft'[31] – a mistaken association that many Jews had come to share.

In spite of its runaway success, *The Occult Philosophy in Three Books* was notably lacking as a sorcerer's manual, offering general principles rather than clear instructions. This was remedied a few decades after Cornelius Agrippa's death by the spurious *Fourth Book,* which Benedetto Blanis had in hand during the winter of 1618–19. On 10 February 1619 he notified Don Giovanni: 'Don Ascanio has returned from the villa safe and well and I immediately arranged to see the *Fourth Book of Cornelius*. I have already gotten my brother Salamone to begin copying it, and we will copy it entirely before I return the original. In the meantime, I am trying to get my hands on the *Key to Raimondo*. Salamone and I will then copy this with all possible diligence and send it to you as quickly as we can.'[32]

Father Ascanio Canacci soon pulled up stakes in Florence and moved on, dying in Siena in late April.[33] The work of the Blanis family scriptorium progressed fitfully at times. Benedetto was unable to do his own copying (somewhat surprisingly, since he wrote his own letters[34]), and Salamone soon gave up on the *Fourth Book of Cornelius* (he did not know Latin, not having the crossover education that his older brother enjoyed). Benedetto then made a terrible miscalculation, enlisting someone from outside their circle to complete the work, 'a priest who is a friend and confidant of mine.' This friend and confidant lost his nerve and blew Benedetto's cover – with disastrous results.[35]

The man was a priest, but that was not the chief problem – priests were often fellow travellers, Orazio Morandi and Ascanio Canacci to name only two.[36] Along with their theological training, many clerics acquired a taste, even a compulsion, for mystic power in its more extreme forms. What mattered most, in the perilous world of Benedetto Blanis, was absolute secrecy born of absolute loyalty. When it got down to it, he could only trust people who were as dependent as he was on Don Giovanni dei Medici.

The Apprentice

On 17 May 1619 Benedetto Blanis heralded a new arrival in their magic circle:

I have some news to share with Your Most Illustrious Excellency regarding a young man named Ferdinando, son of that surgeon who once treated you. He reads Greek very well and can study any book in that language, although he cannot speak or compose verses with the same proficiency as in Latin. In addition, this Ferdinando is well grounded in the Hebrew language, knows how to draw fortifications, taking measurements by sight, and has even studied medicine for some months. I know all of this because he has already become my master of Euclid [Euclidian geometry] and my disciple in Hebrew. He seems a most worthy person to serve Your Most Illustrious Excellency, and he is eager to do so. I can further recommend him because he writes well in ink on paper.

In a postscript, Benedetto remembered to add an essential point, 'He also delights in astrology.'[37] This was a concise portrait of a perennial type that Don Giovanni knew well – the aspiring scholar of modest extraction with an amorphous range of skills and scant means of support. Such poor erudites were endlessly ingenious in their search for patronage, and their letters of petition and recommendation fill the archive of every princely and noble house in Europe.

Ferdinando's qualifications were scarcely news to Don Giovanni dei Medici, since it was he who sent the young man to Benedetto in the first place. On 20 April 1619 Don Giovanni had been approached by 'Luca Magnani, Surgeon from Impruneta, now at the Santissima Annunziata.'[38] In the scheme of contemporary medicine, surgeons were low-level practitioners whose skills in cutting, scraping, bleeding, cupping, and leeching were unhampered by university instruction:

In Florence some years ago, Your Excellency deigned to have me treat the callus from which you were suffering. At that time, you did me innumerable favours, although these were not all as successful as we had hoped. The greatest of these favours, in my mind, was your generous offer to protect and assist me in any situation ... and I would now like to avail myself of your offer on behalf of my son Ferdinando. He is a youth of twenty-eight years, and he would like to be assigned the Church of Quintole[39] which has an annual income of 120 scudi ... For fear of sounding proud or boastful, I will only tell Your Excellency that my son is a practitioner of letters, especially Latin and Greek, and a scholar of Euclid and astrology ... The Most Serene Patron [Grand Duke Cosimo II] had cause to take notice of him last January when my son presented him with an astrological discourse regarding His Highness' birth.[40]

Ferdinando Magnani's astrological discourse was evidently an unsolic-
ited attempt to attract the favourable 'notice' of the ailing grand duke.
However, the competition was fierce, with other such offerings from
Galileo Galilei, Don Orazio Morandi, and (probably) Raffael Gualterotti. While Don Giovanni was ready and willing to help the son of his surgeon, his options were limited since Ferdinando was not an ordained
priest. Luca Magnani summed up the situation on 11 May 1619:

> My son is not a priest as you seem to imagine, although he is twenty-eight
> years old and has worn the habit for more than twenty of those years. This
> is because he lacks the means with which to be ordained, since I am poor
> and he has had no one to protect him. Also, his mastery of Greek letters
> is not yet at the level you assume and I mentioned this only because he is
> now applying himself diligently and can achieve what is required in a few
> months ... I place myself entirely in Your Excellency's hands, if you could
> make it possible for this young man to say Mass.[41]

The evident solution – evident at least to Don Giovanni – was to ar-
range a period of preparatory study[42] with a Jew in the Ghetto. Then, as
Benedetto reported on 15 June 1619, the surgeon's son quickly emerged
as the new copyist in his aspiring scriptorium:

> I would be a sage mathematician if I could make the same progress in
> mathematics that my scholar is making in the Hebrew language. He is
> already beginning to understand it somewhat and will finish the gram-
> mar course in a month or so. Then I will give him some practice in read-
> ing without points [vowels], since that will prove useful when it comes
> to those writings. Helping me copy the *Chiave Raimondina* (*Key to Ramón
> Llull*) will be a good exercise in reading rabbinical script without points,
> and this will also allow Your Excellency to review his work. I do not doubt
> that he will succeed, since we have been applying ourselves assiduously
> ever since Your Excellency let us know your intention.[43]

After many years of trial and hardship, Ferdinando Magnani saw his
fortune made. On 10 August 1619 he enthusiastically thanked Don Giovanni dei Medici:

> I will say no more regarding the favour that Your Excellency has shown
> me by way of Signor Benedetto Blanes, promising to welcome me, protect
> me, and bring me to the priesthood as soon as I master the Greek and He-

brew languages … In three months at most, God willing, I should finish my course of study. Meanwhile, I am awaiting Your Excellency's gracious commands. You will tell me whether I should come to serve you [in Venice] or else remain in Florence for the winter, in order to improve my familiarity with these languages. That would perhaps be best, since I would then be ready to apply myself to the study of Arabic once I head north.[44]

Arabic, the priesthood, and a trip to Venice, all in the service of Don Giovanni dei Medici… The surgeon's son would have done well to cast his own horoscope before making any further plans.

chapter eleven

Curious and Forbidden Books

Passover and Easter

It was sundown on 15 Nissan 5379 – the evening of Friday, 29 March 1619, according to the Gregorian calendar.[1] Benedetto Blanis and his family were gathering for their annual Passover Seder in the Florentine Ghetto. Meanwhile, Jews in every community around the world marked their ancient deliverance from slavery in Egypt and their birth as a distinct nation.[2]

Catholics – at this same moment – were concluding their observance of Good Friday, the anniversary of Christ's death, and preparing for the long vigil that would welcome His rebirth on Easter Sunday. This signalled the end of nearly seven weeks of introspection and spiritual cleansing (Lent), beginning on Ash Wednesday (13 February) then building to a crescendo during Holy Week. Palm Sunday (24 March) commemorated Christ's entry into Jerusalem, Good Friday (29 March) the Crucifixion, and Easter (31 March) the Resurrection.

For Catholics, Holy Week offered a tangible recreation of Christ's last days on earth – taking the believer step by step through the inexorable cycle of the Passion and fostering an intense personal identification with the suffering Redeemer. This process of spiritual renewal was traditionally accompanied by waves of anti-Hebraic zeal, often expressed in violence and bloodshed. The Jews were the irreprobate killers of Christ, as the Church asserted over the centuries, even if their horrific deicide was part of a divinely ordained plan.

In 663, nearly a thousand years before the time of Benedetto Blanis, the Fourth Council of Toledo ruled that 'Jews and Moslems of both sexes ... must not be seen in public on the day of the Passion, nor go about boldly in scorn of the Creator.'[3] By the late Middle Ages, no European Jew in his or her right mind would have set foot out of doors on Good Friday for fear of retribution. In Florence and other Italian cities, there were fiery public sermons throughout Lent and Holy Week, usually delivered by Franciscan preachers – calling down the wrath of God on the Jewish population and demanding their expulsion or worse. The Florentine diarist Pietro Parenti recorded in April 1493, 'With the coming of Holy Week, the preachers were heating things up, saying that the Jews needed to be removed ... Those in the government here were not pleased and they tried to quiet these preachers – but on Easter the preachers insisted on having their own way.'[4]

Meanwhile, there was the infamous 'Blood Libel.' The Jews, it was popularly believed, shared the Christian compulsion to re-enact the martyrdom of Christ but from their own diabolical point of view – through the shedding of innocent Christian blood, especially the blood of children. Entire Jewish communities were devastated in the wake of the falsified ritual murders of Simon of Trent on Holy Thursday of 1475 and Lorenzino of Marostica on Good Friday of 1485. During Holy Week of 1554 a Christian boy was found crucified in a Roman cemetery and a massacre barely averted, although the known perpetrators were not, in fact, Jewish.

Anti-Hebraic sentiment did not reach this fever pitch in Florence during the lifetime of Benedetto Blanis, but Holy Week was still an excellent time for Jews to tread softly around Christian sensibilities. The rigours of Catholic observance ebbed and flowed according to the liturgical calendar – as Benedetto knew well, when he chose to remember.

Days of Scruples

Even during Lent, Benedetto Blanis did not keep a low profile. On 10 March 1619 he offered Don Giovanni a running update on his activities:

> Yesterday in the house of Signor Filippo Capponi, I took part in a debate that lasted four hours with the preacher from Santa Maria Novella and with the theologian of the Capponi family, regarding a sermon of his to which he had invited us ... I therefore hope that Your Most Illustrious Excellency will excuse me when it comes to my current work on that book by Cornelio [Cornelius Agrippa] and the one by Raimondo [Ramón Llull] that I also plan to do. This might take some time, since I cannot work on my own, but I will move things along as quickly and as skilfully as I can.[5]

After Cosimo Ridolfi's death, on 19 January 1619, the big question among his cohorts was the fate of his library – a lovingly assembled collection of arcane treasures. His widow Laudomine Ricasoli Ridolfi was hostile to the occult, as Benedetto reminded Don Giovanni on 24 March (Palm Sunday): 'I will give my fullest attention to the matter of Signora Laudomine's books. She took her husband's dedication to such studies .very badly, so I will focus on the idea of removing this same temptation from her son by selecting the most curious books and getting them out of his way.'[6]

Benedetto Blanis was never at a loss for strategies – particularly when dodging his great nemesis, the Inquisition. For years, he had been walking a tightrope between the Catholic authorities and his Medici patron, and now he was in imminent danger of tumbling off:

> In regard to the Inquisitor, you proved yourself a most accomplished astrologer. As you forecast, it is now necessary for Your Excellency to acknowledge openly that I am working in your service – especially when it comes to books. I wanted that book by Cornelio [the Fourth Part of Cornelius Agrippa's *Occult Philosophy*] to be copied quickly and well, so I passed it on to a priest who is a friend and confidant of mine. However, he brought it back to me on Saturday morning after copying only five pages and he made a scruple of it – telling me that he needed to confess to the Inquisitor and ask his permission to continue. Unfortunately, my brother [Salamone] doesn't know Latin, and even if I read out loud what he needs to write, it is difficult for him to avoid errors. I will, however, think of a way to do what needs to be done as expeditiously as possible.[7]

The words *scrupolo* in Italian and *scruple* in English come from the Latin *scrupulus*, a small sharp, or pointed, stone. A 'scruple' is thus a constant irritant and a source of spiritual discomfort, an 'unfounded apprehension and consequently unwarranted fear that something is a sin which, as a matter of fact, is not.'[8] Benedetto Blanis and Don Giovanni dei Medici were refreshingly free of scruples, but this was not always the case with those around them – particularly during Holy Week.

Benedetto normally approached obstacles at full speed, but even he opted for the better part of valour on 29 March 1619 – Good Friday and the eve of Passover:

> This is the week when religious scruples usually emerge, especially among widows, so I did not want to discuss the books with Signora Lau-

domine. Also, I wanted to await your instructions on how to proceed with the Inquisitor. My friend who was copying the book went to him and confessed, indicating my first name but not my family name. Now a week has passed and I have heard nothing further, so perhaps nothing will come of all this ... As soon as these holidays are over, there will be no lack of copyists – ones who are unhampered by scruples or else have permission. So, we will complete this work, in some way or other. Meanwhile, my brother Salamone and I have started on the *Raimondina* [*Key to Ramón Llull*] and this is more nearly under our control, since it is going into the vulgar tongue [Italian].[9]

Easter and Passover came and went. On the plus side, Benedetto heard only vague rumblings from the Father Inquisitor. On the minus side, he heard nothing at all from Don Giovanni dei Medici. The Jew offered an anxious reminder on 7 April:

In regard to the Inquisitor, it is necessary for you to acknowledge openly that I am working in your service. That priest who was copying Cornelius started having scruples, and he brought the book back to me – so at least I didn't lose the book, which could easily have happened if he examined his conscience a bit sooner. Then he went and confessed to the Inquisitor and identified me by name – so I am lucky not to have been thrown into solitary confinement with all of my books sequestered. The shadow of Your Most Illustrious Excellency perhaps saved me, since the Inquisitor asked our governors [the Jewish governors of the Ghetto] about me and they said ... that I was your servant. The Inquisitor told the governors that he wants to talk with me, at my convenience – so we are delaying as best we can, until I hear back from you and others.[10]

Having waited out 'these days of scruples,' Benedetto was ready to forge ahead with Cosimo Ridolfi's widow. The lady Laudomine told him more or less what he wanted to hear – promising to send her late husband's books to Florence from their Villa at Meleto for appraisal and sale.[11]

Benedetto's great patron was less obliging. Don Giovanni dei Medici would not be going head-to-head with the Catholic authorities, since that was the whole point of using a Jewish agent. Benedetto had no choice but to make the best of a terrifying situation, as he announced on 14 April 1619: 'I received Your Excellency's gracious response to my last two letters, and I was pleased to learn that these were not lost in transit

... I now understand that you are loath to get involved with monks, so I decided to call on the Inquisitor this very morning.'[12]

Holy Cross

The Inquisition had its Florentine headquarters at Santa Croce – Holy Cross – and for a Jew, there was no more daunting prospect than a visit to that notorious place. For centuries, the great Franciscan convent had been a hotbed of anti-Hebraic activity, and its church was the setting for some of the most inflammatory Lenten and Holy Week sermons. The Inquisition, however, was a relatively recent arrival – with its examination rooms, its prisoners, its anonymous investigators, and its relentless bureaucratic efficency.

In 1542 Pope Paul IV founded the *Holy Roman Congregation and Universal Inquisition, known as the Holy Office* (*Sacra Congregatio Romanae et universalis Inquisitionis seu sancti officii*). Its immediate task was to eradicate the dire influence of Protestantism in Catholic lands while functioning as the final court of appeal in matters of faith. The Holy Office (usually identified as the Roman Inquisition, to distinguish it from the older Spanish Inquisition) combined investigative, deliberative, judicial, and pastoral functions – gathering evidence of heretical practice, weighing the guilt or innocence of accused parties, and sentencing those who committed errors to salutary penances for the good of their souls. The Pope presided personally over its operation, coordinating the activities of the Cardinals General who served as the chief judges and advisers.[13]

Outside Rome, the principal agents of the Holy Office were the Father Inquisitors, sent to various cities to ensure local orthodoxy. Their jurisdiction extended only to erring Catholics – at least in theory – leaving Jews to observe their religion as allowed by civil law. In practice, however, there were many ways that Jews could fall foul of the Inquisition. They might be accused of corrupting the faith or morals of Catholics, a charge that could be fitted to almost any situation. They might be denounced as lapsed Catholics – and judaizing after baptism was punishable by death. In any ghetto, there were men and women with complicated life stories, perhaps including Christian assimilation in other lands.

One activity fell squarely within the mandate of the Holy Office – the regulation of books and writings. In 1558 a special Congregation of the Inquisition prepared a list of works detrimental to the Catholic faith or

Catholic morals. Then, a year later, it was published as the first *Index of Prohibited Authors and Books* (*Index auctorum et librorum prohibitorum*), with many editions to follow.[14] In each territory, it was up to the local Father Inquisitor to stop the circulation of proscribed material or at least remove it from impressionable readers. It was also his job to rule on new works presented for publication.

Monsignor Cornelio Priatoni was Father Inquisitor in Florence – the man that Benedetto Blanis faced on 14 April 1619. Inquisitors were awe-inspiring figures in their own jurisdictions, but their powers were tightly regulated by the administration in Rome. In public, they were seldom identified by name – the Father Inquisitor was simply the Father Inquisitor, reinforcing the ideal of an impersonal bureaucracy under divine auspices.

Thanks to a rare memo in the Archepiscopal Archive in Florence, we know more than usual about Cornelio Priatoni's mode of operation.[15] When it came to curious and forbidden books, the protocols were few but clearly expressed:

> In addition to the Index of Prohibited Books, keep a precise updated list of all further books that are banned.[16]
>
> If you receive prohibited or suspended books or other items pertaining to the Holy Office, register them with due diligence.[17]
>
> Do not grant anyone permission to read or keep prohibited books under any pretext.[18]
>
> If writings or other materials related to sorcery are found, they must be burned after you conclude the case against the principal and his accomplices.[19]

Bad Jew

Benedetto's meeting with the Father Inquisitor was as dreadful as anything that he could have imagined:

> I presented myself in the company of our governors and the Inquisitor was not merely stern, he was downright furious. He stated harshly that he had no choice but to imprison me, and I told him that I would certainly not have come if I had known his intention. He did not want to detain me today, the Inquisitor said, since it was my holiday [the Jewish Sabbath] nor tomorrow since it was Sunday. However, he would send for me on Monday if I did not voluntarily present myself for incarceration.[20]

Daniel Calò, Rubino da Palestrina, and Emanuel Pesaro – the governors of the Ghetto – intervened but to no avail:

> There was much general discussion, then the governors gave me a signal to leave the room so that they could try to make some progress. Finally, they called me back. The Inquisitor announced with great severity, right to my face, that I was a bad Jew, which offended me deeply. He did not know me, I told him, so how could he claim a profound understanding of my character, never having talked with me nor even seen me? Others, I concluded, had not been telling him the truth. Finally, we took our leave – with little satisfaction on my part, since he ordered me to return on Monday. My personal resolution, I tell you frankly, was to head for [your villa at] Palvello [near Padua], not back to Santa Croce. The Father Inquisitor, I deduced, had something else in his stomach – not just that book.[21]

If Benedetto knew what else was disturbing the Father Inquisitor, he was not ready to discuss it with Don Giovanni dei Medici. Meanwhile, the governors launched a second round of negotiations at Santa Croce – extracting only a fuller statement of why Benedetto Blanis was a bad Jew:

> We agreed that the governors should return without me, in order to tell the Inquisitor that I was wounded by his bitter words. Then they could try to get his assurance that he would not imprison me. In the end, they got nothing out of him except a lot of words. I was a bad Jew, he said, because I went from one condition to another and did not stay Jewish. That, he said, was his definition of a bad Jew. So, I really don't know where all of this is leading, and I am confused, and I don't know what to do … In my next letter, I will tell you everything that has happened, if I am still able to write letters.[22]

A sudden, startling turnaround then occurred. A week later, on 21 April 1619, Benedetto could put a bright face on things for his patron in Venice:

> Since I know that Your Excellency does not like to intervene with monks, I thank God that I got off with only a bit of house arrest and a fine. To make a long story short, the Father Inquisitor is a great and good man who managed to terrify me out of my wits and make my whole life flash before my eyes. When it got down to it, however, it was only a matter of a few

coins. So, I am now a prisoner in my own home, and I respect this sentence whenever I don't have anything to do outside. The Inquisitor says that he has something to tell me when I see him next, and this will make me realize that he has done me a very great favour.[23]

Benedetto Blanis had a close call – but he got over it quickly. Whatever transpired behind the scenes, he still had unfinished business with the Holy Office. Meanwhile, the Jew was back at the top of his game, playing hide-and-seek with the Inquisition for the sheer love of the sport.

Business as Usual (I)

The Blanis scriptorium remained in operation, as did Benedetto's dealership in banned books. By 28 April 1619 he had found another priest to copy the Fourth Part of Cornelius Agrippa's *Occult Philosophy*, working in his Ghetto home for two hours every day, after giving lessons to his daughters (in keyboard music, it would seem).[24] A few weeks later, even Benedetto had second thoughts – spiriting the manuscript out of Florence so that Don Giovanni could pass it on to a Venetian copyist.[25]

Then there was the library of the late Cosimo Ridolfi. His widow Laudomine hated her husband's occult studies and she hated her husband's occult friends. Meanwhile, she was fiercely protective of her son, six-year-old Niccolò. Benedetto approached her from every possible angle. He did normal Jewish business, selling off used wall hangings and old clothes. He gave her repeated gifts of *acqua d'angiolo* – 'angel water,' a prized medicinal preparation.[26] He even planned a holiday for the widow and her child at Don Giovanni's villa at Montughi, north of Florence.[27]

Laudomine Ricasoli Ridolfi did not know what she wanted and she did not know whom to trust, when it came to her husband's curious and forbidden books. Benedetto's campaign took on a crazy life of its own, as he explained on 19 July 1619:

I saw Signora Laudomine on Wednesday [17 July] at the door to her house [in Florence] and I reminded her about the books. She told me that she had not yet brought them from her villa [at Meleto] but would do so. I swear that I have left nothing untried. This morning, I even called on her to announce that her husband had appeared to me in a dream – begging me to remove all of the books on astrology and distillation from the house so that his son would not waste time and money. I was sure that she would believe my story about the dream and see herself validated as a prophetess, since she always complained about Signor Cosimo's alchemical pastimes. Sooner or later, I will get my hands on those books, whether I buy them myself or have someone else buy them for me. In any case, I will not reveal Your Most Illustrious Excellency's involvement. [28]

Benedetto's stratagems dragged on and on, until even his dream scam wore itself out. After a few months, the widow left for the country – with the Jew in hot pursuit:

I went to see Signora Laudomine at her villa at Meleto, like I said I would – but I found her firmly resolved not to dispose of the books nor anything else ... Finally, by way of a discussion of dreams, I got her to admit that all of the curious books – including the books on distillation – had already been turned over to Father Orazio Morandi.[29]

Laudomine Ricasoli Ridolfi was more likely to trust a priest than a Jew – even a priest who had figured in her late husband's despised magic circle. For years, Don Giovanni dei Medici and Father General Orazio Morandi had shared their arcane pursuits. But now, this high-flying churchman seemed to have an agenda of his own – wanting the library for himself or his friends in Rome.[30]

In Florence, meanwhile, Benedetto found a new copyist – Ferdinando Magnani, an aspiring priest and the son of Don Giovanni's former surgeon. They began swapping lessons in Hebrew for lessons in Euclidian geometry, and Ferdinando soon made himself indispensable in the Blanis family scriptorium:

I am sending Your Most Illustrious Excellency two pages of the *Chiave Raimondina* (*Key to Ramón Llull*), accompanied by the good will of my scholar and his heartfelt devotion to your service. If you find any errors, the blame is entirely mine, since he is only a beginner. I have traded mathematics for copying work in order to supervise him well, and he will send you two pages every week until he finishes.[31]

To encourage Ferdinando's studies, Benedetto bought him a fine Hebrew Bible in four volumes.[32] The young man was a versatile scholar – the Jew enthused – and above all, 'he delights in astrology.'[33]

Divine Favours

'God always sends his favours in due time,'Ferdinando Magnani assured Don Giovanni dei Medici on 7 September 1619. 'When they seem to arrive late, that only enhances their ultimate good – as in Your Excellency's case. Since the Lord God wanted to favour you with children, he gave you a male to compensate for his tardiness.'[34]

'Divine favours can never be said to come late,' Benedetto Blanis echoed a day later. 'I will never tire of expressing the great satisfaction, the supreme pleasure and the infinite joy that I felt last Monday [2 September] when I learned of the birth of so illustrious an offspring. In truth, nature would have done the world a great wrong, had she kept so noble a fruit for herself. I thank the Lord God for such a favour and pray that He will grant him life and greatness.'[35]

In the last days of August 1619 a son was born to Don Giovanni dei Medici and his consort Livia Vernazza. The father was overjoyed to produce an heir at the advanced age of fifty-two. Livia, already twenty-nine, was no less delighted to consolidate her position in his household and – she hoped – the wider world.

The event was greeted with jubilation in a small corner of the Florentine Ghetto, but at the Medici Court the prevailing reaction was shock and horror. The granducal family had been praying that the rumours were true – that this daughter of a Genoese mattress-maker was merely faking her illustrious pregnancy. In hope of confirmation, Niccolò Sacchetti, the Tuscan Ambassador in Venice, had tried and failed to infiltrate Don Giovanni's palace with spies.[36]

In early August Don Giovanni's old friend Don Garzia de Montalvo was dispatched to Venice to block a feared marriage attempt, since the only thing worse than a Vernazza bastard was a legitimate offspring.[37] Montalvo returned to Florence convinced of his success, and Don Giovanni reinforced this belief in a personal letter to his nephew Grand Duke Cosimo II.[38] Then, only a few hours before the birth of Giovanni Francesco Maria dei Medici, Don Giovanni and Donna Livia were secretly married in a local convent.[39]

Divine favours were written large in the heavens for those who could read the language of the stars. 'I gave my scholar the time of birth,' Benedetto informed Don Giovanni, 'and he started to prepare a discourse explicating its circumstances.'[40] 'As you see,' Ferdinando rejoiced, 'these demonstrate – beyond a shadow of doubt – that your son enjoys the very best [astral conjunction] that a great prince could hope for … I am falling behind with the writings of *Raimondo* and cannot send you even a single sheet. Next week, I will make this up to you.'[41]

The *Key to Ramón Llull* was relegated to a distant backburner while Benedetto and Ferdinando applied themselves to this more compelling task. On 15 September Benedetto offered further excuses: 'I hope that Your Most Illustrious Excellency will pardon my scholar's presumption in undertaking this astrological work but the responsibility is mine and for good reason. Since I am unable to enjoy your son's noble presence at first hand, it is a great consolation to learn from the discourse that God grants him long life in the company of his parents.'[42]

On 2 October Ferdinando issued an interim report, telling the doting parents everything they could possibly want to hear:

> In the configuration of this birth, Venus – the chief signifier of the child's Illustrious Lady Mother – is in the sixth house according to the rules of Ptolemy, Book IV, Chapter III ... This is a royal sign in conjunction with Leo, indicating majesty, nobility, magnanimity, elevated thinking, and physical beauty, so that one can truly say that he has species *digna imperio* (traits worthy of an emperor) ... According to the Moon, which is under the ascendancy of Mercury ... it will emerge that he delights in things associated with Mars and Mercury, like military architecture, fires, alchemy, medical and surgical endeavours, and such.[43]

With Mars and Mercury smiling on his birth, the infant was well on his way to becoming a perfect duplicate of his father. Under the onslaught of so much good news, Don Giovanni might have pardoned the presumption of young Ferdinando (age twenty-eight) in making so blatant a play for his favour. But other astrologers were unlikely to be so forbearing – especially in Florence, especially the grand and irascible Raffael Gualterotti (age seventy-six).

Swatting Magnani like a fly was already too much of an honour, as Gualterotti asserted to Don Giovanni on 28 October 1619:

> I doubt that I have the right hour and the right day since I got them from Little Mister Ferdinando who is a flibbertigibbet (*signor Ferdinandino che è un falimbella*). God knows, if he had thirty million in gold, he would make himself master of the world. Meanwhile, if I had four brass farthings (*quattro danari*) worth of good medicine, I believe that I could make two thousand out of them in eight months. Please send them [the coordinates of the birth] so that I can do this work for you, since you already promised them to me.[44]

Gold, brass farthings, and good medicine – this curious reference was alchemical in scope. Gualterotti, meanwhile, was sputtering with exasperation, outraged by Don Giovanni's failure to furnish the essential data for his own authoritative reading of the stars. When Don Giovanni snubbed Gualterotti's letter of 28 October, the senior astrologer had no trouble putting the pieces together – at least in his own mind. Then on 16 November he launched a rambling diatribe against Benedetto Blanis:

> I must complain loudly about those who call themselves mail couriers since I have not yet had a reply to the letter that I wrote you. However, I can also imagine that you were put on guard by my discussion of alchemy, and this presumably reflects the judgment of *Benedetto Brandes*[45] [underlined in the original]. That man has always let me know that Your Most Illustrious Excellency doesn't see much of anything in such studies, only a few odds and ends of no real importance, but I never gave him the least credence since I know to whom he was born and under which stars. *Now he is thundering because I converted a half brother-in-law of his to the true faith. This man is his teacher, and he knows more than Benedetto since he is an Arab by birth and learned in that language. His father was born in Spain and is the nipote [nephew or grandson] of Abram Avenzaar,[46] the famous astrologer and physician. Benedetto Brandes is now carrying arms because he wants to cut me up into little pieces – but this makes me laugh, since I know him for the knave that he is, as well as a traitor and a sorcerer. Therefore, he is no Jew at all but an infamous idolator. In any case, Benedetto's relative is going to be baptized whether Benedetto likes it or not, because he was and is staying in my own house.* But let us return to my letter which might have been lost in transit. In this letter, I asked you for the birth indications of your son, and I also asked you to help me retrieve some small objects in gold that I have there in Venice. Finally, I asked you to let me have those two sheets [the plates from the *Mirror of Truth*] and any others that are now finished.[47]

Knave, traitor, sorcerer … even infamous idolater. The rival astrologer's letter was crazed and barely coherent but his story was at least partially true.

Jews and Converts

On 1 January 1620 there was a grand ceremony in Florence's ancient baptistry. 'Cosimo Suetonio,[48] formerly Joseppe Abenesra, a thirty-

year-old Jew, was baptized by the hand of Monsignor Filippo Salviati, Bishop of Borgo [San Sepolcro].'Cosimo/Joseppe's godmother by
proxy was Dowager Grand Duchess Christine de Lorraine. His godfather and namesake was Grand Duke Cosimo II – represented by Robert Dudley, Earl of Warwick, the most celebrated Protestant convert at
the Medici Court.[49]

A few weeks later, on 26 January, the Jews in the nearby Ghetto
elected their new governors for the coming year. On 1 February their
choices were ratified by the Nine Preservers of the Dominion, an organ
of the Medici government.[50] Benedetto Blanis could now add his name
to a long and distinguished list of family members – going back to his
great-grandfather Laudadio, who headed the first slate of governors
in 1572.[51] Unfortunately, Benedetto had little time to celebrate, as he
explained to Don Giovanni in a distraught letter that same day:

> You should know that a Moorish Jew (*hebreo moresco*) named Josef Hezrà
> is married to the daughter of my mother's brother[52] who lives in Massa
> di Carrara. This Josef disappeared from Florence about seven months ago,
> leaving behind his wife and a daughter who is about a year old. A few days
> later, we heard that he was back in town but he never showed himself in
> the Ghetto. So his wife considered herself to be abandoned and went off to
> her father's house in Massa. Then we heard throughout the city that this
> Josef wanted to be baptized, that he had begun taking instruction last July
> and that he was in fact baptized on the first of January.[53]

Benedetto's cousin from Massa was *aguna* by Jewish law – an abandoned but undivorced wife, with no status and no rights. Her only
option was to return to her father's household and hope that her family could negotiate her release – but her newly Christian husband had
ideas of his own:

> During those six months, that man never enquired after his wife and
> daughter nor made an effort of any kind. Now, however, he has let it be
> known that he wants [my brother-in-law] Moisé Lattone and me to hand
> over his wife. He even initiated proceedings against us with the Inquisi-
> tion but we were released. Then he had us summoned by the Archbishop
> of Florence [Alessandro Marzi Medici] who asked us about this woman.
> We replied that she had gone to her father and the Archbishop was satis-
> fied with our explanation, since we were able to show him an attestation
> from the Florentine customs administration. Her father and brother had

indeed been here in Florence during that time and it was reasonable to assume that they had taken her back home [to Massa].[54]

Failing to make his case by ecclesiastical law, the Moorish ex-Jew tried his luck with civil law – treating the alienation of his wife and child as a crime against persons and property. Meanwhile, he mobilized pious Christian sentiment at the Medici Court:

Now this man [Josef/Cosimo] is causing us even more trouble, working by way of Pitti [the Pitti Palace] to have the case referred to the Eight Magistrates for Protection and Supervision. On 14 January, the Eight sent an official citation giving us fifteen days to hand over the wife and child, so we went to that Magistrature and presented our same arguments verbally. This very morning [now that the fifteen days have elapsed], an order was issued for our arrest, and I suspect that there has been pressure from high-up, since the case seems to be getting hotter and hotter. This Josef has also let it be known that he plans to bring other legal actions against us, alleging many pointless Turkish quibbles of his own invention (*molte vanee turchesche e inventione*).[55]

Benedetto then made his plea to Don Giovanni – evidently unaware that his patron had heard much of the same story from Raffael Gualterotti ten weeks earlier:

Since my conscience is clear, I must not allow myself to be thrown into prison and forced to argue with new converts. Have compassion on me, I beg you, and have compassion on my poor family, who are like helpless insects buzzing around if I am not there to guide them. I was ready to flee Florence, I tell you frankly, but Cavaliere [Camillo] Guidi advised against this and promised to do his best to help me. I now implore you to write a few lines to the Most Illustrious and Excellent Cardinal [Carlo dei Medici], affirming my character and integrity... I beg you, for the love of God, to express your favour for me as soon as possible and save our entire family from ultimate ruin. This is the end to which that Josef is working, along with Albizzo Vecchi, Master of the Pages, and Signor Scipione Ammirato.[56]

By the time Don Giovanni received Benedetto's letter, the situation in Florence had gone from bad to worse. On the night of 3 February the new governor of the Ghetto was hiding out while the police ransacked his house:

Last Saturday [1 February], I troubled Your Most Illustrious Excellency with a long screed, overwhelmed as I was by passion and desperation. Now I am on my knees once again, imploring you for the love of God to render me whatever essential help you can. As you see in the enclosed memorandum, I am being injured by a Jew who has become Christian. Now it is four hours after sunset [around 9 p.m.] on Monday night [3 February], and my house is full of constables ... who are searching through all of my writings and letters and taking them away. I don't know if they are going to seize other things as well, since I am now in the house of Prior [Francesco] Vinta[57] who is favouring me with many undeserved courtesies. If Your Most Illustrious Excellency does not put things right, particularly with the Padroni [Medici Princes], we are facing utter ruin and extermination. I no longer know what I need. I cannot see the light. It is only my firm hope in God and in Your Most Illustrious Excellency that still makes it possible for me to hold a pen ... [Postscript] There are all of the letters that I was keeping for reference from Your Most Illustrious Excellency and from Your Most Illustrious Lady.[58]

Benedetto also sent a formal memorandum to Don Giovanni, focusing on the pathological vindictiveness of Jewish converts to Catholicism:

What we see here is no more than the usual spite that converts manifest towards Jews, whether motivated by true hatred or merely to demonstrate their own devoutness as Christians. This is what occurred four months ago when he [Josef/Cosimo] brought a case to the Inquisition against four of us,[59] and this is what he is doing yet again – manifesting his goodness by way of lawsuits rather than prayer and devotion. The late Grand Duke Ferdinando I [dei Medici] ruled wisely and prudently that baptized Jews could not appear as witnesses in Jewish cases, knowing well the true nature of certain ignorant neophytes. Such enemies and persecutors of the Jewish Nation hope to show themselves more Christian and more devout than the others – not realizing that they are doing the very opposite of imitating Christ.[60]

In Florence or any beleaguered Jewish community, conversion was a constant threat and a relatively frequent occurrence. However deep their convictions, Jews often collapsed under the relentless pressure of ghetto life. Most were poor and many desperately poor, so there were numerous cases of economic accommodation. Others fell victim to personal tensions within the community – like Jacob Pernicca (later Gianlorenzo Laurenzi), a rich and seemingly fortunate young man betrayed by other Jews.[61]

Whatever its origin, conversion was always an act of violence – within the community, within the family, and within the individual – dramatically expressed in the phobic hatreds and fears of New Christians. The usual pattern was for the male head of the household to convert and then insist on taking his dependents with him. The wife would often resist, seeking help from her family and neighbours. Then the husband and his Christian allies – always eager to play out their own spiritual fantasies – would denounce this insidious Jewish interference in the wondrous workings of Divine Grace.

Several inconvenient facts supported Josef/Cosimo's allegations, and Benedetto did his best to neutralize them in his memorandum. The former Jew, he was quick to admit, rented a house (i.e., sublet an apartment) in the Ghetto from Moisé Lattone, his indicted co-conspirator. Moisé, however, never spoke with his tenant's wife nor even saw her (although the woman was related to Moisé by marriage, and there were barely five hundred Jews in Florence). Benedetto also acknowledged his 'incidental' involvement in another recent case. 'A Jew who wanted to convert took his wife with him and one young son. Then a half hour later, the court sent for the other children who happened to be with Benedetto and he turned them over without opposition.'[62]

On 4 February, the day after the ransacking of his house, Benedetto assessed the situation. Police officials, he noted with dismay, were not particularly impressed by his special relationship with Don Giovanni dei Medici:

> Signor Cospi [Anton Maria Cospi, Secretary of the Eight Magistrates] and the Captain [Chief Constable Antonio Maria Milani] should have known about the letters that were going back and forth between me and Your Most Illustrious Excellency. Cospi, I have to say, could have exerted himself more in maintaining control of these letters, without giving way to a baptized Jew who turned spy. The Captain, for his part, could have carried out the order less harshly and with less evident scorn. He might at least have bundled all of the letters together and there was no need to throw everything on the ground, including sacred writings.[63]

Securing Don Giovanni's correspondence was the most immediate concern. For years Benedetto had been running confidential errands of many kinds, and his patron had been facilitating Benedetto's illicit business deals. Don Giovanni's most effective allies in Florence were Cosimo Baroncelli (his major-domo) and Camillo Guidi (secretary to Dowager Grand Duchess Christine de Lorraine). 'Secretary Cospi courteously reminded me that he was your devoted servant,' Cosimo Baroncelli reassured Don Giovanni on 8 February. 'He will not even look at those letters, leaving them in the same sack in which they were taken away. Cospi is now keeping this sack in his own home, and he suggested that I place a seal on it – making absolutely certain that neither he nor anyone else looks at them.'[64]

'None of this should be necessary,' Benedetto declared, 'in response to a petition from a recent convert from Barbery who might even have been a Turk.[65] I note that his toes were cut off, indeed half his feet, which is a frequent punishment among the Berbers.'[66] Benedetto failed to grasp an essential point – conversion was viewed more gratefully at the Medici Court than in the local Ghetto. On 8 February Cosimo Baroncelli updated Don Giovanni dei Medici:

> The crux of the lawsuit is that Benedetto stole this convert's wife, who is Benedetto's cousin, so that she would not become Christian. Signor Cavaliere Guidi is trying to help him with Madama Serenissima [Christine de Lorraine] but that lady is full of spite towards Benedetto, in her zeal to bring this Jewess's soul to the true light of the Holy Faith. So, Benedetto has been ordered to present himself to the authorities ... I made our case as vigorously as I could to the Cardinal [Carlo dei Medici] and asked him to bring his favour to bear on the Eight Magistrates. He will do so, he promised, and he will also try to deflect attention from that book called the *Ortus Nucis* (*Garden of Nut Trees*) and that *Tree of Kabballah* which they found among Benedetto's papers.[67]

Letters were shuttling back and forth between Florence and Venice, with the inevitable delay in transit (usually three days each way). By 8 February 1620 Benedetto was already in jail,[68] as announced by his younger brother Salamone;

> In order to avoid a fine of 600 scudi, Benedetto was forced to present himself to the Eight Magistrates. They immediately put him in secret solitary confinement [in the Bargello prison] at the behest of a Jew who was baptized with the name of Cosimo Suettonio. This Cosimo claims that Benedetto stole his wife who is a relative of ours, but he has no witnesses and no proof – except for false affidavits from Raffaello Gualterotti and his son

the Canon [Francesco Maria Gualterotti]. These two persuaded Cosimo to be baptized, with the inducement of financial need and personal ambition. Cosimo is also favoured by a certain Messer Albizzo Vecchi, Master of the Pages ... Gualterotti and the baptized Jew are now threatening to bring charges of sorcery, magic, and such against Benedetto, all of which is very far from his true nature ... Cavaliere Guidi and Signor Cosimo Baroncelli had been promised that no one would lay hand or eye on the writings taken from Messer Benedetto ... Others, however, claim that they are going to make much of a small handwritten book in Hebrew that they found among his papers. This is called the *Ortus Nucis* and it is a work of speculative Kabbalah, not active Kabbalah. It seems that they are going to show this little book to Messer Alessandro dei Medici who won't even know how to read it, let alone interpret it.[69]

Raffael Gualterotti had already expressed his firm opinion that Benedetto was 'a traitor and a sorcerer... no Jew at all but an infamous idolator.'[70] On 15 February, in a letter to Cosimo Baroncelli, Don Giovanni offered a more nuanced view – demonstrating an impressive familiarity with Kabbalistic matter;

I am always grateful for your services to Benedetto Blanis since I consider him a person of high repute. I have already written to Cavaliere Guidi, enclosing a letter for the Most Illustrious Cardinal [Carlo] dei Medici, and I have written to Messer Albizzo Vecchi since he is casting such aspersions. If you pay another visit to the Cardinal, it would be well for you to explain that the book called *Ortus Nucis* is a work of theology according to the Hebrew Law. The *Tree of Kabbalah* is a kind of chart that passes from Terrestial things through the Natural and the Celestial to the Divine. According to Hebrew Law, this is Speculative Kabbalah, a science associated with philosophy and theology. It is in no way illicit, even for Christians, since there are innumerable permitted books in this field. We are of course dealing with recondite matters, often misunderstood by ignorant people who might cause trouble for our poor Blanis. However, you must realize that he has nothing to fear, if there are no other books than these. Please do whatever you can and keep me informed because I am eager to protect this innocent and reputable man. The senile doddering (*barbogeria*) of Signor Raffael Gualterotti has been a major factor in this persecution, along with the malicious deceit of a certain little canon who happens to be his son.[71]

Don Giovanni did not like to face off with the Inquisition but he was ready and willing to lean on almost anyone else. By 15 February the Jew was back home celebrating: 'Well might I sing to Your Most Illustrious Excellency, *Dominus mihi adiutor non timebo quid faciat mihi homo* (In my trouble I called upon the Lord, and the Lord heard me, and enlarged me). Here in the shadow of your patronage – which Signor Cavaliere Guidi demonstrated to everyone who needed to know – I find that I am free of every harm *et ego dispiciam inimicos meos* (and I will look over my enemies).'[72]

As Benedetto explained, he emerged safe and sound from an elaborately choreographed turf battle: 'An agreement was reached through the mediation of Signor Cosimo Baroncelli and Signor Cavaliere Guidi ... since I never make a move without their advice. I presented myself for incarceration on Friday of last week [7 February] in order to avoid a heavy fine ... The Eight Magistrates wanted to put me in isolation – and that is where I remained from Friday until Wednesday evening [7 through 12 February]. Then, they got me out of jail with a bond of 500 scudi.'[73]

Six days in the Bargello prison while negotiating a settlement was business as usual for the Eight Magistrates. Then, as a matter of principle, the Inquisition also wanted its piece of Benedetto Blanis – although it had no jail of its own and kept its prisoners in the same place;

> On Thursday morning [13 February], the Inquisitor [Fra Cornelio Priatoni] went to [Anton Maria] Cospi and complained that I had been freed without his approval. There was no need to involve the Inquisitor, Cospi replied, since I was not being held at the Inquisitor's behest. However, I am not in hiding so Cospi agreed to send me to the Inquisitor... Once again, I had to present myself for incarceration, and I went to see the Inquisitor and he told me what he wanted and I concurred. The plan was for me to surrender myself on Friday [14 February] before the eighteenth hour [around noon] on pain of a 300 scudi fine, and I would be out of jail in less than three hours. So, I kept my word and the Inquisitor kept his, and I hope that the matter is now over and done with.[74]

Benedetto even managed to extricate himself before sundown and the beginning of the Jewish Sabbath. His letters, writings, and books had already been returned to him[75] on his initial release from the Bargello prison. 'Signor Alessandro Medici, son of Maestro Vitale, looked over the *Ortus Nucis* and other such things, approving them as good and permissible.'[76]

The *Ortus Nucis* was the *Ginat Egoz* (*Garden of Nut Trees*), a classic work by the Spanish Kabbalist Joseph Gikatilla (1248–1310) and one of the most influential expositions of the principles of *gematria* – the permutation of Hebrew words into numerical constructs with far-reaching metaphysical implications. Gikatilla divided his treatise into three sections: the first discusses the names of God, the second the letters of the Hebrew alphabet, and the third the Hebrew vowels. Even if the *Ortus Nucis / Ginat Egoz* was not illicit, it was certainly recondite, as Don Giovanni shrewdly observed.

Alessandro Medici, who pronounced on Benedetto's arcane writings, was the king of Jewish converts in Florence, like his father before him. In 1583, when Ferdinando dei Medici was a cardinal in Rome, he sponsored the baptism of Jehiel da Pesaro – a rabbi and medical doctor in the Florentine Ghetto – adopting him as his son, with the Christian name Vitale and the family name Medici.[77] After Ferdinando's ascent to the Tuscan throne in 1587, Vitale and his sons Antonio and Alessandro Medici all thrived. They accumulated immense wealth and made conspicuous gifts to local churches, commissioning the monumental ciborium on the altar of the Santissima Annunziata, the façade of Ognissanti, and the loggia of San Domenico di Fiesole. Alessandro established himself as the chief expert on Hebraic affairs at the Medici Court, and he was an ubiquitous figure (usually behind the scenes) in everything that had to do with Jews and *conversi*.

After Benedetto's release, Cosimo Baroncelli and Camillo Guidi arranged an audience for him with Cardinal Carlo dei Medici:

> I explained to the Cardinal that I had only one burden left, now that I was free from prison and free from the Inquisition. This was Raffael Gualterotti's ridiculous enmity, which must be caused by the stars since he has no other reason to hate me. Indeed, Gualterotti himself has cited the star under which I was born as the root of the problem. I swear to Your Most Illustrious Excellency that I have not even spoken with him since my return from Venice [in October of 1618], although he claims that I told him that you have not been reading his letters.[78]

Benedetto could look back on an eventful two weeks. He had been fought over by highly placed friends and enemies, been handed back and forth from one jurisdiction to another, and seen the inside of the same prison twice under different auspices. He had faced the Eight Magistrates for Protection and Supervision on the civil side. On the religious side, he had made his way among three distinct and often conflicting authorities: the Inquisition (represented by Monsignor Cornelio Priatoni), the Archdiocese of Florence (represented by Archbishop Alessandro Marzi Medici), and the Tuscan faction at the Court of Rome (represented by Cardinal Carlo dei Medici).[79]

What was this case all about? Was it banned books, astrology, Jewish converts, or something else entirely? Whatever the answer, it did not end with the strategic victory that Benedetto Blanis claimed. By 14 March 1620 Josef Hezrà / Cosimo Suetonio had regained possession of his young daughter – in this world and the next – as recorded in the Florentine baptistry:

> Baptized on this day was Lisabetta, daughter of Cosimo son of Suetonio and his wife Virtuosa de Blandes. She is approximately 13 ½ months old, from the Parish of San Niccolò.[80]

The mother followed in her daughter's footsteps less than three months later, on 7 June:

> The Jew Cristina, formerly Virtuosa daughter of Agnolo Blandes, [blank] years of age, now known as Cristina Alidosi, was baptized on this day by the Most Illustrious and Most Reverend Count Cosimo della Gherardesca, Bishop [of Colle Val d'Elsa]. The Most Serene Cosimo, Grand Duke of Tuscany, was Godfather, represented by the Illustrious Gentleman Rodrigo Alidosi. Madama Serenissima [Christine de Lorraine] was godmother, represented by the lady Lisabetta Bartolini Antinori.[81]

Agnolo Blanis was Benedetto's maternal uncle and also a cousin on his father's side.[82] Virtuosa/Cristina had been adopted by the aristocratic Alidosi family – with a note of lingering irony, at the very least. In 1611 her father Agnolo had tried and failed to perpetrate a bold fraud in collusion with Benedetto's brother Lelio. Hoping to evade Florentine customs duty on a consignment of used clothing from Massa, Agnolo and Lelio infiltrated the baggage train of Ambassador Rodrigo Alidosi who was returning from a diplomatic mission. The police seized hundreds of scudi worth of contraband and imprisoned most of the Blanis family – including Laudadio and his four sons Lelio, Benedetto, David, and Salamone.[83]

On 18 March 1621, this newly Christian family was back in the baptistry with barely a hint of their Jewish heritage: 'Baptized on this day was Francesco son of Cosimo Suedonio and Christina Alidosi from the Parish of San Niccolò.' Robert Dudley, Earl of Warwick, stood as godfather. The godmother was Filippa Vanni Lamberti, wife of the Lucchese Ambassador to the Medici Court.[84]

Business as Usual (II)

In Benedetto's daily life, nothing had changed – at least in his letters to Don Giovanni dei Medici. Once again the Jew was forging ahead, proud of his ability to work the system:

> On Wednesday evening [19 February], I got them to cancel both my fine and the security bond. I am not sending Your Most Illustrious Excellency an instalment of the *Chiave Raimondina* (*Key to Ramón Llull*) at this time, since I removed it from my house in order to avoid difficulties. Now, however, I am resuming work, and I hope to finish it with only another two or three pages. Signora Laudomine has returned [to Florence] and I have had various discussions with her, since she wants me to collect some debts on her behalf. In regard to the books, they are now on their way to Florence from her villa. Signora Laudomine says that she still has all of the curious and prohibited books and has only given Father Don Orazio [Morandi] a few odds and ends ... In dealing with Signora Laudomine, I pretend to suffer from a loss of memory, since letting her think that I believe what she says has turned into a sort of game (*mi fa gioco il credergli*).[85]

Benedetto seemed optimistic as ever, but things were not going well for him and his family, inside the baptistry and out. Their financial plight was growing desperate, as they struggled and failed to collect their usurious loans to Florentine patricians.[86] In the summer of 1619, Ricca Blanis – wife of Benedetto's older brother Lelio – sued to reclaim her dowry, hoping to secure her own property from her husband's creditors.[87] Lelio was then arrested for robbing a recently baptized Jew whose wife had run off to Massa Carrara.[88]

Two renegade wives of local *conversi*, one after the other, absconded to the same place, dangerously implicating the Blanis family. Meanwhile, Benedetto's commerce in banned books was one of the worst-kept secrets in Florence. Under close surveillance by his many enemies, Benedetto needed to shun the occult and cut his ties with Massa until things cooled down – and running true to form, he did exactly the opposite.

On 12 April 1620 (Palm Sunday), Benedetto Blanis updated Don Giovanni dei Medici:

> I am enclosing a page of the *Raimondina* (*Key to Ramón Llull*), signalling Signor Ferdinando [Magnani]'s resumption of this work … In regard to his progress in the Hebrew language, I can say that he reads it well and is achieving a good grasp of the grammar with a solid base of comprehension … In regard to [Signora Laudomine's] books, I really don't have anything to add but my great object is to obtain them for you … Meanwhile, I pray that the Lord God will grant you a good holiday – which I am going to celebrate in Massa di Carrara, where my nephew is taking a wife. I plan to return to Florence, God willing, after the Ottavo di Pasqua, and I pray that He will grant you infinite happiness and contentment on the occasion of this holiday.[89]

Passover began on the evening of 17 April (also Good Friday) and Easter Sunday was 19 April, so *Ottavo di Pasqua* could refer – either or both – to the Octave of Easter and the Eight Days of Passover. When Benedetto returned to Florence, he hit the ground running, as he announced to Don Giovanni on 10 May:

> I had been in Massa di Carrara for many days in order to touch the hand of the wife whom my nephew has taken in that town … Tomorrow, I will go to [the Vallombrosan Monastery at] Ripoli in order to negotiate with the Father General [Orazio Morandi]. Then we will see if we can reach an agreement regarding Signora Laudomine's books … I will send you more of the *Raimondina* in my next letter, since Signor Ferdinando has not been able to work on it recently … In the course of my trip [to Massa], I found some odds and ends of writings for you in the Hebrew language. I can send them as they are or have them translated.[90]

A stimulating battle of wits then ensued. Back in May of 1619, after his first brush with the Inquisition, Benedetto dispatched the manuscript of Cornelius Agrippa's *Occult Philosophy (Part Four)* to Don Giovanni in Venice,[91] without telling its owner, Francesco Maria Maringhi. On 2 June 1620 Maringhi called on him in the Ghetto and Benedetto was ready with a plausible story – during his recent difficulties, he transferred any curious items to the home of an anonymous friend.

'I am delaying him as best I can, so I must ask Your Most Illustrious Excellency to return that book by the surest and quickest means.'[92]

Don Giovanni failed to respond and the Jew spun out his excuses to Maringhi, leading him on a merry chase. But by the end of the month, all of this ceased to matter – Benedetto was back in jail, and there was no more business as usual.

chapter twelve

Prison

Misery and Woe

'Today you find our families in the very depths of misery and woe,' Benedetto's younger brother Salamone lamented to Don Giovanni dei Medici on 2 July 1620:

> You should know that our Messer Benedetto has been *in segreta* for three days now, presumably due to allegations regarding the supposed disappearance of a baptized Jew along with his three-year-old son. Since this baptized Jew is the brother-in-law of another brother of mine, the court is claiming that Messer Benedetto gave him shelter, aid, or counsel ... We had heard this morning that Messer Benedetto was to be brought up for questioning, which seemed good news. Then, alas, they arrested my other older brother [Lelio] who is the brother-in-law of that baptized Jew, leaving our entire household without leadership or guidance.[1]

Lightning struck in the usual place with another neophyte and another child – and once again, much of the action occurred on the road between Florence and Massa Carrara. The 'baptized Jew' was David Finzi and his story is a startling one, even by prevailing *converso* standards.[2]

The tiny principality of Massa Carrara consisted of two nearby towns and it clung to the border of three larger states: the Grand Dukedom of Tuscany, the Dukedom of Modena, and the Republic of Genoa. In 1554 Alberico I Cybo Malaspina (1534–1623) ascended the throne and ruled for nearly seventy years. In 1561 he invited Guglielmo Finzi, a Jew from Reggio Emilia, to settle in his dominion and establish a network of banks, ensuring the flow of credit to his subjects.[3]

The Finzi family flourished under Alberico's relatively benign rule, multiplying and attracting other Jews. By the 1580s these included Salvatore son of Laudadio Blanis, Benedetto's great-uncle.[4] Salvatore and his descendants did well for themselves in Massa Carrara, while maintaining their Florentine connections. There was constant commerce between Jews in those two territories[5] and a brisk exchange of marriageable girls. Alliances between more or less distant cousins were the rule, resulting in densely ingrown family trees.[6] Benedetto, for example, was a Blanis on both sides – his Florentine father and his Massese mother were first cousins, grandchildren of Laudadio the Elder.[7]

In 1595 Benedetto's older brother Lelio found a bride in the customary place, marrying Porzia daughter of Angelo son of Vita Finzi.[8] A few years later, in 1603, Lelio Blanis' brother-in-law David Finzi (brother, that is, of Lelio's wife Porzia) married yet another Porzia Finzi in Massa Carrara – daughter of his own first cousin Prospero (son of Guglielmo).[9] In 1611 Benedetto's brother Lelio married again within the same extended family – selecting Ricca Finzi (daughter of Abramo son of Vita). Ricca was the second cousin of Lelio's first wife Porzia Finzi and also the second cousin of his former brother-in-law David Finzi.[10]

Complications abounded in unions of this kind, and the marriage between Lelio Blanis' Finzi in-laws brought its full share of stress and strain. By 1608 David Finzi (son of Angelo Finzi) and Porzia Finzi (daughter of Prospero Finzi) had separated.[11] The wife reclaimed her dowry, took their three daughters, and left Massa Carrara to live in the Florentine Ghetto – where she reconnected with her husband and produced another daughter and a son. Then on 15 March 1620 there was a sensational public conversion in the local baptistry:

> Cosimo Tacca was baptized on this day, formerly the Jew Davitte son of Angelo Finzi and [mother's name left blank], approximately thirty-eight years old, from Massa di Carrara. The Most Serene Cosimo Medici, Grand Duke of Tuscany, was godfather, represented by Cavaliere Gian Cosimo Geraldini.[12]

Sometimes conversions rippled through a family, sometimes they rushed like a tidal wave.[13] When Cosimo Tacca/David Finzi aproached the font on 15 March 1620, he brought four children with him. There was his son Agnolo Finzi – now named Lorenzo Tacca[14] in honour of his godfather Don Lorenzo dei Medici and their sponsor Pietro Tacca. There were also three daughters – fifteen-year-old Bellafiore, now

Margherita, godmothered by Grand Duchess Maria Magdalena von Habsburg;[15] eleven-year-old Diamante, now Maria Cristiana, godmothered by Dowager Grand Duchess Christine de Lorraine,[16] and fifteen month-old Iudit (Judith), now Agnola Tacca, godfathered by Cardinal Carlo dei Medici.[17] A year earlier, on 1 April 1619, David and Porzia's eldest daughter had already become Maria Francesca Tacca – in a court ceremony in Carrara Cathedral. The elderly Alberico I Cybo Malaspina attended in person while his grand-daughter, Princess Vittoria, stood as godmother.[18]

After his baptism, Cosimo Tacca/David Finzi lost no time in launching a typical *converso* vendetta against his recent neighbours in the Ghetto, as heard by the Florentine police court on 9 April 1620:

> The Magistrates considered the investigation of the Jew Lelio son of Laudadio Blanis [Benedetto's older brother] and the Jew Lustro son of Agnolo from Antwerp, both charged by Davitte, formerly a Jew but now Christian, son of the late Agnolo Fenzi. While this Davitte was secluded in the house of the sculptor Pietro Tacca in order to become Christian, he sent for his wife and family for this same purpose. During that time, the aforesaid [Lelio and Lustro] allegedly entered Davitte's house [in the Ghetto] and appropriated all of his linens and copperware for their own use … The accused asserted that Davitte's wife could have entered the house and appropriated any goods that might be missing, and this Jewess is now in Massa di Carrara. Since there is no evidence to the contrary, the Magistrates absolved the said Lelio and the said Lustro of all charges.[19]

Cosimo/David then experienced a *converso* change of heart – no less sudden and no less typical. The Grand Duke's godson fled the Tuscan capital, taking their son Agnolo/Lorenzo but leaving the three daughters to his wife.[20] Porzia, it would seem, had already decamped to Massa with at least two of the girls, before moving on to Ferrara and taking refuge with her uncle Mosé.[21]

When the dust settled, only Benedetto was left in Florence – in an isolation cell in the Bargello prison. Salamone was now the designated spokesman for the Blanis family, and he quickly focused on the practical realities of the situation, without belabouring his brother's unlikely innocence:

> To tell you the truth, our Benedetto might have had some inkling of this baptized Jew's intentions but no one, I think, will ever prove that he

helped or encouraged him. Information might have come his way, but I don't see the judges insisting that he was obligated to report it. Unfortunately, Prince Don Lorenzo [dei Medici] held the young boy at his baptism and is certain to weigh heavily in this case.[22]

Salomone had no doubt regarding the roots of his brother's predicament:

This all began as the invention of Giambologna's pupil Pietro Tacca. He introduced this baptized Jew and his children to the Christian faith but soon after, the baptized Jew disappeared with his young son. So, these people decided to proceed against my brother [Benedetto] because he is a doctor,[23] one of the governors of the Ghetto and one of the chief supporters of our faith. That Arab Cosimo Suettonio might also be an instigator, since he is my brother's most virulent enemy and is constantly trying to entrap him.[24]

Pietro Tacca (1577–1640), the most gifted follower of the great Giambologna (1529–1608), was First Sculptor to the Grand Duke and the most powerful figure in the Medici art administration. Not only was he a native of Massa Carrara, his brother Monsignor Andrea Tacca was provost of the Collegiata in Massa – the pre-eminent church official in that town.

Benedetto might have been guilty of many things but he was certainly the victim of selective prosecution. Several weeks later, on 27 July, Lelio but not Benedetto was exonerated and released by the civil authorities – even though he was related by marriage to the fugitive *conversa*: 'Item: To be freed from prison, the Jew Lelio son of Laudadio Blanis, arrested on suspicion of having stolen a child but this was found not to be true.'[25]

Not only was Benedetto Blanis not released, he was not even charged. Suspects in high-profile cases were often arrested by the Eight Magistrates and then jailed for the duration, while the interested parties mobilized their friends and supporters. Bringing a charge – *spedire il negozio* or expediting the case, in the language of the time – was an important step forward, like moving from the instructional to the judicial phase in a modern Italian trial. But local powerbrokers, including the Medici themselves, often blocked such due process – keeping suspects in jail and in legal limbo for months and even years.

At the outset, Salomone Blanis was cautiously optimistic: 'From what I have heard, I believe that Cospi [Anton Maria Cospi, Secretary of the Eight Magistrates] will establish the guidelines for this case and he will then inform the Padroni [Medici Princes] next Sunday [12 July]. Unless Their Highnesses tell Signor Cospi to come down hard, we can hope that it will soon be expedited and we now trust Your Most Illustrious Excellency ... to help set these deliberations on a positive course.'[26]

Meanwhile, Benedetto Blanis languished in jail – isolated from his friends and enemies. On 11 July Cosimo Baroncelli noted in a postscript: 'Messer Benedetto Blanis is *in segreta*, so I am sending the letters for him back to Your Excellency.'[27]

The Jew might have been out of sight, but he was not out of mind, and on 16 July Baroncelli dispatched an encouraging report to Don Giovanni. He had called on Cardinal Carlo dei Medici, Don Giovanni's nephew, who promised to assert himself on the prisoner's behalf.[28] Baroncelli then met with the Blanis family and helped them draft a memorandum setting out the facts in the case.[29] Finally, he wrote letters in Don Giovanni's name – on pre-signed blank sheets – to the Attorney General (Auditore Fiscale) and the Secretary of the Eight Magistrates. 'We will then proceed according to your orders, once Benedetto is out [of jail].'[30]

Salamone was only a junior member of the Blanis clan, forced into the spotlight by the incarceration of his two older brothers, Lelio and Benedetto. He made the rounds tirelessly, gathering information and delivering Don Giovanni's second-hand letters of support. Unfortunately, the news that he had to share on 24 July was anything but good:

> Your Most Illustrious Excellency's letters served to sweeten the ministers of the Princes but the malignancy comes from the Princes themselves. Pietro Tacca planted the idea firmly in Madama Serenissima's mind, and now Her Highness absolutely believes that Benedetto spirited away that baptized Jew and his son. We were hoping to effect his liberation through the Auditore Fiscale and Secretary Cospi – but then, both the Nuncio [Papal Ambassador] and the Inquisitor received letters from Cardinal [Roberto] Bellarmino in Rome, telling them to review the case as rigorously as possible. The Father Inquisitor is behaving cruelly, and he has made it known that Benedetto will never be released – unless the child is recovered or at least located.[31]

Pietro Tacca's influence originated in the artistic sphere but soon extended to politics by way of official commissions and state gifts.[32] With

Dowager Grand Duchess Christine de Lorraine, the sculptor shared a taste for strict Catholic observance and the propagation of the Faith through court-sponsored conversions.

The intervention of Roberto Bellarmino (1542–1621) was an alarming development for the Blanis family. The elderly cardinal was a Jesuit, the most authoritative theologian of the Counter-Reformation and one of the most celebrated inquisitors in history – prosecuting such noted heretics as Giordano Bruno (1593–1600) and Galileo Galilei (1615–16).

Don Giovanni managed to co-opt Albizzo Vecchi, Master of the Court Pages.[33] But otherwise, Salamone discovered that his brother's enemies were rapidly outflanking his friends:

> Canon [Francesco Maria] Gualterotti procured those letters from Rome, and he is in league with Pietro Tacca. Meanwhile, that other baptized Jew Cosimo Suettonio made a sworn statement to Cardinal [Fabrizio] Veralli, impugning the Father Inquisitor's handling of my brother Benedetto's previous incarceration a few months ago. In this way, they have spun such a web of conspiracy that mere innocence cannot save him from their perse-cution … Don Lorenzo dei Medici was responsible for baptizing the child, and Pietro Tacca used that to incite the Prince against us.[34] I spoke with Madama Serenissima [Christine de Lorraine] this week and begged her – for the sake of justice – to see that our case was expedited. She replied, 'You may rest assured that justice will be done. Now go (*Andate che non si mancherà di giustitia*).'[35]

In Her Highness' voice, Salamone must have heard the unmistakable sound of an iron door slamming shut. The papal nuncio was renting Don Giovanni's palace in Florence, so Cosimo Baroncelli called on him personally and confirmed everyone's worst fears.[36] In Rome vari-ous factions had attached themselves to the Blanis case, and now they were vying with each other in their severity. In Florence the Medici family was divided – with Don Carlo and Don Giovanni taking Bene-detto's side and Christine de Lorraine and Don Lorenzo opposing him strenuously.

After a month *in segreta*, Benedetto had found a way to move letters in and out of the Bargello, with the evident collusion of the prison staff. By then he had come to doubt his own supporters, and he said as much to Don Giovanni on 1 August:

> This Friday [31 July], the Chancellor of the Inquisition came to see me. I

was expecting to be set free, but they told me that I will never be released from these irons until they find the young son of that man who absconded. This is because Prince Don Lorenzo was responsible for baptizing him ... Your Excellency has already done much, but things are now dragging on inconclusively – perhaps due to your unfortunate absence from Florence. Our Cardinal [Carlo dei Medici] seems less than zealous on my behalf – maybe because of [his brother] Don Lorenzo ... The appeal needs to be written in authoritative terms in Your Excellency's own hand and no one else's, since I don't believe that anyone except Your Excellency truly wishes me well. The whole matter might have been resolved if our Cardinal [Don Carlo] had said a few words in person to the Inquisitor or to Prince Don Lorenzo, but sending a secretary doesn't do the trick ... Signor Baroncelli did what he could, but he was not writing with Your Most Illustrious Excellency's own pen.[37]

Don Giovanni and Cardinal Carlo might have wished Benedetto well, but they were keeping his case at arm's length – using secretaries and inconclusive letters of support. Meanwhile, Benedetto's adversaries were finding the courage to challenge Don Giovanni to his face.

On 8 August 1620 Francesco Maria Gualterotti, son of Raffael and a Canon in Florence Cathedral, was barely civil: 'Malevolent people easily find ways to slander the innocent,' the Canon observed, 'as these Jews have slandered me to Your Excellency.' Then he made some damning charges of his own:

I am well informed regarding the Blandes case, and I do not understand how Your Most Illustrious and Excellent Lordship can declare him innocent. They found the terms of his agreement with that baptized Jew, written out in his own hand, and various letters detailing the execution of their plan. He might have tried to argue against this evidence – but then, they intercepted other letters that he wrote in prison. I know this and the entire city knows this and Their Most Serene Highnesses have held the very documents in their hands. From what I understand, jurisdiction in the case rests entirely with the Court of the Inquisition, where only the truth is admitted.[38]

If Francesco Maria Gualterotti was right about these incriminating letters, Benedetto Blanis had neither a hope nor a prayer. Jurisdiction, however, was not nearly as clear-cut as the canon claimed. The Inquisition might have been moving heavily in Rome but Benedetto was still in Florence, in the Bargello prison, where the Medici held the keys. Francesco Maria closed with a burst of sarcasm that might have made his quarrelsome father proud:

> In his current tribulation, I regret that Blandes finds himself persecuted by Jews more than Christians. Also, it is difficult to dislodge an impression from the minds of the great once it has taken hold. I am telling you this because I see the affection that Your Most Illustrious Excellency has bestowed on this particular servant of yours. If he truly appreciates your favour, he must be in a state of celestial joy.[39]

Rumours were circulating, in Florence and beyond, regarding Francesco Maria Gualterotti's assault on this hapless Jew. On 22 August the canon refuted them categorically, in another letter to Don Giovanni: 'I have absolutely nothing to do with the Benedetto Blandes case ... Since the matter depends largely on the [Medici] Court, we shouldn't be surprised if the doings of a Giant [like the Medici Princes] are sometimes credited to a Pygmy [like myself].'[40]

The canon was playing fast and loose with the truth, some might even say that he was lying through his teeth. Whatever the doings of the local Giants, it was this self-proclaimed Pygmy who pushed the paper, lodging the 'Blandes Case' with the Inquisition in Rome. On 16 July 1620 the Pope and the Cardinals General registered a terse decision in their book of decrees: 'Having read the letters from the Florentine Canon Francesco Maria Gualterotti, dated 4 July, His Holiness ordered the Inquisitor in Florence to proceed to justice against the Jew Benedetto Blandes for seducing recent converts to apostatize from the Faith.'[41]

Even the name 'Blandes' seems a fine Gualterotti/Tacca touch. Benedetto and his Florentine kin normally called themselves 'Blanis,' while 'Blandes' and 'Blanes' prevailed in Massa Carrara.[42] In the decree, there were no specific charges – no names, places, or dates. But a slow poison had been released into the system... The Inquisition would operate in its own way, in its own time, while Benedetto rotted in a Florentine jail.

Beginning of the End

Benedetto Blanis was not the only one whose life was coming apart. Since Don Giovanni's return to Venice from the War in the Friuli in early 1618, his health, career, finances, and personal affairs had been spinning out of control. Tuscan Ambassador Niccolò Sacchetti assessed his predicament on 28 October 1619:

> Signor Don Giovanni has not been feeling well since Saturday [26 October], and on Sunday [27 October] he took to his bed with signs of inflammation in his leg. This gave rise to two or three bouts of fever, and His Excellency took some medicine since he could not continue in this way. Unfortunately, this medicine, induced evacuation which only served to worsen things. Meanwhile, there has been dissension between His Excellency and these gentlemen [in the Venetian government] which could lead to a break in their relations. His Excellency wanted to settle some old accounts from the Friuli War, claiming that he had laid out a great deal of his own money. These Venetians then reacted wildly, blocking even his normal payments. If His Excellency was totally free and not subject in any way to the will of that Livia [Vernazza], he might be inclined to cut his ties to Venice as soon as his military commission expires next year. The day before yesterday, Signor Don Giovanni spoke with me – quite heatedly – regarding these matters.[43]

Like his father Grand Duke Cosimo I (1519–1574), Don Giovanni was a tough and physically resilient individual who worked himself into an early grave. Until the very end, he was subject to dramatic illnesses and no less dramatic recoveries. He also scorned medical advice – which was no bad strategy in the early seventeenth century. On 7 March 1620, at the beginning of Lent, he shared his philosophy with Granducal Secretary Andrea Cioli: 'The best thing, I truly believe, is to beguile the illness by way of amusement ... Since I wanted at least some entertainment on the last Friday of Carnival [27 February], I had a little comedy performed in my own bedroom, even if I had to stay in bed to see it. Now I am well, God be praised, and if the doctors never visit me again, that would be fine with me.'[44]

Meanwhile, Don Giovanni was struggling with his employers, the Venetian Republic – a strict oligarchy with an elected duke (or doge) at the top, combining the capriciousness of despotic rule with the endless accommodation of machine politics. The doge, the senators, and the various councils ran him into the ground – neither meeting his demands nor releasing him from his obligations.

Ambassador Sacchetti briefed Grand Duke Cosimo II on 16 December 1620: 'Don Giovanni appeared before the College on Sunday morning [13 December] and he expressed himself at length – weighing his words carefully but making his position clear. He concluded by asking permission to leave their service, since these gentlemen show him so little consideration. If he has indeed performed so poorly, the Doge should let him go when his current commission comes to an end, although they can claim a grace period of two years ... The Doge immediately acquiesced, but only in very general terms.'[45]

Don Giovanni played with the idea of returning to Florence,[46] of moving to Padua,[47] and finally – more decisively – entering the service of the duke of Mantua as governor of the territory of Monferrato.[48] The Venetians might have wanted him off their payroll but they did not want him taking military and political secrets and going elsewhere. So, they stalled and let his illnesses take their course.

Money was Don Giovanni's most pressing concern since the Venetians had no intention of meeting past obligations, let alone future ones. Meanwhile, his Medici relatives were disinclined to help unless he profoundly modified his personal life – losing his dreadful consort Livia Vernazza. 'I am in grave need of money,' Don Giovanni complained to his old friend and confidant Cosimo Baroncelli. 'I continue spending but am unable to collect what the government owes me ... Soon I will be left without even a house, and I will then have to retire and live in diminished circumstances like a private gentleman, or if worse comes to worst, as a simple citizen. I don't see myself going to live in Florence – not even if they ordered me, asked me, or invited me nicely.'[49]

'Signor Cosimo, we have been living like gypsies for the past seven months,' Don Giovanni lamented on 25 July 1620.[50] Then a few weeks later, unable to afford a new lease, he gave up his palace on the Grand Canal. 'I delayed as long as I could, paying by the month although the landlord wanted to rent for a full year. Meanwhile, there is my young son, who is a great expense and he is now teething ... My lady is pregnant and my own health is uncertain, with inflammation in my leg and congestion and swelling in my throat.'[51] At the beginning of September, Don Giovanni transferred his household to Murano,[52] an outlying island where normally only glass-blowers lived by choice.

By this time Don Giovanni was betting everything on a single get-rich-quick scheme, combining his mastery of alchemical science with his presumed access to the Holy Roman Emperor. 'His Majesty the Emperor is the Grand Duke's brother-in-law,' Don Giovanni noted to Cosimo Baroncelli on 1 March 1620. 'This project is absolutely safe. It can be realized with ease and brought to a satisfactory conclusion because the person who proposed it to me has all of the necessary resources and authority. We are not talking about a confidence trick or castles in the air or false pretenses – but something that is solid, on the up and up and founded in concrete reality.'[53] However exciting Don Giovanni's proposal, it came to naught. Grand Duchess Maria Magdalena von Habsburg, wife of Cosimo II, was dismayed by anything associated with alchemy (including most advanced technology) and politely refused to lobby her brother Emperor Ferdinand II.[54]

'Popular acclaim is mere vanity. People and shit, it's all the same thing. The court is founded on adulation.'[55] Much of this was true, but the sentiments were hardly original and Don Giovanni had been reduced to grumbling like a disgruntled outsider.

While caught in an inexorable downward spiral, he could still enjoy a few moments of fleeting triumph – especially his visit to the Mantuan Court for the Carnival of 1619 and the birth of his first child in August of that year. Both events produced ample grist for the gossip mills in Venice, Florence, and elsewhere. On 29 January 1619 Ambassador Niccolò Sacchetti shared the latest with Granducal Secretary Curzio Picchena:

> A few hours ago, I was given to understand that Signor Don Giovanni had dispatched a special messenger to Mantua with letters responding to the Duke's invitation, apparently begging the Duke [Ferdinando Gonzaga] to send his state barge [*bucentoro*] to transport him there for Carnival ... I was also told that he is taking his lady with him, but I am not quite ready to believe this. For various reasons, I don't see how that woman can possibly be received [at the Mantuan Court] in a manner that Don Giovanni would find agreeable. Many will be curious to learn the details and the outcome – if the visit does in fact take place.[56]

Jaws were soon dropping, all across northern Italy. 'The Duke of Mantua's barge arrived today for Signor Don Giovanni,' Sacchetti informed Florence on 2 February 1619. 'His Excellency will be heading off to Mantua on Tuesday [5 February] for the rest of the Carnival season with his Cleopatra in tow.'[57] On 7 February Grand Duke Cosimo II warned his sister Caterina dei Medici Gonzaga, reigning Duchess of Mantua: 'I consider that woman [Livia Vernazza] to be nothing less than a whore. If I were certain that he had married her, or that he was about to marry her, I should not wish him to be considered a member of this family ever again and I would behave as though I had never known him.'[58]

The Tuscan faction had cause to grit their teeth yet again when Livia and Don Giovanni engendered a male heir, Giovanni Francesco Maria dei Medici. The Venetian government was keen to maintain appearances, so they treated the baptism as a state occasion. 'That baptism took place today,' Ambassador Sacchetti reported on 5 October 1619. 'The principal participant was the Mantuan Ambassador representing his Duke, along with one of the Doge's sons. There were thirty-five other godparents, including senators and members of the leading families here ... The ceremony was a solemn one with fine music – all to satisfy that Lady, who will now be more of a lady than ever.'[59]

Livia Vernazza was universally detested – by none more sincerely than Cosimo Baroncelli, who had entered Don Giovanni's service at the age of twelve in 1581.[60] Years after his comrade's death, Baroncelli unburdened himself in a personal memoir for the instruction of his own sons:

> That female was Genoese, daughter of a certain mattress-maker named Bernardo Vernazza and wife of yet another of the same profession named Battista Granara. Although her birth was of the very lowest, she was insolent and proud to the utmost degree – even daring to pit herself against His Most Serene Excellency the Grand Duke, from whom she received no few insults. She created ugly situations for Don Giovanni but he was so lost in love that he would have done anything for her, considering her most impertinent actions suitable and appropriate. That female sought to banish everyone in His Excellency's service – especially those who had been there longest – bringing in others who were entirely dependent on her.[61]

Don Giovanni's household, in Venice and then Murano, was developing an infamous reputation, as Ambassador Sacchetti noted during the summer of 1619: 'I rarely go to his residence or have any contact there, since the members of my own establishment are treated with suspicion ... In his house, there are now only low people, and they are not to be trusted in any way.'[62] Don Giovanni's secretary[63] Attanasio Ridolfi was a foundling from Florence's Ospedale degli Innocenti[64] – but the Ospedale refused to send more of its young charges, fearing for their safety and moral well-being. In the spring of 1618 Don Giovanni loosed a tirade on Cosimo Baroncelli:

> I wrote to the Innocenti asking for another of those young girls for Signora

Livia, since they had already sent us four others. They were all treated well and raised as carefully as the first gentlewomen of that city [Florence], learning all of the appropriate customs and accomplishments ... Now that the time has come to send the latest girl, this gentleman [the new Prior of the Innocenti] replied in the most offensive manner ... as if my house was the Via del Giardino [Florence's most notorious centre of prostitution] or some rotten brothel.[65]

Apart from the harm to Don Giovanni's reputation (Donna Livia had none to begin with), the uncontrolled coming and going of low people caused collateral damage of other kinds. Their household spun off servants of bad character with far too much inside information – and master and mistress both had a great deal to hide.

On 9 November 1619 Ambassador Sacchetti advised Cosimo II, 'One of Don Giovanni's retainers named [Antonio] Ceccherelli has taken refuge in Your Highness' house [the Tuscan Embassy in Venice] by request of Don Giovanni himself.'[66] Then a week later, Sacchetti reported the full story:

Some months ago, they [the Venetian authorities] imprisoned a certain [Lorenzo] Bartolone for various misdeeds. For many years, he had been a personal servant of Don Giovanni's and I fear that he told them much about His Excellency's affairs. In order to corroborate his own assertions, Bartolone probably mentioned Livia's confidential servant Ceccherelli – inciting the curiosity of these gentlemen. They are now eager to get their hands on Ceccherelli, using the pretext of an old murder that he committed with some other servants of Don Giovanni's.[67]

Sacchetti hoped to make the problem go away by smuggling Antonio Ceccherelli out of Venice, not realizing quite how many devastating secrets he had cut loose. For years, Ceccherelli had managed Livia Vernazza's most clandestine affairs, especially the controversial annulment of her first marriage to Battista Granara (fiercely but unsuccessfully opposed by the Medici).[68] Ceccherelli also witnessed Livia's impromptu marriage with Don Giovanni, hours before the birth of their son Giovanni Francesco Maria.[69]

Lorenzo Bartolone had been moving back and forth between Venice and Florence for several years, more or less in the service of Don Giovanni dei Medici. On 21 July 1618 Cosimo Baroncelli shared the latest Bartolone sighting:

Bartolone appeared [in Florence] and he came to see me on Thursday evening [19 July]. I asked him what he was doing here and he said that he had come to be treated for the pox (*mal franzese*). If he had really come for medical treatment – I warned him – he shouldn't even think of making the rounds of the brothels or hanging out in taverns, since I wouldn't put up with it … Then yesterday morning [20 July], he came to see me again and said that he needed [my help in obtaining permission] to bear arms. Someone who has come for medical treatment – I told him – doesn't need to go around with weapons … I will certainly keep an eye on him and if he doesn't begin his cure within two or three days, I will make sure that he gets what he deserves.[70]

Don Giovanni definitively lost patience with Lorenzo Bartolone in the spring of 1619, after he involved Buonaventura Gualterotti – Raffael's other son – in a thwarted poisoning plot.[71] 'If Bartolone shows up in Florence,' Cosimo Baroncelli assured him, 'it won't be difficult to make him fall into the net … All he has to do is arrive here, then I will see that your order is carried out and he receives his just deserts.'[72]

Cosimo wasted no time, when Lorenzo finally broke cover in June of 1620: 'As soon as Bartolone was seen to alight, they put him in the isolation cells (*prigione segrete*)…The Chief Constable seized him immediately at Your Excellency's behest, without waiting to take him *in flagrante.*'[73]

In Florence the isolation cells of the Bargello prison were filling up with past and present servants of Don Giovanni dei Medici – all of whom had stories to tell. Benedetto Blanis would be joining Lorenzo Bartolone before the end of the month. And if Antonio Ceccherelli was not already *in segreta*, he would be very soon.

Cosmic Battle

By the summer of 1620 Don Giovanni had been away from Florence for five years. Overwhelmed by his own troubles and alienated from the Medici family, he had lost touch with the growing strangeness of daily life at their court. Grand Duke Cosimo II was slowly dying, and his relentless decline eclipsed all other concerns. As seen from the Pitti Palace, a cosmic battle was being waged for the earthly existence of the young ruler (he expired at the age of thirty on 28 February 1621), and the Medici themselves were the principal fighters on the front line.

Cosimo Baroncelli, only a moderately pious individual under normal circumstances, evoked the latest crisis in December of 1619:

We understand that the Most Serene Grand Duke has improved greatly thanks to the continuous prayers that are being offered here. Her Most Serene Highness [Christine de Lorraine], the Most Serene Archduchess [Maria Magdalena von Habsburg], and all the princesses and all the young princes went barefoot in procession from the Pitti Palace to the Santissima Annunziata with the Duchess-to-be of Urbino [Claudia dei Medici] carrying the Cross. God, it seems, wished to fulfil their fervent prayers along with the prayers of the populace since His Highness showed a remarkable recovery at that very time. The doctors had given up all hope of natural remedies, so we see that the Lord God preserved this good prince for the sake of his city and his subjects.[74]

'At court, they keep saying that His Highness is getting better,' Baroncelli noted six months later, on 22 June 1620, 'but that is not the opinion of the medical doctors ... We need to think of the Grand Duke as being eighty years old, and every day that he survives is a special grace from God.'[75] In August the court threw itself into yet another round of desperate pleas for divine intercession:

His Highness has been getting worse and we fear greatly for his life. He is suffering from intense colic pains, he vomits continually, and he has almost no voice, so we are all trembling from the danger that assails him. Madama Serenissima [Christine de Lorraine] stayed with him throughout the night on Monday [3 August] without resting at all, as did the Serenissima Arciduchessa [Maria Magdalena von Habsburg]. We thought that he was ready to depart for heaven, but in response to all the prayers, it pleased the Lord God to leave him with us. That very night, they began the Devotion of the Forty Hours in Serenissima Madama's chapel in the Pitti Palace, and the next morning, they began this same devotion at the Santissima Annunziata. Many prisoners were freed from the Stinche jail,[76] and many other acts of piety and mercy were performed.[77]

'His Highness' illness is considered to have no natural nor ordinary cause,' one courtier observed, 'so there is recourse to spiritual remedies in order to reach where the doctors cannot.'[78] Many in Florence saw this struggle between good and evil, between natural and unnatural causes, in the most concrete terms – someone was trying to murder the Grand Duke through occult means. Benedetto Blanis, in his isolation cell in the Bargello prison, was caught in a real-life witch-hunt – as his brother Salamone explained on 14 August 1620:

> We should be praying to God for the Grand Duke's health, Messer Albizzo Vecchi [Master of the Pages at the Medici Court] tells us, because otherwise our case is hopeless. In this way, he let me know that they suspect someone has cast a spell on His Highness causing the illness. I ask Your Most Illustrious Excellency to consider our strange predicament, since even a good character offers no protection from slander by pestilent tongues. In the end, we hope that God Almighty will spite our many enemies and see that justice is done. Our family has never entertained even the slightest thought contrary to the Padroni [Medici Princes].[79]

Salamone made a desperate effort, travelling to Venice to rally their crumbling defence. Don Giovanni was Benedetto's only earthly hope, but he was then at the lowest point in his own life, packing for his forced move to Murano. If Salamone achieved anything by his journey, it left no trace in Don Giovanni's letters.[80] On 4 September 1620, the day after his return to Florence, he offered a disheartening update:

> I expected to find Benedetto's affairs well on their way to resolution but things, alas, now seem more difficult than ever … We had been working to improve the conditions of his confinement but were told that we were wasting our time. Serenissima Madama [Christine de Lorraine] says that she will not get involved. The Inquisitor says that the case is not his since he did not present it. Cospi [Anton Maria Cospi, Secretary of the Eight Magistrates] says that we should not come to him because he has nothing to do with the matter. Instead, we should commend ourselves to God, who can free us from all these woes … I presented Your Most Illustrious Excellency's letter to Captain Pier Capponi and he replied that the case is pending with the Attorney General (Auditore Fiscale).[81]

The Auditore Fiscale, then Vincenzo Piazza, was the high official who oversaw the administration of Florentine justice. Salamone called on him in person, running headlong into another stone wall. The Auditore already knew everything that he needed to know about the Blanis family, since Christine de Lorraine had recently assigned him to the Sernigi case,[82] their most disastrous adventure in covert usury:[83]

Benedetto's affair was not his, the Auditore said, but if it came his way, he would do what he could. 'Are you Lelio?' he asked me. 'No, I am Salamone,' I answered, 'always ready to serve you.' 'So, you must be the one who went to Venice,' he said, then he wanted to know what I accomplished there. I told him that I begged Your Excellency to assist Benedetto in his present tribulation, and Your Excellency replied that it would serve no purpose – not even a single syllable – since everything was blocked ... However, Benedetto had no need of help, Your Excellency said, since his innocence was help enough. The Sernigi lawsuit was not mentioned.[84]

Benedetto was despised at the Medici Court, and jurisdiction in his case was everywhere and nowhere. 'Asking for justice does not seem an inappropriate demand,' Salamone sighed, 'but justice for us is dead and buried. To our great misfortune, vicious tongues have transmitted false information to the *Padroni* [the Medici Princes], thereby destroying three luckless families.'[85] Information, false or otherwise, was in plentiful supply – as Salamone informed Don Giovanni on 26 September:

A Jew got out of prison where he had been in the company of Antonio Ceccherelli, and he told me that Ceccherelli has been defaming the Illustrious Lady Livia [Vernazza]. Ceccherelli says that your lady was always holed up in her chamber with that woman from Lucca and Benedetto was always there writing. Among his other lies, Ceccherelli said that one morning while Your Lady was dressing, a little parchment scroll fell from around her neck. A girl who was there sweeping picked it up, took it away, opened it and saw that there were Hebrew letters.[86]

Livia Vernazza, Benedetto Blanis, and Jewish sorcery – Ceccherelli was eager to tell the authorities exactly what they wanted to hear, and at least some of it was probably true:[87]

Ceccherelli is relating this and other nonsense, perhaps hoping to buy his freedom with such inventions. He might well have struck a deal of some kind with the Chief Constable (Bargello), since the two of them have developed a close and confidential relationship. Ceccherelli sends for the Bargello whenever he wishes, and they talk together at great length ... Last week, we believed that Benedetto's case was moving ahead. The Inquisitor had already taken it up and was beginning to question him regarding that initial matter of the baptized Jew who absconded – but this latest development with Ceccherelli stopped everything dead.[88]

Salamone then added an urgent postscript: 'While I was writing, I received a note from Messer Benedetto. I enclose it here and I commend it to Your Excellency's attention.' A minuscule sheet of flimsy paper measuring less than 3 by 4 inches,[89] folded and refolded many times, covered with twenty-one lines of writing so tiny as to be almost illegible to the naked eye ... This is the last letter that we have from Benedetto Blanis to Don Giovanni dei Medici, smuggled out of the Bargello prison in Florence:

> My Most Illustrious and Excellent Lord and Patron,
> In these present miseries, I am kept alive by my own innocence and by the hope of Your Most Illustrious Excellency's protection. I bear these misfortunes willingly, hoping that I will be restored to glory at long last in the company of all the innocent while those who speak evil will be destroyed. These hopes will be realized more quickly and easily with your intervention, if you defend me with greater vigour from the pestilent tongues of those who defame and slander me, daring to vociferate against your holy, devout, and pious studies. I refer to Bartolone and Ceccherelli, to give two examples, based on what I have been able to determine while down in this pit. However, I have seen neither of them nor have I been examined since 17 August. If the tribunal calls on me to account for the time that I spent in Your Excellency's company reading, writing, and virtuously studying holy scriptures, you might do well to bring that most precious book, *The Mirror of Truth*, which publicly demonstrates the veracity of all I say. In those printed pages of scholarly doctrine full of Hebraic, Greek, and Latin writings, they will see how you and I passed our time. Here in these conditions, I can do nothing more and you already know my needs better than I can describe them. So, I entrust my family to you with the hope that you will resolve the calamitous misfortune that afflicts it. May God bring you every happiness. Pasqua. Benedetto Blanis.[90]

Pasqua ... Pesach ... Passover ... Easter. In 1621 the Jewish Passover (*Pasqua*) did not come for another six months, until the evening of 5 April and Christian Easter (also *Pasqua*) until sunrise on 11 April.[91] Benedetto was not commenting on a specific holiday, he was making a powerful reference to liberation from physical and spiritual captivity, drawing on many centuries of Jewish experience. From his study of Kabbalah and Hebraic lore, Don Giovanni could recognize its uncanny relevance to Benedetto's predicament.[92]

During this terrible time, Benedetto's disciple Ferdinando Magnani wrote a touching letter to Don Giovanni, conjuring a vision of things past: 'Since Messer Benedetto Blanis has been in jail now for three months, Your Excellency can understand why I have been making such slight progress in the Hebrew language.'[93] Meanwhile, the hunt for Cosimo II's occult assailant had gone off in a very odd direction, as Salamone reported on 3 October 1620:

> I am enclosing a letter from Benedetto, who commends himself to Your Most Illustrious Excellency. Every day he sends us another appeal, so we do not have a single hour of peace. This week in the Ghetto, Doctor da Pellestrina said publicly that a certain monk summoned spirits to find out who had put the spell on the Grand Duke. The spirits replied that it was Madama Serenissima [Christine de Lorraine] – and Your Excellency can now judge whether we should credit sorcery as the cause of his illness.[94]

Doctor Pompilio Evangelisti da Pellestrina (or Palestrina) was a theatrical impresario at the Medici Court, seemingly of Jewish origin.[95] Benedetto's enclosed letter to Don Giovanni does not survive but Salamone was finally exasperated by the futility of his brother's plight. Towards the end of October 1620 he made a last-ditch attempt to unblock the case – or at least, find out what the charges were: 'This week we brought our plea to the Most Reverend Father Inquisitor and begged him to expedite the case. He replied that expediting the case did not depend on him – so we have now lost every hope except for our hope in God.'[96]

Father Inquisitor Cornelio Priatoni was telling the truth – strictly speaking. The Blanis case was firmly lodged in Rome and it no longer depended on him. Even in Florence, the gathering of evidence had been taken out of his hands and assigned to an Adjunct Inquisitor (Vicario), who could be trusted to proceed with exemplary rigour.[97]

The Blanis family was groping through a dense fog of rumours and accusations – surrounded by enemies they could barely see, let alone confront. If the case did not depend on the religious authorities, did it depend on the civil authorities? If it did not depend on Florence, did it depend on Rome? Benedetto, meanwhile, was safely stored away in the Bargello prison, and he was not going home any time soon. Salamone, his dutiful younger brother, had done everything possible, knocking on every imaginable door. All he could do now was dig in for the duration, awaiting the right moment to relaunch his attack.

Salamone continued to write his letters to Venice – now brief and infrequent, usually addressed to Don Giovanni's secretary Attanasio Ridolfi. He kept the line of communication open, even if the chief topic was discount shopping for Livia Vernazza. 'Regarding the wishes of the Most Illustrious Lady,' Salamone Blanis assured Attanasio Ridolfi on 5 February 1621, 'you can tell her that she will discover in me the same willingness to serve that she found in my brother ... I am sending you some samples of taffeta of which I can get 6 or 8 or even 10 braccia [3.8 or 5.1 or 6.4 yards] for 3 lire 6 soldi 8 piccioli per braccio in cash – although it would cost at least 4 lire around the shops. I am also sending you a sample of gold thread ... of which I can get 5 ounces at 5 lire 5 soldi per ounce, more or less.'[98]

At the Medici Court, the resident power brokers had little time to spare for a single renegade Jew. After many false alarms, Cosimo II was finally dying and on 10 February 1621, Christine de Lorraine took extraordinary measures to suppress the current Carnival, banning masked revelry throughout Tuscany. 'Prayers, instead, are to be offered for the health of the Grand Duke.'[99]

On 27 February 1621 (the Friday after Ash Wednesday), Cosimo Baroncelli wrote Don Giovanni dei Medici: 'Now that the rejoicing and jollification of Carnival is over, we can all concentrate on serious things ... But here we had only a meagre Carnival and God knows what Lent will be like, with everyone frightened and afflicted by the grave illness of our Most Serene Patron. Continuous prayers are being offered for his recovery, and may the Lord God answer them for the sake of this State.'[100] Cosimo II, Don Giovanni's nephew, died the very next day. And Ferdinando II, his ten-year-old grand-nephew, ascended the Tuscan throne.

Out of Sight and Out of Mind

After Don Giovanni's retreat to Murano in September of 1620, he was effectively out of sight. Then after the death of Cosimo II in February of 1621, he was also out of mind. Don Giovanni lived the last five months of his life (he died on 19 July 1621) as an isolated figure whose time had come and gone. Although only in his early fifties, he was already an historical relic: the last surviving son of Cosimo I dei Medici, founder of the Grand Dukedom of Tuscany. 'My beard is white,' Don Giovanni observed, 'and I am the oldest of this house, which allows me to offer opinions based on experience'[101] – if anyone was still listening.

In the principal cities of Europe, the local Tuscan communities were staging lavish memorial services for Cosimo II. 'The Florentine nobles here [in Venice] are preparing sumptuous exequies for the late Grand Duke of holy memory,' Ambassador Niccolò Sacchetti informed Ferdinando II. 'They are going to spend three thousand ducats, it is said, and Monsignor Grimani[102] has agreed to sing the solemn Mass. This will be celebrated by at least four bishops positioned around the catafalque, as is customary at the funerals of great princes.'[103]

Sacchetti's letter was addressed to Ferdinando II but the young grand duke almost certainly never saw it. All state correspondence went to the Council of Regents, headed by his mother Maria Magdalena von Habsburg and his grandmother Christine de Lorraine. On 13 March 1621 Cosimo Baroncelli offered Don Giovanni the latest news from the Florentine Court. 'On Thursday morning [11 March], the Senate and the Council of Two Hundred went to swear allegiance to our Most Serene Patron in the usual great room [the Salone dei Cinquecento in Palazzo Vecchio]. His Highness was seated on the usual throne, with his Most Serene Mother at his right hand and His Most Serene Grandmother at his left. The Grand Duke himself spoke a few words and everyone admired his graciousness, but I was too far away to hear.'[104]

In the Cerimonia del Giuramento (Ceremony of the Oath of Allegiance), the chief theme was continuity – and in a very real sense, little had changed. Maria Magdalena was now given pride of place at Ferdinando's right hand, marking the dynastic succession from one Granduchessa Madre to the next.[105] Meanwhile, in the great *saloni* of the Pitti Palace, the Medici State was governed much as before – by an executive committee of two women with their secretaries and advisers. And in the isolation cells of the Bargello prison, Benedetto Blanis was still locked away – out of sight and out of mind – while the same enemies held the key. Amid the wreckage of their lives, the Blanis family had at least one fresh hope – perhaps the rulers of Tuscany were now too busy to obsess over a troublesome little Jew.

Death continued to be a major distraction at the Medici Court. Felipe III, King of Spain and brother-in-law of Maria Magdalena von Habsburg, died in Madrid on 31 March 1621. Closer to home, Don Antonio dei Medici (1576–1621) was coming to the end of his relatively short life, ravaged by years of venereal disease. Back in 1616 at the height of the Pernicca gambling scandal,[106] Benedetto Blanis had already noted, 'I brought [my brother-in-law Moisé Lattone] over to the Casino [di San Marco] on the order of Signor Don Antonio, who is in such a bad way that it is painful to see him.'[107] 'Signor Don Antonio is now *in extremis*,' Cosimo Baroncelli wrote on 24 April 1621, 'and he can go off at any time. On Thursday [22 April], Madama [Christine de Lorraine] went to see him, and they say that he wept bitterly over his miserable state and commended his children to her. Madama promised to keep them under her perpetual protection.'[108]

Don Antonio's death on 2 May 1621 was a dress rehearsal for Don Giovanni's eleven weeks later. Both were recognized bastard sons of grand dukes (Cosimo I in Don Giovanni's case, Francesco I in Don Antonio's),[109] and both were military men with strong inclinations towards the occult. Both also maintained irregular households and produced problematic children – attached by dotted lines to the Medici family tree. Don Antonio's consort was Artemisia Tozzi, a low-born woman from Lucca with whom he had three sons (there were already two daughters from previous relationships). After his death, Tozzi was hustled off to the Florentine Convent of San Clemente where she died in 1643, and their offspring were channelled into respectable military and religious careers. Meanwhile, Don Antonio's extensive property (worth a million scudi in gold, by some estimates) reverted to the grand duke.[110]

Don Giovanni fought the Venetian government until the very end, striving to break their stranglehold on his life and career – when his health was already too far gone for it to make much difference. On 5 April 1621, less than four months before his death, Ambassador Sacchetti advised the grand duke and his surrogates, 'Don Giovanni is thinking of approaching the College yet again for permission to leave but we doubt that he will have better luck than before.'[111]

Don Giovanni's name ceased to figure in the embassy correspondence, and even the Blanis family accepted the inevitable – their great patron was now beside the point. On 4 May 1621 Salamone Blanis made a final perfunctory appeal. David Blanis was on his way to Venice, Salamone explained, to look after some rental properties in the local Ghetto:[112]

> My brother David's imminent trip to Venice has emboldened me to write you these few lines, even though you did not deem my previous letters worthy of reply – the ones that I sent you by way of my brother-in-law in Ferrara. In any case, I beg you to help Benedetto in the prescribed manner or in some other way, if you can do so without prejudice to yourself. This would be an act of charity, raising four families out of the depths of misery.

I am enclosing a little letter from Benedetto who lives with the firm hope of your gracious help.[113]

Benedetto's little letter does not survive, and this is the last known communication between the Blanis family and Don Giovanni dei Medici. If David called on his brother's phantom patron, it left no trace in the archives. All that now remained of their former relationship were a few mutual enemies – with Antonio Ceccherelli in first place.

'That Ceccherelli was long in jail,' Cosimo Baroncelli informed Don Giovanni. 'They kept him there even after the Chief Constable personally let him out of the isolation cells. Then, as a special grace in time of illness, the Most Serene Grand Duke of glorious memory freed him along with many others. Later, however, His Highness saw this Ceccherelli and recognized that he was a bad man, judging by his constitution and his physiognomy.'[114]

'Knaves like Ceccherelli, Bartolone, and others of their ilk want to torment me by harming the things that I hold most dear, especially Signora Livia,' Don Giovanni protested on 19 June 1621.[115] 'Anton Ceccherelli is a dishonourable thief. For a single giulio [a small coin], he would renounce God, murder his own father, and betray Christ. He does not believe in God – as he has said before reliable witnesses – and he regrets any scrap of belief that he might once have had. This is the man who dares bring charges to the Inquisition and offers evidence against the lady he formerly served.'[116]

Antonio Ceccherelli was the star witness against Livia Vernazza, and he was bartering his inside information for everything it was worth. The Medici, meanwhile, were busy planning their mop-up operation in Don Giovanni's household. This was scheduled to begin one second after his death – and if the Inquisition could help, so much the better. On 12 July 1621 Ambassador Niccolò Sacchetti wrote Granducal Secretary Curzio Picchena:

One of Signor Don Giovanni's servants informed me yesterday that His Excellency took to his bed two days ago and is seriously unwell. I hadn't seen him for a long time, so I headed out to Murano late in the day to check on the situation. I found him with a high fever, very apprehensive, and in quite a bad way, as he told me himself ... However, his body is robust and the force of nature is strong. While I was there, his illness reached its crisis with massive sweating and urination ... We will now wait and see what happens after they bleed him this morning.[117]

Sacchetti was summoned back to Murano three days later on 15 July, and he immediately sent an express courier to the Medici Court. Don Giovanni's life hung in the balance, and none of the doctors was willing to predict the outcome. 'His Excellency confessed after I reminded him this morning. He did so willingly and then, without prompting, asked to receive the Holy Sacrament tomorrow.'[118] Everyone was now focusing on the prospect of a good death and looking into the future – none more anxiously than Livia Vernazza.

'That Livia sent me the enclosed note and I am forwarding it to you,' Ambassador Sacchetti told Secretary Picchena. 'When I was leaving His Excellency the other day, she came up to me and made me listen to her. She expressed herself in strong terms and seemed thoroughly overwhelmed. I told her that she should commend herself to God and behave prudently. I repeated this several times, and she seemed to understand me.'[119] Vernazza's note to Sacchetti was almost childlike in its desperation: 'I beg Your Lordship to tell Their Highnesses in Florence about my situation and express my sincere devotion to Their Most Serene House. If they have the chance to experience my humble servitude at first hand, they will not think me so bad a woman as I have been painted.'[120]

The end came quickly, on 19 July 1621, as Ambassador Sacchetti announced to Grand Duke Ferdinando II: 'This morning around the fifteenth hour [10:30 a.m.], Signor Don Giovanni passed to the other life, after receiving all the Sacraments of the Church with great devotion and feeling. Throughout the course of his illness, he was unfailingly patient, his soul rising above matters of life and death since he was totally resigned to our Blessed Lord God.'[121]

Sacchetti, meanwhile, wrote a fuller and franker report to Secretary Picchena – rigorously pruning the moral uplift and getting on with the business at hand:

> He received all of the Church's Holy Sacraments and died with great constancy of soul, leaving all of his servants much afflicted since he had no opportunity to recognize their service in any way. I immediately raced out to Murano so that I could keep an eye on developments there while waiting to learn Their Highnesses' intentions ... Everything is topsy-turvy and Livia is on tenterhooks regarding her own affairs, particularly since His Excellency made no provisions, neither by will nor codicil. She has been in bed with a bit of fever for two days now, and I understand that she is six or seven months pregnant.[122]

Anguished and bedridden, Livia still had the presence of mind to spirit their most valuable possessions out the back door. 'I had to involve myself in many complicated things,' Sacchetti noted in a postscript to his 19 July letter to Picchena, 'since I do not know Their Highnesses' intentions. In particular, I had to block the removal of items from this house. Yesterday, they carried off a cabinet that was believed to contain Livia's jewels but I had already issued orders and had the doors locked. Alessandro delle Rede [the major-domo] brought it back, and then they did their best to quiet that woman.'[123]

Ambassador Sacchetti launched a three-pronged attack – retrieving the money and silverware that Donna Livia had already cached in nearby convents,[124] suppressing the strange and compromising items that were turning up in their household, and bending Donna Livia to the will of the authorities in Florence. Now that Don Giovanni was safely dead, the Venetian government announced a full state funeral for their supreme military leader, putting a good face on a troubled relationship.

The Medici immediately sent Don Garzia de Montalvo back to Venice, (he was the man who had previously tried and failed to dissuade Don Giovanni from marrying his long-time mistress). The simplest solution to the Vernazza problem was immuring her in a Venetian convent, but the local establishments (they discovered) were insufficiently prison-like for their purpose. The Medici wanted her in Tuscany where they could deal with her personally, and they wanted her there as quickly as possible.[125] 'At first, Don Garzia and I were very worried,' Niccolò Sacchetti breathed a sigh of relief on 23 July 1621, 'but he resolved the problem with a single shrewd move. We can't help laughing at the beauty of his ploy':

On Thursday [22 July] a bundle of letters arrived from Florence addressed to Don Giovanni, and I handed them over to Don Garzia. Livia asked for the ones from [Cosimo] Baroncelli, and Don Garzia took these and opened them in her presence. He came to the letter where Baroncelli quoted Their Highnesses. Serious charges, they said, had been levelled against Livia before the Inquisition but they could not interevene because she was outside Tuscany. Don Garzia immediately rose to the occasion, frightening her badly with threats of his own invention ... Yesterday and today, he constantly rehashed these threats ... and this evening at six hours after sunset [around 1a.m.], Livia finally got onto the boat.[126]

Livia's son Giovanni Francesco Maria was sent off to Florence four days later, on 28 July. 'They did not want him to travel with his mother in order to keep her in a submissive frame of mind.'[127] In Livia Vernazza's case, there was much to interest the Inquisition. Antonio Ceccherelli, their presumed informant, knew everything that there was to know about the annulment of her first marriage and her subsequent marriage with Don Giovanni dei Medici. If there had been subterfuge of any kind,[128] she was guilty of the grievous sin of bigamy. Sorcery was another plausible allegation – in league with a notorious Jewish practitioner of the black arts.

Benedetto Blanis was not mentioned by name in any of the letters between Venice and Florence, but souvenirs were turning up every place Ambassador Sacchetti looked. Seven hundred books in ten large crates were sent to Venice from the villa at Palvello. 'Many forbidden ones are dispersed among these,' Sacchetti noted on 24 July, 'including prohibited books of the first class.'[129] On 28 August he warned Curzio Picchena: 'I am sending you a long sheet of vellum full of figures and mysterious Hebrew characters. This can only be a curious item of some kind.'[130] It was, presumably, the *Tree of Kabbalah* (*Tree of the Sephirot*) that Benedetto had copied from an original belonging to his uncle in Lippiano.[131]

Shock followed shock as the embassy staff worked their way through the house in Murano. 'We came upon a strongbox,' Sacchetti reported on 28 September 1621. 'For the sake of His Excellency's memory and reputation, I regret having to send you the things that we found inside':

> There is a quantity of superstitious writings, I don't know if they have to do with Kabbalah or magic or perhaps both – but judging from the little that I saw while packing, these are troublesome items that could contaminate anyone who comes in contact... One thing stunned me beyond all limits. There is a calfskin box with Don Giovanni's arms on the cover and inside that a smaller box bound in iron. I was expecting to find jewels or things of that sort – but instead, I found a bag containing a book placed between two cushions full of aromatic substances. What is written in that book, I will let you see for yourselves in Florence ... Then there is a tiny book and also another book in quarto, both printed in the Hebrew language, and a ring which might be something mysterious ... A little gilded box holds a few miniature portraits, and they say that one of these is of Livia. I packed a large box with 'Confidential Items' written on the top and filled it with smaller boxes containing things that made me suspicious when I looked inside. Also, there is a knife with some characters written on the handle.[132]

Sacchetti's revelations were not limited to the occult. He reclaimed legal and financial documents entrusted to Livia Vernazza's midwife, including a letter written to Livia by Don Giovanni himself. 'This will astonish everyone there in Florence.'[133] Don Giovanni did not leave important scholarly or literary compositions – apart from his unwelcome *Mirror of Truth*[134] – but there were many notebooks and many writings begun and abandoned.[135] 'Among His Excellency's books, we found the draft of a particularly curious work which discusses a way to capture the city of Venice, taking it by surprise ... These gentlemen [of the Venetian government] were not pleased that Signor Don Giovanni entertained ideas of this kind and did not share them while he was still alive.'[136]

Don Giovanni's household was disbanded so quickly that there was no need to dress his servants in mourning[137] – unseemly haste by the standards of the time. On 25 September 1621 Ambassador Sacchetti concluded the sale of his domestic property, realizing the unexpected sum of 4,220 ducats, thanks to a bidding war between Jewish second-hand dealers.[138] Don Giovanni dei Medici was now gone and well on his way to being forgotten. And Benedetto Blanis was still in jail, awaiting justice from man or God.

chapter thirteen

Habeas Corpus?

Why was I brought here for interrogation? I don't know anything about that. I am being kept in the isolation cells, so nobody tells me anything at all. Maybe I am going to be released and that is why I was summoned.[1]

It is at the behest of the Holy Office that I am now incarcerated in the Bargello prison. Since I am a Jew, I have nothing to do with Battista Granara – most of all because I am more of a friend than an enemy to Signora Livia. I profess to live as a good Jew and … I have always told the truth, as I have done throughout the present examination.[2]

Benedetto Blanis testified before the court of the Archbishop of Florence on three occasions: 22 September 1621,[3] 6 October 1621,[4] and 19 January 1622.[5] The authorities were committed to eradicating the last vestiges of Livia Vernazza's long ascendency over the late Don Giovanni, and they already knew how the case needed to end – with the reinstatement of Livia's first marriage to Battista Granara, the annulment of her second 'bigamous' marriage to Don Giovanni, the delegitimization of their son Giovanni Francesco Maria, and the return of all property to the Medici family.[6]

Benedetto's testimony fills more than fifty pages, and it reveals much of the prevailing strangeness of the Medici-Vernazza household. In fact, the Jew fell into his own trap – knowing more than he should about some things while feigning ignorance of others:

The witness [Benedetto Blanis] was warned to think carefully and try to remember whether he ever discussed with Signor Don Giovanni the operations to be carried out in Genoa and exactly what they discussed. It is highly implausible that Signor Don Giovanni did not confer with this witness, considering the confidential intimacy that they shared. In particular, the witness should consider well the method for obtaining depositions [from Genoa] ... and also the proposal to have Livia's husband killed.[7]

When it came to manipulated evidence from Genoa and murder plots, the investigators already had chapter and verse from Antonio Ceccherelli – formerly the chief culprit and now the prosecution's star informant:[8]

The witness [Benedetto Blanis] was warned once again and he was told that they had a statement from Ceccherelli, saying that he was personally involved. The witness knows very well that everything was carried out by order of Signor Don Giovanni. Furthermore, the witness and Ceccherelli went together to meet with Livia's brother at Battista Besenti's inn [in Venice], by order of Signor Don Giovanni, with His Lordship's knowledge, will, counsel, and consent. In this affair, the drafts of the letters originated with Signor Don Giovanni, and they were then written up by Ceccherelli.[9]

According to Ceccherelli, Benedetto was close at hand – helping him prepare fraudulent documents: 'The first words on that paper "This is a copy of the required affidavit" were written by the aforementioned Jew Benedetto Blanis. I can recognize his hand and his mode of writing since I have seen him write on many occasions.'[10] Ceccherelli's identification was confirmed by three other members of Don Giovanni's household.[11]

The investigators had a double mandate: to incriminate Livia Vernazza while deflecting public attention from the late Don Giovanni.[12] Antonio Ceccherelli was in the clear and profiting nicely from his timely testimony.[13] Meanwhile, the Cardinals General of the Inquisition were proceeding against Benedetto on other grievous charges:

12 October 1621 – The Jew Benedetto Blanis was incarcerated by the Holy Office in Florence for encouraging a neophyte to relapse to Judaism. The case was referred to the Inquisitor in that city and the present Council hereby decrees that the said Inquisitor should proceed with full rigour in discovering the ultimate truth in this matter.[14]

Less than three months after the death of Don Giovanni dei Medici, the Inquisition in Rome ruled that their Blanis case was indeed a case.

Somewhere along the way, they decided to overlook the Jew's probable sorcery and certain trafficking in banned books – accusations that would have cast an unhallowed light on the recently deceased.

In the decrees that follow, we hear short, sharp echoes of the inquisitorial process – with a tantalizing lack of supporting data. Dossiers were compiled by local prosecutors and then sent to Rome, including depositions by witnesses and testimony by the prisoners themselves – but little of this contemporary evidence survives:[15]

> 10 November 1621 – In the proceedings against the Jew Benedetto Blanes, under investigation by the Holy Office of the Inquisition in Florence, letters were read from Francesco Maria Gualterotti, dated 31 October 1621. The Vicar of the Holy Office in Florence is to be instructed in writing to keep him in jail, by order of their Most Illustrious Lordships [the Cardinals General].[16]

Canon Gualterotti was still in the thick of things, spurring the prosecutors as vigorously as ever. A second Father Inquisitor then entered the picture:

> 14 December 1621 – In regard to the incarcerated Jew Benedetto Blanis, the Inquisitor in Genoa has sent relevant evidence [to the Inquisitor in Florence] who is authorized to carry this matter through to completion.[17]

Benedetto had spent much of his life scrambling back and forth between Florence and Massa Carrara and that miniature principality fell under the jurisdiction of the infamously harsh Genoese Inquisition.[18] Now that the Vernazza-Granara action was under way (in three dioceses: Florence, Genoa, and nearby Luni-Sarzana), his long association with Don Giovanni and Donna Livia could not have counted in his favour.

There were many cases that the various Inquisitors could have brought against Benedetto but only one went the full distance. On 24 November 1622 the Pope and the Cardinals General weighed the evidence against five defendants. There was 'the Jew Benedetto Blanes incarcerated by the Holy Office in Florence' and also 'the Jews Prospero Finzi, his brother Dante, his wife Sola, and Angelo son of Prospero and Sola, incarcerated by the Holy Office in Genoa':[19]

> They *caused a neophyte* to relapse to Judaism and apostatize from the Chris-

tian faith, together with his wife and son.[20] This case was heard by His Holiness and the authorized Council, which condemned Prospero and Dante to ten years in the galleys for their crime.

This sentence[21] had drastic implications for everyone in Massa Carrara, Jews and Gentiles alike. Dante and Prospero were the acknowledged leaders of the Finzi clan and by extension, the entire Jewish community. Their father Guglielmo Finzi had been the first to settle there in 1561, and he personally created the local banking system. When Dante and Prospero were ordered to the galleys in 1622, there were only two banks in the Cybo Malaspina state – one in Massa and one in Carrara, owned and operated by Dante and Prospero respectively.[22]

In Rome the Pope and the Fathers General enjoined Sola and Angelo[23] – Prospero's wife and son – from interfering with Jewish converts and those taking instruction in the Catholic faith. They barely hinted at a long and dramatic story, presumably documented in case files that no longer exist. In those years, the fate of the entire Finzi family was in play, and it was an open question how many of them would remain Jews. Prospero and Sola had nine children – including Porzia, the recalcitrant wife of David Finzi/Cosimo Tacca.[24] In 1619–20 Porzia, David/Cosimo, and their various offspring ran through a frantic cycle of conversions and deconversions, outraging many at the Medici and Cybo Malaspina courts. Then on 14 March 1621 Flora – another daughter of Prospero and Sola – joined the flock of Finzi *conversi* in a state baptism in Carrara Cathedral.[25]

Whatever Benedetto's relationship with the beleaguered Finzi family, the case against him stalled out on 24 November 1622:

> Although subjected to repeated torture, Benedetto persisted in his denial. He can be dismissed upon payment of a security bond (*fideussione*) to ensure his reappearance – when and if required.[26]

Eight years earlier, at the time of the Pernicca gambling scandal,[27] Benedetto assured Don Giovanni, 'I would suffer any sort of martyrdom rather than jeopardize someone else with my own tongue.'[28] He showed no less fortitude when it came to jeopardizing himself, notwithstanding the Inquisition's celebrated powers of persuasion.

Benedetto's captors were in no hurry to turn him loose. On 6 January 1623 – six weeks after the official decision – Monsignor Filippo Maria Acquanegra, commissioner of the Holy Office in Rome, sent a festive greeting to Monsignor Cornelio Priatoni, Father Inquisitor in Florence. Acquanegra was writing on the Feast of the Epiphany, marking the end of the Christmas season and the beginning of Carnival. His message was as bland and formulaic as a store-bought holiday card, with all of the standard flourishes of the time – then he added a portentous postscript:

> To the Father Inquisitor in Florence
>
>   Most Reverend and Respected Father,
>
>   I offer my most sincere thanks for your gracious affirmation of these happy holidays, and I assure you that I remain committed to your service, should you choose to call on me. This is my perpetual wish and I return the favour of your prayers, hoping that you too receive true and merited consolation. In closing, I kiss your hands ...
>
>   From Rome, 6 January 1623
>
>   Filippo Maria, Commissario del Santo Offitio
>
>   [Postscript] I received the letter from Your Reverence with the information regarding Blanes Hebreo. You would do well not to release him from prison until you hear from us,[29]

Sooner or later, Benedetto was discharged by the Holy Office, presumably on payment of a security bond that the Blanis family could ill afford. However, he was not necessarily released from the Bargello prison, and he remained a continuing presence in the files of the Florentine police court. His notorious *scrocchi, barocchi et usure* – extortionate, twisted, and usurious practices – continued to make their way through the system, duly manipulated by his powerful enemies. In 1623 the Sernigi usury case[30] was finally reaching its disastrous conclusion, with a verdict on 30 August.[31]

Benedetto could hardly have chosen a worse time to fall foul of the law. It was a bad moment for Jews throughout Tuscany, and the Medici were tightening the screws even on privileged Levantines in Pisa and Livorno. On 26 July 1620, less than a month after Benedetto's incarceration in the Bargello, Cosimo II issued an edict that horrified Jewish merchants in these coastal cities. The grand duke and his surrogates stopped short of mandating ghettos in Pisa and Livorno, but they took a giant step in that direction: 'In no way and under no pretext are Jews to cohabit with Christians in the same houses, using the same doors and stairways, even if the rooms and apartments are distinctly separate.'[32] Jews were also denied the use of Christian servants – certainly live-in servants and possibly any servants at all. For people of the merchant class, this would have made life all but impossible; so, they met with the appropriate officials to clarify the situation. Then, having learned the hard lessons of Jewish history, they opted to leave the situation unclear – navigating the ambiguous language of the edict as best they could while waiting for the rigour of enforcement to pass.[33]

When Grand Duke Ferdinando I proclaimed the Livornina in 1593, his goal was to 'encourage and facilitate foreigners who might participate in business and commerce in our beloved city of Pisa and our port and depot of Livorno.'[34] With these words, he inaugurated two decades of unprecedented tolerance, while the Medici granted rights and privileges to almost any Jew who asked for them – all for the greater glory of the Tuscany economy. When Benedetto was arrested, however, the ideology of laissez-faire commerce had worn itself out and the time for saying 'Yes' to Jews had shifted to a time for saying 'No.' Under the stern influence of Christine de Lorraine and Maria Magdalena von Habsburg, the Medici regime was taking a hard look at their special relationship with the killers of Christ – wondering if these marginally welcome guests were actually paying their way.

In the city of Florence, the answer was a resounding 'No!' In the autumn of 1621, while Benedetto was marking the passing days on the walls of his cell in the Bargello prison, the designated Jewish brokers in the local Ghetto emptied the till and skipped town. 'Those Jews Guglielmo and Giuseppe Tesei carried off much property belonging to [Christian] merchants in the Florentine market,' stated Niccolò Sacchetti, the Tuscan Ambassador in Venice on 18 October 1621 – around the time of Don Giovanni's funeral. 'They might already have left here, since they acquired a large sum in Venetian zecchini on Monday [11 October] from one of these traders – as much as five or six thousand in gold.'[35]

On 7 December 1627, after a five-year silence, Benedetto's name reappears amid the terse decrees of the Cardinals General of the Inquisition: 'The Jew Benedetto Blanis asks to be given a formal attestation that he was never sent to justice by the Holy Office in Florence, and he asks to be granted exile from that city. Having read the relevant memoranda, they [the Cardinals General] decided to write the Inquisitor [in Florence] to this effect.'[36]

At long last, a plea bargain was in the works – Benedetto would leave Florence voluntarily, in exchange for the formal closure of his case.[37] He is no longer described as 'incarcerated,' so he was presumably out on a security bond – and its refund might have offered an incentive to the financially devastated Blanis family. A month later, on 4 January 1628, the Cardinals General in Rome deferred to the judgment of the Father Inquisitor in Florence: 'Having read the letters from the Florentine Inquisitor, dated 25 December, the Most Illustrious [Cardinals] will abide by his decision when it comes to favouring (*facere gratiam*) the Jew Benedetto Blanis with the penalty of exile from the city of Florence.'[38]

Exile could be seen as a grace and a favour, since Benedetto was unconvicted rather than innocent, having resisted torture without confessing. In any case, he must have left his native city with a resounding sigh of relief. By the autumn of 1629 Benedetto Blanis was operating in Ferrara where he had a sister and a Finzi brother-in-law.[39] On 27 September he asked Prior Francesco Vinta in Florence to settle an outstanding business obligation.[40] Then, on 8 November 1629, he repeated his plea in even stronger terms:

> As an act of great charity, I beg you to help me in my current need. For eighteen months now, a daughter of mine has been promised in marriage but I have not been able to effect the wedding due to a lack of money. Please help me immediately, for the love of God, and if you cannot send me cash, send me a length of black satin or black woolen cloth or gilded leather or whatever is convenient.[41]

In a Florentine lawsuit of 1641, Benedetto is cited as 'residing in Ferrara.' This was brought by Mirra Blanis – originally from Massa, wife of his brother David[42] – who was seeking to reclaim her dowry: 'The petitioner [Mirra Blanis] has continually asked the Governors of the Jews of Florence to place him [Benedetto] under an edict of excommunication … so that the truth in various matters will come to light.'[43]

During these years Benedetto was not forgotten in his home town. On 15 September 1632 the Archdiocese of Florence issued a *List of the Christian serving women who are presently in the service of Jews in the Ghetto* – including five households with Blanis connections:

Maria is with Moisé Lattone
Angelica is with Davitt Brandis
Argentina is with Lelio Brandis
Dianora is with Doctor Morino, son-in-law of Benedetto Brandis
There is a wet-nurse with Raffaello Brandis.[44]

From time to time Benedetto might have reappeared in Florence as a guest of his daughter and his son-in-law, a medical doctor. Meanwhile, his older brother Lelio and his younger brother David were both heads of households, as was his brother-in-law Moisé Lattone and Raffaello Brandis/Blanis, probably a nephew. Then, a month later, in October of 1632, Benedetto himself began paying rent on apartment number 35 in the Florentine Ghetto – 10 scudi every six months – picking up the lease after the recent death of his father Laudadio. He made regular payments (or at least payments were made in his name) through the end of October 1647, when the lease passed to the heirs of his late brother Lelio Blanis.[45]

Along the way, there was a decisive shift in the balance of power among the various branches of the Blanis family in Florence.[46] In 1621, while Benedetto was in jail, Hayyim Finzi died and was succeeded as both rabbi and chancellor by Moisé Blanis – Benedetto's cousin somewhat removed and a recent arrival in the Ghetto.[47] In February 1622 it was *Cancelliere* Moisé Blanis who registered the latest election of Ghetto governors and reported it to the granducal administration.[48] Moisé figures prominently in a chronology of the Florentine rabbinate that was compiled in 1641 from documents that no longer survive:

> The great rabbi, the honourable teacher, Rabbi Hayyim Finzi, a teacher of righteousness … came here from Pisaro in the year 5371 [1611] … as is seen in the minute-book of the council, and he died in the year 5381 [1621]. And during his days, he had a true helper, the *hakham*, the pious honourable teacher, Rabbi Mosheh ibn Basa mi-Blanis of blessed memory, and he also judged the people until the year of the plague, that is in 5390 [1630].[49]

If Benedetto continued to explore the occult – in Florence, Ferrara, or elsewhere – the relevant documents have not yet risen to the surface. In and around the old Magic Circle of Don Giovanni dei Medici, the most notable survivor was Raffael Gualterotti who died in 1638 at the age of ninety-five. Orazio Morandi had already departed in 1630 – after a meteoric rise and fall, eclipsing even that of Benedetto Blanis. In 1625 Father Orazio definitively transferred his base of operation to Rome, where he served as abbot of the Vallombrosan Monastery of Santa Prassede.[50] He established a lending library featuring 'curious' works and assiduously promoted his astrological talents, casting horoscopes for many members of the Roman elite.[51] In February of 1630, an astrological discourse was circulated in Rome, ostensibly anonymous and ostensibly despatched from Lyons, anticipating the death of Pope Urban VIII Barberini (1568–1644). Morandi's authorship was a badly kept secret and his dire prediction unleashed a furore. Urban VIII took his astrological death sentence very seriously – not only was he Pope, he was an ardent devotee of the extra-Christian arcane. Morandi was arrested, his library at Santa Prassede was ransacked, and he died in the Tor di Nona prison on 7 November 1630 after repeated torture. Although Morandi's death certificate alleged natural causes, few were convinced. 'There is no doubt,' the Roman diarist Giacinto Gigli observed, 'that he was killed by poison administered in his food.'[52]

Benedetto Blanis outlived Don Giovanni dei Medici by twenty-six years, dying in 1647 at the advanced age of nearly seventy.[53] He could claim at least one successor – Ferdinando Magnani, his student of Hebrew and designated copyist of occult texts. Although Ferdinando never became a priest,[54] he did carry on with his linguistic studies and perhaps even his astrology. His chief claim to fame is that he taught Francesco Redi (1626–1697), a celebrated medical doctor, poet, and experimental scientist, who had a crater on Mars named in his honour. In his personal diary from 1648 to 1654, Redi notes that he loaned many books to 'Messer Ferdinando Magnani, formerly my master of the Greek language.'[55]

Notes

1 The Piazza

1 Archivio di Stato di Firenze (ASF), Archivio Mediceo del Principato (MdP) 5150.
2 *The Letters of Benedetto Blanis* Hebreo *to Don Giovanni dei Medici: 1615–21* (University of Toronto Press, 2011).

2 The Palace

1 Francesco Bocchi, *Le Bellezze della Città di Firenze* (Florence, 1591); I cite the expanded edition published by Giovanni Cinelli (1677), 129–40. All translations, unless otherwise stated, are my own.
2 Ibid., 130.
3 ASF MdP 5147, f.285v, 16 Feb. 1618/19 (Cosimo Baroncelli to Don Giovanni dei Medici).
4 During the subsequent reign of Ferdinando II, the coherence of the Medici Court broke down somewhat, as various of the grand duke's brothers made careers that took them out of Florence and developed satellite courts in outlying villas.
5 In the secondary literature, Guidi is usually cited as secretary to Christine de Lorraine. However, in ASF Guardaroba 309, f.4 (a listing of the *salariati di casa*, 1610–20) he is cited simply as a granducal secretary, with Curzio Picchena listed as *primo secretario* from 13 May 1615 and Alessandro Bartolini as secretario di madama from 1 July 1616. During this period, however, tasks and responsibilities were evidently divided in quite a fluid manner among the chief Medici functionaries.
6 Friar Leonard Coquel, Christine's confessor, was a ubiquitous figure in

Medici affairs at this time. Ipolito Coquel, perhaps a relative, was Don Giovanni's 'Furiere e Scr[iva]no di Dispensa' (ASF MdP 5158 f.124, 1 Jan. 1610/11); Sotto Maestro di Casa (ibid., 5158 f.122, 20 Sept. 1611).

7   Ibid., 5154, f.133, 11 July 1579.

8   Montughi is now a northern suburb of Florence, and Don Giovanni's villa is the site of the Museo Stibbert.

9   ASF MdP 5152, f.205v, 5 March 1616.

10 Ibid., 5154, f.173, 17 March 1592.

11 Don Giovanni was the architect of record for the Cappella dei Principi – but ironically enough, he would not be allowed burial space there for himself. In 1621 he was buried in the (now demolished) Church of Santa Lucia in Venice.

12 ASF MdP 5152, f.108r–v, 19 Dec. 1615 (Don Giovanni to Cosimo II).

13 Siro Ferrone analyses Don Giovanni's activity as a theatrical impresario, especially as patron of the Compagnia dei Confidenti, in *Attori mercanti corsari: la commedia dell'arte in Europa tra Cinque e Seicento*, 137–90.

14 ASF MdP 3007, f.235r, 24 July 1621 (Niccolò Sacchetti to Curzio Picchena).

15 Ibid., 5158, f.534.

16 Ibid., 5147, f.589r, 22 June 1620 (Cosimo Baroncelli to Don Giovanni).

17 The most striking documents of Don Antonio's alchemical interests are BNCF MS Magliabecchiana XV, 140, *Segreti sperimentati dall'Illustrissimo et eccellentissimo signor principe don Antonio dei Medici nella sua Fonderia del Casino*, and MS Magliabecchiana XVI, 63–6, *Apparato della Fonderia dell'Illustrissimo et eccellentissimo signor don Antonio Medici, anno 1604*.

18 ASF MdP 5150, f.123r, 9 April 1616 [*Letters*, no. 40].

19 Ibis., 5154, f.141, 6 June 1587.

20 Ibid., 5151, Insert 21, f.67, 5 March 1587/88.

21 Ibid., Insert 20, f.125, 6 July 1611.

22 Don Giovanni's father Cosimo I had married Camilla Martelli and his brother Francesco I had married Bianca Cappello, both of whom were also considered to be little better than whores, but only after the deaths of their very appropriate first wives, Eleonora de Toledo and Johanna von Habsburg.

23 In the letters that I have seen, Don Giovanni is normally addressed as 'Illustrissima Eccellenza,' not 'Serenissimo' or 'Principe.'

24 This was in the context of a sworn deposition in front of the court of the archbishop of Florence on 19 Jan. 1621/22 (ASF MdP 5159, f.677r). A copy of the 'Processo della fuga di Livia dalle Malmaritate' (ibid., 5160, f.183ff, 30 March 1607) verifies the story of the stolen key but identifies her accomplice as Margherita Assereta, another woman who had taken refuge

there from an abusive husband. In ASF MdP 5160, f.341r–f.342v, there is a set of findings regarding Livia's immoral life in Florence; at the conclusion, there is a list of points indicated by number and the annotation, 'Benedetto Blanis hebreo et sopra li altri.'

25   ASF MdP 6108, f.563, translated by Molly Bourne.

26   Benedetto Blanis used this term in ASF MdP 5159, f.677v. *Donna di partito* is often translated as 'party girl'; a more precise translation would be 'woman for whom you can make an offer' or 'woman with whom an arrangement can be made.'

27   ASF MdP 5159, f.598v. This is a copy of a letter from Don Giovanni to Livia dated 17 March 1617. See also Chapter 9 below, 'The Mirror of Truth.'

28   These suits and countersuits are documented in ASF MdP 5159–5162, 6355, and 6357.

29   ASF MdP 5150, f.9, 20 June 1615 [*Letters*, no. 2]. In his memoir (written many years after the event), Cosimo Baroncelli notes that Don Giovanni left for Venice on 12 June 1615 (ASF Misc Med 458, Insert 10, f.161v). Benedetto's letter (written immediately after Don Giovanni's departure from Florence), fixes the date a week later. In fact, Don Giovanni wrote a letter to Cosimo II on 15 June 1615, while still at his Villa at Montughi outside Florence (ASF MdP 5152, f.4). On 26 June 1615, he wrote to Cosimo II from Venice (ibid., f.5).

30   ASF MdP 5159, f.678v–f.679r. For the context of this legal deposition, see Chapter 13 below, 'Habeas Corpus.'

31   In Benedetto's letters, it is often unclear whether he was beginning his days at sunrise or sunset.

32   ASF MdP 5150, f.9, 20 June 1615 [*Letters*, no. 2].

33   ASF MdP 5150, f.11, 21 July 1615 [*Letters*, no. 3].

34   Ibid.

35   See Chapter 6 below, 'The Market.'

36   ASF Magistrato Supremo 4449, f.106r–f.107v, 31 July 1571.

37   ASF MdP 5150, f.11, 21 July 1615 [*Letters*, no. 3]. On 20 May 1617, Cosimo Baroncelli informed Don Giovanni that Camillo Guidi was planning to send him a letter 'entirely drawn from the Psalms of David' (ibid., 5146, f.544).

38   Scholem, *Kabbalah*, 186.

39   It is generally more accurate to refer to the 'Hebrew Bible' rather than the 'Old Testament,' but we are now assessing the Catholic point of view in the late Renaissance.

40   ASF MdP 5159, f.681r.

41   Ibid., 5150, f.5, 1 Aug. 1615 [*Letters*, no. 5].

42 Ibid.
43 Ibid., f.53, 27 Sept. 1615 [*Letters*, no. 12].
44 Benedetto's letter in fact specifies 'l'arciduchessa,' since Maria Magdalena normally maintained her Habsburg title.
45 Mario Bardini was, in fact, Auditore Fiscale, responsible for the administration of the law.
46 ASF MdP 5150, f.53, 27 Sept. 1615 [*Letters*, no. 12].
47 Don Giovanni dei Medici was also an exceptionally vivid letter writer. In the Medici archive, detailed descriptions of events with reported dialogue are encountered most often in ambassadorial dispatches from diplomats stationed in foreign courts.
48 Probably the Augustinian Leonard Coquel, an important figure who has been remarkably little studied.
49 ASF MdP 5150, f.39, 8 Nov. 1615 [*Letters*, no. 17].
50 Ibid.,, f.69, 6 Dec. 1615 [*Letters*, no. 22].

3 The Ghetto

1 Via del Giardino is now Via dell'Ulivo near Santa Croce.
2 ASF MdP 5150, f.61r–f.62r, 16 Aug. 1615 [*Letters*, no. 7].
3 These are the figures cited in the Florentine census of 1622. BNCF Codex E.B., XV: 2, and Codex II, I: 240, 4r and 13r (cited by Siegmund, *From Tuscan Households to Urban Ghetto*, 177).
4 I am grateful to Salvador Salort Pons for this observation. 'Blanis' is not an exclusively Jewish name.
5 Simonsohn, *The Apostolic See and the Jews*, docs. 1212, 1309, and 2927. The family name of 'Blanis' also appears in such variants as 'Blanes,' 'Blandes,' and 'Brandes' (the last is possibly a Portuguese version).
6 Simonsohn, *Apostolic See*, doc. 1372.
7 Ibid., doc. 1776.
8 Ibid., doc. 1483. Laudadio must have been at least in his early twenties when he took the examination, so he was probably born before his family's arrival in Orvieto.
9 Toaff, *The Jews in Umbria*, vol. 3, doc. 2631.
10 Simonsohn, *Apostolic See*, docs. 2098, 2556, 2579, and 2927. Toaff, 'Maestro Laudadio de Blanis e la banca ebraica in Umbria e nel Patrimonio di S. Pietro nella prima metà del cinquecento.'
11 Toaff, *The Jews in Umbria*, vol. 3, doc. 2532. This is specifically a reference to Laudadio's brother Samuele.
12 Ibid., doc. 2462.

13 Ibid., docs. 2540 and 2566.

14 Simonsohn, *Apostolic See*, docs. 1836, 2309, 2945, and 2969.

15 Ibid., doc. 2556.

16 Toaff, *The Jews in Umbria*, vol. 3, docs. 2481 and 2550.

17 Ibid., doc. 2470. In 1558 Agnolo Blanis married Bellotia Montolmo from an affluent Perugia family, receiving a substantial dowry of 600 scudi (doc. 2480).

18 This was registered in a notarial act (ibid., doc. 2481).

19 Jews were allowed to live only in the ghettos of Rome and Ancona under highly restrictive conditions.

20 Salvadori and Sacchetti, *Presenze ebraiche nell'Aretino dal XIV al XX*, 78–9. In 1570 'Messer Samuel de Blanis da Orvieto' was still living in Monte San Savino with a household of eight, as was Laudadio's son, Iacob de Blanis, with a separate household of four (ASF Magistrato Supremo 4450, f.122r).

21 ASF Riformagioni 10, f.22r.

22 In the language of the time, *nipote* could refer to nieces/nephews, great-nieces/great-nephews, and grandsons/granddaughters. We know that Laura was a granddaughter (see note below).

23 Laudadio di Agnolo Blanis (Benedetto's father) married a first cousin – the daughter of his uncle Salvatore, from a branch of the family that settled in Massa Carrara (see below and Chapter 12 below, 'Prison'). Salvatore is known to have had two daughters, Laura and Reche. Laudadio di Moyse Blanis (Benedetto's great-grandfather) lent his son Salvatore money for Laura's dowry and then forgave this debt in his will of 1575. In this same will, he left a dowry-sized bequest to the still unmarried Reche (ASF Notarile Moderno 265, f.30v; cited by Siegmund, *Medici State*, 356, 360, and 393). If Laura was indeed fifteen years old in 1567, she might already have been married but this is not noted in the census. Reche was presumably the younger of the two, which might favour her identification as Benedetto's mother – but we have only approximate information regarding the birth dates and birth order of Benedetto and his siblings. Benedetto seems to have been born around 1580. His brother Agnolo/Lelio was older, while David and Salamone were evidently both younger. Benedetto also had at least two sisters of undetermined age.

24 Laudadio Blanis was called as a witness in an investigation in 1566 of suspected Judaizing by an alleged New Christian. The investigators were particularly concerned that the Psalms were being read in 'Christian letters' (i.e., Spanish) in the *scuola* (ASF Nunziatura Apostolica 842, 9 and 17 Sept., 12 Oct. 1566). Frattarelli Fischer, *Vivere fuori dal ghetto*, 35.

25 ASF Riformagioni 10, f.20r, referring to the household of Lazzero Rabbeno.

See Siegmund, *Medici State*, 165–6, for the various worship centres in pre-Ghetto Florence.

26 For an assessment of this demographic data, see Siegmund, *Medici State*, 223–38.

27 ASF Magistrato Supremo 4450, f.173r.

28 Shulamit Furstenberg Levi explores the real and metaphorical implications of Ghetto space in 'The Boundaries between "Jewish" and "Catholic" Space in Counter-Reformation Florence as seen by the Convert Vitale Medici.'

29 Siegmund, *Medici State*, 223–38.

30 ASF Arte della Seta 13, f.103v, 16 Oct. 1572 (cited by Siegmund, *Tuscan Households*, Appendix 3d).

31 Siegmund (*Tuscan Households*, 221–3) offers an astute assessment of this situation.

32 Ibid., 251.

33 David was a medical doctor who matriculated in the Doctors and Apothecaries Guild in Florence in 1560 (ASF Arte dei medici e speziali, Matricole, v.11, f.128; cited by Cassuto, *Gli Ebrei a Firenze nell'età del Rinascimento*, 185).

34 There is an Agnolo di Salvatore di Magistro Laudadio Hebreo who matriculated in the Florentine Silk Guild on 25 Oct. 1574 (ASF Arte della Seta f.13, 120r; cited by Siegmund, *Tuscan Households*, Appendix 3d). Agnolo di Salvatore was closely involved in commercial affairs with his Florentine relatives (see Chapter 6 below, 'The Market').

35 Agnolo received two dowry payments totalling 500 scudi in 1551 and 1553 (Toaff, *The Jews in Umbria*, vol. 3, doc. 2514).

36 In a legal deposition on 19 Jan. 1621/22 Benedetto described himself to be around forty years old: 'Io di presente mi trovo carcerato nelle Carcere del Palazzo del Bargello ad instanza del Santo Offitio … fo professione di vivere da buon ebreo, e sono figlio di famiglia per esser ancor vivo mio Padre … sono d'età d'anni 40 in circa' (ASF MdP 5159, f.683r). This might imply that Benedetto had not been emancipated by his father and retained dependent status. In another legal deposition, on 13 Jan. 1621/22, Benedetto's older brother Lelio described himself to be around forty-five or forty-six years of age: 'disse essere di età di anno 45 or 46 incirca' (ASF Nove 376, f.364v). Laudadio Blanis had at least six children: Lelio was the eldest son and Benedetto was the second son.

37 Lapini, *Diario fiorentino di Agostino Lapini dal 1552 al 1592*, 171.

38 ASF Nove 16, f.29v–f.30v and f.34r–v. 'Their Lordships' refer to the Nove Conservatori who supervised the auction.

39 Even when left to these rather abnormal market forces, Ghetto rents seem

to have resolved themselves within the expected range for comparable accommodation outside the Ghetto. See Siegmund, *Medici State*, 213–21.

40 In ASF Scrittoio delle Regie Possessioni 6556 (Amminstratione del Ghetto Interno; Libro Maestro 31 for Oct. 1632–37), the numerical sequence of properties goes to 98, although some numbers might be missing in the series and other properties might be unnumbered properties.

41 After Laudadio Blanis' death in 1632, these leases were taken over by his sons Agnolo/Lelio and Benedetto (ASF Regie Possessioni 6556, ff. 89 and 92). Other properties were occupied by Benedetto's youngest brother Salamone (f.74).

42 ASF MS 4449, f.106r–f.107v, 31 July 1571.

43 ASF Magistrato Supremo 4450, f.8r–f.10r.

44 Siegmund, *Medici State*, 68–9. The real meaning of the legislation was in emphasizing the essential role of granducal grace and favour.

45 ACEF, Box D 3.2 folder 3 (cited by Siegmund, *Medici State*, 524nn43–4). As we will see, taverns were dangerous and compromising places for Jews.

46 ASF Otto 277, f.203v, 18 June 1624.

47 For the prosecution of gambling in Florence, see Chapter 8 below, 'Games of Chance.'

48 The appearance of Don Giovanni dei Medici at Benedetto's evening party was quite likely a unique incident.

49 ASF Nove 368, f.378r, no. 32.

50 ASF Otto 255, f.14r, 9 Nov. 1616.

51 Ibid., 5 Dec. 1616.

52 Ibid., f.117r, 12 Jan. 1616/17.

53 Ibid., f.177v, 27 Feb. 1616/17.

54 Ibid., 260, f.87r, 27 Aug. 1618.

55 Ibid., 269, f.181v, 24 Sept. 1621.

56 Ibid., 270, f.228r, 25 Feb. 1621/22.

57 Ibid., 280, f.53r, 20 March 1624/25, and 282, f.121r, 23 Jan. 1625/26.

58 Ibid., 280, f.116v, 29 April 1625.

59 These *magistrati* or magistratures were part of a system that did not have a clear distinction between executive, legislative, and judicial functions. In present-day terms, the Nove carried out mostly executive functions and the Otto judicial ones.

60 The division is clearly expressed in the eighth by-law of 1572 (ASF Nove 13, f.115v–f.118r). In the years that followed, however, there was a marked drift towards bringing all Ghetto matters to the Otto, apart from the annual ratification of the slate of officers and other strictly jurisdictional or administrative issues, which continued to be referred to the Nove. In

particular, the Jews of the Ghetto ceased requesting travel permits from the Nove. Instead, they went to the Otto for dispensations from the *segno* while travelling or remaining outside the Ghetto.

61 In terms of jurisdiction, it seems that the Ghetto was managed in an ad hoc fashion, as a separate corporate entity in some circumstances and as part of the city of Florence in others.

62 ASF Nove 13, f.115v–f.118r, 30 July 1572.

63 ASF Nove 41, f.90v, 26 June 1609.

64 Siegmund, *Medici State*, 254–5. On 4 May 1607 (ASF Nove 39, f.58v), only two governors were registered: Simon di Speranzo Sacerdote and Sabatino di Bigniamino Bondi. Then only two again on 1 Feb. 1619/20 (ibid., 50, f.324v): Benedetto di Laudadio Blanis and Sallomone di Abrami Tedesco. It is always possible that names were occasionally omitted through scribal errors by the secretary of the Nove.

65 The usual title of the executive officers was eventually established as *governatori*, although the terms *deputati* and *governanti* sometimes also appear in the documents. The electoral body was usually referred to as the *Congrega*, but sometimes as the *Governanti*, *Governatori*, and *Deputati*. There was frequent slippage in this nomenclature, implying that the secretary or copyists of the Nove did not much care what the electors and executive officers of the Ghetto called themselves.

66 It is clear that the body of voters and potential governors was quite small. It remains to be determined whether non-voting members of the community could attend meetings and speak.

67 ASF Nove 43, f.145v, 19 Aug. 1611. In the by-laws of 1608 there was a proposal to limit the *Congrega* to eighteen men and tightly structure the election of governors (ibid., 368, f.378v–f.379r).

68 Leone da Modena, *Historia de' riti hebraici*, 46–7.

69 There is consistent documentation for the operation of the Ghetto chancery (or at least the chancery of the Italian synagogue) beginning only in 1652 (ASF Nazione Israelitica 1), by which time there were established rabbis in the Ghetto and the chancery was functioning in a well-organized manner. There was evidently an historical watershed in the administration of the Ghetto in 1639, when Ferdinando II confirmed the legal jurisdiction of the Italian Nation. A good deal of relevant documentation emerged in 1688, during a conflict between the Italian Nation and the administratively subordinate Levantine Nation (ASF Nove 3243).

70 ASF Nove 3243, f.127r–v, 28 Sept. 1688. In 1598 the Ghetto council in Florence prohibited Jews from taking disputes to Christian courts, eliciting a negative response from the granducal authorities (see Siegmund, *Medici State*, 282).

71 There were various incidents of disorder and low-level violence in the Ghetto. However, most cases involving Jews in the files of the Otto di Guardia e Balìa were financial, as discussed here in Chapter 6, 'The Market.'

72 ASF Otto 270, f.138r, 4 Jan. 1621/22.

73 Ibid., 271, f.184v–f.185r, 31 May 1622. This case is recorded under the same date in ASF Auditore Fiscale 2210, f.376r–f.378r. Davitte di Laudadio Blanis, Benedetto's younger brother, is recorded (f.378r) as one of the two guarantors for the 50 lire fine levied against Raffaele di Samuele Levi.

74 Since Zaccheria is described as 'son of Jacobbe from Alba,' Donna Sarra might have been previously married to Jacobbe. Donna Sarra is referred to as 'Donna Sarra di Ventura Todesca socera di detto Raffaello.' I take this to mean 'wife of Ventura,' since that was her current husband's name, although it is also possible that her own father was named Ventura.

75 ASF Otto 271, f.184v–f.185r, 31 May 1622.

76 Ibid.

77 Ibid.

78 ASF Otto 247, f.73v, 29 April 1614. On 10 Oct. 1613 the election of three governors was authorized: Laudadio Blanis, Donato d'Isach Tedesco, and Moyse d'Aronne (ASF Nove 45, f.195v).

79 Ball games were banned in the 1572 by-laws for the Ghetto (ASF Nove 13, f.115v–f.118r), and this ban was reinstated in the 1608 by-laws (ibid., 368, f.374r–f.380v).

80 Ash Wednesday fell on 12 February in 1614. Purim began on Sunday, 23 February, while the Fast of Esther preceded it on Thursday, 20 February. In Florence, however, the chief day of the Carnival celebration is traditionally Berlingaccio or 'Fat Thursday,' not Fat Tuesday.

81 ASF Otto 247, f.73v, 29 April 1614.

82 Ibid., 252, f.174r–v, 13 Jan. 1615/16. Benedetto's older brother is identified as Agnolo Blanis, a form of his name that was used interchangeably with Lelio.

83 In fact, there were serious tensions within the governing class of the Ghetto in 1611, with important developments in the years that immediately followed. See Chapter 4 below, 'The Synagogue.'

84 ASF Otto 252, f.158v, 8 Jan. 1615/16. Laudadio Blanis, Abram di Daniello Calò, and 'the heirs of Donato Tedesco' sought to collect a debt.

85 ASF Nove 45, f.195v, 10 Oct. 1613.

86 ASF Otto 269, f.181v.

87 Judging from Leone da Modena's autobiography, the much larger Venetian Ghetto was more seriously violent. Leone's own son Zebulon was murdered by a Jewish gang in 1622 after an armed confrontation. See Cohen,

trans. and ed., *The Autobiography of a Seventeenth-Century Venetian Rabbi: Leone Modena's 'Life of Judah,'* 119–20.

88 ASF Otto 254, f.67v, 29 July 1616.

89 Ibid., 260, f.118v, 13 Sept. 1618. The reference is to 23 Jan. 1617 Florentine style.

90 Ibid., 247, f.153r, 12 June 1614. This was during the term of the three governors Donato Donati, Moisé son of Aronne, and Laudadio Blanis.

91 Ibid., 260, f.89v, 30 Aug. 1618. Benedetto's brother is identified as 'Agnolo son of Laudadio.'

92 Ibid., 262, f.84r, 30 April 1619.

93 Ibid.

94 Ibid., 267, f.34r, 16 Nov. 1620.

95 Ibid., 256, f.54r, 11 April 1617.

96 Ibid., 261, f.147r, 28 Jan. 1618/19.

97 Ibid., 263, f.17r, 9 July 1619.

4 The Synagogue

1 See Siegmund, *Medici State*, 270 and 507n106.

2 The work was written in 1616–17 but first published in 1637 in Paris, with a second edition in Venice in 1638.

3 The work was conceived as an explanation or 'apology.' See Cohen, 'Leone da Modena's *Riti*,' and the introduction to the most recent edition of Modena's *Les juifs présentés aux Chrétiens*, edited by Le Brun and Stroumsa.

4 Modena, *Riti*, 15–16.

5 This was between David son of Abram from Siena and Michele son of Aronne, as discussed here in Chapter 3, 'The Ghetto.' (ASF Otto 260, f.118v, 13 Sept. 1618.) In a 1721 plan of the Italian synagogue in the Florentine Ghetto (by then, rebuilt and expanded), there is a 'little courtyard, that is to say, uncovered terrace,' up a flight of stairs (ASF Possessioni, vol. XXVI, no. 670, c. CLXV; published by Liscia Bemporad, 'La scuola italiana e la scuola levantina nel Ghetto di Firenze: prima ricostruzione.'

6 Modena, *Riti*, 15–18.

7 ACEF Box D 3.2.4. This is published by Cassuto, 'I piu antichi capitoli del ghetto di Firenze,' *Rivista Israelitica* 9/5–6 (1912): 206.

8 Modena, *Riti*, 3.

9 Ibid., 16–17.

10 Ibid., 18.

11 In a 1721 plan (ASF Regie Possessioni, vol. XXVI, no. 670, c. CLXIV), there are four designated women's galleries in the *matroneo*: (a) Scuola a mezza

Scala della Famiglia Levi, (b) Prima Scuola delle Donne, (c) Altra Scuola delle Donne al 2º piano, and (d) Terza Scuola delle Donne. See Liscia Bemporad, 'Scuola italiana e scuola levantina', Figure 4.

12 ASF Nove 368, f.374r–f.379v, Capitolo 15. In a set of by-laws for the Ghetto ratified by the Nove Conservatori on 30 July 1572, there is a reference: 'when the Jews, men as well as women, gather together and are in their synagogue in order to recite their service, as soon as it is begun, they must keep quiet.' The implication is that women were present in the synagogue in the earliest years of the Florentine Ghetto (ibid., 13, f.115v– f.118r).

13 They ratified them on 8 Jan. 1608/09.

14 Drafts of the 1571, 1572, 1595, and 1608 by-laws are found in ACEF Box D 3.2.4 and were published by Cassuto, 'I piu antichi capitoli del ghetto di Firenze,' *Rivista Israelitica* 9/5–6 (1912): 203–11; 10/1 (1913): 32–40; 10/2 (1913): 71–80. Ratified copies of the 1572 by-laws are found in ASF Nove 13, f.115v– f.118r, 30 July 1572; those from 1578 in ibid., 17, f.202r– v, 13 Nov. 1578; and those from 1608 in ibid., 368, f.374r–f.380v, 8 Jan. 1608/09. The 1595 by-laws were not ratified by the Nove and were probably never presented formally for enactment as law, since the text is notably informal in manner and contains many Hebrew words.

15 ASF Nove 368, f.377r–v, Capitolo 26.

16 ASF Magistrato Supremo (MS) 4450, f.173r.

17 ASF Nove 13, f.118r, 30 July 1572.

18 Ibid., 14, f.95r, 31 July 1573.

19 Ibid., 15, f.95r, 30 July 1574.

20 Ibid., 16, f.106v, 30 July 1575.

21 Siegmund (*Medici State*, 258–9) outlines the coming and going of various individuals who might have had rabbinical status; there is evidence that the ascendancy of the Blanis family was not consistent or uncontested, particularly in the 1580s. The most sensational conversion was probably that of the rabbi and medical doctor Jehiel da Pesaro (subsequently Vitale Medici) in 1582; see Furstenberg Levi, 'The Boundaries between "Jewish" and "Catholic."' .

22 Modena, *Riti*, 37.

23 Ibid., 1–2.

24 Ibid., 37–8.

25 Ibid., 40.

26 Ibid.

27 A rabbi might also function as cantor or prayer leader, if hired specifically for this purpose.

28 Modena, *Riti*, 18.

29 Ibid., 21.

30 Ibid., 91.

31 One of the 1608 by-laws (ASF Nove 368, f.374v, no. 1) refers to 'the del-egate (*deputato*) who goes to officiate at prayer in the morning, at sunset, and in the evening.' *Deputato* can simply mean 'appointed person,' but the term *deputati* was often applied both to the Ghetto governors (then three in number) and the governing elite from which they were selected.

32 ASF Nove 17, f.202r–v.

33 In Italy, only three faculties of medicine normally accepted Jewish stu-dents: at the universities of Padua, Perugia, and Siena.

34 Laudadio the Younger is never referred to in writing as 'Doctor' and Bene-detto only once, in a context that simply means 'man of learning.' On 9 July 1620, while Benedetto remained in jail, his youngest brother Sala-mone Blanis lamented to Don Giovanni dei Medici: 'They [the Florentine Christian authorities] are proceeding against Benedetto because he is a doctor, one of the governors of the Ghetto, and one of the chief supporters of our faith' (ASF MdP 5150, f.411 [*Letters*, no. 202]).

35 The doctorate in medicine was the only public honour that a Jew could achieve that was generally recognized outside the Ghetto. At this time medicine was a learned humanistic study, more abstract than practical, focusing on the theory of the 'humours' and other ancient constructs. Since university instruction took place in Latin, Jewish 'university doctors' were necessarily fluent in that language.

36 In the files of the Nove Conservatori from the late sixteenth and early seventeenth centuries there are numerous records of the confirmation or replacement of *Cancellieri* in towns, villages, and corporations throughout the Florentine dominion, but none for the *Cancellieri* of the Ghetto. These were apparently selected internally and then served for many years with-out substitution.

37 Cassuto, 'I piu antichi capitoli del ghetto di Firenze,' *Rivista Israelitica* 10/1 (1913): 33.

38 ASF Nove 368, f.374v–f.375r. In this passage, the word *Repubblica* was crossed out and substituted with the word *Università*.

39 The oldest surviving plans of both the Italian and the Levantine syna-gogues date from 1721 and are found in the records of the Medici property administration (ASF Possessioni, vol. XXVI). By then the Italian synagogue (the dominant religious and administrative entity in the Ghetto) had been damaged in a disastrous fire in 1670, rebuilt, and significantly enlarged. The 1721 plan shows a suite of three rooms, one large and two small, iden-tified as 'the rooms that were formerly used for the assembly of their gov-

ernment.' The two smaller rooms were presumably used for the storage of community property and probably included the chancery. In fact, the eastern end of the worship space was described as 'the side towards the Chancery (*Cancelleria*)' in the account books from the post-1670 reconstruction. See Liscia Bemporad, 'La scuola italiana e a scuola levantina.'

40 The full name of the magistrature was *Nove Conservatori del Dominio e della Giurisdizione Fiorentina*

41 Modena, *Riti*, 45–6.

42 'Thou shalt not take the name of the Lord thy God in vain.'

43 Levitats, 'Oath *More Judaico* or *Juramento Judaeorum*,' *Encyclopaedia Judaica*, XV, 364–5. Many Christians did not believe that Jews recognized any obligation to tell the truth, especially in their dealings with Christians. In particular, Christians fixated on the implications of the Kol Nidre rite on the eve of Yom Kippur, which seemed to annul all Jewish vows.

44 ASF MdP 5161, f.67r, 22 Sept. 1621, f.269r, 6 Oct. 1621, and 5159, f.672v, 19 Jan. 1621/22.

45 ASF Nove 3243, f.122v. This took place in 1688 in the context of a vehement suit between the Italian and the Levantine nations. Interestingly enough, the rabbi refused to administer the oath, leaving it to the chancellors of the two nations. Tefilin or 'safeguards' are small leather-covered boxes containing inscriptions, attached to the forehead and left forearm with leather bands.

46 Modena, *Riti*, 45.

47 ASF Nove 368, f.374r–f.379v.

48 Ibid., Capitoli 1, 6, and 27.

49 Cassuto, 'I più antichi capitoli del ghetto di Firenze,' *Rivista Israelitica* 10/1 (1913): 32. The job of the *sindaco* was to report infractions to the granducal administration and pay them their share of any resulting fines.

50 Ibid., 35.

51 All of the subsequent bodies of by-laws drafted after 1571 included the reaffirmation of the previous by-laws.

52 ASF Nove 368, f.378v, Capitolo 36.

53 Ibid., f.377r–v, Capitolo 31.

54 Ibid., f.377v, Capitolo 29.

55 The translation is by Cohen, *Autobiography*, 106. In his introductory essay, Howard Adelman notes that Leone da Modena was quite active during his year in Florence apart from his Ghetto duties, teaching distinguished Christians and corresponding widely with scholars (26–7).

56 Gambling emerges as a major theme in his autobiography, and it came near to destroying his life on various occasions.

57 These payments began on 9 Aug. 1611(Siegmund, *Medici State*, 396).

58 For the scant notices on Hayyim Finzi, see ibid., 560nn43–4. It is worth noting that the *responsa* in Moscow, Ginzburg Collection 251 (Institute of Microfilmed Hebrew Manuscripts, no. 45716; cited by Weinstein, *Marriage Rituals Italian Style: A Historical Anthropological Perspective on Early Modern Italian Jews*, 158n12) were apparently issued by a different Hayyim Finzi who lived a generation later. Weinstein (163–4n24) states that he died in the mid-seventeenth century and refers to a eulogy on the anniversary of his death in 1653 (Leningrad, Russian Academy, Oriental Studies Institute, A87; IMHM, no. 52889). The Hayyim Finzi that concerns us died in 1621.

59 Siegmund, *Medici State*, 396–7.

60 ASF Nove 43, f.132r, 3 Aug. 1611.

61 Ibid., f.145v, 19 Aug. 1611. These procedures were mandated by the 1608 by-laws (see Siegmund, *Medici State*, 260).

62 ASF Otto 252, f.174r–v, 13 Jan. 1615/16. On 28 Sept. 1609, the Eight Magistrates imposed a peace bond of 50 scudi on thirteen Jews who were in contention with each other, including Laudadio Blanis and his sons Agnolo, Benedetto, Salomone, and David; Donato Tedesco and his sons Moisé and Agnolo; and Moisé d'Aronne and his son Rubino (ASF Otto 233, f.162v). On 30 Dec. 1608, relatively soon after the arrival of Donato Tedesco and his family in Florence, Lelio Blanis was fined 50 lire and Benedetto Blanis 25 lire for attacking Moisé di Donato Tedesco with their fists; initially Laudadio Blanis, his four sons, his son-in-law Moisé Lattone, Donato di Isacco Tedesco and his son Moisé were all charged (ibid., 230, f.108v).

63 On 10 Feb. 1621/22, the Nove ratified the newly elected board of governors as reported by Moisé Blanis, *Cancelliere*. Moisé, from a collateral branch of the Blanis family, also took over the duties of religious leader from Hayyim Finzi. See Siegmund, *Medici State*, 399.

64 By this time, the Misericordia had evidently emerged as the essential base of elite power in the Ghetto. Leone da Modena and the cantor who succeeded him were also paid by the Misericordia, with these expenditures itemized in their Pinchas (Siegmund, *Medici State*, 559–60nn42–3).

65 Finzi reported this election in his role as *Cancelliere* (ASF Nove 45, f.195v, 10 Oct. 1613).

66 ASF Otto 247, f.73v, 29 April 1614. For this incident, see Chapter 3 above, 'The Ghetto.'

67 ASF MdP 5150, f.61r–f.62r, 16 Aug. 1615 [*Letters*, no. 7]. It is not documented that Benedetto Blanis preached in the synagogue before the advent of Leone da Modena and other professionals. However, it is highly likely that he did so, since he had the desire to preach and was one of the more eru-

dite members of this small community. His precise qualifications are yet to be determined; we do not know where or with whom he studied or if he was specifically trained in the art of preaching.

68 ASF Nove 368, f.375v, no.19.

69 Modena, *Riti*, 18–19, also 2–3.

70 Ibid., 22.

71 See Siegmund, *Medici State*, 562n73, for the *Mahzor ke-fi minhag Kahal Kadosh Roma* (Bologna, 1540).

72 ASF Riformagioni 10, f.20r–f.22v. Lazzero Rabeno was apparently a Rabbi.

73 Frattarelli Fischer, *Vivere fuori dal ghetto*, 35, and Siegmund, *Medici State*, 165–7. The evidence is sparse and somewhat circumstantial – further complicated by the Christian habit of calling almost any recurring gathering of Jews a *sinagoga*. At least one of these featured the reading of the Psalms in Spanish, which triggered an investigation by the Papal Nunzio in 1569, when Doctor Laudadio Blanis was called as an expert witness on Iberian Jewish practice. (ASF Nunziatura 842, 9 and 17 Sept., 12 Oct. 1569.) It is not clear how many of these 'synagogues' supported a full liturgy, including regular Torah readings.

74 ASF Nove 3243, f.78. A copy of this petition, dated 30 June 1688, is one of the documents compiled for a complicated case regarding the relative legal jurisdiction of the Italian and Levantine nations.

75 ASF Nove 3243, f.78 (rescript), dated Nov. 1596.

76 Ibid., f.78r.

77 Ibid., (rescript), dated 7 March 1600/01.

78 Ibid., f.38r, dated 14 March 1600/01.

79 There is a long and complicated story waiting to be written of relations between the Jewish communities in Florence and Pisa/Livorno. Lucia Frattarelli Fischer made a major contribution in her recent book, *Vivere fuori dal ghetto* (2008), which has done much to refocus our view of the forces at work in granducal Tuscany. During the time of Benedetto Blanis and Don Giovanni dei Medici the situation was very much in flux, so I have tried to avoid an overly deterministic reading of specific events.

80 These census figures are taken from ASF MS 4450, f.172 r–v.

81 For the two versions of the Livornina, see Frattarelli Fischer, *Vivere fuori dal ghetto*, 36–51.

82 Ibid., 37.

83 The most dramatic case was that of the 'Martyrs of Ancona.' In 1555–56, eighty Portuguese were arrested for Judaizing by the papal administration in the port city of Ancona, and twenty-five were eventually executed in a public *auto da fe*. These traumatic events shaped the course of Jewish settle-

ment in the Mediterranean for many years to come and formed the immediate context of various actions by the Medici government. Ibid., 30–3.

84 Frattarelli Fischer offers a fascinating discussion of these 'pre-Livornina'
privileges (ibid., 15–36), noting the prevailing climate of secrecy and obfus-
cation.

85 ASF MdP 1170a, Insert 3, f.171r–f.172v, 26 Oct. 1545 (Giorgio Dati to Pier-
francesco Riccio). Frattarelli Fischer, *Vivere fuori dal ghetto*, 17.

86 15 Jan. 1548 in the Florentine style.

87 ASF Misc Med 23, Insert 11, f.2. This is an extract from a finding by Paolo
Vinta, dated 11 April 1577, sent to his brother Belisario Vinta on 7 May
1602. In fact, Francesco I extended important privileges to Jews as Jews,
e.g., 'Sechiel Zaccur et Mordacai suo figlio Hebrei habitanti in Aleppo'
(ASF MdP 6429, f.60, Feb. 1575/76).

88 This particular formulation is my own. Frattarelli Fischer (*Vivere fuori dal
ghetto*, 13–36) offers some fascinating examples of the Medici concealing
privileges to 'New Christians' – not registering them as legally enacted
documents. However, she also demonstrates that there was more of a paper trail than Paolo Vinta realized, although it was not subject to public
scrutiny. On one occasion, in 1551, Cosimo formally registered privileges
to Jews from the east (along with Muslims of various descriptions). In the
case of these authentic *levantini*, Judaizing after baptism would have been
a less immediate issue since they were not coming directly from a Catholic
country (ibid., 29).

89 ASF Misc Med 23, Insert 11, f.2, 7 May 1602 (Paolo Vinta to Belisario
Vinta).

90 Although the *segno* was mandated in Florence, the grand dukes granted
many exemptions.

91 The situation was extremely complex (as Frattarelli Fischer demonstrates),
and there are still many open questions regarding the immediate and
longer term effects of the Livornina. It should not be assumed that this
edict was universally viewed as a major shift in policy by Jews – and others – at the time. Some Jews were probably inclined to take little notice of
general laws or mandates, preferring to operate in the realm of individual
graces and favours, negotiating their own deals with the granducal administration. In ASF MdP 1243, ff.8–10, there is an interesting letter dated 13
Oct. 1593 (four months after the issuance of the Livornina) from Matedia
Menagem in Florence to Granducal Secretary Lorenzo Usimbardi. Matedia
was coordinating the interests of various Levantine Jews in Florence with
pre-Livornina privileges, acting as intermediary between the Consoli del
Mare in Pisa and the granducal administration in Florence. In order to es-

tablish the legal context of the request of Abram Israel, he does not cite the newly issued Livornina; rather, he sends Usimbardi copies of two older documents: (1) the privilege issued in 1556 by Cosimo I 'to all Hebrews of any quality and condition, be they Portuguese or Italian or of other nations' (f.10) and (2) a set of more specific privileges issued by Francesco I in 1583 for Moisé di Sabadullo, Angelo Teseo, and Manuello Lattone (and their households) who wished to live outside the Ghetto in Florence (f.9).

92 David Alben Azzor was, in fact, operating on a very high level, seeking to negotiate full trading and diplomatic relations between Emperor Ahmed I and Grand Duke Ferdinando I. In ASF MdP 940, f.80, 8 March 1607 (evidently1608), there is a letter of presentation to Ferdinando I on behalf of 'David Benaso' from 'Jaffer Bassa Capitanio General de la mar della Maestà del Gran Imperator' in Constantinople. This Ottoman official requests confirmation of Alben Azzor's credentials and his mandate to negotiate on behalf of the Tuscan crown. In f.446, 12 March 1607 (evidently1608), there is another letter of presentation for 'David Abenasor' to Ferdinando I from 'Salagnac' in Pera, who was evidently the French resident ambassador or else the consul of the French Nation in Istanbul.

93 ASF Otto 227, f.60v–f.61r, 22 Aug. 1607. Strictly speaking, the 'Privileges of Livorno and Pisa' should have been determined by the Massari in Pisa and Livorno and then registered by the Consoli del Mare in Pisa; this had already been the subject of a legal confrontation in 1599 (Frattarelli Fischer, *Vivere fuori dal ghetto*, 54–6). However, the habit of relying on granducal grace and favour was deeply rooted.

94 ASF Otto 227, f.60v–f.61r, 22 Aug. 1607. The Otto construed the legal precedents in the same manner when granting Levantine privileges to Samuele Hagges on 10 July 1609 (ASF Otto 233, f.18r) and Emanuello Lattone on 10 Sept. 1609 (ibid., f.128r).

95 The Ghetto was divided into two sections, the Inner Ghetto (Ghetto Interno) and the Outer Ghetto (Ghetto Esterno). Houses and shops in the Outer Ghetto looked onto the Central Market (Mercato Vecchio), had their own entrances, and were occupied both by Jews and Christians. On 27 June 1607 Davit d'Aronne *hebreo levantino* is ordered to surrender a house to Gherson d'Isdrael *hebreo levantino* which might well have been outside the Ghetto since the Otto was involved (ASF Otto 226, f.184v–f.185r). On 16 June 1616 Josef Tiseo (probably Levantine) is described as having a villa at Ponte alle Mosse, in the near outskirts of Florence (ASF MdP 5140, f.387). On 19 and 26 April 1619 Leone di Moise da Prato and Salamone di Leone da Prato (presumably Italians) are ordered to surrender a shop in Via della Nave to Pavolo di Battista Carcani (ASF Otto 262, f.69v and f.76v). On

12 Sept. 1615 Cesare Fabbroni wrote to Don Giovanni dei Medici, in Venice, 'Circa la casa di lung'arno che l'ebreo l'haveva presa per scudi 40, questa al certo non se ne caverà più che 20 o 25 scudi e tutto si farà il meglio che si potrà' (ASF MdP 5140, f.102). In 1573 Graziadio and Abramo di Ventura Leucci (from Pisa) are recorded as having a perfume shop 'sul Canto della via di Martelli' (ASF Arte Medici e Speziali 13, f.91r–v). On 24 July1620 the Otto responded to a request from 'Joseph Uzule *hebreo Levantino*' for various privileges for himself and his servant Isac Coen for the entire Medici State, including 'alloggiare fuora di Ghetto'; this might have been granted but there is a reference to other documents that no longer exist (ASF Otto 266, f.50r).

96 ASF Regie Possessioni 6575, f.32r–v.

97 By 20 July 1612 construction expenses were being authorized 'for setting up the *schola* of the Levantine Nation' (ibid., f.35r–v).

98 ASF Otto 227, f.76r, 3 Sept. 1607. This is the same 'Donato son of Isac Tedesco' who was involved in the scuffle with the Blanis family in 1611 and served as a governor of the Ghetto in 1613–14.

99 ASF Dogana di Firenze 18, f.46v, 22 Oct. 1613. This is an example of regular procedure – with 'Levantine privileges' being granted in Pisa and subsequently extended to Florence. He was perhaps 'Moisé son of Samuele son of Moisé son of Samuele son of Moyse Blanis de Lerda.' Benedetto's great-great-grandfather Moyse Blanis de Lerda had two known sons, Samuele and Laudadio. The latter was Benedetto's great-grandfather who settled in Florence.

100 These dates are expressed in Florentine reckoning. Laudadio's 1617 election was registered on 12 Jan. 1618 Roman reckoning, Benedetto's election on 1 Feb. 1620 Roman, and Salamone's on 1 Feb. 1624 Roman.

101 See Chapter 13 below, 'Habeas Corpus.'

102 The names of Laudadio Blanis' daughters do not appear in any known documents.

103 ASF Otto 250, f.11r, 10 March 1614/15.

5 Memory and Survival

1 ASF MdP 5150, f.131, 2 April 1616 [*Letters*, no. 39]. In Florentine practice, the hours of the day were counted from nightfall, although new days were normally considered to begin at sunrise. In Jewish practice, new days begin at nightfall. In his letters, Benedetto often seems to gravitate between the two systems.

2 Modena, *Historia de' riti hebraici*, 58–9.

3 ASF Otto 270, f.25r, 12 Nov. 1621.

4 ASF MdP 5150, f.9, 20 June 1615 [*Letters*, no. 2]. The man in question was a very eminent one, Medici Secretary Camillo Guidi.

5 Ibid., f.391 (by 26 Sept. 1620) [*Letters*, no. 211]; 26 Sept. was the day before the Jewish New Year of 5381 which began on the evening of 27 Sept. 1620.

6 For the immediate context of this reference, see Chapter 12 below, 'Prison,' and *Letters*, no. 210. '*Pasqua*' is squeezed into the lower right-hand corner of this note, slightly out of line, representing an evident afterthought. The note itself is written on a tiny scrap of paper, measuring 2.85 by 3.55 inches.

7 Modena, *Riti*, 65.

8 Ibid., 66–7.

9 It is worth noting that Leone da Modena originally wrote his *Historia de' riti hebraici* (albeit in Italian) for a Protestant audience in England, where there was likely to be a broader familiarity with the Bible.

10 Presenting only partial quotations (assuming that the reader would complete them from his own knowledge) is a fairly common practice of the time. However, Modena goes beyond this with a concerted avoidance of problematic issues and themes, as part of his 'apologetic' program. Also, he could not take for granted an instant recall of texts from the Old Testament (or 'Jewish Bible') on the part of his Catholic readers, apart from relatively few specialized scholars.

11 Exodus 12:15. Passover is celebrated for seven days in Israel, where the scriptures originated, but for eight days in the diaspora – thus the reference to the 'seventh day.'

12 This passage is somewhat garbled, particularly in regard to the mortar. There might well be a missing phrase.

13 Modena, *Riti*, 68.

14 See Chapter 11 below, 'Curious and Forbidden Books,' section 1, 'Passover and Easter.'

15 ASF MdP 5147, f.787, 29 May 1621.

16 Ibid., 5150, f.91, 25 Sept. 1616 [*Letters*, no. 69]. Sukkot began on Monday, 26 Sept. 1616 (15 Tishri 5377).

17 Modena, *Riti*, 77. In his quote from Leviticus 23:42, Leone's 'etc.' substitutes the essential phrase, 'every one that is of the race of Israel.'

18 There were a number of these terraces in the Ghetto, as documented by the surviving rent accounts in the Archivio di Stato di Firenze, Scrittoio delle Regie Possessioni. The Jews in the Florentine Ghetto were generally forbidden to use the roofs of their houses, since this would compromise their isolation from the surrounding Christian city.

19 ASF MdP 5150, f.321, 29 Sept. 1619 [*Letters*, no. 156].

20 Modena, *Riti*, 72–4.

21 ASF MdP 5150, f.17, 4 Oct. 1615 [*Letters*, no. 13].

22 Modena, *Riti*, 74–6.

23 ASF MdP 5150, f.61r–f.62r, 16 Aug. 1615 [*Letters*, no. 5].

24 Ibid., f.77, 27 Feb. 1615/16 [*Letters*, no. 34].

25 Ibid., f.173, 4 Nov. 1616 [*Letters*, no. 74].

26 See Chapter 6 below, 'The Market.' Unlike many other Jewish businesses, the Blanis' enterprise was not formally incorporated. The Blanis are never cited as '*compagni*' in the files of the Otto di Guardia e Balìa, while we hear of 'Moise Cassuto et compagni levantini,' 'Vito Piazza et compagni tutti hebrei,' 'Abram et Giuseppe di Isdraelle et compagni,' 'Zaccheria, Salvadore, e Prospero Servadio et Compagni ebrei,' 'Lazzero di Lion Pesaro e compagni ebrei,' and 'Danielo Calò hebreo et compagni' – to give some examples.

27 In particular, they were closely involved with the branch of the Blanis family in Massa Carrara.

28 After the death of Laudadio Blanis in 1632, these leases were taken over by his sons Lelio and Benedetto (ASF Regie Possessioni 6556, f.89 and f.92). Other properties were occupied by Benedetto's youngest brother Salamone (f.74).

29 Modena, *Riti*, 3.

30 Ibid., 88. Siegmund (*Medici State*, 346–8) offers evidence of relatively early marriage for men in the Florentine Ghetto.

31 Modena, *Riti*, 89.

32 For 'Doctor Samuel from Fez,' more frequently known as Samuel Hagiz or Chagez, see Chapter 7 below, 'Knowledge and Power.' There is no reference to local Caggesi offspring in the Florentine archive.

33 ASF MdP 5150, f.125, 17 April 1616 [*Letters*, no. 42]. If Samuel had remarried in Massa after the death of a previous wife, we would expect her to be cited as 'sua nuova moglie' or 'la sua moglie adesso,' not 'sua seconda moglie.'

34 Ibid., f.191, 18 Nov. 1617 [*Letters*, no. 104].

35 Ibid., f.219, 23 Dec. 1618 [*Letters*, no. 119].

36 Modena, *Riti*, 90. There are references to a dispute regarding the construction of a *mikveh* in the Florentine Ghetto in ASF Nove 16, 106v, 30 July 1575, and ASF Otto 131, f.262v–f.263r, 5 Oct. 1575.

37 Modena, *Riti*, 91.

38 ASF MdP 5150, f.219, 23 Dec. 1618 [*Letters*, no. 119].

39 Modena, *Riti*, 93.

40 ASF Otto 250, f.11r, 10 March 1614/15.
41 The implication is that David Blanis had business interests on estates out-side Florence. Cosimo Baroncelli was Don Giovanni dei Medici's long-time military companion and probably his closest friend, as well as the major-domo of his Florentine palace and eventually his biographer.
42 Modena, *Riti*, 48.
43 ASF Nove 368, f.375v, no. 14. On 9 Aug. 1622, Giovanni – son and shop-boy of Marco 'called Marco the Jew' – was fined by the Florentine food administration (Grascia) for overcharging on sheep brains. Marco was described as a butcher in the butchers' quarter, and it is unclear whether he was a practising Jew or a convert to Catholicism ('Gio. di Marco detto Marco Ebreo figlio e Garzone di detto Marco Ebreo beccaio in Beccheria,' ASF Auditore Fiscale 2210, f.1011v).
44 Modena, *Riti*, 5 and 50.
45 Ibid., 4–5.
46 Ibid., 47.
47 ASF Otto 227, f.116r, 25 Sept. 1607.
48 Modena, *Riti*, 51.
49 So far, I have not come upon any legal documents relating to Florentine Jews supplying or selling food wholesale or retail, apart from meat. In fact, kosher meat brought into the Ghetto from outside was specifically marked. In a set of by-laws formulated by the Florentine Jewish commu-nity on 3 Aug. 1595, but evidently never ratified by the Nove, the marking of kosher meat is discussed: 'It is understood that no one will dare obtain meat in the slaughterhouse unless it is designated by the shochet with the usual mark' (ACEF Box D 3.2.4; Cassuto, 'I più antichi capitoli,' *Rivista Is-raelitica* 10/1 (1913): 36).
50 ASF Nove 368, f.377r, no. 23.
51 Modena, *Riti*, 51.
52 Wine was less likely to be an everyday beverage for the Germans (who had beer) and the Levantines (who had perhaps lost the habit after living for generations in Muslim lands).
53 In 1552–53 Laudadio evidently sold much of his production on the open market (Toaff, *The Jews in Umbria*, docs. 2540 and 2566).
54 Modena, *Riti*, 53.
55 Ibid., 13–15.
56 Cassuto, 'I più antichi capitoli del Ghetto di Firenze,' *Rivista Israelitica* 9/5–6 (1912): 203–11; ACEF Box D 3.2.4.
57 ASF Nove 17, f.202r–v.
58 Jews writing in Italian did indeed use such terms as *carità, misericordia,* and

elemosine, since there were no ready parallels to *tzdakah* and *mitzvot* in that language.

59 Modena, *Riti*, 30.

60 Ibid. Among various documents associated with a legal action between the Italian and Levantine nations in the Florentine Ghetto in 1688, there are references to the disruption of normal philanthropic activities, beginning with the customary Friday donations to the poor. See ASF Nove 3243, the first of several unnumbered loose sheets at the beginning of the volume.

61 ASF Nove 368, f.377r, no. 24.

62 Ibid., f.374–f.380.

63 Modena, *Riti*, 25. Siegmund (*Medici State*, 387–9) offers interesting comments regarding this custom.

64 Modena, *Riti*, 30.

65 Cassuto, 'I più antichi capitoli del ghetto di Firenze,' *Rivista Israelitica* 10/1 (1913): 33.

66 ASF Nove 368, f.375r, no. 7.

67 Modena, *Riti*, 30–1.

68 See Siegmund, *Medici State*, 393–4. There is a surviving record book for the Compagnia della Misericordia for the years 1610–41 (ACEF Box B 5.1).

69 See Siegmund, *Medici State*, 394–6. These four funds are cited in a list of seventeen account books that were discarded in 1644–55 (ACEF Box E 1.3).

70 Modena, *Riti*, 32–3.

71 For Kabbalah, see Chapter 7 below, 'Knowledge and Power.' In the early years of the seventeenth century, it cannot be taken for granted, without further evidence, that Benedetto was personally influenced by Lurianic Kabbalah.

72 In addition to the testamentary bequest of Ginevra Blanis, there was that of Donna Consola, widow of Daniello Alpelingo from Empoli, which was tied up in litigation for many years. See ASF Otto 247, f.100r, 13 May 1614, and ibid., 260, f.53v, 6 Aug. 1618. Siegmund (*Medici State*, 396), also cites documentation in ACEF Box. 5.I, Opera Pie, misc., folder 32/22.

73 ASF Notarile Moderno Testamenti 767, f.167r–v. Siegmund assesses this will in *Medici State*, 389–95, and reproduces it in Figure 9.

74 Modena, *Riti*, 33.

75 ACEF Box D 3.2.4. Published in Cassuto, 'I piu antichi capitoli del ghetto di Firenze,' *Rivista Israelitica* 9/5–6 (1912): 207.

76 ASF Otto 263, f.17r, 9 July 1619.

77 On 4 Dec. 1608, the Jew Natan Nan was granted special permission to enjoy the privileges of Pisa and Livorno without his family, since living *familiarmente* was part of the terms of the initial privilege (ASF Otto 231, f.57r–v).

6 The Market

1 After completing this chapter, I had the opportunity to read Evelyn Welch's fascinating book, *Shopping in the Renaissance* (2005). Although the scope of her study is far broader than mine, and she focuses on a generally earlier period (1400–1600), her findings sometimes substantiate or qualify my own. I indicate a number of specific instances in the notes to this chapter.

2 The word is *piazzaiolo*, most likely a variant on *pizzicagnolo*.

3 ASF MdP 5150, f.39r, 8 Nov. 1615 [*Letters*, no. 17]. The thousands of *fascine* that caught fire at the *brusciataio* might have been chestnut husks. Another account of the fire was written by Niccola Medici to Don Giovanni on the previous day: 'This morning at the 15th hour [around 7 a.m.], fire struck some of the shops in the Mercato Vecchio on the Ghetto side and four burned down. It would have been a disaster for these unfortunate Jews if this fire occurred at night since they would have been wiped out. As it was, some of those stands belonging to Jews were burned, but they suffered no other damage. However, everything was lost in the shops of the poulterers and the chestnut boilers (*succiolai*)' (ASF MdP 5140, f.164, 7 Nov. 1615). Expenditures for repairing the damage after the fire are noted in ASF Regie Possessioni 6575, f.36v, 4 Feb. 1615/16.

4 ASF Nove 368, f.374v–f.375r, no. 4.

5 Ibid.

6 Ibid., f.376r, no. 16.

7 Ibid.

8 ASF Otto 270, f.187r, 4 Feb. 1621/22. The reference is to 24 March 1620/21.

9 Ibid., 263, f.14r, 6 July 1619.

10 The original statue on top of the column was by Donatello; there is now a copy of a later work by Giovanni Battista Foggini.

11 There was not a permanent structure for the pillory, unlike the kind that was common in England or colonial America. Malefactors were simply tied to an iron ring at the base of the column.

12 ASF Otto 249, f.60r, 1 Dec. 1614.

13 Ibid., 226, f.94, 4 May 1607.

14 Ibid., 261, f.186v, 22 Feb. 1618/19.

15 This is a tentative translation of *due passerini*, an elusive period term.

16 ASF Otto 263, f.165v, 3 Oct. 1619.

17 The guild was the Arte dei Medici e Speziali (Siegmund, *Tuscan Households*, Table 3c). On 26 Sept. 1618 the Jew Agnolo Pesero was given a seal by the Florentine customs administration, allowing him to transport a

box of buttons for sale at the fair in Pisa on behalf of another Jew Ferrante Passini (ASF Dogana Antica di Firenze 333, f.13v).

18 ASF Nove, f.276r, 29 Dec. 1582.

19 ASF MdP 5150, f.424r, 28 June 1620 [*Letters*, no. 198].

20 Ibid., f.403r, 5 Feb. 1620/21 [*Letters*, no. 217].

21 Ibid., f.107r, 2 Aug. 1616 [*Letters*, no. 59], and f.425v, 28 June 1620 [*Letters*, no. 198].

22 Ibid., f.393r, 21 Feb. 1620/21 [*Letters*, no. 218].

23 Don Giovanni sometimes extended his franking and customs privileges to Benedetto for his personal use – but he was evidently concerned that this prerogative not be abused nor taken for granted. See ibid., 5147, f.255v, 29 Dec. 1618 (Cosimo Baroncelli to Don Giovanni).

24 Ibid., f.787, 29 May 1621.

25 Laudadio di Moyse Blanis matriculated as a minor member of the Arte della Seta on 16 Oct. 1572 (ASF Arte della Seta 13, f.103v), and his sister Ginevra matriculated as a minor member on 3 Nov. 1574 (f.120v). Laudadio son of Agnolo Blanis was enrolled as a minor member of the Silk Guild by way of family connections on 25 Aug. 1601. He was then upgraded to major member on that same day (14, f.33r). Lelio (Agnolo) son of Laudadio matriculated on 26 Feb. 1602/3, by virtue of his father's membership (f.51v).

26 Cantini, *Legislazione toscana*, vol. 10 (1804), 65.

27 Ibid., 74.

28 Ibid., 64.

29 Through 1632 (the time of his death), Laudadio di Maestro Agnolo Blanis paid a total annual rent of scudi 33.3.13.18 for property numbers 10, 35, and 81. The shop was number 10, and 35 and 81 were residential apartments (ASF Regie Possessioni 6556, f.49). After Laudadio's death, his son Agnolo took over the lease for the shop and residential property 81 (f.89), while Benedetto took over the lease for residential property 35 (f.92). Through 1633 Salamone Blanis rented three properties (6, 15, and an unnumbered property), for a total of 38 fiorini. In 1634 he relinquished all three of these properties (f.74). In 1643 Benedetto traded apartments with Lazzaro di Jacobe Calò, relinquishing 'le stanze che rispondono sopra l'osteria del Piovano Oste' (6558, f.63).

30 For the general distrust of vendors and resellers, see Welch, *Shopping*, 32–55.

31 Siegmund, *Tuscan Households*, Table 3c.

32 Cantini, *Legislazione toscana*, vol. 9 (1803), 110–11.

33 Ibid., 113.

34 ASF Dogana Antica di Firense 18, f.158r , 14 April 1615.
35 An Agnolo di Salvatore di Magistro Laudadio Hebreo matriculated in the
    Florentine Silk Guild on 25 Oct. 1574 (ASF Arte della Seta 13, 120r; cited
    by Siegmund, *Tuscan Households*, Appendix 3d). In 1613 a Jewish merchant
    from Massa named Agnolo di Blanes was granted permission to travel
    in the Medici State without wearing the *segno* (ASF Otto 251, f.10, 6 July
    1615). Later, Agnolo's daughter Virtuosa married Josef Hezrà – who con-
    verted to Christianity in 1620, with dire results for the extended Blanis
    family. Benedetto identified this Agnolo as his maternal uncle, demonstrat-
    ing the frequent intermarriage between cousins. See below Chapters 11,
    'Curious and Forbidden Books,' and 12, 'Prison.'
36 ASF Dogana Antica di Firenze 17, f.53r, 27 May 1611.
37 Ibid. (all 1611): f.42v, 29 March; f.43r, 8 April; f.46r, 22 April; f.49r, 5 May;
    f.50v, 13 May; f.53v, 27 May (with rescript of 19 Aug.); f.65v, 15 July; f.66v,
    23 July; and f.72r, 18 Aug.
38 Ibid., f.72r, 18 Aug. 1611. In 1635, Chiara, daughter of Mirra and David
    Blandes of Florence, was offered as wife to Abramo Finzi in Massa Cararra
    (Jacopetti, *Ebrei a Massa e Carrara*, 56). Mirra was still alive in 1641, when
    she figures in a lawsuit against Benedetto (ASF Nove 3243, f.81r), and in
    1643, when she lodged an appeal to the governor of Livorno against her
    brother David Franzese (ASL, Governo, 2603, vol. 1, f.739). In 1619 Lelio's
    wife was named Ricca (ASF Otto 263, f.1r, 1 July 1619). We know the
    names of neither of Benedetto's two successive wives: the first one died in
    the autumn of 1617 (ASF MdP 5150, f.191, 18 Nov. 1617 [*Letters*, no. 104]),
    and he remarried in Dec. 1618 (ibid., 5150, f.219, 23 Dec. 1618 [*Letters*, no.
    119]).
39 Cantini, *Legislazione toscana*, vol. 9: 66.
40 ASF Nove 376, f.364v, 22 Dec. 1621.
41 ASF Otto 257, f.14v, 10 July 1617.
42 ASF MdP 5154, f.536, 15 April 1614.
43 ASF Otto 262, f.8r, 5 March 1618/19.
44 ASF Guardaroba 1254, f.489, 4 May 1618, and f.583, 25 May 1618. I would
    like to thank Lisa Goldenberg Stoppato for bringing these references to my
    attention.
45 *Bottonai* and *velettai* appear in the records of three different guilds, the
    Arte della Seta, the Arte dei Linaioli, and the Medici e Speziali. Jewish
    velettai probably edged and finished cloth made by others and also resold
    veils made outside the Ghetto, particularly by cloistered nuns. During the
    crackdown of 1620–22, the Arte della Seta evidently sought to establish
    their control of the button market. In the first weeks of 1622, they found

'Salvadore di Sessa Ebreo' guilty of button making without Guild membership (ASF Auditore Fiscale 2210, f.813r–v, 13 Jan. 1621/22).

46 Cantini, *Legislazione toscana*, vol. 6 (1803), 77.

47 Ibid., vol. 15 (1804), 96.

48 ASF Otto 275, f.107r–v, 18 Aug. 1623.

49 On 22 April 1616 the magistrates treated Laudadio Blanis as the unwitting victim of a thief using a false name (ASF Otto 254, f.120v).

50 Ibid., f.107v, 22 April 1622.

51 Ibid., 250, f.52r, 28 March 1615.

52 Ibid., 259, f.169v, 12 Oct. 1618.

53 His full name was 'Rubino di Moise Basilea detto Mantovano Hebreo' (ibid., 257, f.187v, 24 Oct. 1617).

54 Ibid., 258, f.144r, 12 Jan. 1617/18.

55 Ibid., 258, f.144r, 12 Jan. 1617/18, and 259, f.110r, 23 May 1618.

56 Ibid., 263, f.17r, 9 July 1619.

57 Ibid., 257, f.14v, 10 July 1617.

58 There was a numerous da Pesaro clan in the Florentine Ghetto (although everyone called 'da Pesaro' was not necessarily related), and there were at least two 'Emanuel Pesaro' at this time. The most influential branch of the family was that of Leone da Pesaro; his offspring included an Emanuel (i.e., Emanuel di Leone da Pesaro), and they figure frequently in financial cases in these years. On 16 Oct. 1618 Agnolo Pesaro (the father of Emanuello di Agnolo Pesaro) was granted a two-year exemption from the *segno* (ASF Otto 260, f.174r). On 13 Jan. 1618/19, 'Emanuel di Lion Pesaro' was elected governor (ASF Nove 50, f.318r). 'Manuel [no patronymic] Pesaro' was elected on 20 Feb. 1622/23 (ibid., 54, f.322v), as was 'Manuel [no patronymic] Pesaro' on 16 Feb. 1624/25 (ibid., 56, f.249r).

59 This Moisé Blanis was evidently a descendant of Samuel, the brother of Benedetto's great-grandfather Laudadio, son of Moyse.

60 ASF Otto 275, f.43r, 19 July 1623.

61 They were freed on their own recognizance on the day before the hearing (ibid., f.40r, 18 July 1623).

62 Vismara, *Oltre l'usura: La Chiesa moderna e il prestito a interesse*.

63 Parks, *Medici Money*.

64 ASF Magistrato Supremo (MS) 4450, f.2v–f.5r.

65 Ibid. Around the same time, Pope Pius V made a major move to limit covert lending at interest, with the bull *In eam pro nostro* (1571).

66 Siegmund, *Medici State*, 207–9.

67 Medici, *Omelie fatte alli ebrei di Firenze nella Chiesa di Santa Croce* (1585).

68 Shulamit Furstenberg Levi assesses Vitale Medici's sermons in her insight-

ful and thought-provoking article, 'The Boundaries between "Jewish" and "Catholic" Space in Counter-Reformation Florence as Seen by the Convert Vitale Medici.'

69 Medici, *Omelie*, 6–7.

70 Welch (*Shopping*, 90–2) notes that legitimate commerce often involved delayed payment.

71 Jewelry, textiles, and clothing are frequently cited, along with gold and silverwork, furniture, and tapestries.

72 ASF Otto 257, f.73r, 17 Aug. 1617. The *cedola* was dated 22 March 1616/17.

73 Finance charges for delayed payments on real items would have been considered usurious at that time, no less than charging money for cash loans disguised as delayed purchases.

74 We occasionally hear of Christian usurers, who sometimes shared the action with their Jewish counterparts.

75 Giovanni Francesco degli Albizi (1587–1625) was the son of the deceased Pandolfo degli Albizi (1543–1599).

76 ASF MdP 5150, f.43, 15 Nov. 1615 [*Letters*, no. 19].

77 Ibid., f.44, legal documents (in copy) dated 5 Jan. 1606/07, July 1612 (no day specified), 29 Nov. 1613, and 26 May 1614 [*Letters*, no. 19].

78 Ibid., f.43, 15 Nov. 1615 [*Letters*, no. 19].

79 Ibid., f.69, 6 Dec. 1615 [*Letters*, no. 22].

80 Ibid., 5150, f.79, 22 Nov. 1615 [*Letters*, no. 20].

81 He is described as 'il cavaliere di comenda figliolo del medico di Rimbotti.' The medical doctor was Giovanni Battista Rimbotti, and his son with a benefice in a chivalric order was perhaps Rimbotto Rimbotti.

82 Ibid., f.69, 6 Dec. 1615 [*Letters*, no. 22].

83 Ibid.

84 ASF Otto 249, f.124r, 23 Dec. 1614.

85 ASF MdP 5141, f.1029, 6 Sept. 1620 (Piero Capponi to Don Giovanni dei Medici).

86 ASF Otto 275, f.133v, 30 Aug. 1623.

87 Ibid., f.134v, 30 Aug. 1623. Advancing money on notes of credit (*cedole*) had long been an important activity for the entire Blanis family. For Benedetto's father Laudadio, see, e.g., ibid. (all 1609), 233, f.37v, 21 July; f.139v–f.140r, 16 Sept.; and f.207r–f.208r, 22 Oct.

88 Ibid., 275, f.134v, 30 Aug. 1623.

89 Siegmund (*Medici State*, 312–23) discusses the middling economic status of the Jewish leadership in the first decades of the Ghetto. In a legal deposition on 21 Dec. 1621 Benedetto's older brother Lelio states that he is worth 4,000 scudi, a substantial sum (ASF Nove 376, f.363v–f.364v.) This figure

is difficult to evaluate on its own, since Lelio might have exaggerated his worth in order to enhance his importance (Jews paid a head tax not an income tax). He might also have claimed family property as his own and included uncollectible 'notes of credit.'

90 ASF Otto 228, f.160r, 15 Feb. 1607/08.

91 ASF MdP 939, f.652, 16 Feb. 1607/08. There are letters from 'Dioguo Teixeira' or references to him by others in ibid., 938, ff.140, 276, 560, and 906; 939, f.125; and 941, f.78. I am grateful to Corey Tazzara for bringing this documentation to my attention and for sharing other information regarding mercantile activity in Livorno.

92 Ibid., 939, f.652, 16 Feb. 1607/08.

93 Ibid.

94 Lichtenstein, 'Teixeira de Sampaio, Abraham Senior (formerly Diego)' in *Encyclopaedia Judaica*, XIX, 585–6. Texeira lived from 1581 to1666.

95 For Maggino di Gabriele's extraordinary career, see Frattarelli Fischer, *Vivere fuori dal ghetto*, 39–44, 56–68. Ferdinando I designated Maggino as the first leader of the nascent Livorno community and supported him in various manufacturing enterprises. Subsequently, Maggino launched bold schemes to advance Jewish interests (and his own) in northern Italy and Germany.

96 David Alben Azzor (Abenasor, Benaso) was a Levantine Jew based in Istanbul. On 22 Aug. 1607 he was granted broad commercial and residential privileges in Florence, with reference to a major business venture that was already under way (ASF Otto 227, f.60v–f.61r). Around that time he was seeking to establish formal relations between Grand Duke Ferdinando I and Emperor Ahmed I. On 8 March 1607 (evidently1608), 'Jaffer Bassa Capitanio General de la mar della Maestà del Gran Imperator' in Constantinople wrote a letter to Ferdinando I, to be presented in person by 'David Benaso'; Jaffer requested confirmation of David's credentials from the Grand Duke (ASF MdP 940, f.446). On 12 March 1607 (evidently 1608), 'Salagnac' in Pera (probably Consul of the French Nation) wrote Ferdinando I another letter on behalf of 'David Abenasor' (ibid., f.80).

97 See Frattarelli Fischer, *Vivere fuori dal ghetto*, 105, and Engels, *Merchants, Interlopers, Seamen and Corsairs: The 'Flemish' Community in Livorno and Genoa, 1615–1635*. In the documents, Isaac Lus (Luz, Lussio) is variously described as Flemish, Portuguese, Piedmontese, Jewish, and Catholic. On 22 April 1599 Grand Duke Ferdinando I issued a passport for 'Isach Lus, native of Piedmont, a merchant residing in Livorno' and the crew ('part Italian and part Flemish') of his ship, *Il Paradiso* (ASF MdP 6429, f.92). That same year, Isaac travelled to Russia on a trade mission with credentials

from the Grand Duke and rich gifts for the Emperor of Muscovy (ibid., 67, f.319, and ASF Misc Med 120, Insert 9). On 12 Dec. 1602 Isaac submitted a detailed report to Granducal Secretary Marcello Accolti on the spice trade between Holland and Africa, offering to wrest some of this activity from Spanish control and bring it to Livorno (ASF MdP 938, ff.836–7). In 1604–05 Isaac was operating out of Amsterdam (where the Lus family seems to have been principally based). At that time, he and his father Sion processed a large order, on behalf of Don Giovanni dei Medici, for black Belgian marble for the new granducal burial chapel at San Lorenzo (ASF Alessandri 10, ff.160–78). On 12 May 1603 Grand Duke Ferdinando I issued a passport for Abram Lus, noting that his brother 'Isac Lussio has lived for some years in our territory and in our port of Livorno, where he has kept and keeps a trading house, having always lived as a Catholic' (ASF MdP 72, f.262). This seems a transparent bureaucratic fiction, since it is difficult to imagine anyone mistaking two Portuguese brothers named Isaac and Abram for Catholics.

98 For the Florentine textile industries, see Goldthwaite, *The Economy of Renaissance Florence*, 265–335.

99 For a fuller assessment of these circumstances, see Frattarelli Fischer, *Vivere fuori dal ghetto*, 18–36.

100 ASF MdP 1170a, Insert 3, f.171r–f.172v, 26 Oct., 1545 (Giorgio Dati to Cosimo I). There was an influential figure operating behind the scenes, Pedro de Salamanca (Frattarelli Fischer, *Vivere fuori dal ghetto*, 16). For some early charters (1548–49) reflecting this policy, see Novoa, 'Documents Regarding the Settlement of Portuguese New Chrisitans in Tuscany.'

101 Frattarelli Fischer, *Vivere fuori dal ghetto*, 29; Cassuto, *Gli ebrei a Firenze*, 173–9.

102 ASF MS 4449, f.110v–f.111r. Also, Siegmund, *Tuscan Households*, 327–9.

103 ASF Arte della Seta 3, f.122r, 26 Oct. 1583.

104 Toaff, *La Nazione Ebrea a Livorno e a Pisa: 1591–1700*, 419–35. Also, Cantini, *Legislazione toscana*, vol. 14 (1804), 10–22.

105 Frattarelli Fischer, *Vivere fuori dal ghetto*, 90–2. In the 1590s, Jewish products included silk and cotton cloth, glassware, mirrors, and 'wool caps in the Turkish style.'

106 The Tesei seemed to occupy an intermediate position between the Italians and the Levantines. They enjoyed many of the privileges of Levantines (ASF Arte della Seta 3, f.124v) but also served among the Italian governors of the Ghetto, e.g., Salvador Tesei was ratified on 26 June 1609 (ASF Nove 41, f.90v).

107 Cantini, *Legislazione toscana*, vol. 15, 9.

108 Ibid., 194–6.
109 Ibid., 212–30 (8 Jan. 1621/22). There were also attempts by non-Jews to re-establish commerce with the Ottoman Empire. On 29 Dec. 1618 Cosimo Baroncelli wrote Don Giovanni: 'They are sending a certain Francesco Verrazzano to Constantinople in order to convey cloth (*panni*) in scarlet and other colours in hope that these will be well received and orders will follow for greater quantities, thereby reviving the wool trade in some degree since it has been laid low entirely' (ASF MdP 5147, f.255v).
110 ASF MdP 5147, f.787, 29 May 1621 (Cosimo Baroncelli to Don Giovanni dei Medici).
111 These defendants included Jewish merchants and the Christian producers and middlemen who collaborated with them (ASF Auditore Fiscale 2209, f.810r, 1 Oct. 1620, and 2210, f.812r, 13 Jan. 1621/22).
112 ASF MdP 3007, f.462r–v, 18 Oct. 1621 (Niccolò Sacchetti, Tuscan Ambassador in Venice, to Secretary Curzio Picchena).
113 Another dramatic failure in the Ghetto was that of the da Cagli family. In 1615 they pulled up stakes and went to Ancona, leaving many creditors in Florence. See ASF Otto: 250, f.180r, 29 May 1615; 253, f.84r, 14 April 1616, and f.241v, 18 June 1616; 256, f.89r, 6 May 1617; 258, f.28r, 17 Nov. 1617; 263, f.98r, 5 Sept. 1619, f.189v, 15 Oct. 1619, and f.212v, 25 Oct. 1619; 267, f.182 r, 28 Jan. 1620/21.
114 The young Ferdinando II was Grand Duke, under the regency of his mother Maria Magdalena von Habsburg and his grandmother Christine de Lorraine.
115 ASF Riformagioni 33, f.192r, 17 Oct. 1621. The three governors who signed the letter are Rafaele da Empoli, Leon da Passigli, and Giuseppe di Servadio Jare. A related letter from the consuls of the Silk Guild to the Grand Duke is found at ASF Riformagioni 33, f.178, 20 Oct. 1621. For a subsequent finding of the Eight Magistrates, see ASF Otto 272, f.95v, 25 Aug. 1622.

7 Knowledge and Power

1 ASF MdP 5150, f.159, 15 July 1616 [*Letters*, no. 56]. On 9 July 1616, in a letter to Cosimo Baroncelli, Don Giovanni confirmed Benedettto's task of reorganizing the library (ASF Alessandri 2, f.180r).
2 This is the Pernicca-Lattone-Isdraele-Tesei affair. See Chapter 8 below, 'Games of Chance.'
3 ASF 5150, f.97, 3 Sept. 1616 [*Letters*, no. 66]. Don Giovanni gives instruc-

tions to his *maggiordomo* regarding reorganization of the palace and its contents on 20 Feb. 1616 (modern reckoning) in ASF Alessandri 2, f.94r (and following).

4   ASF MdP 5150, f.95, 16 Oct. 1616 [*Letters*, no. 72].

5   Ibid., f.71, 6 Feb. 1615/16 [*Letters*, no. 30].

6   Ibid., f.13, 25 Oct. 1615 [*Letters*, no. 15].

7   Ibid., f.161, 8 July 1616 [*Letters*, no. 54].

8   Ibid., f.89, 8 Oct. 1616 [*Letters*, no. 71].

9   Ibid.

10   Ibid., f.159, 15 July 1616 [*Letters*, no. 45].

11   Ibid., f.221, 30 Dec. 1618 [*Letters*, no. 120].

12   Ibid., f.219, 23 Dec. 1618 [*Letters*, no. 119].

13   Ibid., f.113, 18 Sept. 1616 [*Letters*, no. 68].

14   Ibid., f.65, 30 July 1616 [*Letters*, no. 58].

15   Federico Barbierato offers many insights into the diffusion of magical books and writings in Venice (see *Nella stanza dei circoli: Clavicula Salamonis e libri di magia a Venezia nei secoli XVII e XVIII*).

16   ASF MdP 5150, f.159, 5 June 1616 [*Letters*, no. 51]. The 'book' in question was presumably an astrological work.

17   From the Latin Vulgate, Isaiah 9:6 (Douai-Reims translation). Livia Vernazza's star-crossed pregnancy ended in miscarriage two weeks later (ASF MdP 5150, f.153, 26 June 1616 [*Letters*, no. 53]). On 18 June 1616 Don Giovanni describes to Cosimo Baroncelli her loss of a five-month-old male child (ASF Alessandri 2, f.174 r).

18   The identity of the 'uncle' is not clear. It might be a brother of his late mother whose family was based in Massa Carrara. Or else, the 'uncle' might be an older cousin, perhaps Moisé Blanis in Florence who was evidently a medical doctor.

19   ASF MdP 5150, f.19, 24 Jan. 1615/16 [*Letters*, no. 28].

20   Ibid., f.81, 27 March 1616 [*Letters*, no. 37].

21   The marchesate was a feudal holding of the Del Monte family. See Toaff, 'Gli Ebrei del Marchesato di Monte S. Maria e Lippiano,' and 'Il commercio del denaro e le communità ebraiche 'di confine' (Pitigliano, Sorano, Monte San Savino, Lippiano) tra Cinquecento e Seicento.'

22   For the range of Kabbalistic charts and diagrams that were being produced in Italy at that time, see Giulio Busi, 'The Visual Kabbalah,' in *Mantova e la Qabbalah / Mantua and the Kabbalah*, 65–74.

23   Kabbalah, in Italy, has been the focus of much scholarly attention in recent years, most notably by Moshe Idel. Many of his relevant articles (originally

published in English) are available in *La Cabbalà in Italia: 1280–1510*. Also by Idel, see 'The Magical and Neo-Platonic Interpretations of the Kabbalah in the Renaissance.'

24 ASF MdP 5150, f.11, 21 July 1615 [*Letters*, no. 3]. See Chapter 2 above, 'The Palace.'

25 Scholem, *Kabbalah*, 102.

26 Ibid., 104.

27 See Idel, 'Italy in Safed, Safed in Italy,' and Busi, 'The Mantuan Kabbalistic Workshop,' in *Mantova e la Qabbalah / Mantua and the Kabbalah*, 49–64. Yosef Avivi assesses the early diffusion of Isaac of Luria's writings in Italy in 'Luria's Writings in Italy to 1620' (in Hebrew), *Alei Sefer* 11 (1984), 91–134. An essential figure in this diffusion was Israel Sarug Ashkenazi, a student of Luria, who was active in Italy in the 1590s and introduced Leone da Modena to his teachings.

28 See Wirszubski, *Pico della Mirandola's Encounter with Jewish Mysticism*. The Institut für Judaistik at the Freie Universität in Berlin and the Istituto Nazionale di Studi sul Rinascimento in Florence are now collaborating on the publication of Flavius Mithridates' Latin translations of kabbalistic texts in Hebrew for Pico della Mirandola.

29 Scholem, *Kabbalah*, 198. Barbierato (*Nella stanza dei circoli*. makes frequent reference to Agrippa's works which were prevalent in Venice.

30 See Chapter 11 below, 'Curious and Forbidden Books.'

31 ASF MdP 5150, f.221, 30 Dec. 1618 [*Letters*, no. 120].

32 Ibid., f.239, 27 Jan. 1618/19 [*Letters*, no. 125].

33 Ibid., f.251, 24 March 1618/19 [*Letters*, no. 130].

34 Ibid., f.221, 30 Dec. 1618 [*Letters*, no. 118].

35 Barbierato (*Nella stanza dei circoli*, 304–27) offers a compelling picture of the Jewish presence in the Venetian occult and the role of the Ghetto in the diffusion of arcane goods and services.

36 This was in the context of a sworn deposition in front of the court of the Archbishop of Florence on 19 Jan. 1621/22 (ASF MdP 5159, f.677r).

37 Benedetto's extraordinary infiltration of Don Giovanni and Livia Vernazza's household emerges most clearly in his legal depositions of 22 Sept. 1621 (ASF MdP 5161, f.67r–f.77v with a copy at f.234r–f.243r); 6 Oct. 1621 (ibid., f.269r–f.272v), and 19 Jan. 1621/22 (ibid., 5159, f.672v–f.683r). In Benedetto's letters to Don Giovanni there are many references to his involvement in matters that went well beyond normal 'Jewish business.'

38 ASF MdP 5150, f.233, 16 Dec. 1618 [*Letters*, no. 120].

39 Zuccarello, *I Vallombrosani in età postridentina: 1575–1669*; Dooley, *The Last Prophecy of Orazio Morandi*.

40 ASF MdP 5149, f.670, 8 Sept. 1618 (from Orazio Morandi at the Abbey in Ripoli). On 12 Oct. 1618 Morandi replied (from Ripoli) to Don Giovanni: 'You thank me for the birth chart ... which I have not yet been able to accompany with the requisite discourses, due to the many obligations of my position' (f.669).

41 Galileo Galilei, *Sidereus Nuncius, or the Siderial Messenger*, 28–35.

42 Raffael Gualterotti was one of the most influential figures at the Medici Court during the late sixteenth and early seventeenth centuries but he has remained almost entirely unstudied, apart from a few older literary encyclopedic works on Tuscan literature, most significantly: Giulio Negri, *Istoria degli Scrittori Fiorentini* (1722), no. 200; Giovanni Cinelli Calvoli, *Biblioteca Volante* (1746), vol. 3: 87. Gualerotti is conspicuous by his absence in the *Dizionario biografico degli Italiani*.

43 Filippo Baldinucci (*Notizie de' Professori*, 1846, vol. 3: 40–1) lists Gualterotti among the 'nobili e letterati' who frequented the studio of the painter Gregorio Pagani.

44 *Feste nelle Nozze del Serenissimo Don Francesco Medici Gran Duca di Toscana et della Serenissima sua Consorte la Signora Bianca Capello* (1579). The dedication to the book is dated 10 Nov. 1579 and the tournament, which was the chief festive element of the wedding, took place on 14 Oct. Gualterotti apparently printed a program that was available at the performance itself. See *Harvard College Library, Department of Printing and Graphic Arts Catalogue: Italian Sixteenth Century Books*, vol. 1: 319n223.

45 The early development of etching in Italy was closely linked to the emergence of the genre of the festival book. A technical study of Gualterotti's illustrations might reveal that many of these were produced in haste with a single acid bath and little retouching in dry-point. In some copies of the *Festivities*, the plates were printed in variously coloured inks.

46 *Descrizione del regale apparato per le nozze della serenissima madama Cristina di Loreno moglie del serenissimo don Ferdinando Medici* (1589), and *Le glorie d'Europa, nelle nozze di Maria Maddalena d'Austria con Cosimo de' Medici Principe di* (1608).

47 *Discorso di Raffael Gualterotti, gentilhuomo fiorentino, sopra l'apparizione de la nuova stella. E sopra le tre oscurazioni del sole e de la luna ne l'anno 1605. Con alquanto di lume del arte del oro, ecc.* (1605).

48 *Scherzi degli spiriti animali, dettati con l'occasione de l'oscurazione de l'anno 1605 di Raffael Gualterotti, ecc.* (1605). 'Animal spirits' are vital forces produced by the bodies of all creatures but also present in the atmosphere and associated with static electricity.

49 In ASF MdP 939, f.311, 23 Feb. 1607/8, Raffael Gualterotti makes an impas-

sioned plea to Secretary Belisario Vinta for granducal patronage on his behalf and that of his sons, referring back to a previous plea two or three years earlier – which would have been at the time of his books on the eclipse of 1605.

50 BNCF Ms. Gal. part VI, vol. VII: 126, 24 April 1610.

51 Ibid. Cimento, vol. XXVII: 11, 6 April 1610. Galileo was also in Pisa at that time, where he had gone to show the Medicean Stars to Cosimo II.

52 ASF MdP 5147, f.237r, 1 Dec. 1618.

53 See Chapter 10 below, 'The Magic Circle.'

54 ASF Alessandri 2, f.352r, 8 Dec. 1618.

55 Ibid., f.355r, 11 Dec. 1618 (Don Giovanni dei Medici to Cosimo Baroncelli).

56 ASF MdP 5147, f.245, 15 Dec. 1618 (Cosimo Baroncelli to Don Giovanni dei Medici). On 26 Jan. 1619 Don Giovanni requested an astrological interpretation of the course of his own life in the coming year from Don Orazio Morandi (ASF Alessandri 2, f.372v).

57 ASF MdP 5141, f.462, 20 April 1619 (Luca Magnani to Don Giovanni dei Medici). Ferdinando Magnani sent his astrological study to Cosimo II some months before Don Giovanni introduced him to Benedetto Blanis. In later years, however, Benedetto showed an intense interest in other of his protégé's astrological undertakings.

58 ASF MdP 5150, f.123, 9 April 1616 [*Letters*, no. 40].

59 Ibid., f.3, 25 July 1615 [*Letters*, no. 4].

60 Calimani, *The Ghetto of Venice*, 155.

61 *The Autobiography of a Seventeenth-Century Venetian Rabbi: Leon Modena's 'Life of Judah,'* translated and edited by Mark Cohen, 108.

62 Ibid., 217.

63 Ibid., 109.

64 Leone da Modena was well known in Florence, having served as Rabbi there in 1609–10. Meanwhile, Benedetto's younger brother David was living in the Venetian Ghetto and renting property from 'Iacobbe d'Anselmo Levi , a Jew of Venice' (ASF MdP 5150, f.3, 25 July 1616 [*Letters*, no. 4], possibly Leone da Modena's son-in-law Jacob, son of Kalonymos Levi.

65 ASF MdP 5149, f.630, 31 Oct. 1615.

66 The translation is adapted from A.E. Waite, 'The Hermetic and Alchemical Writings of Paracelsus' (1894) from *The Coelum Philosophorum*, Part II, 'What Alchemy Is.'

67 ASF MdP 5149, f.627, 8 Aug. 1615.

68 Ibid., 5147, f.579r, 13 June 1620.

69 Waite, 'The Hermetic and Alchemical Writings of Paracelsus' (1894), Preface.

70 ASF MdP 5147, f.521, 7 March 1619/20. Don Giovanni introduced the proposal to Baroncelli on 1 March (ASF Alessandri 2, f.466r), discussed it in
general terms on 2 March (ibid., f.559r) referring to a 'lettera mostrabile'
that does not survive; he replied to Baroncelli on 14 March (ibid., f.416r).
On 15 March, Grand Duchess Maria Magdalena wrote a courteous but
inconclusive letter to Don Giovanni, acknowledging the letter of 1 March
presented by Cosimo Baroncelli (ASF 5138, f.435r).

71 ASF Riformagioni 32, ff.195–6, 30 Aug.–8 Sept. 1619. Also, ASF Dogana di
Firenze 232, f.2r–v, Aug. 1619. By Aug. of 1619, they were also shipping
acqua vite made from spoiled wine from Pistoia to Bologna: ASF Dogana di
Firenze 232, f.2r–v, Aug. 1619, and 334, f.1r, 3 Sept. 1619; f.5r, 15 Sept. 1619;
f.17v, 8 Jan. 1619/20.

72 ASF Riformagioni 32, f.197, 24 Jan. 1619/20.

73 ASF MdP 5150, f.71, 6 Feb. 1615/16 [*Letters*, no. 30].

74 The series of extant letters, from 20 June 1615 until the beginning of this
story on 6 Feb. 1615/16, is complete and consistent without any obvious
gaps. However, we hear only one side of the conversation, since only the
letters from Benedetto to Don Giovanni have been preserved. The tardy
launch of the 'operation' might have been prompted by a pointed inquiry
from Don Giovanni himself.

75 Ibid.

76 I Samuel 28.

77 Exodus 22:18.

78 ASF MdP 5150, f.71, 6 Feb. 1615/16 [*Letters*, no. 30].

79 Ibid., f.73, 7 Feb. 1615/16 [*Letters*, no. 31].

80 Ibid., f.75, 14 Feb. 1615/16 [*Letters*, no. 32].

81 Ibid., f.55, 21 Feb. 1615/16 [*Letters*, no. 33].

82 Ibid., f.77, 27 Feb. 1615/16 [*Letters*, no. 34].

83 Ibid.

84 Ibid., f.33, 13 March 1615/16 [*Letters*, no. 35].

85 Ibid., f.67, 20 March 1615/16 [*Letters*, no. 36].

86 'Hlechamar' does not figure in the standard lists of demons used in
magical invocations, especially the thirty-one cited in Trithemius' *Stega-
nographia* (written c. 1500, first published in 1606), the sixty-nine in Johan
Weyer's *De praestigiis daemonum* (1577), the sixty-eight in Reginald Scot's
The Discoverie of Witchcraft (1584), and the seventy-two in the *Lesser Key
of Solomon* (undated, seventeenth century). Neither does it seem to reflect
the seventy-two names of 'angels' derived from the manipulation of the
letters of the name or names of God (see Barbierato, *Nella stanza dei circoli*,
51–5).

87 I would like to thank Dr Sheila Barker for identifying these materials. In Arabic, the word *Alfarach* means 'conciliation' and the 'Bab Alfarach' or 'Gate of Conciliation' was one of the entrances to the old Jewish quarter in Toledo.

88 ASF MdP 5150, f.81, 27 March 1616 [*Letters*, no. 37].

89 Ibid., f.123, 9 April 1616 [*Letters*, no. 40].

90 Ibid., f.131, 2 April 1616 [*Letters*, no. 39].

91 The unnamed Christian gentleman was probably Cosimo Ridolfi, an influential figure in Don Giovanni's circle in Florence. See Chapter 10 below, 'The Magic Circle.'

92 ASF MdP 5150, f.123, 9 April 1616 [*Letters*, no. 40].

93 Ibid., f.129, 10 April 1616 [*Letters*, no. 41].

94 Ibid., f.125, 17 April 1616 [*Letters*, no. 42].

95 He might have been wearing Levantine or North African dress, which would have looked less *outré* in Venice, or even Livorno, than in Florence.

96 ASF MdP 5150, f.121, 24 April 1616 [*Letters*, no. 43].

97 Ibid., f.87, 8 May 1616 [*Letters*, no. 47].

98 Jacopetti (*Ebrei a Massa e Carrara: Banche Commerci Industrie dal XVI al XIX secolo*) focuses on the demographic and commercial aspects of Jewish life in Massa Carrara and documents the presence of the Blanis family. He does not mention Samuel Caggesi or his wife.

99 In the *Encyclopaedia Judaica*, VIII, 226, Haim Zafrani summarizes the early history of the Hagiz family. A scholar named Samuel Hagiz died in Fez in 1570. Then, around 1590, another scholar named Samuel Hagiz (not necessarily the grandson of the previous Samuel), spent some time in Tripoli before moving on to Venice, where in 1597 he published *Devar-Shemu'el* and *Merakkesh ha-Shem*. Eventually, he settled in Jerusalem. It is possible that this second Samuel Hagiz was the 'Doctor Samuel from Fez' in Florence and Massa Carrara, but it is more likely that Benedetto's colleague was another member of the same extended family (perhaps descended from the first Samuel). For a later chapter in the history of the Hagiz family, see Carlebach, *The Pursuit of Heresy: Rabbi Moses Hagiz and the Sabbatian Controversies*.

100 An anonymous reader of this book (in manuscript) commented: 'Hagiz also lived in Pisa, serving unsuccessfully as rabbi of the Levantine community and then much later as its *hazzan*. During his first stay there in 1602, he was actually reprimanded and threatened with jail by the police for interfering too much in his congregants' affairs, and his strict religious views were generally rejected.' This is fascinating information, as yet unknown to various scholars working in the archives of Pisa and Livorno.

101 A privilege was granted to Dottore Samuele Hagges by Grand Duke
     Cosimo II and duly confirmed by the Otto di Guardia e Balìa on 10 July
     1609 (ASF Otto 233, f.18r), without citing an established residence in
     Pisa, which should have been the basis for the extension of privileges to
     Florence. Lucia Frattarelli Fischer brought a parallel series of documents
     to my attention, regarding the successful request in 1634 by Jacob, son of
     the late 'Dottor Samuele Chagez di Phesa,' for commercial and residential
     privileges in Florence. Jacob cites his father's previous Florentine privi-
     leges (ASPi Consoli del Mare 977, f.79). On 10 Sept. 1610 the Florentine
     Arte della Seta cited a privilege previously granted to 'Samuel Cagges da
     Fes' (ASF Arte della Seta 3, f.124v). On 15 Nov. 1624, the Otto cited the
     'gratia ottenuta sino dell'anno 1609' by 'Dottore Samuel Hagges Ebreo'
     (ASF Otto 279, f.20r).
102 In 1610–11, 360 scudi were spent on 'the house that is being newly built
     in the Mercato Vecchio although considered to be in the Ghetto, by order
     of His Most Serene Highness, for the use of Doctor Samuele from Fez.'
     Doctor Samuel's new home is specifically described as 'over the oil shop
     in the Mercato Vecchio facing the discount meat stand'(ASF Regie Posses-
     sioni 6575, f.32r–v).
103 ASF Regie Possessioni 6556, f.14. 'Dottor Samuello Agies di Fessa' paid
     scudi 5–4–1 every six months, from 31 Oct. 1632 through 30 April 1637,
     for apartment number 46 – or at least this money was paid in his name,
     since he had died by 1634. On 25 Jan. 1633/34, Granducal Secretary
     Andrea Cioli, replying to the Consoli del Mare in Pisa, acknowledged the
     1609 privileges of the late 'Dottor Samuele Chagez di Phesa' on behalf of
     his son Jacob (ASPi Consoli del Mare 977). Cioli cites in detail the previ-
     ous privileges, granted by Cosimo II and ratified by the Florentine Otto
     di Guardia e Balía on 10 July 1609. It is interesting to note that in 1609,
     Doctor Samuel requested the privilege 'granted to Jews for the entire
     state' – implying that he did not yet enjoy the privileges (guaranteed by
     the Livornina) automatically extended to Jews who were official residents
     of Pisa and Livorno. I am grateful to Lucia Frattarelli Fischer for bringing
     this Pisan documentation to my attention.

8 Games of Chance

1 ASF Pratica Segreta 16, f.78r, 24 Oct. 1602. The legislation refers specifically to paintings by well-known artists. For this and other related documents, see Barzman, *The Florentine Academy and the Early Modern State*,
   268–78.

2 Francesco Bocchi, *Le Bellezze della Città di Firenze* (1591). I cite the expanded edition published by Giovanni Cinelli (1677), 5.

3 Ibid., 124.

4 Ibid., 350.

5 Ibid., 213.

6 ASF Otto 263, f.176v, 10 Oct. 1619.

7 In the *Dizionario Etimologico Italiano*, vol. V: 3796, the *tiorba* is described as a 'sorta di grande liuta che sarebbe stato inventato, secondo G.B. Doni (a. 1640), verso il 1575 da Antonio Naldi, detto il Bardella.' Bardella was the 'guardaroba della musica' at the Medici court.

8 'Gratiadio' was perhaps a scribal error for 'Laudadio,' indicating Laudadio di Agnolo (Lelio) di Laudadio Blanis. (Names, particularly Jewish names, were frequently garbled in administrative and legal records.) Daniello was probably the son of Elia Passigli, representative of another distinguished Ghetto family (ASF Otto 260, f.174). Brian Pullan (*The Jews of Europe and the Inquisition of Venice, 1550–1670*, 292–3) discusses the conversion of Abram, son of Guglielmo Teseo from Florence, in 1619 at the age of ten and the later efforts of his uncle Giuseppe to block his inheritance of family property.

9 ASF Otto 180, f.139r, 15 May 1625.

10 Ibid., 270, f.154, 14 Jan. 1621/22.

11 Ibid., 279, f.81v, 14 Dec. 1624.

12 Ibid., 270, f.189v, 9 Feb. 1621/22.

13 Cantini, *Legislazione toscana*, vol.13 (1804), 192 (7 Jan. 1585/86).

14 ASF Otto 255, f.26v, 14 Nov. 1616.

15 Ibid., 247, f.31v, 24 March 1613/14.

16 Cantini, *Legislazione toscana*, vol. 14 (1804), 328 (18 Sept. 1606).

17 ASF MdP 5140, f.387, 26 March 1616.

18 See Chapter 6 above, 'The Market.'

19 In ASF MdP 1243, f.8, 13 Oct. 1593, Matedia Menagem reports to Granducal Secretary Lorenzo Usimbardi on the flourishing state of 'Pernica d'Ancona' who has established a household in Florence and deserves full privileges from the grand duke.

20 ASF MdP 5141, f.1029, 6 Sept. 1620 (Piero Capponi to Giovanni dei Medici).

21 For this legal formula, see Calvi, 'Donne, orfani, famiglie di fronte alle istituzioni,' esp. 444–9.

22 ASF MdP 5150, f.153, 26 June 1616 [*Letters*, no. 53].

23 In a legal deposition of 21 Dec. 1621, Moisé Lattone describes himself as being thirty-six years old (ASF Nove 376, f.365v).

24 ASF MdP 5150, f.153, 26 June 1616 [*Letters*, no. 53]. The magistrates refer to this escape in their eventual finding in the case (ASF Otto 254, f.121v, 22 Aug. 1616).

25 ASF MdP 5150, f.153, 26 June 1616 [*Letters*, no. 53].

26 Ibid., 5146, f.299, 2 July 1616 (Cosimo Baroncelli to Don Giovanni).

27 Ibid., 5150, f.163, 10 July 1616 [*Letters*, no. 55].

28 Ibid., 5146, f.309, 16 July 1616.

29 Ibid., 5150, f.159, 15 July 1616 [*Letters*, no. 56].

30 ASF Otto 254, f.40r, 15 July 1616; ASF MdP 5150, f.159, 17 July 1616 [*Letters*, no. 56]; ASF Otto 254, f.91v, 11 Aug. 1616.

31 ASF MdP 5150, f.157, 22 July 1616 [*Letters*, no. 57]. Benedetto is quoting Secretary Marsili.

32 Latin Vulgate, Psalm 17:40.

33 ASF MdP 5150, f.105, 5 Aug. 1616 [*Letters*, no. 60]. It would appear that Moisé Lattone spent some time in Don Giovanni's palace as well as in the Casino di San Marco, unless there was another brother-in-law involved.

34 ASF MdP 5150, f.101, 14 Aug. 1616 [*Letters*, no. 61], ASF Auditore Fiscale 55, f.53v, 12 Aug. 1616.

35 ASF Otto 254, f.121v, 22 Aug. 1616.

36 Ibid.; ASF Auditore Fiscale 55, f.64v, 3 Sept. 1616.

37 ASF Otto 254, f.121v, 22 Aug. 1616. The Magistrates presented this as a moderate sentence, admitting mitigating factors like Jacob Pernicca's denial of the gambling. The Magistrates heard a rather similar Christian gambling case on 6 Nov. 1618, regarding the sixteen-year-old Francesco di Giulio Pitti who was victimized by Niccolò di Giannozzo Vaini (ibid., 260, f.9r).

38 ASF MdP 5150, f.29, 27 Aug. 1616 [*Letters*, no. 63]; ibid., f.117, 2 Sept. 1616 [*Letters*, no. 64].

39 Ibid., f.115, 7 Sept. 1616 [*Letters*, no. 67].

40 ASF Auditore Fiscale 55, f.98v, 17 Nov. 1616. The 50 scudi pay-offs were assessed 'per il inventore' – which would seem to mean the initiator of the case.

41 ASF Otto 2561 (Registro di Suppliche 1612–17): 'Jacob del già Juda pernica ebreo. S.A. vuole che habiti nel ghetto, et gli concede in oltre tutti li privilegij, et habilità che haveva il Padre, nel resto non altro———no. 241 ^[in margin] segue sotto la lettera R^ Jacob pernicca ebreo concedesi con che in Firenze habiti in ghetto. 2 7bre 1617 n.o 365.'

42 I did not find a record of Juda Pernicca's baptism in Opera di Santa Maria del Fiore, Registri Battesimali 31 and 32.

43 ASF Scrittoio delle regie possessioni 6575 (Entrate e Uscite del Ghetto Interno dal 1588 al 1632), Libro D, f.12v: 'Addì 24 dicembre 1618 ... Da Jacobbe di Juda Pernica gia ebreo [?detto], oggi Gianlorenzo Laurenzi scudi tre di moneta r[icevu]to Giovanni Buratti——scudi 3.' In this same account book (f.32r–v), there are references to reconstruction work on a Ghetto dwelling carried out for Juda Pernicca in 1609–10.

44 Opera di Santa Maria del Fiore, Registri Battesimali 254, f.50, 11 Feb. 1619/20. This records the baptism of Maddalena, daughter of 'Lorenzo Laurenzi' and Caterina di Matteo Lapi of the Parish of San Frediano. There was a distinguished godfather, Granducal Secretary Lorenzo Usimbardi.

45 ASF Otto 254, f.121v, 22 Aug. 1616. Everyone involved in the case was Christian.

46 Ibid., 272, f.217r, 29 Oct. 1622.

47 For example, the case of 'Pietro Turco batezzato' (ibid., 254, f.179v, 24 Sept. 1616).

48 For example, the case of 'Bartolomeo di Antonio' (ibid:, 269, f.37r, 17 July 1621).

49 Ibid., 272, f.217r, 29 Oct. 1622. This sentence and subsequent rescripts are confirmed in ASF Auditore Fiscale 2211, f.65r, 29 Nov. and 5 Dec. 1622, and 16 Sept. 1625.

50 ASF Otto 273, f.2v, 3 Nov. 1622, and f.52v, 5 Dec. 1622.

51 Ibid., f.19v, 14 Nov. 1622.

52 Ibid., f.52v, 5 Dec. 1622; and 283, f.22r, 14 March 1625/26.

9 The Mirror of Truth

1 For this reason, we have relatively little documentation from this period. Benedetto was not writing letters to Don Giovanni. He is not mentioned in any of Don Giovanni's other correspondence from that time, nor is he mentioned in any of the letters to Florence from the Tuscan Embassy in Venice.

2 Since Jews could not own real estate in Venice, these 'properties' would have consisted of leases in perpetuity, called *Jus gazakà* in the local parlance, blending legal Latin and Talmudic Hebrew (Calimani, *Ghetto of Venice*, 135). These properties constituted the dowry of David Blanis' wife, Mirra Galli de Franzesis (Jacopetti, *Ebrei a Massa e Carrara*, 56 and 172).

3 ASF MdP 5150, f.3, 25 July 1615 [*Letters*, no. 4].

4 It is possible that Benedetto was also summoned to Venice to assist in resolving the problem of Livia Vernazza's first marriage to Battista Granara (see below) but this is a less compelling argument. Benedetto might have

drifted into these activities because he was on the spot and part of the daily life of the Medici-Vernazza household.

5 As Federico Barbierato demonstrates, in *Nella stanza dei circoli: Clavicula Salamonis e libri di magia a Venezia nei secoli XVII e XVIII*, occult activity was widespread in Venice – with a major Jewish participation – and it permeated many aspects of daily life.

6 ASF MdP 5150, f.69, 6 Dec. 1615 [*Letters*, no. 22].

7 Ibid., f.35, 28 Nov. 1615 [*Letters*, no. 21]. We cannot identify this 'gentleman' conclusively but he is likely to have been Cosimo Ridolfi (see Chapter 10 below, 'The Magic Circle').

8 Don Giovanni was in the Friuli by Feb. 1617 (ASF Alessandri 2, f.218r, 16 Feb. 1617, letter to Cosimo Baroncelli from the camp in Meriano). He was back in Venice by 6 Jan. 1618 (f.268v).

9 ASF MdP 5150, f.189, 14 Aug. 1617 [*Letters*, no. 103].

10 Ibid., f.191, 18 Nov. 1617 [*Letters*, no. 104].

11 Ibid., f.211, 21 Jan. 1617/18 [*Letters*, no. 107]. The quote is Proverbs 16:15.

12 Ibid., f.223, 3 Feb. 1617/18 [*Letters*, no. 108].

13 There is a gathering of legal documents regarding the rental of these furnishings (including two copies of the inventory) in ASF Alessandri 10, Insert 56 (ff.206–14). The stock came from Iseppo Esperiel and Iacob Moretto in Padua, with the contract brokered by Guglielmo della Baldosa in Venice. The 'Palazzo del Clar.mo Trevisam per mezzo il Draghetto di S. Jhieremia' no longer exists. Since it had windows overlooking the canal, it might have occupied part of the site of the present Palazzo Labia.

14 For the Venetian Ghetto, see Concina, Camerino, and Calabi, *La Città degli Ebrei: Il Ghetto di Venezia–Architettura e Urbanistica*. For its historical, social, and cultural context, see see Pullan, *The Jews of Europe and the Inquisition of Venice*, the collected articles of Ravid in *Studies on the Jews of Venice, 1382–1797*, and Davis and Ravid, eds., *The Jews of Early Modern Venice*.

15 Calabi, 'The "City of the Jews,"' esp. 33–5.

16 In Davis and Ravid, eds., see Pullan, 'Jewish Banks and the Monte di Pietà,' and Arbel, 'Jews in International Trade'; Calimani, *Ghetto*, 116–28. Although Florentine Jews were actively involved in illicit moneylending, Venetian Jews had a range of legitimate options that facilitated other more questionable, and lucrative, activities.

17 Harrán, 'Jewish Musical Culture: Leone Modena.'

18 Paraphrased from Mark Cohen's translation in *The Autobiography of a Seventeenth-Century Venetian Rabbi: Leone Modena's 'Life of Judah,'* 131. Modena preached this particular sermon on 28 April 1629. The reference is to Gaston, Duke of Orléans (1608–1660), brother of Louis XIII. Benjamin Ravid

offers an interesting collation of comments by foreign (non-Italian) visitors in, 'Christian Travelers in the Ghetto of Venice: Some Preliminary Observations,' in *Studies on the Jews of Venice, 1382–1797*, 111–50. Also, Calabi, 'City of the Jews,' 45–8.

19 Calimani, *Ghetto*, 196. The quote is from Giulio Morosini's *Via della Fede* (1683). Regarding Christian participation in Jewish festivals in Venice and Jewish participation in Christian festivals, see Pullan, *Jews of Europe*, 163–4. If Purim occurred during Lent, it offered Christians a context for evading its prohibitions.

20 Barbierato (*Nella stanza dei circoli*, 304–27) offers a compelling picture of the Jewish presence in the Venetian occult.

21 Cohen, *Autobiography*, 160–2 and 169.

22 Barbierato, *Nella stanza dei circoli*, 309–11.

23 Concina, 'Dal "Geto de rame" al "Geto dove habita li ebrei,"' in Concina et al., *La Città degli Ebrei*, 11–49.

24 Favero and Trivellato ('Gli abitanti del ghetto di Venezia in età moderna: dati e ipotesi') summarize the demographic data for the Venetian Ghetto from 1516 to 1797. They propose a population of nearly 3,000 before the plague of 1630 (p. 41), based on the 2,420 Ghetto residents registered in the 1632–33 census, plus 454 plague deaths, plus an upward correction for a tendency towards growth. This calculation would not include Jews who were only passing though – like Benedetto Blanis himself.

25 These are the figures cited in the Florentine census of 1622. BNCF Codex E.B., XV: 2, and Codex II: I.

26 ASF Otto 252, ff.174r–v, 13 Jan. 1615/16.

27 ASF MdP 5150, f.71, 6 Feb. 1615/16 [*Letters*, no. 30] and following. This, at least, is how Benedetto cast Doctor Samuel from Fez in his letters to Don Giovanni.

28 Ibid., f.153, 26 June 1616 [*Letters*, no. 53] and following.

29 On 3 June 1615 Francesco Accolti (Venice) wrote Don Giovanni (Florence), discussing the rental of the 'Palazzo del Illustrissimo Moro,' who was represented in this transaction by Zuane (Giovanni) Landi. The palace is described as facing onto the Grand Canal with another canal along one side (ASF MdP 5135, f.22r–v). The Moro family had several palaces in Venice; it seems likely that Don Giovanni rented the one in Dorsoduro at the intersection of the Grand Canal and the Rio Malpaga.

30 ASF MdP 3004, f.1227, 6 Jan. 1618.

31 Ibid., f.1235v, 13 Jan. 1618 (Amb. Asdrubale Montauto in Venice to Cosimo II).

32 Ibid., f.1231r, 9 Jan. 1618 (Amb. Asdrubale Montauto to Cosimo II).

33 Ibid., 5150, f.391, 26 Sept. 1620 [*Letters*, no. 211].

34 Ibid., 5159, f.681r.

35 Ibid., f.679v–f.680r.

36 Ibid., 5149, f.670, 8 Sept. 1618.

37 Ibid., 5141, f.497, 1 June 1619.

38 There are many letters from Pietro Cecconcelli to Don Giovanni in ibid. For the discussions of Greek and musical type from Venice, see f.512r, 21 June 1619 and following.

39 Ibid., f.44r, 15 June 1618 (Jacques Callot in Florence to Don Giovanni in Venice); f.79r, 14 July 1618 (Callot to Don Giovanni). ASF Alessandri 2, f.300r, 7 April 1618 (Don Giovanni in Venice to Cosimo Baroncelli in Florence); f.303r, 28 April 1618 (Don Giovanni to Baroncelli). Don Giovanni also corresponded with the printmaker Lorenzo Parigi (ASF MdP 5141, f.3r, 31 March 1618, and following).

40 One possibility is that a number of engraved plates (illustrations or tables) were printed while the text remained in manuscript. The plates would have represented the most difficult and expensive part of the operation.

41 ASF MdP 3007, f.388r, 18 Sept. 1621.

42 In ibid., 5158, ff.546–7, there are references to the disposal of Don Giovanni's books after his death. Some of these were sold, others taken by Don Lorenzo and Cardinal Carlo dei Medici, 'and there are the three chests of books, most of which are prohibited. Offers cannot be accepted for these nor can they be sold, and an order will be issued as to where they are to be sent.'

43 Orazio Petrobelli, *Specchio di Verita* (1626). Petrobelli later resumed this theme in *L'ebreo conuinto* (1642). Later, Giovanni Battista Comastri published an alchemical concordance, *Specchio della verità* (Venice, 1683). In the Biblioteca Apostolica Vaticana there is a manuscript *Speculum Veritatis* (Cod. Lat. 7286) from probably the early seventeenth century, including twelve naively executed pen drawings but without significant accompanying texts.

44 This was probably Benedetto's longest experience of a non-Jewish environment, apart from his various incarcerations. While travelling, he probably stayed in Christian inns. He might also have been a guest in the homes of aristocratic amateurs of the occult, especially at their villas outside the city.

45 ASF MdP 5159, f.681r. In another legal deposition (ibid., 5161, f.77v), he calculates his departure from Venice to have been in Oct. – which corresponds with what we know from his letter of arrival in Florence (ibid., 5150, f.354, 20 Oct. 1618 [*Letters*, no. 110]).

46 Ibid., 5161, f.76v.

47 Ferrone, *Attori mercanti corsari: la commedia dell'arte in Europa tra Cinque e Seicento*, 137–90.
48 ASF MdP 5161, f.74v–f.75r.
49 Ferrone, *Attori mercanti corsari*, 142.
50 Benedetto describes her as a '*donna di partito*' in ASF MdP 5159, f.677v.
51 Ibid., 5161, f.75r.
52 Ibid., f.75r–v.
53 Ibid., f.75v.
54 Ibid., f.75v–f.76r.
55 Ibid., 5159, f.681v.
56 Ibid., f.682r.
57 Ibid., 5161, f.272r–v.
58 Ibid., 5150, f.231, 21 Aug. 1618 (Benedetto Blanis in Ferrara to Don Giovanni in Venice [*Letters*, no. 109]).
59 There might have been other letters that did not survive, but Benedetto was living in Don Giovanni's own house and he probably had little occasion to write.
60 ASF MdP 5147, f.158r, 4 Aug. 1618 (Cosimo Baroncelli in Florence to Don Giovanni in Venice); ibid., 3012A, f.110r, 17 Aug. 1618 (Cosimo II in Florence to Amb. Niccolò Sacchetti in Venice); f.112r, 19 Aug. 1618 (Sec. Curzio Picchena in Florence to Amb. Sacchetti). Albizi's ostensible mission was to congratulate the new Doge Antonio Priuli on his election but this was to be more than a simple exchange of courtesies. In May of 1618 the Venetian government had thwarted a coup d'état instigated by the Spanish ambassador, leaving diplomatic relations in disarray.
61 If Don Giovanni had wanted to put a confidential word in Albizi's ear before his arrival in Venice, his stop in Ferrara would have offered an opportunity – and a Jew might have had the advantage of seeming an unlikely messenger. In Venice, Albizi would be staying at the Tuscan Embassy, where any contact would be noticed.
62 ASF MdP 5150, f.231, 21 Aug. 1618 [*Letters*, no. 109].
63 After the annexation of Ferrara in 1598, the Este family moved their court to Modena. In Ferrara the Jews enjoyed thirty years of relative calm under papal governance. Then in 1627 the Roman authorities created a Ghetto and imposed serious restrictions on the Jewish population.
64 The names of the women in the Blanis family are seldom recorded.
65 This took place on 15 Aug., Feast of the Ascension of the Virgin. After the disastrous fire of 1618, the fair was relocated to the less flammable setting of the 'Pavaglione,' an arcaded market in the centre of town.
66 ASF MdP 5150, f.231, 21 Aug. 1618 [*Letters*, no. 109].

67 ASF MdP 3006, f.54r, 15 Sept. 1618. The surgeon was a Frenchman named Belriguard, sent by Dowager Grand Duchess Christine de Lorraine (ibid., 5138, f.342r, 11 Aug. 1618, Christine de Lorraine to Don Giovanni).

68 Ibid., 3006, f.57r, 15 Sept. 1618 (Niccolò Sacchetti to Cosimo II).

69 Ibid., f.65r, 22 Sept. 1618 (Niccolò Sacchetti to Cosimo II).

70 Ibid., 5150, f.354, 20 Oct. 1618 [*Letters*, no. 110].

71 Ibid., f.225, 4 Nov. 1618 [*Letters*, no. 112].

72 ASF MdP 5150, f.219, 23 Dec. 1618 [*Letters*, no. 119].

73 Ibid. Don Giovanni agreed to let him send the leather from Florence to Venice under his personal seal, exempting him from excise duty. However, as Cosimo Baroncelli noted on 29 Dec. 1618, 'Messer Benedetto … is so grief-stricken and so overwhelmed by the loss of his first [wife] that he didn't even mention sending anything at this time' (ibid., 5147, f.255). Benedetto borrowed 100 scudi from the Florentine silk merchant Matteo Galli. In Venice, the Jew Abram Copio (or Coppio) was to broker the sale of the gilded leather.

74 Ibid., 5150, f.368, 6 Jan. 1618/19 [*Letters*, no. 121]. The writings that Benedetto sent cannot be identified and are unlikely to have survived.

10 The Magic Circle

1 ASF MdP 5147, f.237r, 1 Dec. 1618 (Cosimo Baroncelli to Don Giovanni dei Medici); see Chapter 7 above, 'Knowledge and Power.'

2 ASF Alessandri 2, f.355r, 11 Dec. 1618 (Don Giovanni to Cosimo Baroncelli).

3 See Chapter 9 above, 'The Mirror of Truth.'

4 ASF MdP 5150, f.220, 23 Dec. 1618 [*Letters*, no. 119].

5 Ibid., f.221, 30 Dec. 1618 [*Letters*, no. 120].

6 Ibid., f.368, 6 Jan. 1618/19 [*Letters*, no. 121].

7 The reference is to Cornelius Agrippa von Nettesheim's *De Occulta Philos-ophia* (1531); see Chapter 7, above, 'Knowledge and Power.'

8 Baroncelli's villa was near to Florence and was usually referred to as at 'Mezza Strada' – perhaps near Strada in Chianti.

9 ASF MdP 5150, f.243, 13 Jan. 1618/19. Benedetto offered to translate the *Chiave di Raimondo* into the '*volgare*,' which is usually taken to mean Italian. In this context, it might possibly indicate Latin, since Jews normally referred to Hebrew as *la lingua sacra*.

10 ASF MdP 5150, f.145, 19 Jan. 1618/19 [*Letters*, no. 123].

11 Ibid., 5147, f.266, 19 Jan. 1618/19. On 10 March 1618, Don Giovanni asked Cosimo Baroncelli to send his greetings to Orazio Morandi and to forward a letter or packet (*plico*) to Cosimo Ridolfi (ASF Alessandri 2, f.274).

12　ASF Raccolta Sebregondi 4474.
13　ASF Alessandri 2, f.372, 26 Jan. 1619. Cosimo Baroncelli sent Don Giovanni a long and highly emotional reply on 2 Feb. 1618/19 (ASF MdP 5147, f.276r–v).
14　ASF MdP 5141, f.47r, 25 June 1618.
15　Although Cosimo Baroncelli, Don Giovanni's major-domo, was sympathetic towards arcane studies and consistently supportive of those who engaged in them, he was not necessarily an adept in his own right but certainly a 'fellow traveller.'
16　See Chapter 7 above, 'Knowledge and Power.'
17　Galileo's heliocentric theory was formally condemned by the Inquisition on 24 Feb. 1616.
18　ASF Alessandri 2, f.94r, 20 Feb. 1616 (Don Giovanni to Cosimo Baroncelli). There would seem to be a subtext here, particularly in the last sentence, 'voglio dire che credo costà come quà le neve comenciaranno a deleguarsi onde i procacci tornaranno a lor ordine senza strafalcioni.' Among the possible readings is a play on *procacci* meaning mail carriers and *procaci* meaning 'the audacious' or 'the shameless.' Also possible is a reference to Galileo's *Siderius Nuncius* (*Starry Messenger*) of 1609 where he announced the discovery of the Medicean Planets.
19　Orazio Grassi, *Libra astronomica et philosophica* (1619).
20　ASF MdP 5150, f.61, 16 Aug. 1615 [*Letters*, no. 7].
21　On 25 Jan. 1618/19, Baroncelli described Canacci's age as 'said to be seventy-one' (ibid., 5147, f.269).
22　Ibid., 5132A. There is a large insert of unbound letters including letters from Ascanio Canacci to Don Antonio dei Medici dated (all 1605) 29 June, 25 July, 6 Aug., 3 and 24 Sept., and 29 Oct. Also, letters from Zeferiel Tommaso Bovio to Don Antonio dated 14 and 31 March and 14 Sept., 1605, and 1 Nov. 1606. It does not seem that the *Teatro* was ever published. See Luti, *Don Antonio de' Medici e i suoi tempi*, 163–4.
23　ASF MdP 5150, f.251, 24 March 1618/19 (Benedetto Blanis to Don Giovanni) [*Letters*, no. 130].
24　Ibid., f.269, 22 Dec. 1619 (Benedetto Blanis to Don Giovanni) [*Letters*, no. 168].
25　Ibid., f.239, 27 Jan. 1618/19 (Benedetto Blanis to Don Giovanni) [*Letters*, no. 125].
26　Ibid., 5147, f.269, 25 Jan. 1618/19 (Cosimo Baroncelli to Don Giovanni).
27　Ibid., 5150, f.237, 10 Feb. 1618/19 (Benedetto Blanis to Don Giovanni) [*Letters*, no. 127].
28　For Hebrew translations of Ramón Llull and their context, see Hames,

'Jewish Magic with a Christian Text: A Hebrew Translation of Ramon Llull's *Ars Brevis*.' Hebrew was the essential language of Kabbalah, and the raw material of the intricate alpha-numerical permutations practised even by non-Jewish adepts. Hebrew, however, was not the language in which Llull and later Christian Kabbalists wrote, usually opting for Latin texts studded with Hebrew characters, words, and charts.

29 The city of Cologne was of Roman foundation, originally known as 'Colonia Agrippa.' Cornelius' name was therefore a latinized reference to his birthplace.

30 This translation of the Trithemius letter is adapted from that of 'J.F.,' probably John French, published in London in 1651. The following translations of the *De occulta philosophia libri tres* are also by 'J.F.'

31 Scholem, *Kabbalah*, 198.

32 ASF MdP 5150, f.237, 10 Feb. 1618/19 (Benedetto Blanis to Don Giovanni) [*Letters*, no. 127]. The idea of translating the *Chiave Raimondina* into 'the vulgar language' was soon abandoned in favour of a straightforward copy in Hebrew.

33 'In Siena Messer Ascanio passed on to the better life.' MdP 5150, f.333, 28 April 1619 (Benedetto Blanis to Don Giovanni) [*Letters*, no. 135].

34 This issue often arises in Benedetto's letters to Don Giovanni. Back in 1616, he was unable to write the labels himself for the books in Don Giovanni's palace library (ASF MdP 5150, f.65, 30 July 1616 (Benedetto Blanis to Don Giovanni) [*Letters*, no. 58]. It is possible that Benedetto had a problem with eyesight and was unable to focus on two different objects at once.

35 See Chapter 11 below, 'Curious and Forbidden Books.'

36 In Venice, as Federico Barbierato demonstrates (*Nella stanza dei circoli*, esp. 162–7 and 206–36), priests and monks played an active role in the diffusion of arcane practices and, more particularly, arcane books and writings.

37 ASF MdP 5150, f.273, 17 May 1619 [*Letters*, no. 138].

38 Ibid., 5141, f.462, 20 April 1619.

39 Perhaps a reference to Quintole near Fiesole with the parish church of San Pietro.

40 ASF MdP 5141, f.462, 20 April 1619.

41 ASF MdP 5141, f.470, 10 May 1619. On 10 May 1619 Captain Piero Capponi wrote to Don Giovanni on behalf of Luca Magnani (ibid., f.468).

42 It is not clear whether Don Giovanni also offered direct financial assistance to Ferdinando Magnani, although this is seemingly implied.

43 ASF MdP 5150, f.271, 15 June 1619 [*Letters*, no. 142].

44 Ibid., 5141, f. 551, 10 Aug. 1619.

11 Curious and Forbidden Books

1 The first full day of Passover was Saturday, 30 March 1619.
2 For the observance of Passover in Benedetto Blanis' day, see Chapter 5 above, 'Memory and Survival.'
3 Calimani, *Ghetto*, 24.
4 Cassuto, *Gli Ebrei a Firenze*, 378 (Document XIX). The most popular of these preachers was Bernardino da Feltre who was, in fact, expelled by the Florentine civil authorities. In the aftermath of this tumult, the Monte di Pietà was founded in Florence in order to end Jewish usury.
5 ASF MdP 5150, f.217, 10 March 1618/19) [*Letters*, no. 129].
6 Ibid., f.251, 24 March 1618/19) [*Letters*, no. 130].
7 Ibid.
8 'Scruples.', *Catholic Encyclopedia* (Robert Appleton: New York), 1907–13, XIII, 640.
9 ASF MdP 5150, f.380, 29 March 1619) [*Letters*, no. 131].
10 Ibid., f.303, 7 April 1619) [*Letters*, no. 132]. These 'others' are not identified but they are presumably Benedetto's contacts in Florence and at the Medici Court.
11 Ibid.
12 Ibid., f.362, 14 April 1619) [*Letters*, no. 133].
13 There were thirteen cardinals general at the time of Benedetto Blanis.
14 The *Index* was discontinued in 1966.
15 Archivio Arcivescovile di Firenze, TIN 51.22 (undated, c.1610–20): 'From the Most Illustrious and Reverend Cardinals General of the Inquisition; Orders for carrying out the activities of the Holy Office, as communicated by the Most Reverend Father Monsignor Cornelio Priatoni, Inquisitor, to the present Vicar of the Holy Office.' In 1612 Priatoni gave the imprimatur of the Holy Office to Galileo Galilei's seminal treatise on physics, *Intorno alle cose che stanno su l'acqua o che in quella si muovono*, 'Fra Cornelio Inquisitor for Florence, 5 April 1612. To be printed by order on this day.'
16 Ibid., f.78v.
17 Ibid.
18 Ibid.
19 Ibid.
20 ASF MdP 5150, f.362, 14 April 1619 (Benedetto Blanis to Don Giovanni)) [*Letters*, no. 133].
21 Ibid.
22 Ibid.

23 Ibid., f.370, 21 April 1619) [*Letters*, no. 134].
24 Ibid., f.333, 28 April 1619 (Benedetto Blanis to Don Giovanni)) [*Letters*, no. 135]. The expression *lettioni di tasto* is unclear. Since the reference is to two young women, the most likely interpretation would involve playing a keyboard (*tastiera*) instrument. *Tasto* can also refer to 'testing' or 'sampling,' with possible reference to merchandise or precious metals; this seems less likely in the context.
25 Ibid., f.273, 17 May 1619 (Benedetto Blanis to Don Giovanni)) [*Letters*, no. 138]. Federico Barbierato (*Nella stanza dei circoli*, 188–94) describes the Venetian world of scribes and copyists who were often clerics and often reproduced forbidden books, including magical treatises.
26 ASF MdP 5150, f.333, 28 April 1619 (Benedetto Blanis to Don Giovanni)) [*Letters*, no. 135].
27 Ibid., f.273, 17 May 1619 (Benedetto Blanis to Don Giovanni)) [*Letters*, no. 138].
28 Ibid., f.293, 19 July 1619) [*Letters*, no. 147].
29 Ibid., f.277, 17 Nov. 1619) [*Letters*, no. 163].
30 Ibid.
31 Ibid., 5150, f.337, 14 July 1619) [*Letters*, no. 146]. The implication is that Magnani was copying the *Chiave Raimondina* in the original Hebrew and the project for an Italian translation was abandoned.
32 Ibid., f.307, 27 July 1619 (Benedetto Blanis to Don Giovanni)) [*Letters*, no. 148].
33 Ibid., f.273, 17 May 1619) [*Letters*, no. 138].
34 Ibid., 5141, f.591, 7 Sept. 1619.
35 Ibid., 5150, f.343, 8 Sept. 1619) [*Letters*, no. 153].
36 Ibid., 3006, f.414r, 17 Aug. 1619 (Niccolò Sacchetti to Curzio Picchena).
37 Ibid., f.399r, 6 Aug. 1619 (Niccolò Sacchetti to Cosimo II).
38 Ibid., 5161, f.10r–f.11r, 11 Aug. 1619. Although Livia's marriage to Battista Granara had been annulled, Don Giovanni insisted that he had no intention of marrying her himself.
39 This hasty union was widely rumoured throughout Venice and at the Medici Court, but it was only verified two years later, after Don Giovanni's death. See ibid., 3007, f.316r, unsigned and undated but presumably from Ambassador Niccolò Sacchetti in 1621.
40 Ibid., 5150, f.343, 8 Sept. 1619) [*Letters*, no. 153].
41 Ibid., 5141, f.591, 7 Sept. 1619 (Ferdinando Magnani to Don Giovanni).
42 Ibid., 5150, f.315, 15 Sept. 1619) [*Letters*, no. 154].
43 Ibid., 5141, f.618, 2 Oct. 1619 (Ferdinando Magnani to Don Giovanni).

44 Ibid., f.652, 28 Oct. 1619 (Raffael Gualterotti to Don Giovanni).

45 'Brandes' apears occasionally in documents, and it might be a Portuguese variation of the Spanish (or Catalan) 'Blanis.'

46 Gualterotti might be proposing that the convert was a descendent of the celebrated Spanish Jew Abraham ben Meir ibn Ezra (1092–1167). If so, he has garbled his facts since Ibn Ezra lived five centuries earlier and was not a physician.

47 ASF MdP 5141, f.679, 16 Nov. 1619 (Raffael Gualterotti to Don Giovanni).

48 Jewish and Muslim converts to Catholicism were often given recognizably artificial names that no 'Old Christian' would have. 'Cosimo' acknowledges his godfather the Grand Duke. 'Suettonio' presumably refers to the Roman historian and biographer Gaius Suetonius Tranquillus.

49 Opera di Santa Maria del Fiore, Registri Battesimali 32, f.102, 1 Jan. 1619/20.

50 ASF Nove 51, f.324, 1 Feb. 1619/20. Two new governors are recorded rather than the usual three: Benedetto di Laudadio Blanis and Sallomone di Abrami Tedesco. It is possible that one name was omitted by the secretary of the Nove.

51 We don't know Benedetto's exact date of birth but it is likely that he had turned forty, since the Jewish community in Florence (and elsewhere) tended to choose mature leaders.

52 This was Agnolo son of Salvatore son of Laudadio Blanis, with Laudadio (the elder) being Benedetto's great-grandfather.

53 ASF MdP 5150, f.291, 1 Feb. 1619/20) [Letters, no. 175].

54 Ibid.

55 Ibid.

56 Ibid.

57 In ASF Miscellanea Medicea 19, Insert 2, there is correspondence regarding business relations between the Vinta and the Blanis families, esp. f.14, 8 Nov. 1629 and f.16, 27 Sept. 1629 (both Benedetto Blanis in Ferrara to Francesco Vinta in Florence).

58 ASF MdP 5150, f.364, 3 Feb. 1619/20) [Letters, no. 176].

59 These four are perhaps Benedetto Blanis, Moise Lattone, and Josef Hezrà's wife and daughter – unless charges were brought against her father and brother.

60 ASF MdP 5150, f.430, 'Narrazione dello stato in che si trovava ms. Benedetto Blanis hebreo di Febbraio 1620' (Roman dating)) [Letters, no. 177].

61 See Chapter 8 above, 'Games of Chance.'

62 ASF MdP 5150, f.430) [Letters, no. 177]. Benedetto seems to be offering a highly selective account of the conversion of David Finzi and his family,

originally from Massa Carrara. These events were soon to figure prominently in Benedetto's life. See below and Chapters 12, 'Prison,' and 13, 'Habeas Corpus.'

63 ASF MdP 5150 f.327, 4 Feb. 1619/20) [*Letters*, no. 178]. For a Jew, throwing sacred writings on the ground would have been a major offence.

64 Ibid., 5147, f.510, 8 Feb. 1619/20.

65 Benedetto seems to be implying that Josef Hezrà might have been a Muslim at some point.

66 ASF MdP 5150, f.327, 4 Feb. 1619/20) [*Letters*, no. 178].

67 Ibid., 5147, f.511, 8 Feb. 1619/20.

68 If Benedetto was formally cited on his arrival at the Bargello or on his release, this should be recorded in ASF Otto 264 (1 Nov. 1619 through 28 Feb. 1619/20) which was damaged in the 1966 flood and cannot be consulted.

69 ASF MdP 5150, f.265, 8 Feb. 1619/20 (Salamone Blanis to Don Giovanni)) [*Letters*, no. 179]. Ferdinando Magnani also wrote Don Giovanni on Benedetto's behalf (ibid., 5141, f.793, 8 Feb. 1619/20).

70 Ibid., f.679, 16 Nov. 1619.

71 ASF Alessandri 2, f.526, 15 Feb. 1620. In ASF MdP 939, f.311, 23 Feb. 1607/8, Raffael Gualterotti makes an impassioned plea to Secretary Belisario Vinta for granducal patronage on his own behalf and that of his sons, citing his declining mental and physical powers. In fact, he reached the age of ninety-five, living until 1638.

72 ASF MdP 5150, f.295, 15 Feb. 1619/20) [*Letters*, no. 180]. Benedetto is citing Psalm 117:5–7.

73 ASF MdP 5150, f.295, 15 Feb. 1619/20) [*Letters*, no. 180].

74 Ibid.

75 His papers were evidently seized again at the time of his next imprisonment in late June. When he testified before the court of the Archbishop of Florence on 22 Sept. 1621, he took it for granted that the authorities had possession of the letters that Don Giovanni had written to him (ASF MdP 5161, f.77v).

76 ASF MdP 5150, f.295, 15 Feb. 1619/20) [*Letters*, no. 180].

77 For Vitale Medici, see Furstenberg Levi, 'The Boundaries between "Jewish" and "Catholic."'

78 ASF MdP 5150, f.295, 15 Feb. 1619/20) [*Letters*, no. 180].

79 Until 1568 the tribunal of the Inquisition in Florence consisted of the Archbishop of Florence, the Papal Nuncio, and the Father Inquisitor. After 1568 cases were managed only by the appointed inquisitor from Rome. Little documentation survives from the Florentine office of the Inquisition, and it is difficult to determine its inner workings.

80 Opera di Santa Maria del Fiore, Registri Battesimali 254, f.134, 14 March
    1619/20. Cosimo Suettionio is an unusual name, and the registrar evident-
    ly assumed that 'Cosimo di Suettonio' was intended.
81 Ibid., f.105, 7 June 1620.
82 In the 1611 smuggling case (see Chapter 6 above, 'The Market') the defend-
    ant is identified as 'Agnolo son of Salvadore Blanis' (ASF Dogana Antica
    di Firenze 17, f.53r, 27 May 1611). Benedetto's grandfather Agnolo di
    Laudadio Blanis had a brother named Salvatore di Laudadio who settled
    in Massa Carrara. For this branch of the Blanis family, see Jacopetti, *Ebrei a
    Massa e Carrara*, 57–8.
83 See Chapter 6 above, 'The Market.'
84 Opera di Santa Maria del Fiore, Registri Battesimali 33, f.35, 18 March
    1620/21. The presence of the ex-Protestant Robert Dudley would seem to
    reflect the converso context.
85 ASF MdP 5150, f.311, 22 Feb. 1619/20) [*Letters*, no. 181].
86 See Chapter 6, 'The Market.'
87 ASF Otto 263, f.1r, 1 July 1619; f. 29v, 16 July 1619; and f.60r, 9 Aug. 1619.
88 This was Porzia di Prospero Finzi, whose husband Davitte Finzi converted
    on 15 March 1620, along with their four children. See below Chapters 12,
    'Prison,' and 13, 'Habeas Corpus.'
89 ASF MdP 5150 f.434, 12 April 1620) [*Letters*, no. 189].
90 Ibid., f.432, 10 May 1620) [*Letters*, no. 190].
91 Barbierato (*Nella stanza dei circoli*) frequently cites the works of Cornelius
    Agrippa, demonstrating that they were already widely circulated in Ven-
    ice.
92 ASF MdP 5150, f.426, 2 June 1620) [*Letters*, no. 194].

12 Prison

1 ASF MdP 5150, f.409, 2 July 1620) [*Letters*, no. 120].
2 Brian Pullan (*The Jews of Europe and the Inquisition of Venice, 1550–1670*,
   243–312) offers a fascinating range of case studies regarding Jewish conversion and reversion. Although he focuses principally on Venice, he
   reveals broader social, economic, cultural, and psychological patterns that
   are immediately relevant to the Blanis case.
3 Around the same time, Alberico I Cybo Malaspina also authorized a Monte di Pietà, a pawnbroking operation under religious auspices (Jacopetti,
   Ebrei a Massa e Carrara, 2–3 and n7).
4 There is no evidence that Salvatore di Laudadio Blanis ever resided in the
   Florentine Ghetto (See Chapter 3 above, 'The Ghetto'). Salvatore's connec-

tions with Massa Carrara date back to 1581 at least (Jacopetti, *Ebrei*, 57 and n147).

5 For example, on 6 July 1615, the Otto di Guardia e Balìa allowed seven Jews from Massa Carrara, including six members of the Finzi family, to do business in Florence for limited periods without wearing the *segno*. These were 'Prospero Finis, Vita son of Abram Finis, Salamon Finis with his son Gratiadio, Dante Finis with his son Guglielmo.' As legal precedent, the Otto cited a previous concession on 23 July 1613 to 'Agnolo di Blanes and Agnolo di Sera, Jews and merchants living in Massa' (ASF Otto 251, f.10v, 6 July 1615).

6 Significant inbreeding was to be expected, considering the limited number of Jewish families, especially in the smaller communities.

7 See Chapter 11 above, 'Curious and Forbidden Books.' Benedetto refers to Virtuosa, daughter of Agnolo di Salvatore di Laudadio Blanis, as 'the daughter of my mother's brother who lives in Massa di Carrara' (ASF MdP 5150, f.291, 1 Feb. 1619/20) [*Letters*, no. 175].

8 Jacopetti, *Ebrei*, 46 and n85, cites the marriage contract. ASM, ANM, Cortile A., b.376, f.31. Also see, Jacopetti, *Ebrei*, 426–7 for a genealogical tree of the Finzi family.

9 For the story of David and Porzia Finzi, see Jacopetti, *Ebrei*, 44–6.

10 It is not clear whether Porzia Finzi, wife of Lelio Blanis, died or was divorced before Lelio's subsequent marriage with Ricca Finzi in 1611. (A polygamous second marriage seems less likely.) Porzia, daughter of Angelo Finzi, married Lelio son of Laudadio Blanis from Florence in 1595 (according to Jacopetti, *Ebrei*, 46). Ricca daughter of Abramo Finzi, married Agnolo son of Laudadio son of Agnolo Blanis from Florence in 1611 (p. 42). The two bridegrooms must have been the same person, since Agnolo and Lelio are both variants of Angelo (the Italian equivalent of the Hebrew Mordechai). In the extant documentation, Benedetto's older brother is cited as 'Lelio' and 'Agnolo' with no evident preference. In Florence, at that time, there is no indication of another Lelio/Agnolo son of Laudadio Blanis.

11 Porzia's stated motive for dissolving the union was David's spendthrift habits and his inability to earn a living (Jacopetti, *Ebrei*, 44).

12 Opera di Santa Maria del Fiore, Registri Battesimali 32, f.103, 15 March 1619/20. All of the godparents at this group baptism were represented by proxies. All of the converts are identified as hailing from Massa di Carrara.

13 Pullan (*Jews of Europe*, esp. 275–312) presents many cases – often traumatic – of wives, children, and even parents caught up in the conversion of (male) heads of households. Furstenberg Levi analyses some of these same

issues in the Florentine context in 'The Boundaries between "Jewish" and "Catholic Space."'

14 Opera di Santa Maria del Fiore, Registri Battesimali 32, f.141, 15 March 1619/20. The boy's age is left blank.

15 Ibid., 254, f.154, 15 March 1619/20.

16 Ibid.

17 Ibid., 254, f.90, 15 March 1619/20. Margherita/Bellafiore and Maria Cristiana/Diamante probably also took the family name of 'Tacca' but this is not stated in the baptismal record.

18 Many details remain to be clarified regarding the Finzi conversions. The date of Maria Francesca's baptism in Carrara was 1 April 1619 (Roman style), while her father and four siblings were baptized on 15 March 1619 (Florentine style), which is to say 15 March 1620 (Roman style). Maria Francesca Tacca's sponsor was probably Captain Bernardo di Jacopo Tacca, the oldest brother (it would seem) of the sculptor Pietro di Jacopo di Bernardo Tacca. Maria Francesca is described as being fifteen years of age at the time of her conversion (Jacopetti, *Ebrei*, 44). A year later, Margherita Tacca is also described as being approximately fifteen years old. It is just possible that Maria Francesca and Margherita are the same person, but it is difficult to imagine the same girl undergoing two high-profile baptisms – unless there was some question regarding the validity of the first one or a desire to increase the numbers at the Florentine spectacle.

19 ASF Otto 265, f.66r, 9 April 1620. It was presumably in regard to this case that Lelio was jailed by the Eight Magistrates, then released on a security bond of 200 scudi on 18 March 1620 (ASF Otto 265, f.25r).

20 It is not clear where Davitte/Cosimo settled, presumably not in Massa Carrara. Agnolo/Lorenzo was presumably his eldest and probably only son, since he bore the name of Davitte's father.

21 In 1626 Margherita and Maria Christina entered the convent of Santa Maria degli Angeli in Florence, with the financial aspects managed by Bernardo Tacca (Jacopetti, *Ebrei*, 44). It does not seem that their mother Porzia Finzi ever converted to Catholicism. It is worth noting that Benedetto Blanis had a sister in Ferrara, married to Salamon Finzi – which might indicate a family link (see Chapter 9 above, 'The Mirror of Truth').

22 ASF MdP 5150, f.409, 2 July 1620) [*Letters*, no. 200]. Strictly speaking, Don Lorenzo was godfather by proxy and did not 'hold' his young namesake.

23 Benedetto was not a medical doctor, so 'dottore' is to be taken in the more strictly Jewish sense of 'man of learning'; see Chapter 4 above, 'The Synagogue.'

24 ASF MdP 5150, f.411, 9 July 1620) [*Letters*, no. 202].

25 ASF Otto 266, f.53v, 27 July 1620.

26 ASF MdP 5150, f.411, 9 July 1620) [*Letters*, no. 202].

27 Ibid., 5147, f.600, 11 July 1620 (Cosimo Baroncelli to Don Giovanni). This presumably refers to Don Giovanni's letter to Benedetto of 4 July 1620 (ibid., 5150, f.422) [*Letters*, no. 201]), which is the only letter from him to Benedetto that survives. This responds to Benedetto's letter of 28 June (ibid., f.420) [*Letters*, no. 199]), the last before his incarceration. Don Giovanni addressed Benedetto as 'Molto Magnifico,' a respectful non-patrician form of address that normally went with the title of 'Messer.'

28 Cardinal Carlo was also the godfather of Iudit Finzi / Agnola Tacca (Opera di Santa Maria del Fiore, Registri Battesimali 254, f.90, 15 March 1619/20).

29 This memorandum is not preserved with the other Blanis papers.

30 ASF MdP 5147, f.605, 16 July 1620.

31 Ibid., 5150, f.389, 24 July 1620) [*Letters*, no. 204].

32 In 1613 Pietro Tacca's brother-in-law Antonio Guidi travelled to Paris, accompanying the monumental bronze Equestrian Statue of Henri IV that he completed after the death of Giambologna. In 1616 his brother Monsignor Andrea Tacca, provost of the Collegiata at Massa, escorted his equally monumental bronze Equestrian Statue of Felipe III to Madrid. This was treated as a full diplomatic mission, and Monsignor Andrea took advantage of the opportunity to lobby for the confirmation of Alberico Cybo-Malaspina, prince of Massa, as a grandee of Spain. Members of the Tacca family controlled the lucrative salt trade between the Medici territory of Avenza and Massa Carrara. (ASF Pratica Segreta 23, f.417, 20 Nov. 1622, 'Sale del Avenza in Lunigiana a Antonio et Bernardo Tacca di Carrara ministri per l'offitio del Sale di Firenze che si distribuisce a' sudditi del Prinicpe di Massa'.) According to ASF Sebregondi 5092, Pietro di Jacopo Tacca became a Florentine citizen on 14 March 1616 (citing Cittadinario Fiorentino manoscritto 419).

33 ASF MdP 5150, f.389, 24 July 1620 (Salamone Blanis to Don Giovanni) [*Letters*, no. 204]. Also, ibid., 5141, f.1015, 15 Aug. 1620 (Albizo Vecchi to Don Giovanni). In ASF Depositeria Generale: Parte Antica 1521, f.125, he is listed among the salariati di corte as 'Reverendo ms. Albizzo Vecchi m.o de Paggi.'

34 After Don Giovanni's marriage to Livia was annulled, in June 1622, Don Lorenzo became his uncle's heir – at the expense of Don Giovanni and Donna Livia's 'illegitimate' son, Giovanni Francesco Maria.

35 ASF MdP 5150, f.389, 24 July 1620) [*Letters*, no. 204].

36 The Nuncio was Monsignor Pietro Valier, a Venetian; see ASF MdP 5147, f.619, 25 July 1620, and ASF MdP 5147, f.624, 1 Aug. 1620 (Cosimo Baroncelli to Don Giovanni).

37 Ibid., 5150, f.405, 1 Aug. 1620) [*Letters*, no. 205].
38 Ibid., 5141, f.991, 8 Aug. 1620.
39 Ibid.
40 Ibid., 5141, f.1022, 22 Aug. 1620 (Canon Francesco Maria Gualterotti to Don Giovanni).
41 Rome: Archivio della Congregazione per la Dottrina della Fede (Inquisition), Decreta S.O. 1620, f.259, feria quinta Die 16 julij 1620. Cardinals Roberto Bellarmino and Fabrizio Veralli (cited in previous letters) both took part in this meeting of the council. Mons. Alejandro Cifres, Dr Daniel Ponziani, and Fabrizio De Sibi were unfailingly gracious in helping me navigate the Archive of the Congregation for the Doctrine of the Faith (Inquisition). Francesco Bustaffa, a fellow researcher, generously assisted me with some challenging documents.
42 The genteel forms of 'de Blandes' and 'de Blanes' are frequently encountered in Massa Carrara, but less frequently in Florence.
43 ASF MdP 3006, f.486r, 28 Oct. 1619 (Amb. Niccolò Sacchetti to Sec. Curzio Picchena).
44 Ibid., 5151, f.185r, 7 March 1620.
45 Ibid., 3006, f.852r, 16 Dec. 1620.
46 Ibid., f.102r, 10 Nov. 1618 (Niccolò Sacchetti to Cosimo II).
47 Ibid., f.239v, 2 March 1619 (Niccolò Sacchetti to Cosimo II). Don Giovanni was already renting a villa at nearby Palvello.
48 Ibid., 3007, f.59r, 23 Feb. 1621 (Niccolò Sacchetti to Cosimo II).
49 ASF Alessandri 2, f.472r, 26 Dec. 1620.
50 Ibid., f.542r, 25 July 1620.
51 Ibid., f.453r, 15 Aug. 1620 (Don Giovanni to Cosimo Baroncelli).
52 ASF MdP 3006, f.748v, 5 Sept. 1620 (Niccolò Sacchetti to Cosimo II).
53 ASF Alessandri 2, f.466r, 1 March 1620 (Don Giovanni to Cosimo Baroncelli).
54 ASF MdP 5147, f.521, 7 March 1619/20 (Cosimo Baroncelli to Don Giovanni). For further documentation, see Chapter 7 above, 'Knowledge and Power,' the section: 'Silver, Gold, and Grappa.'
55 ASF Alessandri 2, f.456r, 5 Sept. 1620 (Don Giovanni to Cosimo Baroncelli).
56 ASF MdP 3006, f.192r, 29 Jan. 1619 (Niccolò Sacchetti to Curzio Picchena). At this time, Don Giovanni's interest in assuming the governorship of the contested border territory of the Monferrato was presumably under discussion.
57 Ibid., f.202r, 2 Feb. 1619.
58 Ibid., 6108, fol. 563, 7 Feb. 1619; translated by Molly Bourne.
59 Ibid., 3006, f.463r, 5 Oct. 1619 (Niccolò Sacchetti to Curzio Picchena).

60 According to Baroncelli's own memoir (ASF Misc Med 458, Insert 10), he
   was born on 18 Sept. 1569, was held at his baptism by Cosimo I and Johanna von Habsburg (wife of Francesco I), and became Don Giovanni's page
   in 1581 at the age of eighteen. In fact, Baroncelli would have been twelve
   not eighteen in 1581, which was a more normal age for a page.

61 ASF Misc Med 458, Insert 10, f.178r/f.41 (there are two numbering systems). In regard to the expulsion of Don Giovanni's most faithful servants,
   Baroncelli goes on to say, 'Against me alone she did not prevail, due to the
   reverence and love that His Excellency bore me and the many obligations
   that he acknowledged.' Nonetheless, at the time of Livia Vernazza's rise,
   Cosimo Baroncelli elected to leave Don Giovanni's principal household
   and return to Florence.

62 ASF MdP 3006, f.414r, 17 Aug. 1619.

63 In a legal depositon on 16 Jan. 1621/22, Benedetto Blanis explained, 'In the
   city of Venice, I know that a certain Attanasio Ridolfi served Signor Don
   Giovanni as secretary but without the title of secretary' (ibid., 5159, f.675r).

64 Ibid., 3006, f.414r, 17 Aug. 1619. It might seem that Attanasio Ridolfi was
   thus not a member of the distinguished patrician family of that name nor
   a relative of Cosimo Ridolfi and Donna Laudomine. However, on 18 Feb.
   1622, in the context of the trial that resulted in the annulment of Livia
   Vernazza's marriage to Don Giovanni, he was called in to identify the
   handwriting in various letters, including those of Antonio Ceccherelli and
   Benedetto Blanis. At that time, he is identified as 'Ill.re sig.r Athanasio
   di Antonio Ridolfi nobile fiorentino' (ibid., 5159 f.130r). In 1638 Atanasio
   Ridolfi was sent to Spain as agent of Cardinal Carlo dei Medici (ibid., 2640,
   Insert 398, 19 Feb. 1637/38).

65 ASF Alessandri 2, f.279r (dated March 1618, with no day specified).

66 ASF MdP 3006, f.498v, 9 Nov. 1619. Antonio Ceccherelli entered the *ruolo*
   of Don Giovanni's household on 1 July 1615 (right after Don Giovanni's
   arrival in Venice) without a title, earning the rather low salary of 3 scudi a
   month (ibid., 5158, f.145, 1 Oct. 1615).

67 Ibid., 3006, f.503v–f.504r, 16 Nov. 1619 (Niccolò Sacchetti to Cosimo II).

68 See Chapter 9 above, 'The Mirror of Truth.' Ceccherelli's activities are amply documented in the papers of the case to reverse the annulment of Livia
   Vernazza's first marriage to Battista Granara in ASF MdP 5159, 5160, and
   5161. Ceccherelli turned on his former mistress, emerging as the chief witness against Livia and her interests.

69 ASF MdP 3007, f.316r–f.317r (unsigned and undated, presumably written
   by Attanasio Ridolfi shortly after the death of Don Giovanni dei Medici).

70 Ibid., 5147, f.149v, 21 July 1618 (Cosimo Baroncelli to Don Giovanni).

71 ASF Alessandri 2, f.374r, 1 April 1619 (Don Giovanni to Cosimo Baron-celli).
72 ASF MdP 5147, f.337r, 9 April 1619.
73 Ibid., f.585r, 20 June 1620.
74 Ibid., f.489r, 7 Dec. 1619 (Cosimo Baroncelli to Don Giovanni).
75 Ibid., f.590v, 22 June 1620 (Cosimo Baroncelli to Don Giovanni). According to Baroncelli, this observation was made by Cavaliere Camillo Guidi and repeated to him by Papal Nunzio Pietro Valier.
76 The Stinche was the central prison where convicted criminals served out their sentences. The Bargello was primarily a holding facility for those whose cases were *sub judice*. Ill prisoners were often sent from the Bargello to the Stinche which was considered a healthier and more comfortable facility.
77 ASF MdP 5147, f.628r, 8 Aug. 1620 (Cosimo Baroncelli to Don Giovanni).
78 Ibid., 5140, f.1015, 15 Aug. 1620 (Albizzo Vecchi to Don Giovanni).
79 Ibid., 5150, f.399, 14 Aug. 1620 (Salamone Blanis to Don Giovanni) [*Letters*, no. 207].
80 Only one reference has come to light, in a 29 Aug. 1620 letter from Cosimo Baroncelli to Don Giovanni, 'In regard to Blanis' brother, I will say nothing further since he has arrived there [in Venice]' (ASF MdP 5147, f.634).
81 Ibid., 5150, f.397, 4 Sept. 1620) [*Letters*, no. 208].
82 Ibid., 5141, f.1029, 6 Sept. 1620 (Piero Capponi to Don Giovanni).
83 See Chapter 6 above, 'The Market.'
84 ASF MdP 5150, f.395, 10 Sept. 1620 (Salamone Blanis to Don Giovanni)) [*Letters*, no. 209]. On 18 Sept. 1620, Moisé Lattone, Benedetto's brother-in-law, was released from the Bargello prison on payment of a 500 scudi security bond. The reason for his detainment is not stated (ASF Otto 266, f.192, 18 Sept. 1620).
85 ASF MdP 5150, f.397, 4 Sept. 1620) [*Letters*, no. 208].
86 Ibid., f.391, 26 Sept. 1620) [*Letters*, no. 210].
87 See Chapter 9 above, 'The Mirror of Truth.' Benedetto's own statements support the allegation that he was often in Livia's chamber writing.
88 ASF MdP 5150, f.391, 26 Sept. 1620) [*Letters*, no. 210]. Ceccherelli eventually became the chief informant against Livia Vernazza in the investigation of the annulment of her first marriage to Battista Granara; see Chapter 13 below, 'Habeas Corpus.'
89 The exact measurement is 2.85 by 3.55 inches (73 by 91 mm).
90 ASF MdP 5150, f.391, by 26 Sept. 1620) [*Letters*, no. 211]. Benedetto's note is attached to Salamone's letter of 26 Sept.

91 Shavuot, which was often called *Pasqua del Pentecoste* in Italian, began on the evening of 26 May. It is worth noting that the letter arrived on the day before the Jewish New Year (5381) which began on the evening of 27 Sept.

92 For Passover, see Chapter 5 above, 'Memory and Survival.' In Kabbalah, Passover has a profound relevance to spiritual liberation, and Don Giovanni should have been aware of this. In his explanation to Cosimo Baroncelli of the significance of Joseph Gikatilla's *Ortus Nucis / Ginat Egoz* (ASF Alessandri 2, f.526, 15 Feb. 1620), he demonstrated an impressive familiarity with the general context of Kabbalah; see Chapter 11 above, 'Curious and Forbidden Books.'

93 ASF MdP 5141, f.1003, 12 Sept. 1620.

94 Ibid., 5150, f.31, 3 Oct. 1620) [*Letters*, no. 213].

95 Dottore Pompilio Evangelisti da Pellestrina was a ubiquitous figure at the Medici Court in these years. Ferrone et al., *Comici dell'Arte: Corrispondenze*, 219, describe him as 'cavaliere di piacere al servizio dei Medici (1596).' In ASF Guardaroba 309, f.10r, he is listed among the *salariati* at the Medici Court as 'Cavaliere di Piacere: Pompilio Evangelisti da Palestrina detto il dottore.' 'Dottore' is written over another word which might possibly have been 'buffone.' 'Da Palestrina' was a frequent Jewish surname after the expulsions from Lazio. 'Pompilio Evangelisti' has the oddly synthetic feel of many converso names, juxtaposing classical and Christian references.

96 ASF MdP 5150, f.413, 23 Oct. 1620 (Salamone Blanis to Don Giovanni)) [*Letters*, no. 214].

97 Salomone Blanis (ASF MdP 5150, f.389, 24 July 1620) [*Letters*, no. 204]) and Cosimo Baroncelli (ibid., 5147, f.624, 1 Aug. 1620) both comment on the Roman authorities' moves to curtail Priatoni's perceived leniency. In the Archivio Arcivescovile in Florence (TIN 51.22, f.78ff.), there is a long memorandum (undated) governing the activity of Priatoni's 'vicario.' The involvement of the 'Vicario Sancti offici Florentiae' in the Blanis case is specifically cited in the Archive of the Congregation of the Doctrine of the Faith, Decreta S.O. 1621, f.362, 10 Nov. 1621.

98 ASF MdP 5150, f.403r, 5 Feb. 1620/21) [*Letters*, no. 217].

99 ASF Nove 1017, f.357, 10 Feb. 1620/21 (Benedetto Barchetti to Niccolò dell'Antella).

100 ASF MdP 5147, f.726r, 27 Feb. 1620/21.

101 ASF Alessandri 2, f.316r, 8 Oct. 1618 (Don Giovanni to Cosimo Baroncelli).

102 This is probably Antonio Grimani who became Patriarch of Aquilea in 1622.

103 ASF MdP 3007, f.116r, 27 April 1621. This took place on 25 May 1621.

104 Ibid., 5147, f.730v, 13 March 1620/21.

105 Almost immediately after the death of Cosimo II, Maria Magdalena von Habsburg began signing the decisions of the Camera Fiscale which oversaw the rule of law within the Grand Dukedom and would ultimately be responsible for the prosecution of the Blanis case, if it was tried by a civil court. The decisions of the Camera Fiscale were often written up by her personal secretary Orazio della Rena (ASF Camera e Auditore Fiscale 959 and 960).

106 See Chapter 8 above, 'Games of Chance.'

107 ASF MdP 5150, 26 June 1616 (Benedetto Blanis to Don Giovanni) [*Letters*, no. 53].

108 Ibid., 5147, f.757v, 24 April 1621 (Cosimo Baroncelli to Don Giovanni).

109 Don Giovanni was legitimized by his father, at least in legal terms, although he remained outside the grand ducal line of succession. Don Antonio was technically legitimate since his mother Bianca Cappello was married to Francesco I and had been crowned as grand duchess. However, there were serious doubts regarding the circumstances of Don Antonio's birth, and Bianca Cappello was repudiated by the Medici family after her death in 1586. In real terms, his position was that of a legitimized bastard.

110 ASF MdP 5147, f.770r, 8 May 1621 (Cosimo Baroncelli to Don Giovanni).

111 Ibid., 3007, f.93r, 5 April 1621 (Niccolò Sacchetti to Ferdinando II).

112 Jacopetti, *Ebrei*, 56 and 172.

113 ASF MdP 5150, f.440, 4 May 1621) [*Letters*, no. 220].

114 Ibid., 5147, f.801r, 26 June 1621 (Cosimo Baroncelli to Don Giovanni).

115 ASF Alessandri 2, f.607r, 19 June 1621 (Don Giovanni to Cosimo Baroncelli).

116 Ibid., f.577v, 19 June 1621 (Don Giovanni to Cosimo Baroncelli).

117 ASF MdP 3007, f.210r, 12 July 1621.

118 Ibid., f.211r, 15 July 1621 (Sacchetti to Ferdinando II).

119 Ibid., f.217r, 15 July 1621.

120 Ibid., f.218r, 15 July 1621 (Livia Vernazza to Niccolò Sacchetti).

121 Ibid., f.219r, 19 July 1621.

122 Ibid., f.220r, 19 July 1621.

123 Ibid., f.222r, 19 July 1621 (Postcript to the letter on f.220).

124 Ibid., f.252r, 31 July 1621 (Niccolò Sacchetti to Curzio Picchena).

125 Ibid., f.239r, 21 July 1621 (Niccolò Sacchetti to Curzio Picchena).

126 Ibid., f.244r, 23 July 1621 (Niccolò Sacchetti to Curzio Picchena).

127 Ibid., f.236r, 24 July 1621, and f.252r, 31 July 1621 (Niccolò Sacchetti to Curzio Picchena).

128 The staff of the Tuscan Embassy began a methodical search for documents relevant to the marriage of Don Giovanni and Livia Vernazza, with
particular attention to the role of Antonio Ceccherelli. ASF MdP 3007,
f.316r (unsigned and undated but evidently by Attanasio Ridolfi; also,
ibid., copy of the record of the baptism of (Giovanni) Francesco Maria
from the registry of the church of San Gervaso in Venice. In the subsequent hearings – which featured Benedetto Blanis as a witness – Livia's
antagonists sought to prove that she married Battista Granara of her own
free will and that any contrary evidence had been falsified. This is documented in ASF MdP 5159, 5160, 5161, and 5162.

129 ASF MdP 3007, f.235r, 24 July 1621 (Niccolò Sacchetti to Curzio Picchena).

130 Ibid., f.325r, 28 Aug. 1621.

131 Ibid., 5150, f.19, 24 Jan. 1615/16 (Benedetto Blanis to Don Giovanni)) [*Letters*, no. 28]; see Chapter 7 above, 'Knowledge and Power.'

132 Ibid., f.388r, 18 Sept. 1621 (Niccolò Sacchetti to Andrea Cioli).

133 Ibid.

134 See Chapter 9, 'The Mirror of Truth.'

135 ASF MdP 3007, f.235r, 24 July 1621 (Niccolò Sacchetti to Curzio Picchena).

136 Ibid., f.413r, 25 Sept. 1621 (Niccolò Sacchetti to Curzio Picchena). In ibid.,
5158, ff.546–7, there are references to the disposal of Don Giovanni's
books after his death, with specific reference to three boxes of mostly
prohibited ones.

137 Ibid., 3007, f.235r, 24 July 1621 (Niccolò Sacchetti to Curzio Picchena).

138 These were Guglielmo della Baldosa and Isacco Luzzato (ASF MdP 3007,
f.413r, 25 Sept. 1621, Niccolò Sacchetti to Curzio Picchena). The proceeds
of Don Giovanni's estate were assigned to Don Lorenzo dei Medici, cutting out the repudiated wife and son of the deceased.

13 Habeas Corpus

1 ASF MdP 5159, f.673r–v, 19 Jan. 1621/22.

2 Ibid., f.683r, 19 Jan. 1621/22.

3 Ibid., 5161, f.67r–f.77v. There is another copy of this deposition on f.234r–
f.243r. On 17 Sept. 1621 Niccolò dell'Antella wrote Alessandro Vettori
(both in Florence) explaining that Chief Constable Anton Maria Cospi had
been ordered to release Benedetto Blanis for questioning (ibid., f.129r).
On 8 Oct. 1621 Antonio Ceccherelli (Fortezza di Susolo) wrote Alessandro Vettori (Florence), saying that he was pleased to learn that Benedetto
Blanis had confirmed his own testimony (ibid., f.329r).

4 Ibid., f.269r–f.272v.

5 Ibid., 5159, f.672v–f.683r.
6 There is extensive documentation of this case in ASF MdP 5159, 5160, 5161, and 5162. In June 1622 the marriage of Livia Vernazza and Don Giovanni dei Medici was annulled; Don Giovanni's property was awarded to his nephew Don Lorenzo (who was the godfather of Agnolo Finzi / Lorenzo Tacca and an adversary of Benedetto Blanis); see Chapter 12 above, 'The Prison.'
7 ASF MdP 5161, f.76r.
8 Coincidentally or not, considering his involvement in Genoese matters, Antonio di Fillipo Ceccherelli was from Cecina di Fivizzano, in the Medici State but on the Ligurian border.
9 ASF MdP 5161, f.76v–f.77r.
10 Ibid., 5159, f.164, 18 March 1622. Ceccherelli was testifying before the Court of the Bishop of Sarzana-Luni. The document is dated '1621 die. ven 18 martij,' evidently *ab incarnatione*, since 18 March fell on a Thursday in 1621 and on a Friday in 1622.
11 These were Attanasio Ridolfi (ibid., f.130r, 18 Feb. 1621/22), Gabriele Ughi (ibid., f.133r–v, 18 Feb. 1621/22), and Filippo Renzi (ibid., f.135v, 19 Feb. 1621/22).
12 The ecclesiastical courts that were reviewing the Vernazza-Granara annulment did not hesitate to acknowledge Don Giovanni's role in fabricating documentation and even plotting murder. However, the late Don Giovanni was not on trial, nor were his co-conspirators, so there was no reason for their guilt to become a public concern. The only substantive issue was whether Livia Vernazza had married Battista Granara of her own free will. In that case, the previous annulment could be overturned since it presupposed Livia's non-consent.
13 Antonio Ceccherelli's role as a prosecution informant is documented in the working papers of the Vernazza case in ASF MdP 5159, 5160, 5161, and 5162.
14 Rome: Archivio della Congregazione per la Dottrina della Fede (Inquisition), Decreta 1621, f.329, 3 Oct. 1621.
15 I have looked for relevant Inquisitorial material, with limited success, in the Archivio Arcivescovile in Florence and the Archive of the Inquisition in Rome. There might also be relevant material in the Archivio Arcivescovile in Genoa, where I have not looked.
16 Rome: Archivio Fede (Inquisition), Decreta 1621, f.362, 10 Nov. 1621.
17 Ibid., f.407, 14 Dec. 1621.
18 The Inquistor in Florence, a Franciscan, was also responsible for Siena and Pisa. The Inquisitor in Genoa, with jurisdiction over Massa Carrara, was a Dominican.

19 Rome: Archivio Fede (Inquisition), Decreta 1621–22, f.264v, 24 Nov. 1622. This is a copy of the less easily legible version at ibid., Decreta 1622, f.352v–f.353r.

20 This would seem to refer to the case of Porzia Finzi, David Finzi, and their son Agnolo, but there were other conversions between Florence and Massa in these years.

21 Dante and Prospero Finzi immediately began negotiating their sentence with the Inquisition. A 1,000 scudi fine was substituted for service in the galleys (ibid., Decreta 1623, f.86v, 8 March 1623). Then there was an ongoing discussion of the terms of payment: see (all 1623) ibid., f.183r, 23 May; f.190v, 31 May; f.234v, 5 July; and f.301r, 8 Nov. In ibid., Decreta 1624, f.100r, 22 June 1624, they are cited as 'Dantis, et Prosperis de fintis Judaeorum de Massa,' and their appeal for delayed payment is refused. In April 1627 Dante sold 50% of the Massa bank (Jacopetti, *Ebrei*, 97).

22 Jacopetti, *Ebrei*, 7.

23 In 1629 Angelo son of Prospero and Sola made a Jewish marriage. Also in 1629 Prospero and Sola's granddaughters (the daughters of David and Porzia Finzi) entered a Florentine convent (ibid., 55).

24 See Chapter 12 above, 'Prison.'

25 Flora took the name of Maria Elisabetta Staffetti; her godparents were Ferdinando Cybo and Vittoria Cybo Pepoli (Jacopetti, *Ebrei*, 54).

26 Rome: Archivio Fede (Inquisition), Decreta 1621–22, f.264v, 24 Nov. 1622.

27 See Chapter 8 above, 'Games of Chance.'

28 ASF MdP 5150, f.163, 10 July 1616) [*Letters*, no. 55].

29 Florence, Archivio Arcivescovile, TIN 17.10, f.2, 6 Jan. 1623 (Filippo Maria Acquanegra to Cornelio Priatoni). On the outside of the sheet, there is a secretarial summary: 'Rome 6 Jan. 1623, The Commissioner of the Holy Office offers thanks for the festive greetings and for the favour done for Maggioli. He approves what was done in regard to the Jew Blanes.' I would like to thank Dr Rossella Tarchi who helped me find this and other documents in the Archivio Arcivescovile.

30 See Chapter 6 above, 'The Market.'

31 ASF Otto 275, f.134v, 30 Aug. 1623.

32 ASF Riformagioni 32, f.420, 26 July 1620.

33 Ibid., f.423, 3 Aug. 1620; f.424, 3 Aug. 1620, and f.425, 12 Aug. 1620. In 1621 Jews were also excluded from taking medical degrees at the University of Pisa, a ban that remained in force until 1738 and the end of Medici rule (Salvadori, *Breve storia degli ebrei toscani*, 71).

34 Salvadori, *Breve storia*, 49–56.

35 ASF MdP 3007, f.462r–v, 18 Oct. 1621 (Niccolò Sacchetti to Curzio Picchena).

36 Rome: Archivio Fede (Inquisition), Decreta S.O. 1627, f.211r, 7 Dec. 1627.

37 During these years, the case against the Finzi in Massa Carrara was evidently settling out as well. Porzia daughter of Prospero and Sola Finzi had apparently returned from Ferrara, and at least two of her daughters were reclaimed for the Catholic faith (Jacopetti, *Ebrei*, 54–5).

38 Rome: Archivio Fede (Inquisition), Decreta S.O. 1628, f.12r, 4 Jan. 1628.

39 This was Salamone Finzi. 'Salamone' was a recurring name among family members in Massa Carrara – but there were many other Finzi, particularly in the Emilia Romagna. The Massese branch originally came from Reggio Emilia.

40 ASF Misc Med 19, Insert 2, f.16, 27 Sept. 1629. This was the same man with whom Benedetto took refuge on 3 Feb. 1620 (ASF MdP 5150, f.364, 3 Feb. 1619/20) [*Letters*, no. 176]).

41 ASF Misc Med 19, Insert 2, f.14, 8 Nov. 1629. There are a few other documents in this folder regarding Vinta's business dealings with Laudadio and Lelio Blanis and Moisé Lattone.

42 ASF Dogana Antica di Firenze 17, f.72r, 18 Aug. 1611. In 1635, Chiara daughter of Mirra and David Blandes of Florence was offered as wife to Abramo Finzi in Massa Cararra (Jacopetti, *Ebrei*, 56).

43 ASF Nove 3243, f.81r, 8 May 1688, 'Supplica di Mirra Blanes rescritta a gl'ord.i a 26 luglio 1642.' This refers to a case before the Otto di Guardia e Balìa and perhaps involves Mirra's rental properties in Venice. In 1635 these had been resettled on her (and David Blanis') daughter Chiara (Iacopetti, *Ebrei*, 56 and 172–3). Mirra also had properties in Livorno that were the focus of litigation with her brother David Franzese, as cited in a supplication to the governor of Livorno in 1643. Her son Jacob acted as her legal proxy (ASL, Governo, 2603, vol. 1, f.739). I am grateful to Corey Tazzara for bringing this document to my attention.

44 Archivio Arcivescovile di Firenze, CCR.Monte del Sale.23.16.

45 ASF Regie Possessioni 6556, f.92; , 6557, f.72; 6558, f.66 and also ff.178–9.

46 It is probable that various members of the Blandes/Blanes family from Massa Carrara settled, or resettled, in Florence. Jacobetti (*Ebrei*, 58) notes that the Blandes/Blanes are no longer documented in Massa Carrara after 1617. Names like Moisé and Giuseppe Blanis, which become prominent in the Florentine Ghetto after that time, seem characteristic of the Massa Carrara branch of the family.

47 In 1613 Moisé registered as a Levantine in Pisa and then settled in Florence with Levantine privileges (ASF Dogana di Firenze 18, f.46v, 22 Oct. 1613).

48 ASF Nove 53, f.422r, 10 Feb. 1621/22.

49 Translated from the original Hebrew by Siegmund, *Medici State*, 399. The

manuscript is in Rome in the Archives of the United Jewish Communities of Italy, ms. 123, II, ff.119–20.

50 Zuccarello, *Vallombrosani*, 168.

51 See Dooley, *Morandi*, for an assessment of Morandi's career strategies and the context in which he operated.

52 Gigli, *Diario romano (1608–70)*, 118.

53 In 1647 Benedetto ceased paying rent on an apartment in the Florentine Ghetto, and the lease was assumed by his nephews (Benedetto had no sons).

54 In Redi's *La Vacchetta: Libro di Ricordi*, 3 (7 May 1648), 5 (30 May 1648), 6 (14 August 1648), 7 (6 November 1648) and 13 (14 May 1654). Ferdinando is referred to as 'Messer' and 'Signore' but not 'Padre' or 'Reverendo,' implying that he did not take priestly orders.

55 Ibid. The formula 'già mio maestro di lingua greca' appears in the four entries for 1648. The books that Redi borrowed from Magnani were all in the area of Greek language and culture.

Bibliography

Agrippa, Cornelius (Heinrich Cornelius von Nettesheim). *Three Books of Occult Philosophy*. Trans. by John French. London, 1651.

Avivi, Yosef. 'Luria's Writings in Italy to 1620' (in Hebrew), *Alei Sefer* 11 (1984), 91–134

Arbel, B. 'Jews in International Trade,' in Robert Davis and Benjamin Ravid, eds., *The Jews of Early Modern Venice*. Baltimore: Johns Hopkins University Press, 2001, 73–96.

Baldinucci, Filippo. *Notizie de' professori del disegno …* Florence: Batelli, 1846.

Barbierato, Federico. *Nella stanza dei circoli: Clavicula Salamonis e libri di magia a Venezia nei secoli XVII e XVIII*. Milan, 2002.

Barzman, K. *The Florentine Academy and the Early Modern State*. Cambridge: Cambridge University Press, 2000.

Bocchi, Francesco. *Le Bellezze della Città di Firenze*. Expanded ed. by Giovanni Cinelli Calvoli. Florence, 1677.

Bonfil, Robert. *Jewish Life in Renaissance Italy*. Berkeley: University of California Press, 1994.

– *Rabbis and Jewish Communities in Renaissance Italy*. Oxford: Oxford University Press, 1990.

Bracket, John. *Criminal Justice and Crime in Late Renaissance Florence, 1537–1609*. Cambridge: Cambridge University Press, 1992.

Busi, Giulio. *Mantova e la Qabbalah / Mantua and the Kabbalah*. Milan, 2001.

Calabi, Donatella. 'The "City of the Jews,"' in Robert Davis and Benjamin Ravid, eds., *The Jews of Early Modern Venice*. Baltimore: Johns Hopkins University Press, 2001, 31–49.

Calimani, Riccardo. *The Ghetto of Venice*. Milan, 1995.

Calvi, Giulia. 'Donne, orfani, famiglie di fronte alle istituzioni,' in *Storia della Civilità Toscana*, vol. 3. Florence: Le Monnier, 2003, 441–60.

Cinelli Calvoli, Giovanni. *Biblioteca Volante.* 2nd ed. Venice, 1746.

Cantini, Lorenzo. *Legislazione toscana raccolta e illustrate.* Florence, 1800–1808.

Carlebach, Elisheva. *The Pursuit of Heresy: Rabbi Moses Hagiz and the Sabbatian Controversies.* New York: Columbia University Press, 1990.

Cassuto, Umberto. *Gli Ebrei a Firenze nell'età del Rinascimento.* Florence, 1918.

– 'I più antichi capitoli del ghetto di Firenze,' *Rivista Israelitica* 9/5–6 (1912): 203–11; 10/1 (1913): 32–40: 10/2 (1913): 71–80.

Cipolla, Carlo. *Money in Sixteenth Century Florence.* Berkeley: University of California Press, 1989.

Cohen, Mark. 'Leone da Modena's *Riti*: A Seventeenth Century Plea for Social Toleration of Jews.' *Jewish Social Studies* 34/4 (1972): 287–321.

– trans. & ed. *The Autobiography of a Seventeenth-Century Venetian Rabbi: Leon Modena's 'Life of Judah.'* With a historical note by Howard Adelman and Benjamin Ravid. Princeton: Princeton University Press, 1988.

Comastri, Giovanni Battista. *Specchio della verità.* Venice, 1683.

Concina, Ennio, Ugo Camerino, and Donatella Calabi. *La Città degli Ebrei: Il Ghetto di Venezia-Architettura e Urbanistica.* Venice, 1991.

Davis, Robert, and Benjamin Ravid, eds. *The Jews of Early Modern Venice.* Baltimore: Johns Hopkins University Press, 2001.

Del Col, Andrea. *L'Inquisizione in Italia: Dal XII al XXI Secolo.* Milan, 2006.

De Roover, Raymond. *The Medici Bank. Its Organization, Management, Operations and Decline.* New York: New York University Press, 1948.

Diaz, Furio. *Il Granducato di Toscana: I Medici* (Storia d'Italia, XIII) UTET. Turin, 1987.

Dooley, Brendan. *The Last Prophecy of Orazio Morandi.* Princeton: Princeton University Press, 2002.

Engels, Marie-Christine. *Merchants, Interlopers, Seamen and Corsairs: The 'Flemish' Community in Livorno and Genoa, 1615–1635,* Hilversum: Uitgeverij Verloren, 1997.

Fasano, Guarini. *Lo stato mediceo di Cosimo I.* Florence, 1973.

– *L'Italia moderna e la Toscana dei principi: Discussioni e ricerche storiche.* Mondadori, 2008.

Favero, Giovanni, and Francesca Trivellato. 'Gli abitanti del ghetto di Venezia in età moderna: dati e ipotesi.' *Zakhor: rivista di storia degli Ebrei d'Italia* 7 (2004): 9–50.

Ferrone, Siro. *Attori mercanti corsari: la commedia dell'arte in Europa tra Cinque e Seicento.* Turin, 1993.

Ferrone, Siro, Claudia Buratelli, Domenica Landolfi, and Anna Zinanni. *Comici dell'Arte: Corrispondenze.* Firenze, 1993.

Frattarelli Fischer, Lucia. *Vivere fuori dal ghetto: Ebrei a Pisa e Livorno secoli XVI–XVIII.* Turin, 2008.

Furstenberg Levi, Shulamit. 'The Boundaries between "Jewish" and "Catholic" Space in Counter-Reformation Florence as seen by the Convert Vitale Medici.' *Italia-Studie ricerche sulla storia, la cultura e la letteratura degli ebrei d'Italia* 18 (2008): 65–90.

Galasso, Cristina. *Alle origini di una comunità. Ebree ed ebrei a Livorno.* Florence, 2002.

Galilei, Galileo. *Sidereus Nuncius.* Venice, 1610.

– *Intorno alle cose che stanno su l'acqua o che in quella si muovono.* Florence, 1612.

– *Sidereus Nuncius, or the Siderial Messenger.* Trans. by Albert van Helden. Chicago: University of Chicago Press, 1989.

Gigli, Giacinto. *Diario romano 1608–70.* Edited by G. Ricciotti. Rome, 1958.

Goldthwaite, Richard. *The Economy of Renaissance Florence.* Baltimore: Johns Hopkins University Press, 2009.

Grassi, Orazio. *Libra astronomica et philosophica.* Rome, 1619.

Gualterotti, Raffael. *Feste nelle Nozze del Serenissimo: Don Francesco Medici Gran Duca di Toscana et della Serenissima sua Consorte la Signora Bianca Capello.* Florence, Giunti, 1579.

– *Descrizione del regale apparato per le nozze della serenissima madama Cristina di Loreno moglie del serenissimo don Ferdinando Medici.* Florence: Padovani, 1589.

– *Discorso di Raffael Gualterotti, gentilhuomo fiorentino, sopra l'apparizione de la nuova stella. E sopra le tre oscurazioni del sole e de la luna ne l'anno 1605. Con alquanto di lume del arte del oro, ecc.* Florence: Giunti, 1605.

– *Scherzi degli spiriti animali, dettati con l'occasione de l'oscurazione de l'anno 1605 di Raffael Gualterotti, ecc.* Florence: Giunti, 1605.

– *Le glorie d'Europa, nelle nozze di Maria Maddalena d'Austria con Cosimo de' Medici Principe di Florence.* Florence: Tosini, 1608.

Hames, Harvey. 'Jewish Magic with a Christian Text: A Hebrew Translation of Ramon Llull's *Ars Brevis.' Traditio* 54 (1999): 283–300.

Harrán, Don. 'Jewish Musical Culture: Leone Modena,' in Robert Davis and Benjamin Ravid, eds., *The Jews of Early Modern Venice.* Baltimore: Johns Hopkins University Press, 2001, 211–30.

Harvard College Library, Department of Printing and Graphic Arts Catalogue: Italian Sixteenth Century Books. Cambridge: Harvard University Press, 1974.

Idel, Moshe. 'The Magical and Neo-Platonic Interpretations of the Kabbalah in the Renaissance,' in Bernard Cooperman, ed., *Jewish Thought in the Sixteenth Century.* Cambridge: Harvard University Press, 1983, 186–242.

– 'Major Currents in Italian Kabbalah between 1560 and 1660,' in D. Ruderman, ed., *Essential Papers on Jewish Culture in Renaissance and Baroque Italy*. New York: New York University, 1992, 107–69.
– *Kabbalah, New Perspectives*. New Haven: Yale University Press, 1988.
– 'Italy in Safed, Safed in Italy,' in David Ruderman and Giuseppe Veltri, eds., *Cultural Intermediaries: Jewish Intellectuals in Early Modern Italy*. Philadelphia: University of Pennsylvania Press, 2004, 239–69.
– *La Cabbalà in Italia: 1280–1510*. Florence, 2007.
Israel, Jonathan. *European Jewry in the Age of Mercantilism*. Oxford: Oxford University Press, 1989.
Jacopetti, Ircas Nicola. *Ebrei a Massa e Carrara. Banche, Commerci, Industrie dal XVI al XIX secolo*. Florence: EDIFIR, 1996.
Lapini, Agostino. *Diario fiorentino di Agostino Lapini dal 1552 al 1592*. Edited by Giuseppe Odoardo Corazzini. Florence, 1900.
Levitats, Isaac. 'Oath *More Judaico* or *Juramento Judaeorum*,' *Encyclopaedia Judaica*, (2nd ed.). New York: Macmillan, 2007, XV, 364-5.
Lichtenstein, Aaron. 'Teixeira de Sampaio, Abraham Senior (formerly Diego)' in *Encyclopaedia Judaica* (2nd ed.), Macmillan Reference USA, 2007, XIX, 585–6.
Liscia Bemporad, Dora. 'La scuola italiana e la scuola levantina nel ghetto di Firenze: prima ricostruzione.' *Rivista d'arte* 38 (1986): 3–48.
Liscia Bemporad, Dora, and Anna Marcella Tedeschi Falco. *Toscana. Itinerari ebraici. I luoghi, la storia, l'arte*. Venice, 1995.
Litchfield, R. Burr. *Emergence of a Bureaucracy: The Florentine Patricians, 1530–1790*. Princeton: Princeton University Press, 1986.
– *Dalla Repubblica al Granducato: il nuovo assetto socio-spaziale di Firenze, 1551–1632*. Florence, 1991.
Luti, Filippo. *Don Antonio de' Medici e i suoi tempi*. Florence: Olschki, 2006
Luzzati, Michele. *La casa dell'Ebreo. saggi sugli Ebrei a Pisa e in Toscana nel medioevo e nel Rinascimento*. Pisa, 1985.
Medici, Vitale. *Omelie fatte alli Ebrei di Firenze nella chiesa di Santa Croce, et Sermoni fatti in piu compagnie della detta città*. Firenze, 1585.
Modena, Leone da. *Historia de' riti hebraici: Vita & osservanza de gl'Hebrei di questi tempi*. Bologna 1979: reprint of 1678 Venice edition.
– *Les Juifs presentes aux chretiens: ceremonies et coutumes qui s'observent aujourd'hui parmi les Juifs*. Edited, with an Introduction by Jacques Le Brun and Guy Stroumsa. Trans. by Richard Simon. Paris, 1998.
Morosini, Giulio. *Via della Fede*. Rome, 1683.
Negri, Giulio. *Istoria degli Scrittori Fiorentini*. Florence, 1722.

Novoa, James Nelson. 'Documents Regarding the Settlement of Portuguese New Chrisitans in Tuscany.' *Hispania Judaica Bulletin* 5 (2007): 261–70.

Paracelsus Theophrastus Philippus Aureolus Bombastus von Hohenheim. *Coelum Philosophorum*. Trans. by Arthur Edward Waite. London, 1894.

Parks, Tim. *Medici Money*. New York: Atlas Books, 2005.

Petrobelli, Orazio. *Specchio di Verita (sic) comprobato con la Sacra Scrittura, con l'autorità degli rabbini, & con ragioni efficacissime. Nel quale chiaramente si vede Che gli hebrei hanno perso la vera intelligenza della sacra Scrittura. Che Dio è trino in persone & uno in essenza. Chel Messia è Dio & huomo insieme. Ch'egli venir voleva per patire e morire in redimer l'humana natura...* Venice: Ghirardo and Iseppo Imberti, 1626.

– *L'ebreo conuinto. Cioè breue raccolto d'efficacissime raggioni fondate nella Sacra Scrittura, & auttorità de rabbini, con le quali si proua il poco intendimento che hanno gl'ebrei della scrittura.* Venice: Turrini, 1642.

Pieraccini, Gaetano. *La Stirpe de' Medici di Cafaggiolo: Saggio di Ricerche sulla Trasmissione Ereditaria dei Caratteri Biologici*. Florence, 1925.

Prosperi, Adriano. 'L'inquisizione fiorentina dopo il Concilio di Trento.' *Annuario dell'istituto storico italiano per l'età moderna e contemporanea* 37–38 (1985–86): 97–124.

– 'L'inquisizione romana e gli Ebrei,' in Michele Luzzati, ed., *L'Inquisizione e gli Ebrei in Italia*. Rome, 1994, 67–120.

Pullan, Brian. *The Jews of Europe and the Inquisition of Venice*. Oxford: Blackwell, 1983.

– 'Jewish Banks and the Monte di Pietà,' in Robert Davis and Benjamin Ravid, eds., *The Jews of Early Modern Venice*. Baltimore: Johns Hopkins University Press, 2001, 55–72.

Ravid, Benjamin. *Studies on the Jews of Venice, 1382–1797*. Ashgate, 2003.

Redi, Francesco. *La Vacchetta: Libro di ricordi di Francesco Redi*. Edited by Ugo Viviani. Arezzo, 1931.

Roth, Cecil. *The Jews in the Renaissance*. Philadelphia, 1959.

Ruderman, David. *Kabbalah, Magic and Science: The Cultural Universe of Sixteenth Century Jewish Physician*.Cambridge: Harvard University Press, 1988.

– *Jewish Thought and Scientific Discovery in Early Modern Europe*. New Haven: Yale University Press, 1995.

Ruderman, David, ed. *Essential Papers on Jewish Culture in Renaissance and Baroque Italy*. New York: New York University Press, 1992.

Salvadori, Roberto. *Breve storia degli ebrei toscani IX–XX secolo*. Florence, 1995.

Salvadori, Roberto, and Giorgio Sacchetti. *Presenze ebraiche nell'Aretino dal XIV al XX*. Florence, 1990.

Scholem, Gershom. *Kabbalah*. Plume Books, 1987.

Siegmund, Stefanie. *From Tuscan Households to Urban Ghetto: The Construction of a Jewish Community in Florence, 1570–1611*. Ph.D. dissertation, Jewish Theological Seminary of America, 1995.

– *The Medici State and the Ghetto of Florence*. Stanford University Press, 2006.

Simonsohn, Shlomo. *The Apostolic See and the Jews*. Toronto: Pontifical Institute of Mediaeval Studies, 1988–91.

Toaff, Ariel. 'Gli Ebrei del Marchesato di Monte S. Maria e Lippiano.' *Annuario di Studi Ebraici* 7 (1977): 45–72.

– 'Il commercio del denaro e le communità ebraiche di confine Pitigliano, Sorano, Monte San Savino, Lippiano tra cinquecento e seicento,' in *Italia Judaica*. Rome, 1986, 99–117.

– *The Jews in Umbria*. New York, 1993.

– 'Maestro Laudadio de Blanis e la banca ebraica in Umbria e nel patrimonia di S. Pietro nella prima netà del Cinquecento.' *Zakhor: rivista di storia degli Ebrei d'Italia* 1 (1997): 95–111.

– *Pasque di Sangue*. Bologna, 2008.

Toaff, Renzo. *La Nazione Ebrea a Livorno e a Pisa: 1591–1700*. Florence, 1990.

Vismara, Paola. *Oltre l'usura: La Chiesa moderna e il prestito a Interesse*. Soveria Mannelli: Rubettino Editore, , 2004.

Vivanti, Corrado ed. *Gli ebrei in Italia. Annali II*. Turin, 1996.

Waite, Arthur Edward (translator and editor). *The Hermetic And Alchemical Writings Of Paracelsus*. London, 1894.

Weinstein, Roni. *Marriage Rituals Italian Style: A Historical Anthropological Perspective on Early Modern Italian Jews*. Leiden: Brill, 2004.

Welch, Evelyn. *Shopping in the Renaissance*. New Haven: Yale University Press, 2005.

Wirszubski, Chaim. *Pico della Mirandola's Encounter with Jewish Mysticism*. Cambridge: Harvard University Press, 1989.

Zafrani, Haim. 'Hagiz' (family), in *Encyclopaedia Judaica* (2nd ed.). New York: Macmillan, 2007, VIII, 226.

Zuccarello, Ugo. *I Vallombrosani in età postridentina: 1575–1669*. Brescia, 2005.

Index

ramifications, where several different members might have the same name in the same generation, e.g.,

Index